Computer Graphics and Geometric Modeling for Engineers

Computer Graphics and Geometric Modeling for Engineers

Vera B. Anand

Clemson University

John Wiley & Sons, Inc.

New York ▪ Chichester ▪ Brisbane ▪ Toronto ▪ Singapore

Acquisitions Editor   Charity Robey
Marketing Manager   Debra Riegert
Copyediting Supervisor   Richard Blander
Production Manager   Lucille Buonocore
Senior Production Supervisor   Savoula Amanatidis
Text Designer   Sheila Granda
Cover Photo   Courtesy of PDA Engineering Inc.
Illustration Coordinators   Sigmund Malinowski and Jaime Perea
Manufacturing Manager   Andrea Price

This book was set in Garamond by Waldman Graphics and printed and bound by
South East Printing Pte Ltd.

Library of Congress Cataloging in Publication Data:

Anand, Vera B., 1938–
    Computer graphics and geometric modeling for engineers / Vera B. Anand.
        p.   cm.
    Includes bibliographical references and index.

    1. Computer graphics.   2. Engineering models—Data processing.
    I. Title.
    T385.A49   1993
    006.6'02462—dc20
                                                92-36055
                                                CIP

Printed in Singapore

10 9 8 7 6 5 4 3

0471514179

*To my father, who encouraged me to
pursue an engineering career.*

Preface

Computer graphics and geometric modeling play a fundamental role in instruction for engineering design. It is an acknowledged fact that the computer is needed for data storage and numerical processing. Computer-aided modeling, on the other hand, strengthens the engineer's ability to think through a design, because it eases the process of establishing both conceptual trade-offs at the preliminary design stage, and the choice of parts to bracket a specific design.

Computer graphics allows a full description of an engineering component to be stored in a CAD system. This captures both the visual and quantitative aspects of object creation. Geometric modeling describes an object by means of mathematical and abstract relationships, and focuses on the efficient computer representation of geometry. Both are integral parts of the engineering education process.

This textbook teaches the basic principles and techniques of computer graphics and geometric modeling from the point of view of engineering applications. The text is, therefore, aimed for engineers, although some generic computer graphics topics are also covered, since they are needed as background information essential to an overall understanding of the material. It is designed as a one- or two-semester course at the junior, senior, or graduate levels.

TEXTBOOK ORGANIZATION

It would be difficult to cover all the information contained in this book in a one-semester course. It is possible, however, to group the chapters in various ways that match the time allocated to a class. Some possible arrangements are suggested here.

One-semester undergraduate course: use Chapters 1, 2, 3, 4, 5, 6; parts of 7 and 8; and selected topics of 10, 11, 13.

Two-semester undergraduate course: use Chapters 1, 2, 3, 4, 5, 6, 7, 8; parts of 10, 11, 12, 13.

One-semester graduate course: cover Chapters 1, 2, 3, 4, 5, 6, 7 and 8 at a faster pace; add Chapter 9, and give more coverage to Chapters 10, 11, 12, 13.

If more emphasis is needed on geometric modeling topics, Chapters 10, 11, and 12 should be thoroughly covered.

All suggested sequences include Chapters 1 through 6, since they contain fundamental material on graphics hardware, software, standards, and geometric transformations. Chapter 7 is very important for an understanding of data structures used in the creation of geometric models, and Chapter 8 describes the three-dimensional viewing pipeline, including projections, viewing parameters, and clipping. Both Chapters 7 and 8 can be shortened and tailored to a specific sequence without loss of continuity.

Chapter 9 discusses various topics relating to visual realism, including hidden line/surface removal, shading and coloring. Although it is important for gaining an insight on the works of graphics systems, it can be omitted in an engineering environment with no undue continuity problems.

Chapters 10 and 11 discuss in detail various representational methods for curve and surface design. An in-depth coverage of these topics is given, and instructors can choose at will the representations that best suit the sequence used in their course.

Chapter 12 covers fundamentals of solid modeling theory and applications, and can be easily partitioned to fit any sequence of topics. The description of a simple solid modeling system given in section 12.12 can be either omitted or included at the discretion of the instructor.

Chapter 13 describes specific engineering applications of computer graphics/geometric modeling, including contouring, graphical simulation of articulated robots, and automatic generation of finite element meshes. Various other applications are suggested for possible implementation. It should be an essential component of any sequence used.

INSTRUCTIONAL SUPPLEMENTS

Ancillary instructional materials are supplied with this textbook, including a color slide set and an instructor's manual. The color slide set reproduces all color figures contained in Chapter 1, plus a variety of other 35mm slides relating to engineering applications. It will be useful in giving students an overview of the subject matter as an introduction to the course. The instructor's manual contains not only solutions to all numerical problems listed at the end of the chapters, but also transparency masters with many of the figures from the text.

ACKNOWLEDGMENTS

This textbook originated from a set of classnotes I used for several years at Clemson University. Many students contributed to the development of these notes and commented on the textbook drafts, in particular Aravinth Babu, Mukund Rajagopalan, Prasad Manne and Viswanath Dasari. Without their selfless dedication this book would not have been written.

Many thanks are due to the reviewers, whose comments and guidance greatly improved the final version of this text. In particular, Ronald Barr, University of Texas at Austin; Robert Mabrey, Tennessee Technological University; Gunther Schrack, University of British Columbia; and Robert Koretsky, University of Portland, were very thorough in the review of the complete manuscript. A number of selected chapters were also reviewed by Michael B. Atkins, Western Michigan University; Edward N. Ferguson, University of Maine; Mark Henderson, Arizona State University; Bruce P. Johnson, University of Nevada-Reno; Warren N. Waggenspack, Jr., Louisiana State University; and J. K. Wu, University of Iowa.

A special thank you is due my husband, Subhash Anand, who not only contributed to the technical content, but also helped me during the time-consuming process of polishing the manuscript. His patience and encouragement during the creation of this book were invaluable.

Finally, I wish to thank the staff at Wiley for their assistance and co-operation in the various phases of production of this text, particularly my editor, Charity Robey, for her sustained support and belief in this project.

September 1992   **Vera B. Anand**

Contents

Chapter 1

Introduction

The engineering environment has been revolutionized by the advent of computer technology. Computer graphics has been placed at the forefront of this revolution and plays a fundamental role in engineering design and communication. It is the element that transforms numerical computer solutions into physical interpretations needed for the design of engineering parts, or for illustration of complex phenomena. In its relation to other areas of computing, computer graphics can be represented as shown in Figure 1.1 [1]. It can be used whenever a visual representation of objects, relations, data values, positions, and so forth, is needed. In engineering applications, however, these visual cues may not be the final result. A model, most frequently a geometric model describing size and shape of an object, is often the intended result. Geometric modeling can be defined as the process of constructing a complete mathematical description of the shape of a physical object. The visual display and manipulation of this model is done through computer graphics techniques. An understanding of both

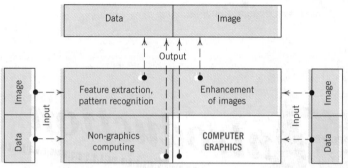

FIGURE 1.1 Relationship of computer graphics to other areas of computing.

$$\text{geometric modeling} \longrightarrow \text{model creation}$$

and

$$\text{visual display} \longrightarrow \text{computer graphics}$$

is of utmost importance to engineers.

Interactive computer graphics was introduced in the 1950s, and major automotive companies immediately began to explore its potential for industry. During the period 1960 to 1980, computer graphics received a major boost with the appearance of the computer as a tool in industrial and educational settings, and not exclusively in research laboratories. The development of the Sketchpad system by Ivan Sutherland in 1962 demonstrated the use of the computer in creating and modifying drawings interactively. By the mid-1970s, its ability to improve productivity secured the role of computer graphics in industrial, government, and academic settings. During 1980 to 1990 the use of the microprocessor became widespread and computer-aided design became a de facto standard in industry and academia. New computer-aided design/computer-aided manufacturing (CAD/CAM) technology allowed research to be conducted in theories and algorithms for computer-aided design, with a major focus on the expansion of CAD/CAM systems into widespread engineering applications. The decade of the 1990s will probably integrate and automate design in a more complete fashion. Visual perception will be an important area of study, since it is essential in the creation and manipulation of models of objects and in the simulation of phenomena occurring in three-dimensional space.

1.1 COMPUTER GRAPHICS/GEOMETRIC MODELING APPLICATIONS

Computer graphics and geometric modeling can be used to accomplish most tasks that require visual representation of numerical data or the creation of images of objects [2]. Major engineering applications fall into the following areas:

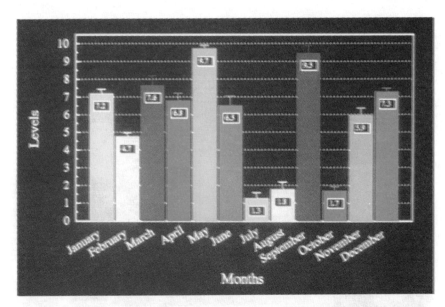

FIGURE 1.2 A bar graph as an example of presentation graphics. (Courtesy of TriMetrix, Inc.)

Presentation Graphics. The processes of communication and decision making are everyday events in the engineering environment. Graphs and charts are valuable tools in these areas and represent an important application of computer graphics, as shown in Figure 1.2.

Two-dimensional Layout and Design. Engineering applications such as circuit board and integrated circuit design, facilities and plant design,

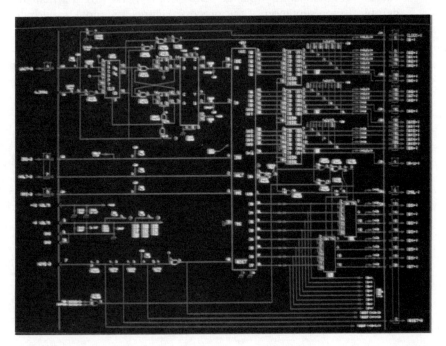

FIGURE 1.3 Electronic circuit design. (Courtesy of Tektronix, Inc.)

FIGURE 1.4 Real-time process control monitoring. (Courtesy of Precision Visuals, Inc.)

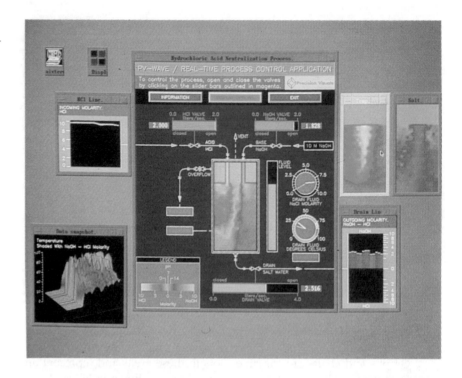

process control, and so forth, are ideally suited for computer graphics use. In process control, for example, a human operator performs checks on a constantly updated status display, showing a schematic graphical representation of the process. Figures 1.3 and 1.4 illustrate some of the uses of computer graphics systems.

FIGURE 1.5 Surface and contour plot. (Courtesy of TriMetrix, Inc.)

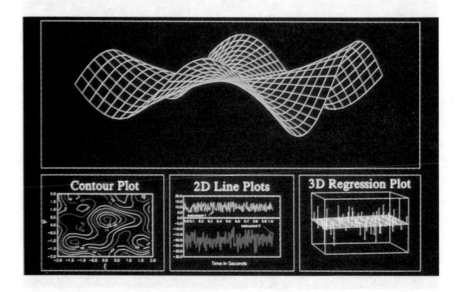

Data Analysis. Many times the most important information to be obtained from a set of data is buried under a large volume of numerical detail. Computer graphics allows for the rapid presentation of complex data, easy change in viewing directions, and the use of color to extract new information. Various types of data representations are used in engineering applications, including two-dimensional contour, line and scatter plots, as shown in Figures 1.5 and 1.6. A three-dimensional continuous mesh surface plot, shown in Figure 1.7, models the underground water table based on the location and water level information of various wells. Computational fluid dynamics data can be much better understood through the use of graphical images. Figure 1.8 represents supersonic airflow streaming over an airfoil, with colored bands indicating shock waves emanating from the flow. Figures 1.9, 1.10, and 1.11 are also examples of fluid dynamic data. In Figure 1.10 various types of visual techniques are employed, including a three-dimensional vector field plot and a cutaway isosurface. Figure 1.12 shows a four-dimensional image, defining the interplay of turbo speed, exhaust, torque, and boost pressure in an engine test. Structural analysis of stress, heat transfer, deformation, and other properties are also well described by visual techniques. Figures 1.13 (*a,b,c*) and 1.14 (*a,b*) are examples of these applications.

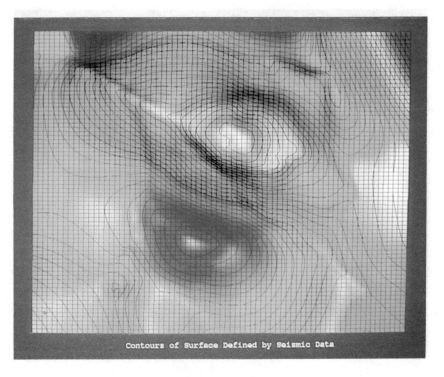

FIGURE 1.6 Contour plot of seismic data. (Courtesy of Engineering Computer Graphics Lab, Brigham Young University.)

FIGURE 1.7 Continuous mesh surface plots. (Courtesy of Precision Visuals, Inc.)

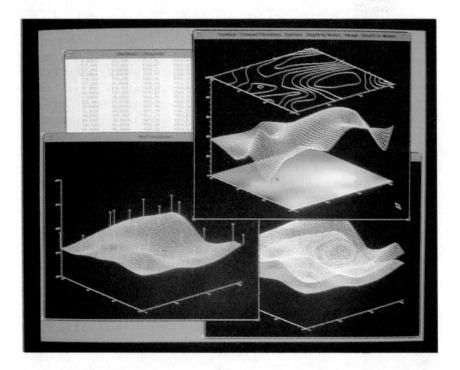

FIGURE 1.8 Image of supersonic airflow streaming over an airfoil. (Courtesy of Precision Visuals, Inc.)

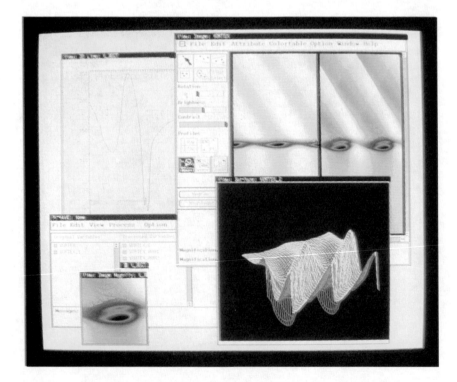

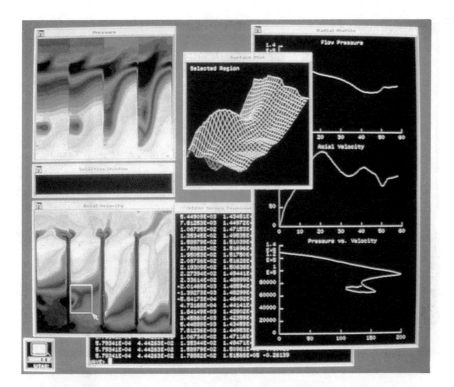

FIGURE 1.9 Interactive analysis of computational fluid dynamics data. (Courtesy of Precision Visuals, Inc.)

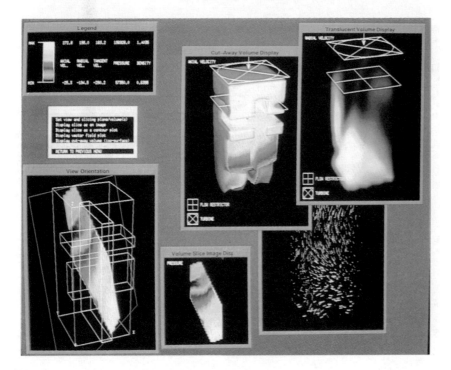

FIGURE 1.10 Fluid flow through a turbine shown as a collection of visuals. (Courtesy of Precision Visuals, Inc.)

FIGURE 1.11 Curve-mesh data points used to generate regular gridded arrays of air pressure and velocity. (Courtesy of Precision Visuals, Inc.)

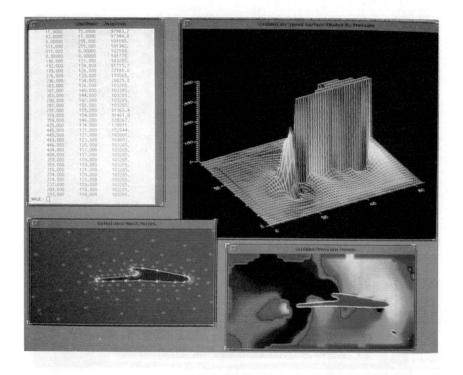

FIGURE 1.12 Four-dimensional image, highlighting the interplay of turbo speed, exhaust, torque and boost pressure in an engine test. (Courtesy of Precision Visuals, Inc.)

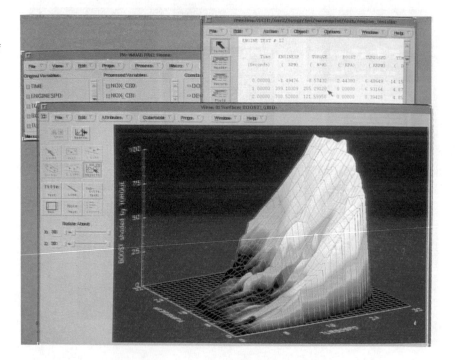

Three-dimensional Modeling and Design. Computer graphics systems are capable of realistic three-dimensional modeling and simulation. Computer models may be easier and cheaper to produce than a physical model and can identify major design weaknesses with minimal cost and without danger to human life. They have become standard tools in the designer's workbench. Figure 1.15 (*a,b,c*) shows wireframe and solid models of the rear swing arm of a motorcycle, and its relationship to the rest of the assembly. Similar modeling techniques are used in creating the solid model for the compact disk player in Figure 1.16 (*a,b,c*), the automobile brake subassembly in Figure 1.17 (*a,b,c,d*), and the prototype AMTRAK seat in Figure 1.18 (*a,b*). The solid model of the turbine shown in Figure 1.19 includes the results of analysis performed on the blades. The connector flange in Figure 1.20 is modeled with the use of texture techniques to produce a more realistic image.

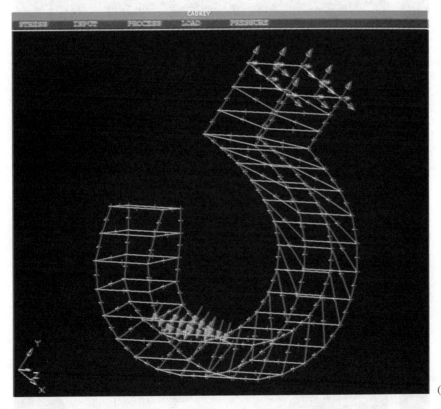

FIGURE 1.13 Boundary element analysis of a hook, showing (*a*) boundary conditions and (*b,c*) stress plots. (Courtesy of Cadkey, Inc.)

(a)

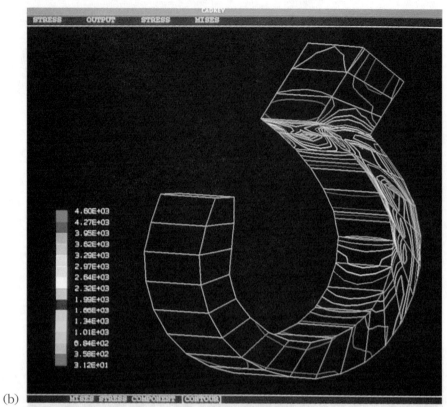

(b)

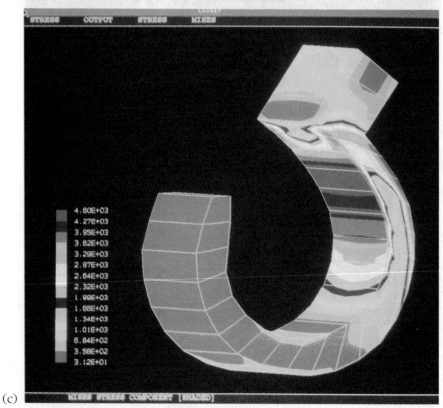

(c)

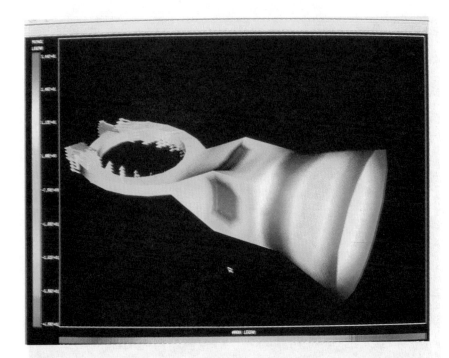

(a)

FIGURE 1.14 Arrows showing displacement results (a,b) after finite element analysis of an aircraft part. (Courtesy of Engineering Computer Graphics Lab, Brigham Young University.)

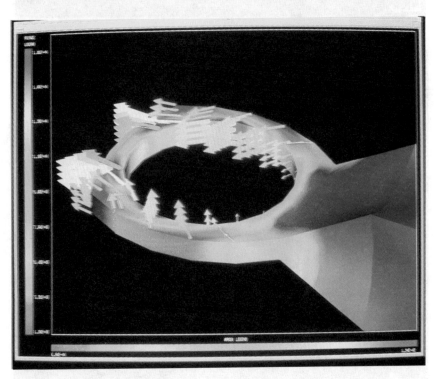

(b)

FIGURE 1.15 Rear swing arm subassembly of a motorcycle, showing (a) solid model of the part, (b) its relationship with the overall assembly, and (c) additional views. (Courtesy of Cadkey, Inc.)

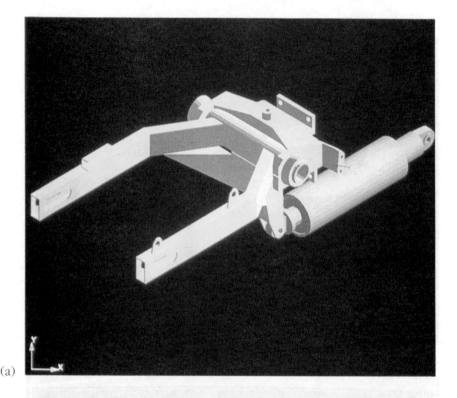

(a)

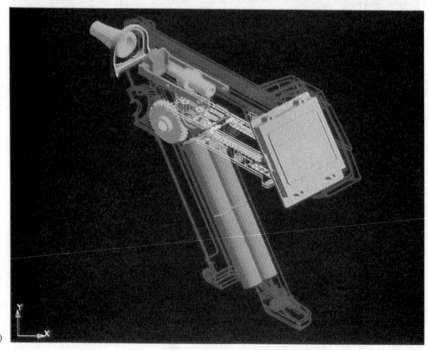

(b)

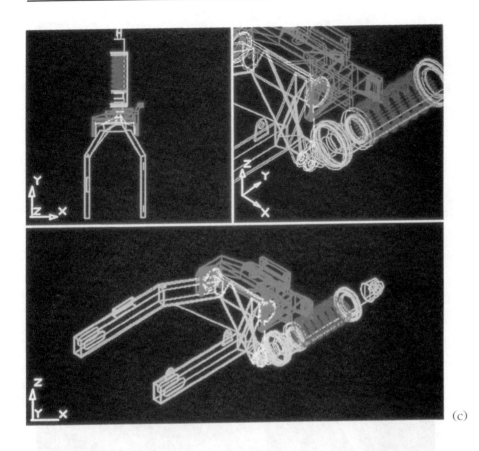

(c)

FIGURE 1.16 Compact disk player assembly, showing (a) solid model, (b) translucency, and (c) exploded view. (Courtesy of Structural Dynamics Research Corporation.)

(a)

FIGURE 1.16 (continued)

(b)

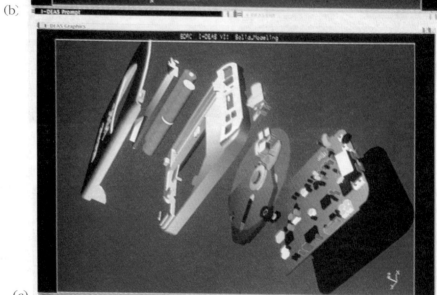

(c)

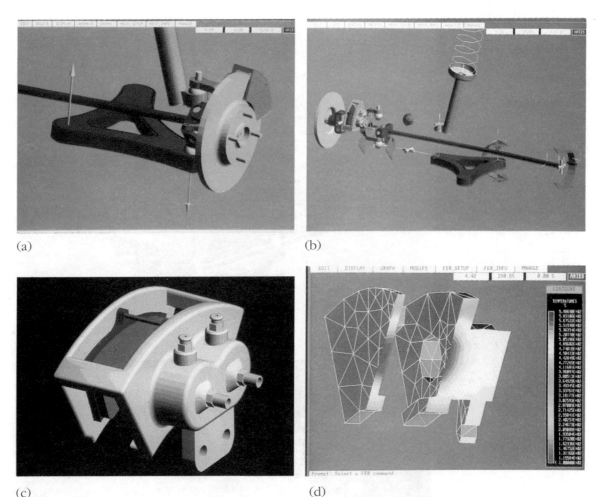

(a)

(b)

(c)

(d)

FIGURE 1.17 Automobile front-end assembly, showing (*a*) solid model, (*b*) exploded view, (*c*) solid model of brake subassembly, and (*d*) finite element analysis results on brake subassembly. (Courtesy of Aries Technology, Inc.)

Computer graphics and geometric modeling have become one step in the integration of planning, design, and manufacturing into a continuous process. A major goal of design/manufacturing is to expand CAD/CAM systems beyond simple geometric design and concentrate more in the areas of engineering applications. Freeform surface generation and solid modeling have expanded the use of CAD/CAM systems, and new design and manufacturing algorithms and capabilities are expected to continue this expansion in the future.

FIGURE 1.18 Solid model of prototype AMTRAK seat (*a*) and close-up of food tray adjustment mechanism (*b*). (Courtesy of Aries Technology, Inc., and Coach and Car Equipment Corp.)

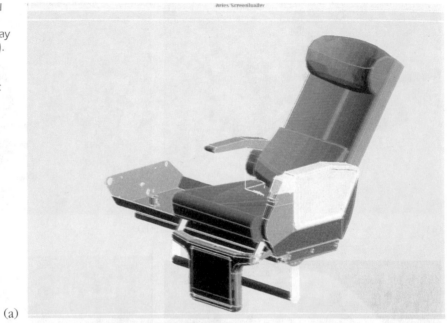

(a)

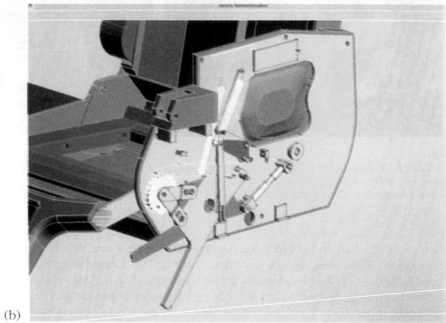

(b)

FIGURE 1.19 Solid model of a turbine, including results of finite element analysis performed on the blades. (Courtesy of PDA Engineering, Inc.)

FIGURE 1.20 Solid model of a connector flange. (Courtesy of PDA Engineering, Inc.)

Chapter 2

Computer Graphics Hardware

In modern days computers have been added to the graphic tool chest as an additional and effective tool in the design and drafting process. Computer graphics can be thought of as a collection of computer hardware and application programs directed to one specific goal—the creation of pictures. The hardware plays an essential role in setting the capabilities of the computer graphics system as it limits efficient communication between the designer and the computer. An analogy would be the difference between driving a car having a manual transmission and one with an automatic transmission. The degree of interaction between driver and automobile is controlled by the capabilities of the hardware, in this case the car itself.

In very general terms, computer graphics hardware can be classified into four categories: input, storage, transmission, and output. The graphical information is first transferred to the computer system by any of a number of special types of input devices. It is then stored internally in specific formats that depend on the device type used and is finally transmitted to the appropriate output device for viewing.

Several hardware-related parameters are important in computer graphics and differentiate graphics systems from other standard computer hardware. Among these are the various technologies for image production and image quality, the need for color and spatial representation, and the variation in media-type, size, and speed of output devices.

In the late 1980s, the advent of inexpensive microprocessors prompted major advances in graphics technology. These advances include the creation of subsystems that can be used as graphics accelerators, allowing the performance of complex three-dimensional graphics functions at the hardware level.

2.1   DISPLAY TECHNOLOGY AND GRAPHICS SYSTEMS

The display terminal in a computer graphics system is the main link of communication between the user and the system. Various types of technologies are used in the composition of graphics display devices. Figure 2.1 shows a classification chart. Each of the devices mentioned in the chart has advantages and disadvantages which must be considered when choosing a display device for a specific application. Among these are cost, resolution, color, and interactivity capabilities [2].

Resolution refers to the ability of the display to show details. Current displays reach a resolution of about 1280 × 1024, where the numbers refer to separately distinguishable spots on the screen. The total number of colors available and the number of colors that can be displayed at any one time are also important. The latter can vary from 8 to 4096 simultaneous colors from a total available of up to 16 million. Interactivity points to two capabilities of the display: (1) the ability to manage interactive input devices and (2) its

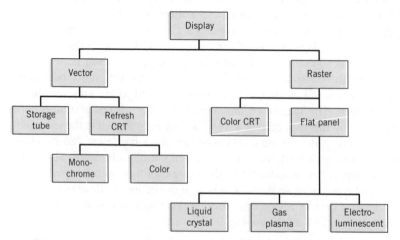

FIGURE 2.1 Technologies used in the composition of graphics display devices.

range of dynamics, that is, how well can the system provide the impression of movement.

2.1.1 Cathode Ray Tube (CRT)

The basic display device used in computer graphics systems is the Cathode Ray Tube (CRT). It consists of a vacuumed glass tube ending in a conical-shaped screen. Its main components are a base with connector pins, an electron gun, a focusing system, horizontal and vertical deflection plates, and a phosphor-coated screen, as shown in Figure 2.2. The display appears when the electron gun emits a beam of electrons that passes through the focusing and deflection systems before reaching specified locations on the screen. The beam can be repositioned at very fast rates due to the weightlessness of the electrons.

The screen of the CRT is coated with a phosphorous material that is agitated when hit by the electron beam, causing the spot to lighten. This phosphorous material is made of a mixture of various substances such as sulphur, silicon, and silver. The light emitted by the phosphor fades very quickly as the beam moves to another location. To give the viewer the appearance of a continuous image, the electron beam must repeatedly redraw (refresh) the picture on the screen over the same spots. The period of time in which the phosphor is active is termed *persistence* and is equivalent to the time needed to decay to one-tenth of the original intensity. This value differs for different types of phosphors, depending on the composition of the phosphorous material, as shown in Table 2.1. For display types that are expected to "store" information on the screen, a long-persistence phosphor is used, typically phosphor P7 on the table. On the other hand, if a quick update of the display is needed, a low-persistence phosphor is used, such as P31 or P4.

To maintain the brightness of a portion of the screen for a long period of time, the phosphor must be repeatedly activated or "refreshed" by the electron beam. If the phosphor is not refreshed, a condition called "flicker" will occur causing the image to fade between refresh cycles on the screen. A phosphor of low persistence is useful for animation, whereas higher persistence phosphors are useful for displaying complex static pictures.

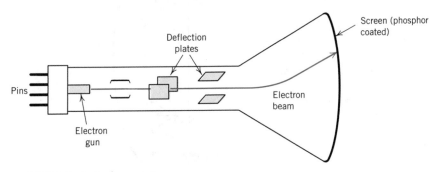

FIGURE 2.2 Cathode ray tube.

TABLE 2.1

Phosphor	Color	Persistence
P1	Yellow–Green	24 msec
P2	Yellow–Green	35–100 μsec
P4	White	60 μsec
P7	Green/White	300 μsec
P22-B	Blue	22 μsec
P31	Green	40 μsec
P39	Yellow–Green	150 μsec

2.1.2 Storage Tube

Storage tube displays, although no longer manufactured, were largely responsible for the first graphics revolution. Their development occurred in the 1960s, when Tektronix introduced the Direct View Storage Tube (DVST). This device has the ability to retain an image on the screen without the need for refreshing. Two kinds of electron guns are used in the operation of storage tube displays. One is a flood gun, which continuously bombards the screen with electrons in order to maintain the phosphors at a minimum level. The other is a single stroke-writing gun which accesses specific positions on the screen and activates the phosphors beyond the minimum level of excitation (see Figure 2.3). Continued operation of the flood guns keeps the image on the screen for a long period of time, without refreshing. The display is erased by raising the voltage on the entire screen, producing a "flash" usually associated with this erasure process and causing the screen to be saturated with the flood electrons.

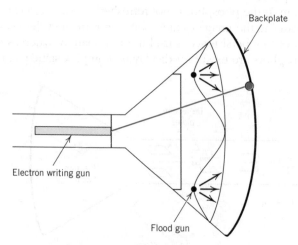

FIGURE 2.3 Direct view storage tube.

FIGURE 2.4 Vector refresh display.

Storage tubes can display a large amount of data at one time. They offer addressable resolution of up to 4096 × 4096. Their low cost, due to the lack of complex refresh electronic circuitry, was a major breakthrough at the time of their introduction. However, they do not have color capability and can produce only a static display, that is, the whole screen has to be erased for any modifications on the image to appear. Their inability to perform selective image erasures, and the reduction in the cost of computer memory in the past years, have led to a decline in the use of DVST systems.

2.1.3 Vector Refresh Displays

The vector refresh display (also called random, calligraphic, or stroke display) generates a picture by directing a beam of electrons to random points on the screen, and connecting them in vector form, as shown in Figure 2.4. The phosphor used has low persistence, and the screen has to be refreshed many times per second to avoid flickering. In addition to the CRT, the vector refresh system requires a display buffer and a display controller. The display buffer stores the information required to create the picture, and the controller sends this information to the vector generator which transforms it into corresponding positions of the beam on the screen. The process depends on the size of the display buffer and the speed of the controller [3]. Figure 2.5 shows one possible configuration of this process.

Vector refresh displays allow the change of any element of a picture in the display buffer. Because the phosphor used on the CRT screen has low persistence, each refresh cycle can be used to modify the original image. This type of display is, therefore, very useful in representing dynamic motion. Vector displays also produce a very bright and clear picture and have a high resolution. However, not only is their cost high, but they do not have the capability of displaying areas filled with color. Their use was common until the mid-1980s, when continuous advances in raster technology made raster the preferred type of display.

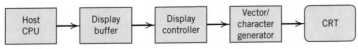

FIGURE 2.5 A vector refresh system.

FIGURE 2.6 Raster scan
display.

2.1.4   Raster Scan Displays

In the early 1970s, inexpensive raster graphics based on television technology gave a boost to the computer graphics field. In contrast to the two types of displays previously described, which are line drawing devices, the raster display is a point plotting device. This type of computer graphics terminal evolved from TV technology and benefits from the accumulated experience of the TV industry.

The screen of the raster scan display is divided into an *XY* matrix of dots, referred to as picture elements or *pixels*. This "pointillist" method creates pictures out of individual points that are either "on" or "off." The beam in the CRT moves horizontally, starting at the upper left corner of the display, and progressing from left to right at sequential vertical levels (Figure 2.6). The process is repeated until the entire screen is covered, and the beam is then returned to the upper left corner to start a new scan. The image is formed on the screen by varying the intensity of the beam as it travels. If a specific location on the screen is to be part of the picture, the beam passes the spot at full intensity, and returns to minimum intensity when traveling over spots that are to remain dark.

The limiting factor in this type of display is the need to address each pixel individually. As the beam moves across the display it must receive instructions on the intensity level required at different points to produce the image. The modulation levels for each pixel are stored in a digital memory called a refresh or frame buffer (Figure 2.7). Whenever a scan line is swept, a controller picks information from the refresh buffer, converts it to an analog voltage, and sends the voltage to a beam-intensity amplifier. The process of creating the information stored on the frame buffer (Figure 2.7), changing the geometric information describing an object into raster format data, is called *scan conversion* or *rasterization*. Several scan-conversion algorithms exist, most of them implemented at the hardware level for the sake of speed. To create a line, for example, an algorithm is used that highlights pixels in the proximity of the line.

Because each pixel in the raster display must have its own memory location, large amounts of storage are necessary for such systems, representing a limiting factor. A secondary effect produced on the image is the "stairstepped" appearance of diagonal lines, usually called the *aliasing effect* (Figure 2.8). The true line cannot be represented exactly, as in the vector displays, because of the discretization of the display surface. All that can be

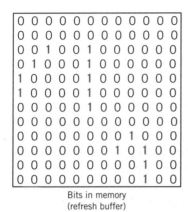 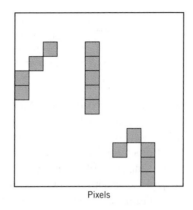

Bits in memory
(refresh buffer)

Pixels

FIGURE 2.7 *The composition of the frame buffer.*

done is to find the best fit of pixels to the true line. Several methods of antialiasing have been developed to reduce this problem, using various intensity levels to blend the edges of lines [3].

Raster displays are capable of presenting bright pictures and are particularly useful when color is introduced. Systems developed over the last few years have shown improvements in resolution, and begin to approach the performance of vector refresh displays. Raster displays are unaffected by picture complexity and can show dynamic motion.

2.1.5   Advances in Raster Architecture

In recent years major advances in semiconductor technology have given a boost to the general development of computer architecture. These advances are reflected in the modification and improvement of graphics systems, allowing for considerably faster image creation [3].

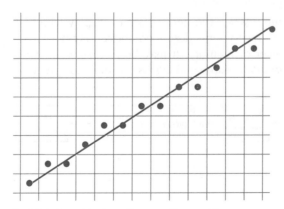

FIGURE 2.8 *Aliasing effect on diagonal lines.*

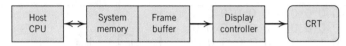

FIGURE 2.9 A simple raster display system.

Peripheral display processors. A simple raster display system contains a central processing unit (CPU), main memory, frame buffer, display controller, and CRT, as shown in Figure 2.9. In such a simple system, the burden of all computations necessary for the manipulation of the display falls on the single host CPU. One possible strategy to improve this process is to use a *peripheral display processor* with its own memory and a direct link to the host CPU, as shown in Figure 2.10. Two processors will, therefore, be in use:

- The general-purpose CPU
- A separate, special-purpose processor used to perform graphics functions

In addition, three memory areas contribute to the efficiency of the system:

- Main memory
- Display processor memory
- Frame buffer memory

The use of peripheral processors to perform graphics operations is common in current graphics systems.

Integrated graphics processors. Recent developments in the use of dense Very Large Scale Integration (VLSI) technologies have allowed the inclusion of added graphics support directly to the main CPU. In this case, a single chip can perform all the functions normally managed by the host CPU, in addition to high-level graphics functions. An effective graphics system can therefore be created with very few parts—the CPU, memory, and a video system. Continued improvements in VLSI technology will give rise to further advances in graphics systems.

Multiprocessing. When the need arises to display large databases at relatively fast rates, the systems described above may not have sufficient computational power or memory. It may be necessary to use concurrent processing, or *multiprocessing* making use of multiple processing units. If the

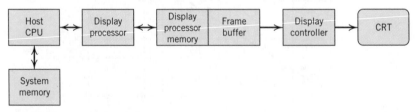

FIGURE 2.10 Raster display system with dedicated display processor and memory.

units are set up in series, so that the output of one becomes the input of the next, the process is named *pipelining*. If they are arranged in parallel, it is called *parallelism*. When using one or the other of these configurations, it is important to partition the data into appropriate stages, so that computations can be performed sequentially or independently, depending on the configuration used. Almost all high-level graphics systems today make use of multiprocessing. More information on their use in accelerating the performance of graphics functions at the hardware level will be given in Section 9.3.

2.1.6 Color Raster Displays

Color displays operate in a manner similar to that of monochrome displays, except that combinations of phosphor colors are used when generating an image. Basically, three beams illuminate three different types of phosphors, red, green, and blue (RGB). Variations in these colors are obtained by combining the primary colors to produce secondary hues.

In most color raster displays three electron guns are used, usually arranged in a triangular pattern as shown in Figure 2.11. The red, green, and blue phosphor dots are also arranged in this pattern. A perforated metal grid, referred to as a *shadow mask*, is placed between the phosphor and the electron guns, so that each gun excites only its corresponding phosphor. The shadow mask has small holes where the beams converge. By passing the beams through the mask, they are prevented from hitting more than one phosphor dot. The blue beam, for example, can only strike a blue dot. Var-

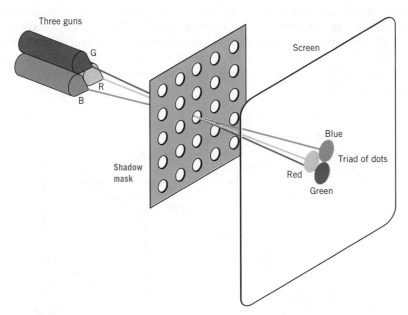

FIGURE 2.11 *Use of shadow mask in color raster displays.*

TABLE 2.2

Colors	Bits/Pixel
4	2
8	3
16	4
256	8
1024	10
4096	12
≈16 million	24

iations in the intensities of the beams result in different intensities of the primary colors, giving rise to many hues.

To show color in a raster CRT, it is necessary to modify the frame buffer [4]. As mentioned previously, each pixel of the raster display has a memory location associated with it, stored in the frame buffer. A minimum of one memory bit is stored for each pixel in the display. This is usually referred to as a *bit plane*. Each bit in this single bit plane can only have two values, either 0 or 1, so that a monochrome image is the result. Figure 2.7 shows a single bit plane. Color is incorporated into the frame buffer with additional bit planes. If N bit planes exist, then 2^N intensity levels can be produced at any one time or 2^N colors. Table 2.2 shows the correspondence between the number of bit planes and the number of available colors. Figure 2.12 shows the effect of systems with three bit planes. A minimum of three bit planes is necessary to generate color graphics, one for each of the three primary colors—red, green, blue. The information stored in the bit planes is used to activate the three electron guns of the color displays. Each pixel on the screen has three bits to describe its intensity level, so eight colors can be assigned as shown in Table 2.2. All combinations of bits that produce eight colors are shown in Table 2.3.

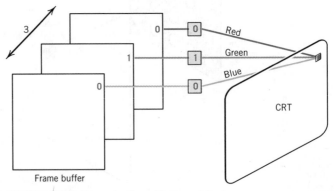

FIGURE 2.12 Frame buffer with three bit planes.

TABLE 2.3

	Red	Green	Blue
Black	0	0	0
Red	1	0	0
Green	0	1	0
Blue	0	0	1
Yellow	1	1	0
Cyan	0	1	1
Magenta	1	0	1
White	1	1	1

Since additional memory planes allow for a wider range of colors and pixel intensities, it is convenient to give the user some flexibility on the choice of which colors to use. One method is to use a *lookup table* (LUT). The memory address in the LUT contains an expanded number of bits that can be mapped to the pixel coordinates on the display, as shown in Figure 2.13. The bit planes are read into the frame buffer, and the resulting number is matched to a programmable position in the LUT. A pixel value is used,

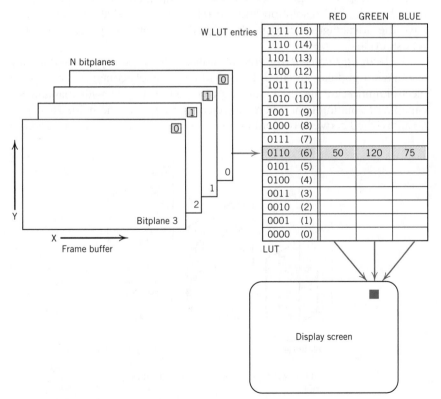

FIGURE 2.13 Frame buffer with LUT.

therefore, not to control the electron beam directly, but rather as an index into the LUT. If N bit planes exist, the LUT must have at least 2^N entries, possibly more (notice that "W" LUT entries exist in Figure 2.13), in which case only 2^N different pixel intensities would be available at any one time. The LUT can be reprogrammed as needed, so all colors in the palette are made available to the user in different combinations [5].

2.1.7 Flat Panel Displays

Most graphics displays in use today are of the CRT type. However, because CRTs tend to be bulky, heavy, and limited in size, flat panel displays have been receiving much attention. Among the most popular of these are plasma panels and electroluminescent and liquid crystal displays.

Plasma panels are formed by an array of small neon bulbs, which can be activated or deactivated, and kept in this state until specifically instructed to change it. Each point can be uniquely addressed and turned on or off without a refresh cycle. The panel consists of three glass plates, as shown in Figure 2.14, with the neon bulbs in the middle plate and strips of an electrical conductor placed vertically and horizontally on the other two layers. Individual bulbs are activated by matrix addressing and adjustment of voltages on the corresponding lines of the front and back plates. Plasma panels typically have limited resolution and are relatively expensive. However, they have the advantage of being very rugged and able to operate without a refresh cycle.

Electroluminescent displays are similar to the plasma panel in that they also have a gridlike structure. Front and back panels contain a layer of an electroluminescent material, such as zinc sulfide doped with manganese, capable of emitting light when subjected to a high electric field. This layer is sandwiched between two orthogonal sets of electrodes, as shown in Figure

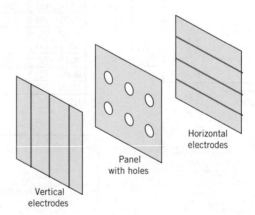

Horizontal electrodes

Panel with holes

Vertical electrodes

FIGURE 2.14 Schematic diagram of a plasma panel.

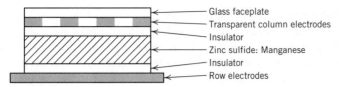

FIGURE 2.15 *Schematic diagram of an electroluminescent flat display.*

2.15. Points on the panel are activated by matrix addressing and a high voltage placed across the selection lines. This type of display has a characteristically bright, yellow-orange color, and can be turned on and off quickly. It is sometimes used in portable laptop computers.

Liquid crystal displays (LCD) are also commonly used in portable computers, as an alternative to the CRT. They are formed by several layers: two polarizers (horizontal and vertical), two grid wires (horizontal and vertical), one layer containing the liquid crystal, and one reflective layer. All layers are placed together to form a thin panel, as shown in Figure 2.16. If no electric field is applied at a specific matrix address, the polarizers are able to pass light and brighten the spot on the display. If an electric field is present, the molecules forming the liquid crystal take a new alignment and light is not passed, creating a dark spot. In the past, LCD displays have been mostly monochrome; color displays show low contrast and lack brightness. Nowadays, however, new color LCD panels make use of active-matrix technology with thin-film transistors at each pixel position to improve color contrast and brightness [6].

2.2 INPUT DEVICES

Input devices can be considered the primary means for creating images on a computer graphics system. They allow users to enter data in more visual form, as against the character-by-character alphanumeric input mode. Graphic input devices are primarily used to locate points and lines, usually through cross-hair cursors on the screen. Another function is to select menu items or manipulate parts of constructed images on the screen. This variety of operations and lack of standardization may be confusing at times. An understanding of the operation and features of the various devices may provide some clarification [7].

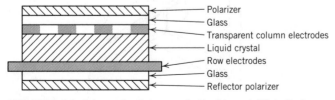

FIGURE 2.16 *Schematic diagram of a liquid crystal flat display.*

Digitizers are frequently available graphic input devices. They operate by moving a cursor unit over a flat surface and sensing each cursor position. The surface of most digitizers contains wires embedded in orthogonal directions that emit coded electrical or acoustical signals. The signals are received and translated by the cursor into digital coordinate data, which are then transmitted to the computer. The cursor units are usually free moving and consist of a flat puck or a pen-shaped stylus connected to the tablet.

Image scanners are fully automated digitizers that bypass the need for good hand-eye coordination on the operator's part. A scanner sweeps across a drawing or illustration with a camera and light-beam assembly, and turns the graphics into a pictorial database. The operator need only set the system, which then proceeds in a fully automated mode. Special settings are used to eliminate smudges or any other undesirable background tones.

Lightpens are used for direct interaction with the CRT screen. The pen consists of a stylus containing a photocell which emits an electronic signal on sensing light when placed on the terminal screen. The signal is sent to the computer for determination of the exact location being addressed on the screen.

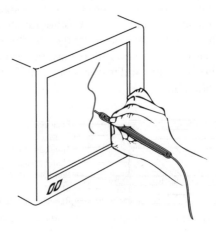

Touch-sensitive screens also work by direct user-interaction with the CRT—a screen overlay is able to sense the physical contact of the operator's fingers on the screen.

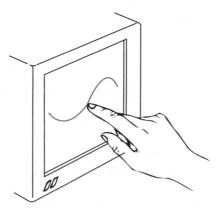

Joysticks, trackballs, and mice are potentiometric devices. They contain several variable resistors that send signals to the computer, indicating device positions. Such devices rely on the operator's hand-eye coordination.

Voice data entry, allowing voice interaction with computers, is becoming an acceptable alternative to the traditional data entry methods. Current systems use standard interfaces and high-level software for ease of installation. The process of voice storage and retrieval is as follows:

(a) While recording, incoming voice signals are converted into digital code.

(b) The code is transformed by breaking it into frequency components of the voice spectrum and is then stored.

(c) In the playback mode, a message address is sent to the voice system and the corresponding spectrum is retrieved. This spectrum is decoded and sent to a digital-to-analog converter, so that the analog voice signal can be reproduced by a loudspeaker or the like.

More information about input devices can be found in [7].

2.3   OUTPUT DEVICES

At the end of any computer modeling, a hard copy is usually obtained for further analysis or examination by the user. A number of hard-copy output devices exist, as described in Table 2.4. The most common types are differentiated in Table 2.5 by media type, media size, resolution, and the like.

TABLE 2.4

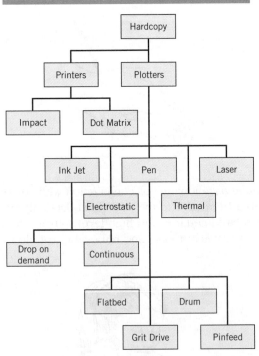

TABLE 2.5 Characteristics of Output Devices

	Dot Matrix	Ink Jet	Laser	Electrostatic	Thermal	Pen
Media type	Paper	Paper, trans-parencies	Paper, trans-parencies	Coated paper, translucent film	Paper, poly-ester film	Paper, mylar, transparencies, film
Media size	A-Size to 11 × 14 in.	A-Size, 34 × 44 in.	A-Size, 11 × 14 in.	8 to 44 in. wide—unlimited length	A-Size & 11 × 17 in.	A-Size to 70 × 192 in. (flatbed)
Resolution	120 to 240 dpi*	60 to 240 dpi	300 dpi or higher	200 to 508 nibs per in. (200 to 400 for color)	60 to 300 dpi	.0005 to .005 in. per addressability
Imaging technology	Pins impact paper through ribbon	Continuous stream or "drop on demand"	Xerography (laser charges selenium drum)	Toner particles adhere to charged paper	Heated polymer ribbon lays ink on paper	Ballpoint, felt, ink pens
Plotting speed	Very slow	1.5 min per page for A-Size; 30 min for largest	Varies, depending on imaging engine	Very fast, 0.5 to 3 in. per second	1 to 3 min per page	Slow; pens move from 3 to 24 in. per sec

*dpi = dots per inch.

Dot-matrix printer.   The printing mechanism of dot-matrix printers is a set of 7 to 24 stiff wires arranged on a print head that moves horizontally across the paper. These printers work as raster devices and require scan-conversion of vector images. Color output is achieved by the use of multicolored ribbons. Additional colors can be realized by striking two areas of the ribbon over the same spot on the paper.

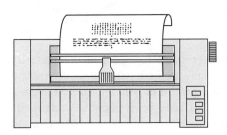

Ink-jet plotters (printers) are also raster-scan devices, providing low-cost color output. Their basic mechanism consists of ink jets placed on a head that moves across the page and sprays ink of different colors. The nozzles are connected to separate chambers by very small channels, surrounded by piezoelectric crystals. An electric impulse applied to the crystals causes a slight jerk, shooting one ink droplet. The resolution of the ink-jet plotter is controlled by the size of the droplet or the nozzle from which it originates. The nozzle is usually small, leading to potential clogging problems.

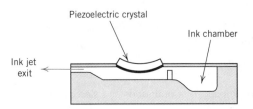

Laser plotters (printers) are raster-scan devices in which a laser beam scans a rotating, positively charged drum coated with selenium. The portions of the drum touched by the beam lose their charge, leaving positive charges only where the paper is to become black. A powdered toner sticks to the positively charged areas and is transferred to the paper. A microprocessor on the laser printer performs the scan conversion needed for rasterization.

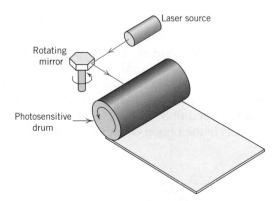

Electrostatic plotters (printers) are devices that place a negative charge on parts of a specially treated paper and then deposit a positively charged liquid toner on the paper. The toner covers and darkens the parts of the paper that have been negatively charged. This is a raster type of device, often containing a processor to perform the rasterization.

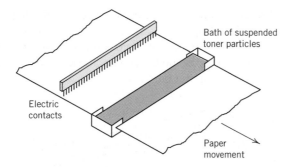

Thermal plotters (printers) are devices similar to the electrostatic plotters, except that a ribbon coated with wax-base ink is heated enough to allow the wax to melt and place the ink on a sheet of paper. This is also a raster device.

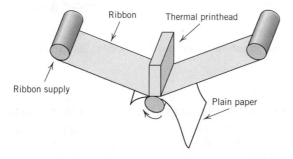

Pen plotters are devices whereby a pen is moved over a sheet of paper in random fashion. The two most common types of pen plotters are the *flatbed* and the *drum*.

A *flatbed plotter* accesses x,y positions on a flat platform by moving an arm suspended over the plotter bed. On the arm is placed a pen-mount that moves along its length. The pen can be lowered or raised, depending on whether a line is to be drawn or the pen is to be relocated. The paper is usually held on the platform by an electrostatic charge or vacuum.

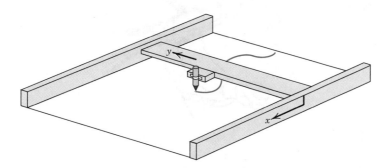

A *drum plotter* is somewhat more complex than the flatbed, although their basic modes of operation are similar. In a drum plotter the paper is stretched over a drum so that there is no slippage. The drum rotates forward and backward while the plotting head slides over a fixed arm, accessing all points on the paper.

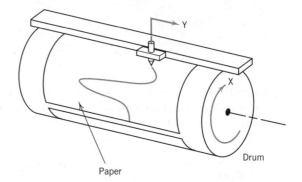

More detailed information about hard-copy devices can be found in [1,5].

2.4 NEW GRAPHICS TECHNOLOGIES

The way we interact with computers may change dramatically in the future because of a new technological wave called virtual reality, artificial reality, cyberspace, or telepresence. Regardless of the name used, the difference

FIGURE 2.17 Schematic diagram of a virtual reality apparatus.

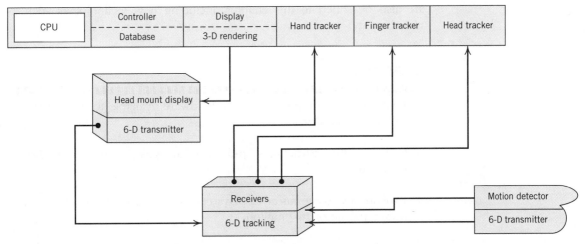

FIGURE 2.18 Major hardware components of virtual reality systems.

between this approach and a standard computer simulation falls in the realm of the user's experience of the model. In virtual environments, the graphics display changes dynamically in response to body movements. Interaction is achieved via a headset that provides a "window" into the simulation model as shown in Figure 2.17. A series of small screens are placed on the headset through which an image of the model is displayed in front of the user's eyes. As the user moves his or her head, the headset displays the corresponding image of the simulation model. Additional motion detection is obtained through fiber-optic sensors that detect wrist, hand, and finger movements, or body suits that detect "full" body movements. Figure 2.18 shows the five major hardware components of virtual reality systems [8].

Research on this technology is working toward faster rendering for images, probably through the use of three-dimensional graphics coprocessors; the ability to scan eye movement more precisely and project color images directly onto the user's retina, eliminating the need for display screens; smaller head gear, perhaps simply a pair of wraparound glasses; multisensory feedback devices with real-time tactile feedback providing sensory cues.

The ultimate goal of virtual reality is to have the user become a part of the simulation itself. This will become possible as the different technologies needed, such as imaging and rendering, merge with each other.

SUMMARY

Basics of display technology are described in this chapter, with particular emphasis on color raster displays. Major advances in raster architecture, including multiprocessing, allow modern graphics systems to perform high-level graphics functions at an accelerated rate. Input and output technologies are also described in this chapter, including new technologies such as virtual reality.

EXERCISES

1. Inventory the computer graphics hardware available to you, listing all technical characteristics.

2. Compare the advantages and disadvantages of all major display technologies.

3. Explain how some raster displays can present 256 simultaneous colors from a palette of 16.7 million.

4. Search the literature for up-to-date details on new hardware technologies, such as virtual reality.

5. Study in detail the advantages of multiprocessing and compare the use of pipelining or parallelism in various commercial systems.

Chapter 3

Computer Graphics Software— Standards

Because the purpose of computer graphics is the creation and manipulation of graphics scenes, it is important to be able to evaluate and modify these scenes in an interactive, fast-responsive way. Interactive computer graphics is needed, therefore, to give human control to the graphics process.

In the previous chapter, a description of computer graphics hardware highlighted important aspects of the physical devices that constitute a computer graphics system. Figure 3.1 shows how these devices fit into an overall interactive graphics system. Application programs, normally written in high-level languages, issue instructions in terms of the graphics requirements of the user. Graphics support packages implement interaction, easing communication between the user and the physical devices. The role of the support package (or graphics library, as it is also called) is to reduce the involvement of the user with the specifics of each physical device by providing a high-level interface.

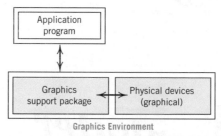

Graphics Environment

FIGURE 3.1 An interactive graphics system.

There are two ways in which a designer or engineer interacts with these graphics systems [9]:

- By accessing the graphics library through a high-level language such as FORTRAN or C, in a programming mode. The graphics library functions are invoked from the high-level language, following the schematic approach shown in Figure 3.1. An example in FORTRAN is shown in Figure 3.2.

- By using interactive modeling programs, written with the goal of satisfying a generic need, in which the graphics functions are accessed by the user without the need for programming. In this case, the process of accessing the graphics support libraries is hidden from the user, who interacts with the software through a specified user interface, and not through the source code. This "black box" approach is described by the schematic diagram in Figure 3.3 [10,11]. An example of this type of interaction is shown in Figure 3.4.

One of the major requirements for a computer graphics system as described here is that applications, portable to any physical system, be developed without hardware in mind. To attain this portability, standardization of the graphics environment at the functional level is necessary, providing language and device independence. Figure 3.5 illustrates a model for standardizing the graphics environment.

```
          CALL     OPEN SEGMENT('?picture')
C         INSERT LINES TO CREATE UNIT SQUARE
          CALL     INSERT LINE (-.5,.5,0,.5,.5,0)      ⎫  Library
          CALL     INSERT LINE (.5,.5,0,.5,-.5,0)      ⎬  functions
          CALL     INSERT LINE (.5,-.5,0,-.5,-.5,0)    ⎪  used to
          CALL     INSERT LINE (-.5,-.5,0,-.5,.5,0)    ⎭  create line
          CALL     PAUSE()
          CALL     CLOSE SEGMENT()
          STOP
          END
```

FIGURE 3.2 FORTRAN code using library functions.

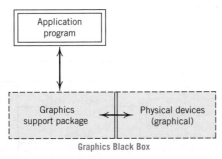

Graphics Black Box

FIGURE 3.3 "Black box" approach to graphical output.

The programming language interface level in this model specifies the boundary between an application program and a graphics support package. It establishes the language bindings to various high-level languages, such as FORTRAN or C, making the functions in the graphics library appear to the programmer like standard library functions. The example in Figure 3.2 shows this binding process to FORTRAN.

Device independence allows a graphics application program to run on hardware of various types. This is accomplished through "logical" input and output devices available to the application software through the graphics support package, and mapped to the actual physical devices at execution time. More details on these logical devices are given in Section 3.1.4.

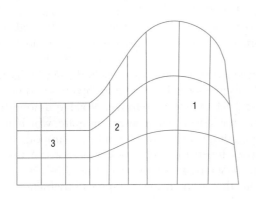

COMMAND	NAME	DISPLAY	ACTIVE	WINDOW	VIEW	SET/SHOW	PLOT	MODE

MODE	
GEOMETRY	1
ANALYSIS MODEL	2
ANALYSIS	3
RESULTS	4
NEUTRAL	5
STOP	6
	7
	8
	9

FIGURE 3.4 Example of interactive modeling programs.

ENTITY LABELS	COLOR CONTROL	SOLID SHADING	HARD COPY	END	MAIL
SPLIT SCREENS	SPECTRUM CONTROL	FILL HIDE	RASTER IMAGES	HELP	
ACTIVE SCREENS	LOOKUP TABLES	HIDDEN LINE PLOT	ERASE SCREEN		

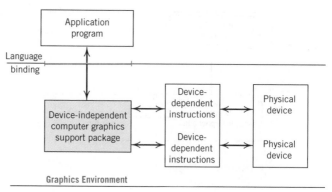

FIGURE 3.5 *Model for standardization of the graphics environment.*

The major portion of the standardization effort at the application programmer's level is found within the computer graphics support package. Several graphics standards have been developed over the years, including CORE (1977, revised 1979) and GKS (Graphical Kernel System, adopted 1984–1985), developed particularly to address the need for standardized two-dimensional input and output. Some of these became official standards, accepted by the American National Standards Institute (ANSI), the International Standards Organization (ISO), and others. These first efforts were followed by new standards addressing the needs of three-dimensional applications with a high level of interactivity. GKS-3D added three-dimensional capabilities to the existing GKS standard. PHIGS (Programmer's Hierarchical Graphics System, 1984) and PHIGS+ include more powerful three-dimensional graphics functions and the ability to interactively create and manipulate complex graphics data. PHIGS+ makes full use of raster concepts, including rendering capabilities, as described in Chapter 9. It also includes support for the parametric curves and surfaces described in Chapters 10 and 11.

De facto graphics standards have also resulted from industry acceptance of specific interfaces proposed by various companies and not available within the official standards mentioned above. Notable among these is a system like X-Windows, a window management program, which, in addition to creating and manipulating variable-sized windows, supports a variety of input functions and two-dimensional graphics operations. A three-dimensional extension of the X-Windows system was started in 1987 and named PEX, supporting various three-dimensional graphics capabilities.

3.1   STANDARDIZED GRAPHICS FUNCTIONS

Standards like GKS and PHIGS make use of several commonly used graphics functions that are typically accessed through a collection of linkable library

FIGURE 3.6 Object A is built by combining B, C, and D, where C is formed by combining E and F.

object programs. The standards attempt to describe an all-inclusive set of graphics functions, but it is obvious that any given set may be insufficient for some specific application. A graphics programmer must always rely on appropriate manuals for details on these functions, and must check on their completeness for implementation on each application.

The graphics database is an integral part of each standard description. PHIGS, for example, uses a hierarchical structure—that is, a structure where a complex model is built from a combination of small elements, as shown in Figure 3.6. A more thorough description of a hierarchical structure is given in Chapter 7.

Finally, to achieve device independence, the graphics standard must be able to receive and send data from/to various input and output devices. To accomplish this task, the standards make use of the concept of a logical workstation.

3.1.1 Logical Workstations

A workstation [12] is an abstract graphics device that provides a logical interface between the application program and the physical device. It must not be confused with the terms "graphics workstation" or "engineering workstation," which apply to graphics hardware that satisfies specific configurations. A logical workstation can be of three classes:

- Input only, with at least one logical input device and no output capability
- Output only, having only one display area available and no input capability
- Input/output, combining the characteristics of both the above

Several types of physical devices may be used with each workstation class. Once a logical workstation is activated, the user can send to it the results of his graphics implementation. The final effect should be the same whether the physical device associated with the workstation is a drum plotter or a terminal screen.

The concept of the logical workstation is embedded in both GKS and PHIGS. However, each standard handles the storage of graphics data used by the workstation differently. Graphics data are different from the applica-

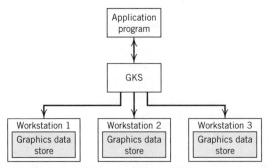

FIGURE 3.7 GKS stores graphics data at the workstation level.

tion model data that are maintained by the application program in a form suitable for its manipulation. The graphics data are maintained by the graphics support package in a form suitable for *graphics* manipulation and rendering.

PHIGS has a centralized location in which the graphics data are stored; from there the data are sent to individual logical workstations. GKS, on the other hand, stores the graphics data at the workstation level. Figures 3.7 and 3.8 show these different organizations. In PHIGS, the workstation can be selectively activated or deactivated while maintaining a single copy of the graphics data. This approach is very suitable for interactive systems using large volumes of data that need to be continuously updated.

3.1.2 Device Independence

To achieve portability, the standards establish for an application program minimal changes that allow it to address various input or output devices. Initially, the programmer establishes a modeling coordinate system in which the object is described, usually referred to as the *World Coordinate* (WC) *system.* Next, the programmer specifies a *Normalized Device Coordinate* (NDC) *system,* defining by two-dimensional square areas the viewing surfaces on which the image will appear. The normalized device coordinates

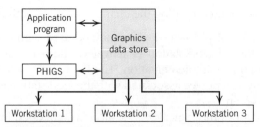

FIGURE 3.8 PHIGS stores graphics data at a centralized location.

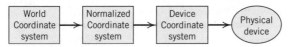

FIGURE 3.9 *Device independence in the process of picture creation.*

are subsequently transformed to device coordinates. The application programmer interacts with the normalized coordinate system in a consistent manner, no matter what physical output device is used. Device independence in the production of the image of objects is thus obtained. Figure 3.9 shows this process of picture creation, which will be described in more detail in Chapter 5. Suffice it to say for now that one of the ways to achieve device independence is through the normalization of the viewing area.

3.1.3 Output Functions

All graphics standards provide a series of output primitives with which complex scenes are created. These primitives can be two- or three-dimensional lines, markers, or the like, as shown in Figure 3.10.

The graphics standard implementation supplies the application programmer with output primitive functions such as

DRAW_POLYLINE(SetOfPoints)

which will draw straight line segments connecting the indicated set of points.

These primitives provide only geometric information. In order to define color, linetype, and so forth, drawing attributes are defined and associated

PHIGS Primitive	Definition	Example
Polyline	A point sequence defining a set of connected lines.	
Polymarker	Symbols placed at specific locations.	
Text	A character string placed at a given location.	STANDARD
Fill area	A polygonal interior area, without edges, filled in a variety of possible styles.	
Fill area set	A complex, polygonal area, with or without edges, filled in a variety of possible styles.	

FIGURE 3.10 PHIGS output primitives.

PHIGS Polyline Attributes

Attribute	Definition
Linetype	Selects a line style, such as: solid _____ dashed - - - - - - - - center — - — - —
Linewidth	Selects a line thickness as a multiple of a workstation's nominal line width.
Polyline Color Index	Selects a line color through a workstation color table.

FIGURE 3.11 Attributes to polyline primitive.

with each primitive through a "SET <attribute>" function. Figure 3.11 shows the attributes to the polyline primitive. Appropriate attributes are available for all other output primitives [12,13,14].

3.1.4 Input Functions

Device independence requires that a variety of physical input devices be used by the software with minimal modification of the application program. To accomplish this, logical input devices or input functions are used, representing physical input devices that possess similar characteristics. Logical input devices can be divided into six input classes, differentiated by the type of data values the logical device returns to the application program [12,14]. Figure 3.12 lists these logical input classes. Each can utilize more than one

Class	Logical Data Values Returned
Locator	Indicates a position and/or orientation in world coordinates.
Valuator	Provides scalar values.
Choice	Selects from a number of possible choices and returns a non-negative number.
Stroke	Provides a sequence of positions in world coordinates.
Pick	Selects a displayed entity, providing a pick status and path.
String	Provides a character string.

FIGURE 3.12 Logical input classes.

Logical Device or Logical Function	Physical Devices
(1) Locator	Tablet
	Mouse
	Trackball or crystal ball
	Joystick
	Joyswitch
	Touch panel
	Sonic tablet 2D/3D
	Noll box
(2) Valuator	Rotary potentiometer (DIAL)
	Slide potentiometer
	Control dials
	Levers
(3) Pick	Light pen
	Data tablet stylus
(4) Choice	A separate bank of buttons.
(5) String	Alphanumeric keyboard
(6) Nontraditional devices	Speech recognizers

FIGURE 3.13 Correlation between logical and physical input devices.

physical device associated with it. Figure 3.13 shows the correlation between the logical and physical input devices.

Each logical input device can be operated in one of three possible input modes, that is, there are three different ways in which the application pro-

Mode	Definition
REQUEST	An input function in REQUEST mode causes GKS or PHIGS to attempt to read a logical input value from a specified logical input device. The program waits until this input is entered or until a break action is performed by the end user.
SAMPLE	GKS or PHIGS returns the current input value, without waiting for operator input.
EVENT	The latest available event report, containing the identification of a logical input device and its logical input value, is removed from the input queue maintained by both GKS and PHIGS.

FIGURE 3.14 Operating modes for logical input devices.

Segment Attributes
(modify segment as a whole)

Transformation ⟶ Translation, rotation, scaling

Highlighting ⟶ Normal or highlighted

Vsibility ⟶ Visible or invisible

Priority ⟶ Front or back (position with respect to viewer)

FIGURE 3.15 Global segment changes.

gram can receive information from the device. Figure 3.14 describes the operating modes available in GKS and PHIGS [12,14].

3.1.5 Subpictures

In the process of creating, modifying, and displaying a graphical scene, it may be useful to break the scene into elements or subpictures. These elements behave somewhat like a subprogram in a computer program—they can be duplicated at any time or a complex scene can be divided into a collection of simpler ones. In addition, subpictures can be manipulated or transformed to construct complex pictures. The creation of subpictures establishes a defined structure for graphics data.

PHIGS and GKS handle subpictures differently. GKS provides a single-level data structure named a *segment*. In broad terms, a segment is a collection of graphical primitives as described in previous sections. The application program creates a segment with a function Open_Segment, inserts primitives into it, and closes the segment with a Close_Segment. For identification, each segment is assigned an integer 'segment name.' Once the segment has been created, its contents cannot be modified, although some changes that affect the segment as a whole can be implemented. Figure 3.15 describes the global segment changes. Historically, GKS segments have been used to represent

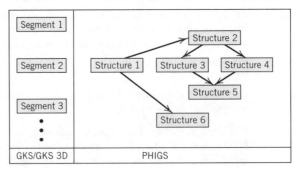

FIGURE 3.16 Comparison of graphics data structuring in GKS and PHIGS.

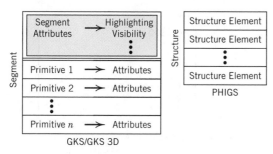

FIGURE 3.17 GKS and PHIGS handling of segmentation.

information about the graphics image rather than information about the model.

PHIGS organizes graphics data in *structures*, controlled by the application program. Each structure contains *structure elements*, which represent output primitives, attributes, transformations, application-specific data, and so forth. A unique identifier is given to each structure for later reference. PHIGS's structures are defined at the graphics model level, not the image level. The organization of graphics data in PHIGS is multilevel, or hierarchical, with structures relating to each other in a hierarchical network. More details on hierarchical data structures are given in Chapter 7.

Figure 3.16 compares the graphics data structuring of GKS and PHIGS [15]. The content of each segment or structure also varies between the two standards, as shown in Figure 3.17. GKS binds the attributes to the primitives at creation time, before they are retained in the graphics data structure. A segment must be recreated to be able to change primitive attributes. In PHIGS, primitives and attributes are separate elements, bound only when the structure is being executed or "traversed" for display. Figure 3.18 shows this difference in attribute binding between the two standards.

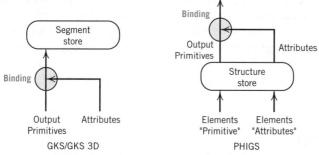

FIGURE 3.18 Difference in attribute binding between GKS and PHIGS.

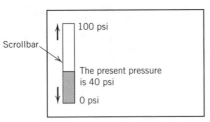

FIGURE 3.19 Example of the use of a Scrollbar function as a Valuator logical input.

3.2 GRAPHICAL USER INTERFACE

Graphical user interface (GUI) may be the area of computing wherein graphics will make its major impact. Primitive functions for graphics user interaction are not provided in GKS or PHIGS. Other systems, such as X-Windows, have this capability. Graphics interaction tools provide primitives for user interaction and are available to the application program. For example, the SCROLLBAR function is activated in sample mode, as shown in Figure 3.19. This function presents an area of the screen where a slide bar can be adjusted by mouse input. The function is set up as a logical input device operating in sample mode, and can be used to read the value shown on the screen. This type of user interaction facility relieves the application programmer from performing a series of routine programming tasks. Many existing packages providing user interface function capability also have access to device-independent graphics functions such as are available in GKS or PHIGS. X-Windows, for example, combines the user interface facility with two-dimensional graphics primitives in a device-independent mode [16,17].

SUMMARY

This chapter addressed the role of device-independent graphics, highlighting the need to reduce the user's involvement with physical device specifics. The GKS and PHIGS graphics standards represent attempts to describe a complete set of graphics functions for use in a variety of applications. They differ primarily in their structure and in the types of applications for which each is best suited.

EXERCISES

1. Check on the types of graphics support systems available to you, including graphics libraries and interactive modeling programs.

2. If a graphics library is available, how will you access it from the programs you write?

3. Prepare a report on the development of GKS (GKS3D) and PHIGS (PHIGS +), explaining in detail the differences in the structure of the two standards.

4. Verify the use of standards on the development of the graphics library available to you. Check on the correlation between the input and output functions of the library and those of GKS or PHIGS.

5. Examine any interactive CAD system containing two-dimensional primitives (line, circle, etc.) in a menu structure. Explain how logical input classes, such as Locator and Pick, are used when selecting these primitives and placing them in the graphics area of the screen.

6. Check on the availability of windowing systems at your institution. Describe any graphics primitives present in these systems and the forms of GUI.

Chapter 4

*T*wo-Dimensional Coordinate Geometry

Many engineering problems are solved by means of two-dimensional representations of a model. Among these are standard kinematic problems, such as the motion of a slider-crank mechanism or the calculation of shear and bending moments in a structural element, as shown in Figure 4.1. To represent these problems, graphics systems must give the user the capability of creating geometric entities such as lines, circles, and the like, and of transforming these entities, changing their size, position, or orientation in an organized and efficient way. Such geometric transformations play a crucial role in the creation and viewing of models and form an integral part of all current CAD systems.

4.1 REPRESENTATION OF TWO-DIMENSIONAL GEOMETRY

In computer graphics, the shape and size of two-dimensional objects are characterized by two-dimensional numerical descriptions tied to a coordinate sys-

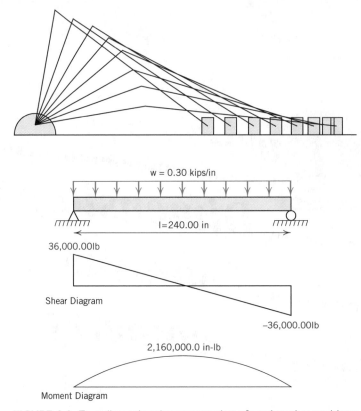

w = 0.30 kips/in

l=240.00 in

36,000.00lb

Shear Diagram

−36,000.00lb

2,160,000.0 in-lb

Moment Diagram

FIGURE 4.1 Two-dimensional representation of engineering problems.

tem, usually the familiar x,y cartesian coordinates. A set of geometric transformations can then be applied to the model to shift, resize, or reorient it.

The basic element of any two-dimensional model is a point. A line, for example, is represented by its two endpoints, and a surface is represented by several of its points. All two-dimensional representations can, therefore, be defined by a set of x,y coordinates or points, considered an elementary component of any model.

Figure 4.2 shows the representation of a triangle by the x,y coordinates of its vertices.

This triangle could also be represented by a [3 × 2] matrix, as follows:

$$[P]_{\text{TRIANGLE}} = \begin{bmatrix} x_1 & y_1 \\ x_2 & y_2 \\ x_3 & y_3 \end{bmatrix} \tag{4.1}$$

where each x,y pair is a position vector relative to the specified coordinate system. The matrix notation is very useful for geometry definition and manipulation in computer graphics applications; it would be convenient, there-

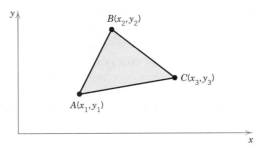

FIGURE 4.2 Triangle represented in an *xy*-coordinate system.

fore, if all geometric transformations could also be represented in this form. The use of ordinary cartesian coordinates, however, precludes this possibility, since, as will be seen in the following sections, some geometric transformations are obtained by matrix multiplication and others by vector addition. To avoid this problem, homogeneous coordinates have been traditionally used in place of ordinary cartesian coordinates in computer graphics and geometric modeling.

The representation of points in homogeneous coordinates provides a unified approach to the description of geometric transformations, even allowing for their implementation into graphics hardware. To understand homogeneous coordinates, imagine a two-dimensional ordinary coordinate point P_1 (x_1,y_1) lying in three-dimensional space as shown in Figure 4.3. Points on the ray connecting P_1 to the origin of the coordinate system can be described through a parameter h, such that:

$$P(x, y, z) = P(hx_1, hy_1, h) \qquad (4.2)$$

Any two-dimensional point can be represented by one of the points along the ray in three-dimensional space (called *homogeneous space*), except the one at the origin ($h = 0$). The ordinary coordinates correspond to the point

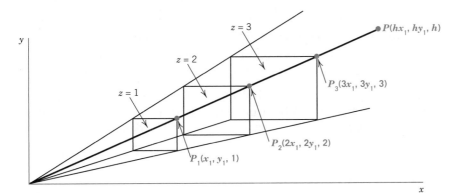

FIGURE 4.3 Three-dimensional representation of homogeneous space.

where the ray crosses the $z = 1$ plane. Different points in ordinary coordinates are represented by different rays in homogeneous space.

In homogeneous coordinates, therefore, a point is represented as $P(hx, hy, h)$. As an example, consider the point $P(2,4)$ in ordinary coordinates. The following homogeneous representations all identify the same point: $P(4,8,2)$, $P(6,12,3)$, $P(2,4,1)$. Given the homogeneous coordinates of a point as $P(m,n,h)$, the ordinary coordinates can be found by the representation $P(m/h, n/h, 1)$, and

$$x = \frac{m}{h}$$

$$(4.3)$$

$$y = \frac{n}{h}$$

When using homogeneous coordinates, points in two-dimensional space are represented by $[n \times 3]$ matrices, where n is the number of vertices in the object. The triangle shown in Figure 4.2 can now be described as

$$[P]_{\text{TRIANGLE}} = \begin{bmatrix} x_1 & y_1 & 1 \\ x_2 & y_2 & 1 \\ x_3 & y_3 & 1 \end{bmatrix}$$

$$(4.4)$$

4.2 TWO-DIMENSIONAL TRANSFORMATIONS

A geometric transformation involves the calculation of new coordinates for the points forming an object from their original to their transformed positions. It relocates every point according to specified rules. Scaling, translation, rotation, and so forth, can therefore be accomplished by simply transforming the coordinates of specific points. These transformations do not deform the object during motion and are called *rigid body transformations*. For each of the original points, one and only one transformed point is obtained.

Geometric transformations can be studied in two ways:

Object transformation changes the coordinates of the points forming the object, without altering the underlying coordinate system.

Coordinate system transformation creates a new coordinate system and then represents all points forming the object in this different system.

These two approaches are equivalent; coordinate transformations operate in the reverse sense from object transformations. It is common in computer graphics to use object transformations. They will be described in the following sections.

4.2.1 Scaling

The scaling transformation allows an object to change by expanding or contracting its dimensions. Scaling constants in the x and y directions provide

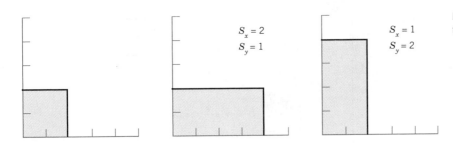

$S_x = 2$
$S_y = 1$

$S_x = 1$
$S_y = 2$

FIGURE 4.4 Scaling transformation.

changes in length. If larger than one, these constants represent expansion, and if smaller than one, they represent contraction. Also, they are always positive, since negative values produce what is referred to as *reflection*.

Mathematically, the scaling transformation of a point $P(x,y)$ into $P^*(x^*, y^*)$ can be written as

$$x^* = x \cdot S_x$$

(4.5)

$$y^* = y \cdot S_y$$

or, in matrix form,

$$[x^* \quad y^* \quad 1] = [x \quad y \quad 1] \begin{bmatrix} S_x & 0 & 0 \\ 0 & S_y & 0 \\ 0 & 0 & 1 \end{bmatrix}$$

(4.6)

Figure 4.4 shows examples of the effect of this transformation on a square. If the scaling factors applied in the x,y directions are different, changes in both size and shape occur, as shown in Figure 4.4. CAD systems always include a command "scale" to perform this function.

Scaling in the form just described is called *scaling about the origin*, since each point on the object changes its size, location, or both, with respect to the origin. It is said to be uniform if the scaling factor in the x and y directions are equal. This is equivalent to the "magnify" command found in CAD systems, which allows the user to magnify a specific area on the display screen.

4.2.2 Translation

The ability to move parts of a model is an essential feature of any graphics system. Consider, for example, displaying the movement of a piston inside a cylinder (or a set of objects connected to one end of the piston). The various positions of the piston and its elements can be conveniently and efficiently represented as a translation from the original to a new position. CAD systems usually perform this transformation under "move" and "copy" commands, depending on whether the original object is deleted or retained.

Translations cause an object to be displaced in a specific direction by a specific amount, as shown in Figure 4.5. Mathematically, this can be expressed as

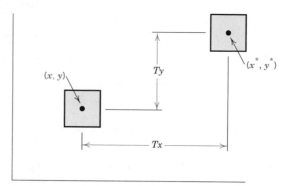

FIGURE 4.5 Translation transformation.

$$x^* = x + T_x$$
$$y^* = y + T_y$$
(4.7)

or, in matrix form,

$$[x^* \quad y^* \quad 1] = [x \quad y \quad 1] \begin{bmatrix} 1 & 0 & 0 \\ 0 & 1 & 0 \\ T_x & T_y & 1 \end{bmatrix}$$
(4.8)

The advantage in using homogeneous coordinates is apparent here; with ordinary coordinates rigid body translations could not be represented in matrix form.

4.2.3 Rotation

Rotation is an important geometric transformation in computer graphics. It is frequently used to enable the viewer to see an object from different directions, or to create entities arranged in a circular array. CAD systems use commands such as "rotate" and "array" to perform these operations.

The rotation transformation is a rotation about the origin of the coordinate system by a specified angle θ. Consider a point $P(x,y)$, as shown in Figure 4.6, rotated to position $P^*(x^*, y^*)$ by an angle θ. Since a convention about the direction of rotation must be adopted, assume that counterclockwise (CCW) rotations are positive and clockwise (CW) are negative. The transformed position P^* of point P due to rotation can be calculated by the use of simple trigonometric relations:

$$x = r \cos \phi$$
$$y = r \sin \phi$$
(4.9)

where ϕ and r are the parameters shown in Figure 4.5, and

$$x^* = r \cos (\phi + \theta) = r \cos \phi \cos \theta - r \sin \phi \sin \theta$$
(4.10)
$$y^* = r \sin (\phi + \theta) = r \sin \phi \cos \theta + r \cos \phi \sin \theta$$

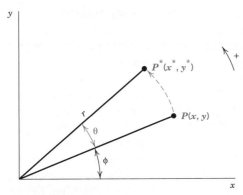

FIGURE 4.6 Rotation of a point.

Substituting x and y for their respective values:

$$x^* = x \cos \theta - y \sin \theta$$

$$y^* = x \sin \theta + y \cos \theta$$

or, in matrix form,

$$[x^* \quad y^* \quad 1] = [x \quad y \quad 1] \begin{bmatrix} \cos \theta & \sin \theta & 0 \\ -\sin \theta & \cos \theta & 0 \\ 0 & 0 & 1 \end{bmatrix}$$

Figure 4.7 shows a simple engineering example, the representation of a four-bar mechanism. The rotation transformation can be conveniently used to define the movement of the links by varying incrementally the value of the angle θ. Since the length of the moving links is fixed, the locus of any point on these links is a circle.

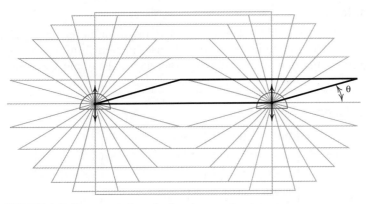

FIGURE 4.7 Representation of a four-bar mechanism.

4.3 COMPOSITE TWO-DIMENSIONAL TRANSFORMATIONS

Most two-dimensional problems require not one but a series of transformations to accomplish the desired goal. This series could include, for example, a change in scale followed by a translation or a rotation. The matrices representing each individual transformation are multiplied in a specified order, or concatenated, and are then applied to the point matrix to obtain the new positions for each point. The computational time involved in matrix multiplication is reduced by this approach—without concatenation each matrix would have to be multiplied separately with the point matrix as done in Example 4.1. Special care must be taken regarding the order in which the matrices are multiplied because some of the operations may not be commutative. Sequential rotations, for example, are not commutative; the order of operations affects the final result. The following examples demonstrate the approaches to setting composite transformations.

Example 4.1

Rotate the rectangle formed by points $P_1(1,1)$, $P_2(2,1)$, $P_3(2,3)$, $P_4(1,3)$ 30° CCW about the point $S(3,2)$.

Solution

The solution involves the following sequence of transformations:

1. Translation of S to the origin, which automatically moves the rectangle to a new position. (This can also be described as a movement of the origin to point S.)
2. 30° rotation, CCW.
3. Translation of S back to its original position.

Figure 4.8 shows the implementation of these steps. See Example 4.2 for a solution to this problem using concatenation.

Example 4.2

For models described by a large number of points, a more computationally efficient way to accomplish composite transformations is to first multiply all the matrices and only then apply the point matrix. Example 4.1 would then be solved as follows.

Solution

$$[T] = \begin{bmatrix} 1 & 0 & 0 \\ 0 & 1 & 0 \\ -3 & -2 & 1 \end{bmatrix} \begin{bmatrix} 0.866 & 0.5 & 0 \\ -0.5 & 0.866 & 0 \\ 0 & 0 & 1 \end{bmatrix} \begin{bmatrix} 1 & 0 & 0 \\ 0 & 1 & 0 \\ 3 & 2 & 1 \end{bmatrix}$$

$$= \begin{bmatrix} 0.866 & 0.5 & 0 \\ -0.5 & 0.866 & 0 \\ 1.4 & -1.23 & 1 \end{bmatrix}$$

And

$$[P]^* = [P][T] = \begin{bmatrix} 1 & 1 & 1 \\ 1 & 3 & 1 \\ 2 & 3 & 1 \\ 2 & 1 & 1 \end{bmatrix} \begin{bmatrix} 0.866 & 0.5 & 0 \\ -0.5 & 0.866 & 0 \\ 1.4 & -1.23 & 1 \end{bmatrix}$$

$$= \begin{bmatrix} 1.77 & 0.13 & 1 \\ 0.77 & 1.87 & 1 \\ 1.63 & 2.37 & 1 \\ 2.63 & 0.63 & 1 \end{bmatrix}$$

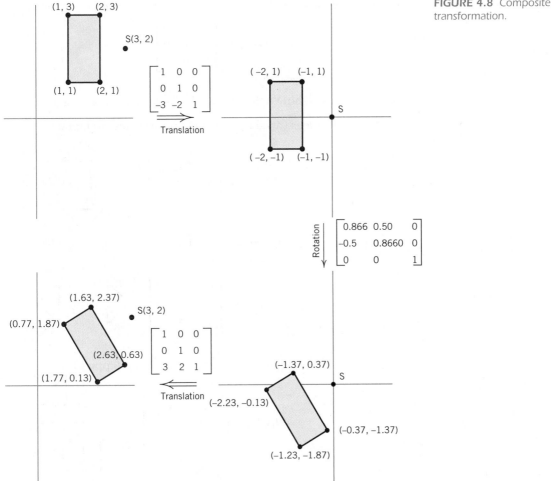

FIGURE 4.8 Composite transformation.

4.4 OTHER TRANSFORMATIONS

In addition to the primary types of two-dimensional transformations–scaling, translation, and rotation–other types can also be studied. Of these, the most common are reflection and shearing.

4.4.1 Reflection

The concept of reflection (or mirroring) can be understood by thinking of images in a mirror. The reflection transformation is useful in the construction of symmetric objects. For example, one half of the object may be created and then conveniently reflected to generate the whole picture, as shown in the construction of the truss in Figure 4.9. CAD systems always contain the command "mirror" to perform this operation.

Reflection can occur about a point or about a line. The reflection matrix relative to the x,y axes or the origin can be written in matrix form as

$$[T_{\mathrm{RFL}}] = \begin{bmatrix} a & 0 & 0 \\ 0 & b & 0 \\ 0 & 0 & 1 \end{bmatrix}$$

The following cases show different possible reflections of a triangle.

About the x axis (x values are kept and y values are flipped:)

$$[T_{\mathrm{RFL}}]_x = \begin{bmatrix} 1 & 0 & 0 \\ 0 & -1 & 0 \\ 0 & 0 & 1 \end{bmatrix}$$

About the y axis (y values are kept and x values are flipped:)

$$[T_{\mathrm{RFL}}]_y = \begin{bmatrix} -1 & 0 & 0 \\ 0 & 1 & 0 \\ 0 & 0 & 1 \end{bmatrix}$$

About the origin (both x and y values are flipped:)

$$[T_{\mathrm{RFL}}]_o = \begin{bmatrix} -1 & 0 & 0 \\ 0 & -1 & 0 \\ 0 & 0 & 1 \end{bmatrix}$$

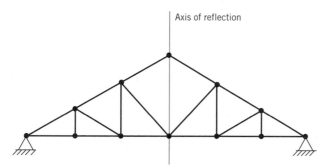

FIGURE 4.9 Use of reflection in modeling symmetric objects.

Other reflections through general lines or points are also possible. The reflection of the triangle about line $y = x$ shows one of these cases.

Reflection About the Line $y = x$

$$[T_{\text{RFL}}]_{(y=x)} = \begin{bmatrix} \cos 45° & -\sin 45° & 0 \\ \sin 45° & \cos 45° & 0 \\ 0 & 0 & 1 \end{bmatrix} \begin{bmatrix} 1 & 0 & 0 \\ 0 & -1 & 0 \\ 0 & 0 & 1 \end{bmatrix} \begin{bmatrix} \cos 45° & \sin 45° & 0 \\ -\sin 45° & \cos 45° & 0 \\ 0 & 0 & 1 \end{bmatrix}$$

⇓
Line rotation
to x-axis, CW
⇓

⇓
Reflection
about x-axis
⇓

⇓
Line rotation
back to original
position
⇓

$$[T_{\text{RFL}}]_{(y=x)} = \begin{bmatrix} 0 & 1 & 0 \\ 1 & 0 & 0 \\ 0 & 0 & 1 \end{bmatrix}$$

Example 4.3

Mirror the line segment formed by points $A(-1,-1)$ and $B(2,1)$ around the axis described by $x = -2$. Sketch the line before and after the transformation.

Solution

The steps in the solution are:

1. Move the axis ($x = -2$) to coincide with the y axis.

2. Mirror line AB about the y axis.

3. Move the mirroring axis to its original position.

The following matrices will implement these steps:

$$[T] = \begin{bmatrix} 1 & 0 & 0 \\ 0 & 1 & 0 \\ 2 & 0 & 1 \end{bmatrix} \begin{bmatrix} -1 & 0 & 0 \\ 0 & 1 & 0 \\ 0 & 0 & 1 \end{bmatrix} \begin{bmatrix} 1 & 0 & 0 \\ 0 & 1 & 0 \\ -2 & 0 & 1 \end{bmatrix} = \begin{bmatrix} -1 & 0 & 0 \\ 0 & 1 & 0 \\ -4 & 0 & 1 \end{bmatrix}$$

Applying this concatenated matrix to the point matrix yields the mirrored points.

$$\begin{bmatrix} -1 & -1 & 1 \\ 2 & 1 & 1 \end{bmatrix} \begin{bmatrix} -1 & 0 & 0 \\ 0 & 1 & 0 \\ -4 & 0 & 1 \end{bmatrix} = \begin{bmatrix} -3 & -1 & 1 \\ -6 & 1 & 1 \end{bmatrix}$$

The transformed positions are

$$A^* \, (-3, \, -1)$$

$$B^* \, (-6, \, 1)$$

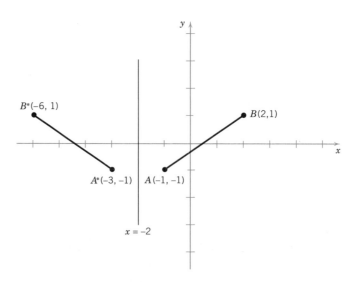

4.4.2 Shearing

The shearing transformation changes the value of a coordinate by adding to it a linear function of the other coordinate. The general shearing matrix is

$$[T_{\text{SH}}] = \begin{bmatrix} 1 & b & 0 \\ c & 1 & 0 \\ 0 & 0 & 1 \end{bmatrix}$$

The shearing of a square is described below for a few specific cases:

The x direction shear (affects only the x coordinate):

$$[T_{\text{SH}}]_x = \begin{bmatrix} 1 & 0 & 0 \\ \text{SH}_x & 1 & 0 \\ 0 & 0 & 1 \end{bmatrix}$$

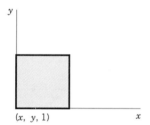

$(x, y, 1)$

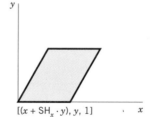

$[(x + \text{SH}_x \cdot y), y, 1]$

The y direction shear (affects only the y coordinate):

$$[T_{\text{SH}}]_y = \begin{bmatrix} 1 & \text{SH}_y & 0 \\ 0 & 1 & 0 \\ 0 & 0 & 1 \end{bmatrix}$$

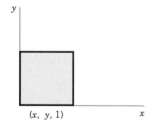

$(x, y, 1)$

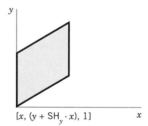

$[x, (y + \text{SH}_y \cdot x), 1]$

4.5 ENGINEERING APPLICATIONS

As stated at the start of this chapter, many engineering problems can be solved by considering only a two-dimensional representation of the space conditions. The following examples reflect this two-dimensional approach to problem solving. In each case, two possible ways of reaching a solution are given [18,19]:

- By developing a computer program which uses appropriate equations and transformations, or
- By using an existing CAD system, where the values required are interactively input by the user. In this case, macro programming within the CAD system can automate the process considerably.

Example 4.4

For the plane stress condition shown, calculate the magnitude of the principal stresses and their direction.

Solution

This problem can be solved graphically by means of a Mohr's circle, where the stress condition on each plane is represented by a point on the circle. The original stresses are plotted with the normal stress, σ, along the horizontal axis and the shear stress, τ, along the vertical axis. Two points, P_1 and P_2, representing stresses on two mutually perpendicular surfaces, are located in the position shown in Figure 4.10. For this problem, P_1 (6,6) and P_2 ($-10,-6$). The Mohr's circle is drawn with center at point C and radius CP_1. The principal stresses σ_1 and σ_2 are found at the intersection of the circle with the x-axis, and the maximum shearing stress is equal to the radius of the circle. The direction of the major principal stress, σ_1, is half the angle 2ϕ

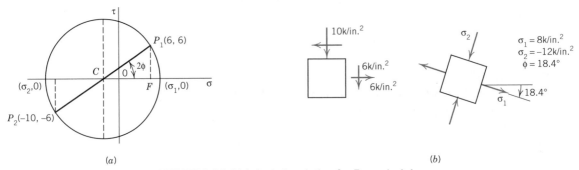

FIGURE 4.10 Mohr's circle solution for Example 4.4.

shown on the Mohr's circle. Figure 4.10 shows these principal stresses for the numerical values given in this problem. In addition to its use in determining principal stresses, the Mohr's circle can be employed for finding the eigenvalues of symmetric matrices. The reader is encouraged to obtain more information on the Mohr's circle from any text on mechanics of materials [20].

The process of drawing the Mohr's circle can be automated through a computer program. The user inputs the values of σ and τ to create the circle, from which the magnitudes and directions of the principal stresses are obtained. Figure 4.11 shows a flowchart for this procedure. When implementing this flowchart, it is convenient to add an algorithm to display the stressed element in its original and rotated positions, as shown in Figure 4.10.

Another way of solving this problem is to use an interactive CAD system, where the user creates the Mohr's circle using the "circle" command and obtains the desired stress values directly from it. The magnitude of the principal stresses, for example, can be found by locating the intersection of the Mohr's circle with the σ axis, using a "snap to intersection" command. Its direction can be measured with a "measure angle" command. As mentioned earlier, the use of macro programming automates this process.

Example 4.5

Create a graphical display for the slider-crank mechanism shown, indicating the various positions of the mechanism as the angle θ varies from $0°$ to $90°$. Find the locus of point M, midpoint of link PQ.

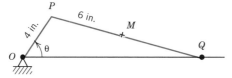

Solution

This problem can be solved through a computer program that will perform the required rotations of the crank. The user inputs the geometry of the mechanism and the increments for the angle θ. The position of point M should be found for each rotational increment, connected and displayed, as shown in Figure 4.12.

Another approach is to use an interactive CAD system, as mentioned in Example 4.4. The user creates the mechanism with a "line" command and rotates the crank OP incrementally. For each new position of point P the location of Q is found as the intersection of a circle of radius PQ, centered at P, and line OQ. A command such as "snap to intersection" can be used for this purpose. Once all midpoint locations have been found, the locus is obtained by connecting the points with straight line segments or an interpolating curve as described in Chapter 10. Here, again, the use of macro programming automates the process.

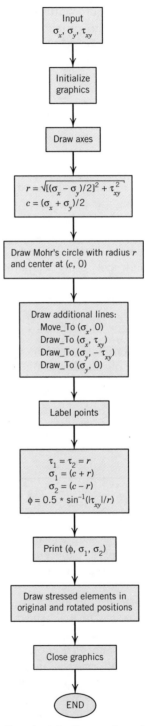

FIGURE 4.11 Flowchart for the creation of a Mohr's circle.

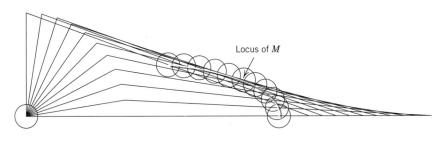

FIGURE 4.12 Locus of midpoint for Example 4.5.

Locus of *M*

SUMMARY

Two-dimensional representations of models, typical in the solution of many engineering problems, are studied in this chapter. Various rigid body transformations, such as rotation, scaling, translation, and reflection, are defined and correlated to specific commands used in modern CAD systems. It is shown that two-dimensional transformations can be effectively used in solving a variety of engineering applications.

EXERCISES

1. Given a triangle with the following coordinates for its vertices: $A(3,1)$, $B(1,3)$, and $C(3,3)$, rotate it by $90°$ about an axis passing through point $P(2,2)$ and determine the new coordinates for A, B, and C.

2. Show that a circle, when subjected to the transformation given by matrix

$$[T] = \begin{bmatrix} 1.5 & 0 & 0 \\ 0 & 0.75 & 0 \\ 0 & 0 & 1 \end{bmatrix}$$

   does not remain a circle. What is the transformed shape?

3. Magnify the triangle given in Exercise 1 to twice its size while maintaining point C in its original position. Calculate the transformed coordinates of the three points.

4. Derive the appropriate matrix for reflection about a line given in slope-intercept form, where the slope is m and the y intercept is $(0,c)$.

5. A circle is defined by the equation

$$(x_1)^2 + (y_1)^2 = 1$$

   Find its equation in terms of x,y coordinates, assuming that in the x_1,y_1 coordinate system x_1 is equal to $4x$, and y_1 is equal to $2y$. Does the circle remain a circle?

6. Write the series of transformations (in matrix form) that are needed to place the square shown in Figure 4.13, reduced to half its size, into the position shown in Figure 4.14, where the center of the square is at (2, − 2).

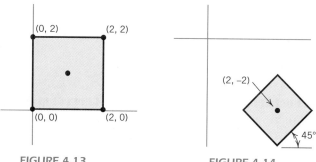

FIGURE 4.13   FIGURE 4.14

7. Use a graphics library to develop a computer program to display the 4-bar mechanism shown in Figure 4.7, varying θ from 0° to 360°, by increments of 30°. Solve the same problem using an interactive CAD system.

8. Develop a computer program to implement the Mohr's circle shown in Figure 4.11. Draw the two-dimensional stressed element in its original and rotated positions, including the stress vectors. Experiment with a CAD system to find stresses at any plane by using the Mohr's circle.

9. Implement an algorithm to output Figure 4.12. The user input should be the geometry of the mechanism and the angular increment. Use a CAD system to solve the same problem, for the specific values given in Example 4.5.

Chapter 5

Two-Dimensional Viewing Operations

A geometric model is a numerical description of an object including its size, shape, and other properties. A model description is most conveniently achieved in an unbounded cartesian coordinate system, where units can be associated with the x, y coordinate values. Obtaining a graphical image of the geometric model on the display screen requires a two-step approach.

1. The model is converted into a coordinate system that fits the screen.

2. Decisions are made relative to how much of the model is to appear and where it should appear on the screen. Step 2 will be discussed in Section 5.1.

To perform the first step outlined above, two coordinate systems are used, defined below.

World Coordinate (WC) system is a right-handed cartesian system used by the application program and indicating the actual coordinates of an

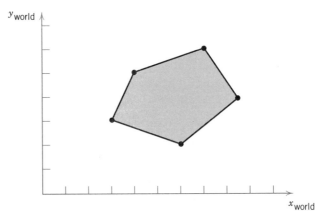

FIGURE 5.1 World Coordinate (WC) system.

object, as shown in Figure 5.1. The transformations described in the previous chapter (rotation, scaling, and so forth) can be directly applied in world coordinates.

Device Coordinate (DC) system corresponds to the actual device used, and relates to the device's surface where the image of the object will appear, as shown in Figure 5.2.

The transformation from world coordinates to device coordinates depends on the type of display device used. Therefore, an application program developed for one computer system may not work on another, unless a driver translates the geometric data describing the model into device-specific coordinates which vary from one display device to another. This variation causes difficulties in the use of application software because of the lack of portability. Also, general methods for computer graphics applications tend to lose importance in the face of device concerns.

In an effort to place device-related details in the background, a uniform interface to applications was developed through a device-independent driver, described in an appropriate coordinate system. Graphics standards such as GKS or PHIGS (Chapter 3) define these coordinates.

FIGURE 5.2 Device Coordinate (DC) system. (*a*) 1040 × 1040 resolution. (*b*) 240 × 320 resolution.

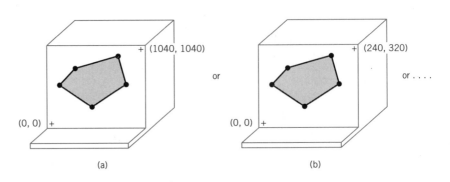

The *Virtual* or *Normalized Device Coordinate (NDC) system* is defined for an idealized graphics device. The display surface of this device is typically made to correspond to a unit square, with the origin in the lower left corner, as shown in the accompanying figure.

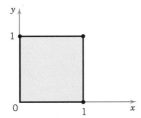

GKS establishes a general process of coordinate transformations, shown schematically in Figure 5.3 [14]. The model is described initially in world coordinates by the application program. It then undergoes a viewing transformation which changes its coordinates from WC space to NDC space. At this point the model can be shown in any of a number of display devices, because NDC is independent of the type of display used. Finally, a transformation onto device coordinates occurs, reflecting the limitations of the display used. The representation now becomes hardware dependent.

During this process of coordinate transformations, the application program may ask GKS to show only parts of a picture. A cutting process known as *clipping* is applied to remove the parts that are not to be displayed. In GKS, clipping does not occur during the normalization transformation; it is delayed until the output primitives are to appear on the viewing surface of a workstation. More details on this operation are given in Section 5.2.

5.1 WINDOW-TO-VIEWPORT MAPPING

The previous section explained that decisions must be made to determine which parts of an object are to appear on the display screen, and where they

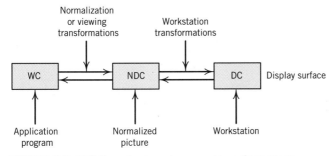

FIGURE 5.3 GKS Coordinate systems and transformations.

FIGURE 5.4 Window and viewport definitions.

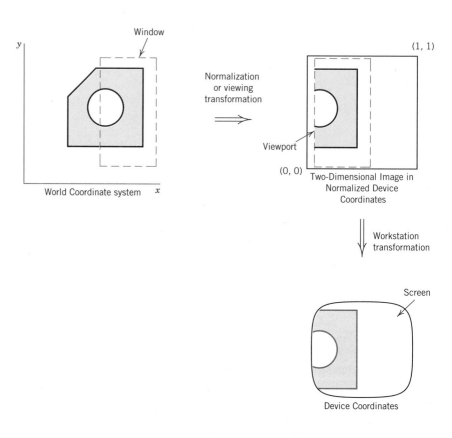

should appear. These decisions are reached by choosing two rectangular regions, one in WC—the window—and the other in NDC—the viewport.

GKS defines a *window* as a rectangular region of the world coordinate space, and the *viewport* as a rectangular region of the normalized device coordinate space. Figure 5.4 shows an example of both. The normalization or viewing transformation indicated in the figure, also referred to as *window-to-viewport-mapping*, maps the window onto the viewport. Obviously, the mapping is carried over to the device through a workstation transformation.

FIGURE 5.5 Window-to-viewport mapping.

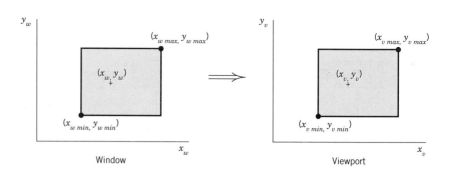

A window-to-viewport mapping can be expressed by the following relationships, based on elements shown in Figure 5.5:

$$\frac{x_v - x_{vmin}}{x_{vmax} - x_{vmin}} = \frac{x_w - x_{wmin}}{x_{wmax} - x_{wmin}} \tag{5.1}$$

and

$$\frac{y_v - y_{vmin}}{y_{vmax} - y_{vmin}} = \frac{y_w - y_{wmin}}{y_{wmax} - y_{wmin}} \tag{5.2}$$

So that

$$x_v = (x_w - x_{wmin})\left(\frac{x_{vmax} - x_{vmin}}{x_{wmax} - x_{wmin}}\right) + x_{vmin} \tag{5.3}$$

$$y_v = (y_w - y_{wmin})\left(\frac{y_{vmax} - y_{vmin}}{y_{wmax} - y_{wmin}}\right) + y_{vmin} \tag{5.4}$$

The terms

$$\left(\frac{x_{vmax} - x_{vmin}}{x_{wmax} - x_{wmin}}\right) \quad \text{and} \quad \left(\frac{y_{vmax} - y_{vmin}}{y_{wmax} - y_{wmin}}\right) \tag{5.5}$$

are constant for all points being mapped, and are simply scaling factors in the x and y directions, S_x and S_y. If $S_x \neq S_y$, distortions occur in the picture. The concept of *aspect ratio* refers to this situation. For the rectangular window or viewport described previously, the aspect ratio of each is given by the ratio of width to height:

$$AR = \frac{x_{max} - x_{min}}{y_{max} - y_{min}} \tag{5.6}$$

If the aspect ratios of both window and viewport are the same, then $S_x = S_y$ and there will be no distortion of the picture. For circular features special care must be taken, or circles will appear as ellipses on the display screen. Figure 5.6 shows examples of window-to-viewport mapping for different conditions. Notice that the parameters inside the parentheses are (x_{min}, x_{max}, y_{min}, y_{max}). The "zooming" effect shown in Figure 5.6 is obtained by mapping a smaller window to the whole viewport. It gives the impression that the user is located closer to the object.

Example 5.1

Find the transformation matrix that will map points contained in a window whose lower left corner is at (2,2) and upper right corner is at (6,5) onto a normalized viewport that has a lower left corner at $(\frac{1}{2},\frac{1}{2})$ and upper right corner at (1,1).

FIGURE 5.6 Examples of window-to-viewport mapping.

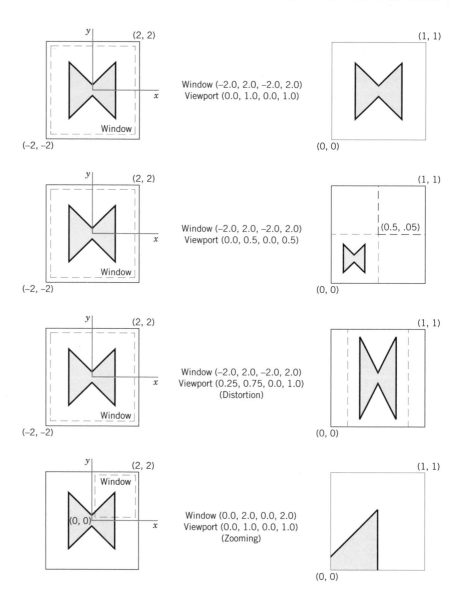

Window (−2.0, 2.0, −2.0, 2.0)
Viewport (0.0, 1.0, 0.0, 1.0)

Window (−2.0, 2.0, −2.0, 2.0)
Viewport (0.0, 0.5, 0.0, 0.5)

Window (−2.0, 2.0, −2.0, 2.0)
Viewport (0.25, 0.75, 0.0, 1.0)
(Distortion)

Window (0.0, 2.0, 0.0, 2.0)
Viewport (0.0, 1.0, 0.0, 1.0)
(Zooming)

Solution

The window/viewport parameters are

$$
\begin{aligned}
x_{w\min} &= 2 & x_{v\min} &= \tfrac{1}{2} \\
x_{w\max} &= 6 & x_{v\max} &= 1 \\
y_{w\min} &= 2 & y_{v\min} &= \tfrac{1}{2} \\
y_{w\max} &= 5 & y_{v\max} &= 1
\end{aligned}
$$

Therefore, based on Eqs. 5.3 and 5.4,

$$S_x = \frac{1 - 1/2}{6 - 2} = \frac{1}{8}$$

$$S_y = \frac{1 - 1/2}{5 - 2} = \frac{1}{6}$$

Equations 5.3 and 5.4 can be rewritten as:

$$x_v = (x_w - x_{wmin}) s_x + x_{vmin}$$

$$y_v = (y_w - y_{wmin}) s_y + y_{vmin}$$

Or, in matrix form,

$$[x_v \quad y_v \quad 1] =$$

$$[x_w \quad y_w \quad 1] \begin{bmatrix} S_x & 0 & 0 \\ 0 & S_y & 0 \\ (-s_x \cdot x_{wmin} + x_{vmin}) & (-s_y \cdot y_{wmin} + y_{vmin}) & 1 \end{bmatrix}$$

And the transformation matrix becomes:

$$M_{map} = \begin{bmatrix} \frac{1}{8} & 0 & 0 \\ 0 & \frac{1}{6} & 0 \\ \frac{1}{4} & \frac{1}{6} & 1 \end{bmatrix}$$

5.2 TWO-DIMENSIONAL CLIPPING

As shown in Figure 5.4, there may be times when only a portion of the total model is to be displayed. In that case, the window is used to clip the visible parts of WC space, much like cutting part of a picture from a magazine. This process is known as clipping. It can be considered a geometric transformation and involves the cutting of all lines or curves that cross the boundaries of the window. Only portions of each entity will be displayed on the screen. Clipping, therefore, breaks each element of the picture into visible and invisible parts and discards the parts that are invisible. If clipping is not employed, the portion of the image falling beyond the limits of the display may appear in the opposite side, as shown in Figure 5.7. Although less likely to occur in present-day hardware, this wraparound effect should be avoided.

The algorithms used in the clipping process depend entirely on the shape of the window. For the case studies in this chapter, it will be assumed that the window is rectangular, with sides parallel to the principal coordinate axes.

5.2.1 Point Clipping

Point clipping is easily accomplished by checking the coordinates of the point against the boundaries of the window. If the window is defined by its

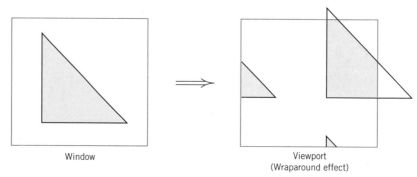

Window   Viewport
(Wraparound effect)

FIGURE 5.7 Wraparound effect.

four corners, that is, left (L), right (R), top (T), and bottom (B), as shown in Figure 5.8, a point $P(x,y)$ will be visible if all the following inequalities are satisfied:

$$x_L \le x \le x_R \tag{5.7}$$

$$y_B \le y \le y_T \tag{5.8}$$

If one of the inequalities does not hold, the point will not be displayed. Although this is a simple decision, it would be inappropriate to break an object into the totality of its points for display purposes. There are more efficient algorithms that take into account the existence of lines and polygons in the object's structure.

5.2.2   Line Clipping

The algorithms used for line clipping can be divided into two parts:

1. Check all line segments and separate those that intersect the window boundaries.

2. Clip the line segments obtained from step 1 by calculating their intersections with the window boundaries.

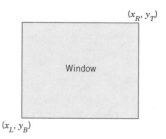

(x_R, y_T)

Window

(x_L, y_B)

FIGURE 5.8 Window boundaries.

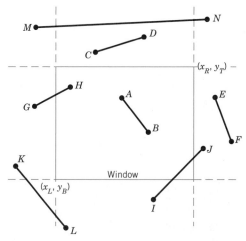

FIGURE 5.9 Placement of various line segments with respect to the window boundaries.

Step 1 can be accomplished by dividing all line segments into the following categories:

1. *Visible.* Both endpoints of the segment fall within the window boundaries. Line segment *AB* in Figure 5.9 falls in this category. This line is displayed without further checks.

2. *Invisible.* If both endpoints are outside one of the window boundaries, the line is removed from the display. A line segment from $P_1(x_1,y_1)$ to $P_2(x_2,y_2)$ is not visible if one of the following inequalities holds:

$$x_1 \text{ and } x_2 < x_L$$
$$x_1 \text{ and } x_2 > x_R \tag{5.9}$$
$$y_1 \text{ and } y_2 < y_B$$
$$y_1 \text{ and } y_2 > y_T$$

Line segments *CD* and *EF* in Figure 5.9 satisfy one of these inequalities.

3. *Indeterminate.* The line segment does not fall into any of the two previous categories and should be considered for clipping. Segments *GH*, *IJ*, and *KL* in Figure 5.9 are examples.

5.2.2.1 Cohen–Sutherland Algorithm

The Cohen–Sutherland algorithm is a simple and efficient procedure for determining the category in which a specific line segment falls with respect to the rectangular window boundaries. The algorithm is developed in two stages:

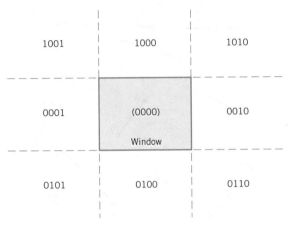

FIGURE 5.10 Codes for line endpoint regions.

1. A 4-bit code is assigned to the endpoints of the line segment being checked, based on nine regions that include and surround the window, as shown in Figure 5.10. Each bit of the code is set to 1 (true) or 0 (false), starting with the leftmost one, so

Bit 1 = 1   endpoint of the segment is above the window
Bit 2 = 1   endpoint of the segment is below the window
Bit 3 = 1   endpoint of the segment is to the right of the window
Bit 4 = 1   endpoint of the segment is to the left of the window

Obviously, if the bit code is (0000), the endpoint is inside the window or on its boundaries. All bit codes are assigned to the endpoints of the line segments by comparing each endpoint coordinate against the coordinates of the window boundaries.

2. The endpoints of the line segment are checked with respect to each other. If the same bit is set to "true" or "1" at both endpoints, the segment is invisible. For example, a segment *EF* with endcodes (1010) and (0010) is located to the right of the window, as can be seen in Figure 5.11. On the other hand, if both endcodes are (0000) the line segment is contained inside the window. An indeterminate segment is one with bits set to 1 in different locations, such as segments *AB* and *CD* in Figure 5.11: (1000) and (0010). These segments may or may not cross the window boundaries. Line *AB* is invisible, but line *CD* is partially visible and must be clipped.

A special logic, called the *bitwise logical AND*, is used when checking the cases described previously. It assumes the following is valid when checking the endpoint codes bit by bit.

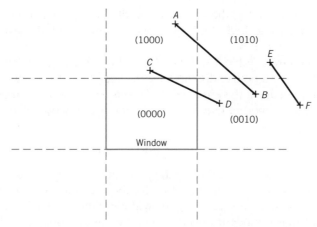

FIGURE 5.11 Examples of the use of endpoint codes for checking line visibility.

Endpoint 1		Endpoint 2		Bitwise logical AND
0	and	0	⟶ false ⟶	0
0	and	1	⟶ false ⟶	0
1	and	0	⟶ false ⟶	0
1	and	1	⟶ true ⟶	1

Based on this logic, the visibility of the segment is determined as follows:

Visible ⟶ Both endpoint codes are (0000).

Invisible ⟶ Bitwise logical AND of the endpoint codes is not (0000).

Indeterminate ⟶ Bitwise logical AND of the endpoint codes is (0000), but each individual endpoint does not have a (0000) code.

TABLE 5.1

Line	Endpoint Codes		Logical AND	Comments
1	1000	1001	1000	Invisible
2	0101	0100	0100	Invisible
3	0000	0000	0000	Visible
4	1001	0110	0000	Check
5	0001	1000	0000	Check

Using the AND operator, the endpoints of all line segments under consideration are thus checked. Table 5.1 gives examples of the calculations needed for this operation.

As can be seen from Table 5.1, if the bitwise logical AND is (0000), the line will be visible only if both endpoints have the code (0000). Otherwise, partial visibility may occur. In this case, the endpoints are passed to a routine that determines the point(s) of intersection with the window boundaries.

5.2.2.2 Intersection Calculations and Clipping

One of the simplest ways of finding the point of intersection between a line segment and a window boundary is to solve the equations representing both the line and boundary. For a rectangular window aligned with the coordinate axes, not all four boundaries need be checked at one time [21]. By determining which bit code of the bitwise logical AND is not zero, the window boundary where the intersection will occur can be found as follows:

$$\text{For bit } 1 = 1 \longrightarrow \text{intersection with } y = y_{\text{T}}$$
$$\text{For bit } 2 = 1 \longrightarrow \text{intersection with } y = y_{\text{B}}$$
$$\text{For bit } 3 = 1 \longrightarrow \text{intersection with } x = x_{\text{R}}$$
$$\text{For bit } 4 = 1 \longrightarrow \text{intersection with } x = x_{\text{L}}$$

Figure 5.12 shows this process for two line segments. The intersection is found by setting parametric equations for both the line segment and the window boundary. For a line segment joining $P_1(x_1,y_1)$ and $P_2(x_2,y_2)$ the equations are

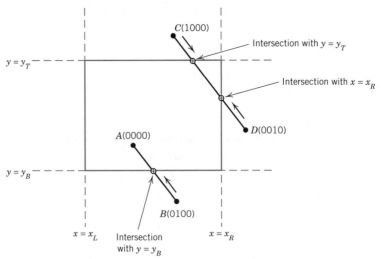

FIGURE 5.12 Isolating the appropriate window boundaries for intersection calculations.

$$x = x_1 + t(x_2 - x_1) \tag{5.10}$$

$$0 \le t \le 1$$

$$y = y_1 + t(y_2 - y_1) \tag{5.11}$$

At the window boundaries the equations become $x = $ constant or $y = $ constant. The intersection point is found by calculating the value of t in either Eq. 5.10 or 5.11, and substituting it in the other equation.

Example 5.2

For the rectangular window boundaries given as $x_L = 2$, $y_B = 2$, $x_R = 8$, $y_T = 8$, check the visibility of the following segments using the Cohen–Sutherland algorithm and, if necessary, clip them against the appropriate window boundaries.

Line AB: $A(3,10)$ $B(6,12)$
Line CD: $C(4,1)$ $D(10,6)$

Solution

Step 1. Set up the endcodes of the two lines

Line AB $A(3,10) \longrightarrow (1000)$
                    $B(6,12) \longrightarrow (1000)$
        Logical AND $\longrightarrow (1000)$
                        INVISIBLE

Line CD $C(4,1) \longrightarrow (0100)$
                    $D(10,6) \longrightarrow (0010)$
        Logical AND $\longrightarrow (0000)$
                    INDETERMINATE

Step 2. Clipping of line CD.

(a) Endpoint C has a code of (0100). Since bit 2 is not zero, intersection must be found with the boundary $y = y_B = 2$. The parametric equation of line CD is

$$x = 4 + t(10 - 4) = 4 + 6t \tag{1}$$

$$y = 1 + t(6 - 1) = 1 + 5t \tag{2}$$

Substituting $y = 2$ in Eq. 2 yields the value of

$$t = \tfrac{1}{5} = 0.2$$

And

$$x = 4 + \tfrac{1}{5}(6) = 5.2$$

Intersection point:

$$I_1\ (5.2,2)$$

(b) Endpoint D has a code of (0010). For bit 3 not equal to zero, the intersection with the boundary $x = x_R = 8$ must be found. Substituting $x = 8$ in Eq. 1 yields

$$8 = 4 + 6t \therefore t = \tfrac{4}{6} = 0.667$$

And

$$y = 1 + 5\left(\frac{2}{3}\right) = \frac{3 + 10}{3} = 4.33$$

Intersection point:

$$I_2 \ (8,4.33)$$

Since both I_1 and I_2 lie on the window boundary, their endcodes are (0000) and (0000), respectively. The line segment is, therefore, visible between the two intersection points.

5.2.2.3 Midpoint Subdivision

Midpoint subdivision is a useful method of numerical analysis, an alternative to finding the point of intersection between the line segment and the window boundaries by equation solving. The line segment is separated at its midpoint, and the two resulting segments are checked for visibility and possible clipping. If not totally visible or invisible, the segment is again bisected and the process continues until the intersection with the window boundary is found within the specified tolerance. Figure 5.13 gives an example of this process. If the endpoints of the line segment are $P_1(x_1, y_1)$ and $P_2(x_2, y_2)$, each midpoint $P_m(x_m, y_m)$ is found by the following expression:

$$x_m = \frac{x_1 + x_2}{2} \qquad y_m = \frac{y_1 + y_2}{2} \tag{5.12}$$

Midpoint subdivision can be efficiently implemented in hardware because division by two is accomplished by a simple bit shift to the right. For example, (0100) is the 4-bit binary representation of the number four. A shift to the right yields (0010), which represents $2 = \tfrac{4}{2}$. When implemented in hardware,

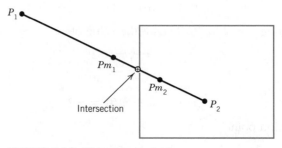

FIGURE 5.13 Midpoint subdivision.

the midpoint subdivision process involves only integer values. When implemented in software, it may be slower than the direct calculation method.

Example 5.3

A window is defined by the coordinates of its lower left corner (2,2) and upper right corner (8,6). A line segment from $A(4,3)$ to $B(10,5)$ is to be clipped against this window. Find the endpoint codes of the line and their AND logical intersection. If needed, calculate the points of intersection of the line against the window boundaries by the midpoint subdivision method.

Solution

Based on the coordinates of the window boundaries, the endpoint codes of the lines are:

$$A \longrightarrow (0000)$$
$$B \longrightarrow (0010)$$

The logical AND intersection is (0000), so the line must be checked for clipping. The following table implements the midpoint subdivision method. When the line segment is bisected, both halves are checked against the window boundaries for possible further subdivision.

LINE AB: $A(4,3)$, $B(10,5)$

Subdivisions	Midpoint	Segment Chosen for Further Subdivision
1	7,4	(7,4) to (10,5)
2	(8.5,4.5)	(7,4) to (8.5,4.5)
3	(7.75,4.25)	(7.75,4.25) to (8.5,4.5)
4	(8.13,4.38)	(7.75,4.25) to (8.13,4.38)
5	(7.94,4.31)	(7.94,4.31) to (8.13,4.38)
6	(8.03,4.34)	(7.94,4.31) to (8.03,4.34)
7	(7.99,4.33)	

Since the x coordinate is equal to 8 at the window boundary, the intersection can be approximated as (8,4.33).

5.2.2.4 Comparison of Line Clipping Methods

The part of the clipping process that takes most computational time is the intersection calculation with the window boundaries. The Cohen–Sutherland algorithm reduces these calculations by first discarding the lines that can be trivially accepted or rejected. The intersection with the window boundaries is then found and used to break the original line into two new segments which are checked again for possible trivial acceptance or rejection. The process continues until all line segments, original and new, are checked.

Midpoint subdivision is a special case of the Cohen–Sutherland algorithm where the intersection calculation is not done by equation solving but by a midpoint approximation method. This method is particularly suitable for hardware implementation, which is very fast and efficient.

There are other algorithms for line clipping, such as the Cyrus–Beck and the Liang–Barski algorithms. They are widely described in the literature [22]. Specialized algorithms for polygon clipping have also been developed [22].

5.3 APPLICATION PROBLEMS

The concepts described in this chapter are part of all computer graphics systems. Viewing transformations and clipping must be performed before graphical images can be displayed on a computer screen. The following examples highlight the use of these concepts.

Example 5.4

Given the geometry of the connecting rod shown below, generate its image by dividing the computer screen into three viewports, so that

(a) The lower half of the screen shows the full rod.

(b) The upper left quarter shows the left end of the rod.

(c) The upper right quarter shows the right end of the rod.

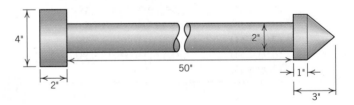

Solution

A computer program is developed to create this image through the appropriate viewing transformations. At the start, a geometric description of the rod is prepared and stored, in world coordinates. Using a graphics library, the three windows (WC) and three viewports (NDC) are created in pairs, satisfying the conditions of the problem. The following are possible combinations that will create the desired entities:

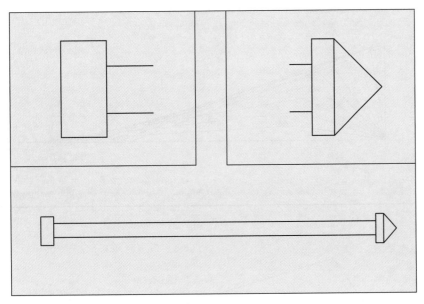

FIGURE 5.14

Lower half: set_window $(-0.5,65.,-5.,5.)$
                 set_viewport $(0.,1.,0.,0.5)$

Upper left: set_window $(-5.,5.,-4.,5.)$
                 set_viewport $(0.,0.5,0.5,1.)$

Upper right: set_window $(50.,60.,-4.,5.)$
                 set_viewport $(0.5,1.,0.5,1.)$

In most graphics libraries, clipping is performed automatically during the window-to-viewport mapping. Figure 5.14 shows the result of this implementation.

Another solution to this problem could be obtained by means of an interactive CAD system, with the ability to divide the screen in various viewports. In this case, a full geometric description of the rod would be prepared on the screen. The commands needed to create three viewports would then be invoked and, on the upper left and upper right viewports, a zooming operation would display only the appropriate ends of the rod.

Example 5.5

The slider-crank problem described in Example 4.5 can be modified, so that separate viewports display the mechanism in its various positions and the locus of the follower midpoint, as shown in Figure 5.15. The problem could be further enhanced by using additional viewports where various parameters such as the angular velocities and accelerations of the links are plotted.

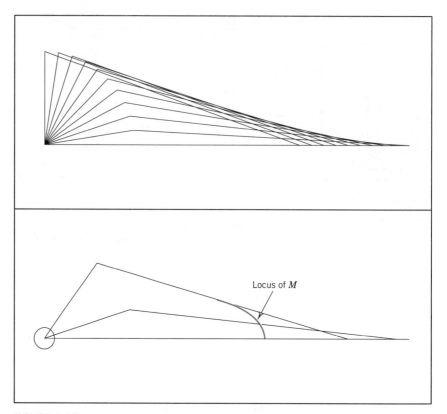

FIGURE 5.15

SUMMARY

Chapter 5 described the process of mapping the geometric model of an object from a world coordinate system convenient for design and modeling into the coordinate system of the display device. The need to use an intermediate, normalized coordinate system to achieve device independence was stressed. A description was also given of clipping algorithms that discard portions of the model not meant to appear on the display screen.

EXERCISES

1. Use a series of transformations in matrix form (translation, scaling, translation) to derive the window-to-viewport-mapping relationships, also known as the normalization transformation.

2. Find the normalization transformation matrix which maps the rectangle $A(1,0)$, $B(4,3)$, $C(3,4)$, $D(0,1)$ to the normalized viewport shown in the accompanying figure.

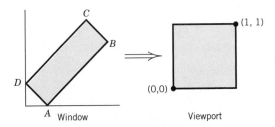

3. Suppose a window is defined as $(-20,20)$, $(60,60)$ in the world coordinate system. Consider a line segment whose two endpoints are given by $(-30,0)$ and $(80,40)$ and

(a) Determine the logical AND of the endpoint bit codes.
(b) Find the intersection of the line segment with the appropriate window boundaries.
(c) Assume that a viewport is defined by $(10,30)$ and $(200,130)$. Find the viewport coordinates for the intersection points.

4. In Problem 3, will the window size compared to the viewport size produce any distortions on the image of objects? Explain your answer.

5. A window is defined by the coordinates of its lower left corner $(2,2)$ and upper right corner $(6,8)$. A line segment from $A(3,1)$ to $B(7,5)$ is to be clipped against it. Find the endpoint codes of the line segment and their bitwise logical AND. Calculate the points of intersection of the line against the window boundaries, if any, by the midpoint subdivision method.

6. Establish the equations that will transform the area of a geographical map covering four square miles into a normalized viewport $(0,0)$ to $(1,1)$.

7. Use a graphics library to develop a program that outputs Figure 5.14. Obtain the same output by using an interactive CAD system.

8. Solve the slider-crank problem given in Example 5.5, placing the output in two viewports as shown in Figure 5.15.

Chapter 6

Three- Dimensional Coordinate Geometry

S ome engineering problems, such as those involving graphs, certain maps, cross-sectional views of objects, and the like, can be considered two-dimensional. However, most problems relating to engineering design deal with three-dimensional objects. A variety of shapes or patterns is normally used to create the final three-dimensional shapes, which can be represented in the display screen as a framework of lines, a combination of flat polygonal surfaces, or a combination of solid primitives. For certain applications, such as the design of automobile or aircraft bodies, special design parameters are used to modify three-dimensional surface patterns until specific criteria are met.

Whatever method is used, the three-dimensional object is usually created in a three-dimensional world coordinate system and then mapped onto the two-dimensional system of the display. Manipulation, viewing, and creation of the object's image require the use of three-dimensional geometry and coordinate transformations.

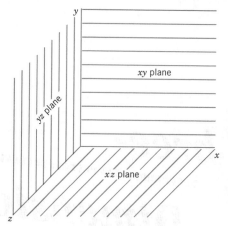

FIGURE 6.1 Representation of the three principal orthogonal planes.

6.1 COORDINATE SYSTEMS

Points in the three-dimensional world are represented by a three-dimensional coordinate system which can be considered an extension of the two-dimensional system used in Chapter 4. In the two-dimensional world, the xy plane contained the whole object. In three dimensions, an additional orthogonal z axis is introduced, creating two other principal planes, xz and yz, as shown in Figure 6.1.

The orientation of the coordinate axes in the three-dimensional system can be either "right-handed" or "left-handed". The right-handed system is modeled by a right hand with the thumb placed in the direction of the z axis, the fingers curling from the positive x axis to the positive y axis (see Figure 6.2).

The left-handed system locates the z axis as shown in Figure 6.3. If the left hand is placed with the fingers curled from the positive x axis to the positive y axis, the thumb will point to the positive z axis.

FIGURE 6.2 Right-handed coordinate system.

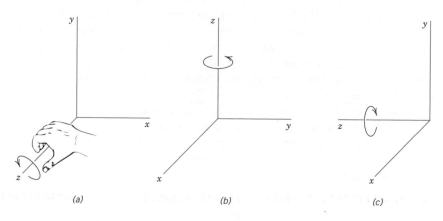

(a)   (b)   (c)

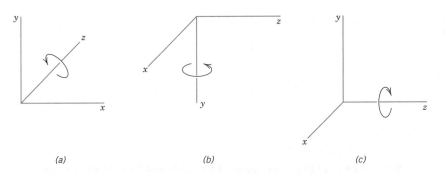

(a)   (b)   (c)

FIGURE 6.3 Left-handed coordinate system.

Engineering problems are conventionally solved in a right-handed co-ordinate system, and the world coordinate system is therefore considered to be right-handed. Many computer graphics systems, however, make use of the left-handed system, with an xy image plane and the positive z axis into the screen. This causes increasing positive values of z to recede from the viewer.

In addition to the Cartesian system, other coordinate systems can be used to define a three-dimensional object, such as cylindrical or spherical coordinates. These can be implemented in some graphics systems and are useful in specific applications. For the most part, however, three-dimensional objects will be described here in the Cartesian reference system.

6.2   REPRESENTATION OF THREE-DIMENSIONAL GEOMETRY

The basic geometric element in three dimensions is the same as in two di-mensions, a point, requiring in three dimensions an additional coordinate. Figure 6.4 shows a tetrahedron in three-dimensional space.

The concept of homogeneous coordinates is applied to the object's description, as in two-dimensional geometry. The tetrahedron can, therefore,

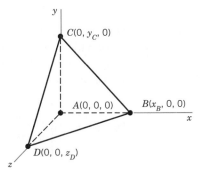

FIGURE 6.4 Representation of a tetrahedron.

be represented by a 4 × 4 matrix, as follows:

$$[P] = \begin{bmatrix} 0 & 0 & 0 & 1 \\ x_B & 0 & 0 & 1 \\ 0 & y_C & 0 & 1 \\ 0 & 0 & z_D & 1 \end{bmatrix} \tag{6.1}$$

6.3 THREE-DIMENSIONAL TRANSFORMATIONS

Transformations in three-dimensional space are executed by the same methods used in two-dimensional space, with the addition of the z coordinate. In homogeneous coordinates they are represented by a 4 × 4 matrix of the type

$$\begin{bmatrix} A & B & C & 0 \\ D & E & F & 0 \\ G & H & I & 0 \\ J & K & L & S \end{bmatrix} \tag{6.2}$$

This matrix can be partitioned as follows:

$$\begin{bmatrix} 3 \times 3 & \vdots & 3 \times 1 \\ \cdots & \vdots & \cdots \\ 1 \times 3 & \vdots & 1 \times 1 \end{bmatrix} \tag{6.3}$$

The 3 × 3 submatrix on the upper left allows for scaling, reflection, shearing, and rotation. The lower left 1 × 3 submatrix produces translation and the 1 × 1 on the lower right produces "uniform global scaling." The 3 × 1 on the upper right is presently simply used as part of the homogeneous representation. Chapter 8 will demonstrate that this submatrix produces *perspective transformations.*

6.3.1 Scaling

The scaling transformation is obtained by placing values along the main diagonal of the general 4 × 4 transformation matrix. Both local and global scaling can be obtained in this way. A point $P(x, y, z, 1)$ is scaled to $P^*(x^*, y^*, z^*, 1)$ by the following transformation:

$$[x^* \quad y^* \quad z^* \quad 1] = [x \quad y \quad z \quad 1] \begin{bmatrix} A & 0 & 0 & 0 \\ 0 & E & 0 & 0 \\ 0 & 0 & I & 0 \\ 0 & 0 & 0 & 1 \end{bmatrix} \tag{6.4}$$

This is usually called *scaling with respect to the origin* and is an extension of the two-dimensional scaling described in Section 4.2.1. If the scaling factors

A,E,I are different from each other, the image of the object is distorted. Otherwise, a change in size occurs, but the original proportions are maintained. This type of overall scaling can also be obtained by the transformation

$$[x^* \quad y^* \quad z^* \quad 1] = [x \quad y \quad z \quad 1] \begin{bmatrix} 1 & 0 & 0 & 0 \\ 0 & 1 & 0 & 0 \\ 0 & 0 & 1 & 0 \\ 0 & 0 & 0 & s \end{bmatrix} \qquad (6.5)$$

$$= [x \quad y \quad z \quad s]$$

Notice that when global scaling is used, the fourth column of the transformed point matrix may not be equal to 1. As explained in Section 4.1, this matrix should be normalized so that the corresponding x, y, z values become the standard cartesian coordinates. To obtain these cartesian coordinates, Eq. 6.5 is modified as follows:

$$[x \quad y \quad z \quad s] = \begin{bmatrix} \dfrac{x}{s} & \dfrac{y}{s} & \dfrac{z}{s} & 1 \end{bmatrix}$$

For s values larger than one, this reduces the size of the object. To enlarge it, a factor of $1/s$ should be used on the scaling matrix. The final coordinates would then be

$$[sx \quad sy \quad sz \quad 1] \qquad (6.6)$$

Example 6.1

Consider the 2-in. cube shown in Figure 6.5. The homogeneous coordinates of the cube are represented in matrix form as

$$[P] = \begin{bmatrix} 0 & 0 & 0 & 1 \\ 2 & 0 & 0 & 1 \\ 2 & 2 & 0 & 1 \\ 0 & 2 & 0 & 1 \\ 0 & 0 & 2 & 1 \\ 2 & 0 & 2 & 1 \\ 2 & 2 & 2 & 1 \\ 0 & 2 & 2 & 1 \end{bmatrix}$$

Apply a scaling matrix to reduce it to a unit cube.

Solution

The scaling matrix needed to transform this 2-in. cube into a unit cube is

$$[T_{SC}] = \begin{bmatrix} \frac{1}{2} & 0 & 0 & 0 \\ 0 & \frac{1}{2} & 0 & 0 \\ 0 & 0 & \frac{1}{2} & 0 \\ 0 & 0 & 0 & 1 \end{bmatrix} \qquad (a)$$

or

$$[T_{SC}] = \begin{bmatrix} 1 & 0 & 0 & 0 \\ 0 & 1 & 0 & 0 \\ 0 & 0 & 1 & 0 \\ 0 & 0 & 0 & 2 \end{bmatrix} \qquad \text{(b)}$$

Either of these scaling transformations applied to the original cube yields the desired result. Using matrix (b):

$$[P^*]_{\substack{\text{UNIT} \\ \text{CUBE}}} = \begin{bmatrix} 0 & 0 & 0 & 1 \\ 2 & 0 & 0 & 1 \\ 2 & 2 & 0 & 1 \\ 0 & 2 & 0 & 1 \\ 0 & 0 & 2 & 1 \\ 2 & 0 & 2 & 1 \\ 2 & 2 & 2 & 1 \\ 0 & 2 & 2 & 1 \end{bmatrix} \begin{bmatrix} 1 & 0 & 0 & 0 \\ 0 & 1 & 0 & 0 \\ 0 & 0 & 1 & 0 \\ 0 & 0 & 0 & 2 \end{bmatrix} = \begin{bmatrix} 0 & 0 & 0 & 2 \\ 2 & 0 & 0 & 2 \\ 2 & 2 & 0 & 2 \\ 0 & 2 & 0 & 2 \\ 0 & 0 & 2 & 2 \\ 2 & 0 & 2 & 2 \\ 2 & 2 & 2 & 2 \\ 0 & 2 & 2 & 2 \end{bmatrix}$$

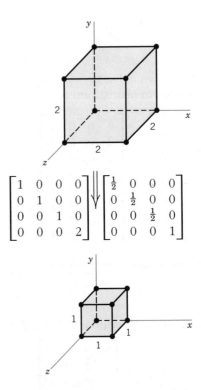

$$\begin{bmatrix} 1 & 0 & 0 & 0 \\ 0 & 1 & 0 & 0 \\ 0 & 0 & 1 & 0 \\ 0 & 0 & 0 & 2 \end{bmatrix} \Updownarrow \begin{bmatrix} \frac{1}{2} & 0 & 0 & 0 \\ 0 & \frac{1}{2} & 0 & 0 \\ 0 & 0 & \frac{1}{2} & 0 \\ 0 & 0 & 0 & 1 \end{bmatrix}$$

FIGURE 6.5 Scaling of a cube.

Or, in standard form

$$[P^*]_{\substack{\text{UNIT} \\ \text{CUBE}}} = \begin{bmatrix} 0 & 0 & 0 & 1 \\ 1 & 0 & 0 & 1 \\ 1 & 1 & 0 & 1 \\ 0 & 1 & 0 & 1 \\ 0 & 0 & 1 & 1 \\ 1 & 0 & 1 & 1 \\ 1 & 1 & 1 & 1 \\ 0 & 1 & 1 & 1 \end{bmatrix}$$

The same result would have been obtained if matrix (a) had been used.

6.3.2   Translation

The following transformation matrix translates a point (x, y, z) to a new point (x^*, y^*, z^*) through (J,K,L):

$$[x^* \quad y^* \quad z^* \quad 1] = [x \quad y \quad z \quad 1]\begin{bmatrix} 1 & 0 & 0 & 0 \\ 0 & 1 & 0 & 0 \\ 0 & 0 & 1 & 0 \\ J & K & L & 1 \end{bmatrix} \tag{6.7}$$

The values of J, K, L represent the relative movement of the point in the x, y, z directions. Figure 6.6 shows the effect of translating a unit cube with one vertex at the origin to a new position in space determined by the given translation matrix. Each vertex is translated by the same amount so that, in matrix form, the transformed coordinates of the cube become

$$[P^*]_{\text{CUBE}} = \begin{bmatrix} 0 & 0 & 0 & 1 \\ 1 & 0 & 0 & 1 \\ 1 & 0 & 1 & 1 \\ 0 & 0 & 1 & 1 \\ 0 & 1 & 1 & 1 \\ 1 & 1 & 1 & 1 \\ 1 & 1 & 0 & 1 \\ 0 & 1 & 0 & 1 \end{bmatrix} \begin{bmatrix} 1 & 0 & 0 & 0 \\ 0 & 1 & 0 & 0 \\ 0 & 0 & 1 & 0 \\ 2 & 2 & 0 & 1 \end{bmatrix} = \begin{bmatrix} 2 & 2 & 0 & 1 \\ 3 & 2 & 0 & 1 \\ 3 & 2 & 1 & 1 \\ 2 & 2 & 1 & 1 \\ 2 & 3 & 1 & 1 \\ 3 & 3 & 1 & 1 \\ 3 & 3 & 0 & 1 \\ 2 & 3 & 0 & 1 \end{bmatrix} \tag{6.8}$$

6.3.3   Rotation

Rotations in three dimensions are important in understanding the shape of an object or in verifying different angles of a design. They are more complex than their two-dimensional counterparts, because an axis of rotation rather than a point of rotation must be specified. Rotations about arbitrary axes can be decomposed into simple rotations about the three principal coordinate axes, and are established by following procedures similar to those used for two-dimensional rotation.

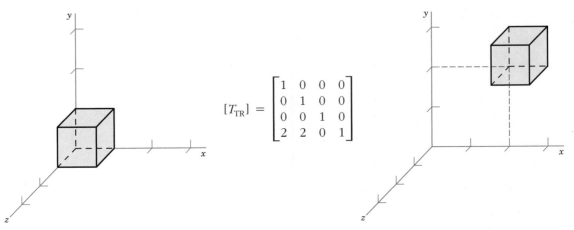

$$[T_{TR}] = \begin{bmatrix} 1 & 0 & 0 & 0 \\ 0 & 1 & 0 & 0 \\ 0 & 0 & 1 & 0 \\ 2 & 2 & 0 & 1 \end{bmatrix}$$

FIGURE 6.6 Translation of a unit cube.

Figure 6.7 shows the three basic positive rotations about the coordinate axes. The coordinate system is right-handed and CCW rotations are assumed positive when looking along the axis toward the origin. For two-dimensional applications, the axis of rotation was essentially the z axis. Expanding the matrix derived in Section 4.2.3 yields the z axis rotation in three dimensions,

$$[T_R]_z^\theta = \begin{bmatrix} \cos\theta & \sin\theta & 0 & 0 \\ -\sin\theta & \cos\theta & 0 & 0 \\ 0 & 0 & 1 & 0 \\ 0 & 0 & 0 & 1 \end{bmatrix} \tag{6.9}$$

which produces the following mapping:

$$x^* = x\cos\theta - y\sin\theta$$

$$y^* = x\sin\theta + y\cos\theta \tag{6.10}$$

$$z^* = z$$

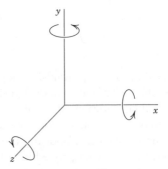

FIGURE 6.7 Positive rotations about the coordinate axes.

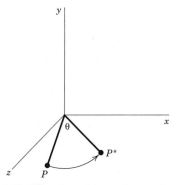

FIGURE 6.8 Rotation about the
y axis.

In a similar manner, a rotation of θ degrees about the *y* axis can be obtained by the following equations, derived from Figure 6.8.

$$x^* = x \cos \theta + z \sin \theta$$

$$y^* = y \qquad (6.11)$$

$$z^* = -x \sin \theta + z \cos \theta$$

or

$$[T_R]_y^\theta = \begin{bmatrix} \cos \theta & 0 & -\sin \theta & 0 \\ 0 & 1 & 0 & 0 \\ \sin \theta & 0 & \cos \theta & 0 \\ 0 & 0 & 0 & 1 \end{bmatrix} \qquad (6.12)$$

The rotation about the *x* axis, derived from Figure 6.9, is

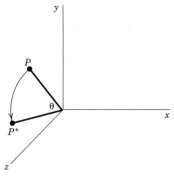

FIGURE 6.9 Rotation about the
x axis.

$$x^* = x$$

$$y^* = y \cos \theta - z \sin \theta \qquad (6.13)$$

$$z^* = y \sin \theta + z \cos \theta$$

or

$$[T_R]_x^\theta = \begin{bmatrix} 1 & 0 & 0 & 0 \\ 0 & \cos \theta & \sin \theta & 0 \\ 0 & -\sin \theta & \cos \theta & 0 \\ 0 & 0 & 0 & 1 \end{bmatrix} \qquad (6.14)$$

It is worthy of note that the sign of the sine terms appears reversed in the matrix $[T_R]_y^\theta$ from those in the other two matrices, as a result of the right-handed convention.

Example 6.2

Consider a chamfered block as shown in Figure 6.10. Points P_1 to P_{10} define the geometry of the block and can be written in matrix form as follows:

$$[P] = \begin{bmatrix} -10 & -3 & -4 & 1 \\ -10 & 1 & -4 & 1 \\ -8.5 & 3 & -4 & 1 \\ 10 & 3 & -4 & 1 \\ 10 & -3 & -4 & 1 \\ -10 & -3 & 4 & 1 \\ -10 & 1 & 4 & 1 \\ -8.5 & 3 & 4 & 1 \\ 10 & 3 & 4 & 1 \\ 10 & -3 & 4 & 1 \end{bmatrix}$$

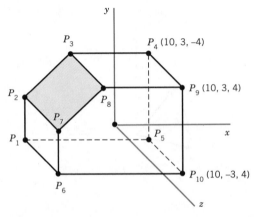

FIGURE 6.10 Geometry of a chamfered block.

Rotate the block so that the bottom plane, defined by points P_1, P_5, P_{10}, and P_6, is parallel to the xy plane.

Solution

To make plane $P_1P_5P_{10}P_6$ parallel to the xy plane, the rotation could be expressed as CCW about the x axis by 90°. The appropriate matrix is given by

$$[T_R]_x^\theta = \begin{bmatrix} 1 & 0 & 0 & 0 \\ 0 & \cos\theta & \sin\theta & 0 \\ 0 & -\sin\theta & \cos\theta & 0 \\ 0 & 0 & 0 & 1 \end{bmatrix}$$

For $\theta = 90°$ this matrix becomes:

$$[T_R]_x^{90°} = \begin{bmatrix} 1 & 0 & 0 & 0 \\ 0 & 0 & 1 & 0 \\ 0 & -1 & 0 & 0 \\ 0 & 0 & 0 & 1 \end{bmatrix}$$

The matrix of transformed points is

$$[P^*] = \begin{bmatrix} -10 & -3 & -4 & 1 \\ -10 & 1 & -4 & 1 \\ -8.5 & 3 & -4 & 1 \\ 10 & 3 & -4 & 1 \\ 10 & -3 & -4 & 1 \\ -10 & -3 & 4 & 1 \\ -10 & 1 & 4 & 1 \\ -8.5 & 3 & 4 & 1 \\ 10 & 3 & 4 & 1 \\ 10 & -3 & 4 & 1 \end{bmatrix} \begin{bmatrix} 1 & 0 & 0 & 0 \\ 0 & 0 & 1 & 0 \\ 0 & -1 & 0 & 0 \\ 0 & 0 & 0 & 1 \end{bmatrix} = \begin{bmatrix} -10 & 4 & -3 & 1 \\ -10 & 4 & 1 & 1 \\ -8.5 & 4 & 3 & 1 \\ 10 & 4 & 3 & 1 \\ 10 & 4 & -3 & 1 \\ -10 & -4 & -3 & 1 \\ -10 & -4 & 1 & 1 \\ -8.5 & -4 & 3 & 1 \\ 10 & -4 & 3 & 1 \\ 10 & -4 & -3 & 1 \end{bmatrix}$$

Figure 6.11 shows the object after the 90° rotation, viewed along the z axis.

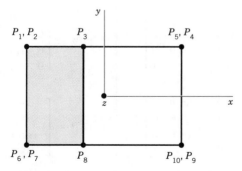

FIGURE 6.11 Chamfered block after 90° CCW rotation about the x axis.

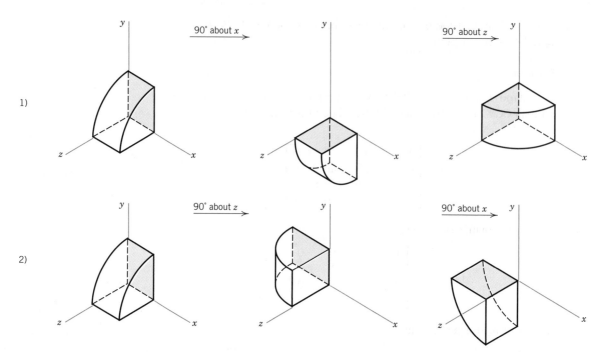

FIGURE 6.12 Order of rotations affects the final position of an object.

FIGURE 6.13 Summary of rotation matrices about the three coordinate axes.

ROTATION MATRICES: Right-handed system looking along the appropriate axis toward the origin

CCW	CW
$[T_R]_z^\theta = \begin{bmatrix} \cos\theta & \sin\theta & 0 & 0 \\ -\sin\theta & \cos\theta & 0 & 0 \\ 0 & 0 & 1 & 0 \\ 0 & 0 & 0 & 1 \end{bmatrix}$	$[T_R]_z^\theta = \begin{bmatrix} \cos\theta & -\sin\theta & 0 & 0 \\ \sin\theta & \cos\theta & 0 & 0 \\ 0 & 0 & 1 & 0 \\ 0 & 0 & 0 & 1 \end{bmatrix}$
$[T_R]_x^\theta = \begin{bmatrix} 1 & 0 & 0 & 0 \\ 0 & \cos\theta & \sin\theta & 0 \\ 0 & -\sin\theta & \cos\theta & 0 \\ 0 & 0 & 0 & 1 \end{bmatrix}$	$[T_R]_x^\theta = \begin{bmatrix} 1 & 0 & 0 & 0 \\ 0 & \cos\theta & -\sin\theta & 0 \\ 0 & \sin\theta & \cos\theta & 0 \\ 0 & 0 & 0 & 1 \end{bmatrix}$
$[T_R]_y^\theta = \begin{bmatrix} \cos\theta & 0 & -\sin\theta & 0 \\ 0 & 1 & 0 & 0 \\ \sin\theta & 0 & \cos\theta & 0 \\ 0 & 0 & 0 & 1 \end{bmatrix}$	$[T_R]_y^\theta = \begin{bmatrix} \cos\theta & 0 & \sin\theta & 0 \\ 0 & 1 & 0 & 0 \\ -\sin\theta & 0 & \cos\theta & 0 \\ 0 & 0 & 0 & 1 \end{bmatrix}$

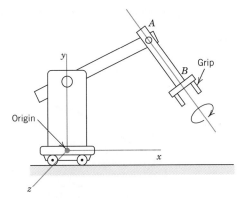

FIGURE 6.14 Robot grip rotates about axis *AB*, not one of the principal axes.

Care must be exercised when applying rotation matrices sequentially. The order in which the rotations are performed affects the result. In Figure 6.12 the final position of the wedge after sequence 1 is different from the final position after sequence 2. This is because matrix multiplications are in general noncommutative. Figure 6.13 summarizes the rotation matrices about the three coordinate axes.

6.3.3.1   Rotations about Arbitrary Axes

Rotations about arbitrary axes in space are frequently found in engineering. Figure 6.14 illustrates an aspect of this fact—the robot grip rotates about axis *AB*, inclined with respect to the principal axes and not through the origin. This type of rotation is obtained by first using a sequence of translations and simple rotations that will make the arbitrary axis coincide with one of the principal coordinate axes; second, by performing the desired rotation; and third, by returning the axis to its original position. The sequence of steps is given as follows.

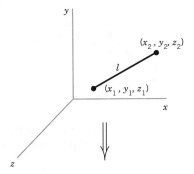

1. Translate the arbitrary axis so that one of its endpoints coincides with the origin.

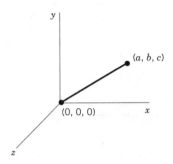

2. Perform rotations about the x and y axes to align the arbitrary axis with the positive z axis.

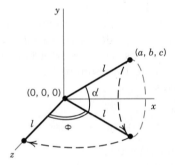

3. Rotate about the z axis by the desired angle θ.

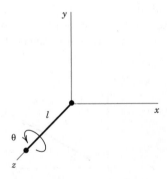

4. Apply reverse rotations about the y and x axes. This will bring the arbitrary axis back to its original position from the origin.

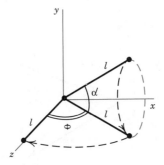

5. Apply the reverse translation to place the arbitrary axis back in its initial position in space.

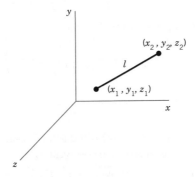

All these transformations are then concatenated into a single matrix expressed by

$$[T_R]_{ARB} = [T_{TR}][T_R]_x^\alpha[T_R]_y^\phi[T_R]_z^\theta[T_R]_y^{-\phi}[T_R]_x^{-\alpha}[T_{TR}]^{-1} \qquad (6.15)$$

The individual transformation matrices in this expression can be found through geometric considerations.

1. Translation $[T]$ is given by

$$[T_{TR}] = \begin{bmatrix} 1 & 0 & 0 & 0 \\ 0 & 1 & 0 & 0 \\ 0 & 0 & 1 & 0 \\ -x_1 & -y_1 & -z_1 & 1 \end{bmatrix} \qquad (6.16)$$

2. To establish the rotation matrix about the x axis it is necessary to calculate the angle of rotation α. Figure 6.15 illustrates that the angle α can be found in the projection of the arbitrary axis onto the yz plane.

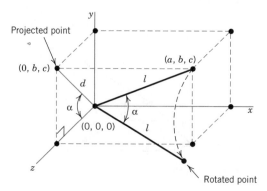

FIGURE 6.15 Angle of rotation α can be found in the projection of the arbitrary axis on plane *yz*.

From this projection,

$$\sin \alpha = \frac{b}{\sqrt{b^2 + c^2}} = \frac{b}{d}$$

$$\cos \alpha = \frac{c}{\sqrt{b^2 + c^2}} = \frac{c}{d}$$

(6.17)

Noticing the positive (CCW) direction of rotation about the *x* axis, the transformation matrix can be written as

$$[T_R]_x^\alpha = \begin{bmatrix} 1 & 0 & 0 & 0 \\ 0 & \cos \alpha & \sin \alpha & 0 \\ 0 & -\sin \alpha & \cos \alpha & 0 \\ 0 & 0 & 0 & 1 \end{bmatrix} = \begin{bmatrix} 1 & 0 & 0 & 0 \\ 0 & c/d & b/d & 0 \\ 0 & -b/d & c/d & 0 \\ 0 & 0 & 0 & 1 \end{bmatrix}$$

(6.18)

3. The angle of rotation ϕ about the *y* axis is shown in Figure 6.16.

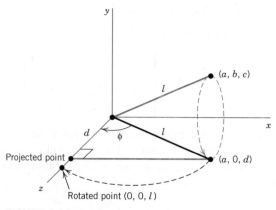

FIGURE 6.16 Angle of rotation ϕ.

$$\sin \phi = \frac{a}{l}$$

(6.19)

$$\cos \phi = \frac{d}{l}$$

Notice that the indicated rotation about the y axis is negative (CW) and $l = \sqrt{a^2 + b^2 + c^2}$. The value of d was found as $\sqrt{b^2 + c^2}$. This is indeed the z coordinate of the rotated point on the xz plane, as can be shown very simply by the following relationships derived from the geometry of Figure 6.16:

$$l^2 = a^2 + b^2 + c^2 \qquad l^2 = a^2 + d^2$$

(6.20)

or

$$a^2 + b^2 + c^2 = a^2 + d^2$$

which yields the expected result

$$d = \sqrt{b^2 + c^2}$$

(6.21)

The clockwise rotation about the y axis is given by the matrix

$$[T_R]_y^\phi = \begin{bmatrix} \cos \phi & 0 & \sin \theta & 0 \\ 0 & 1 & 0 & 0 \\ -\sin \phi & 0 & \cos \phi & 0 \\ 0 & 0 & 0 & 1 \end{bmatrix} = \begin{bmatrix} d/l & 0 & a/l & 0 \\ 0 & 1 & 0 & 0 \\ -a/l & 0 & d/l & 0 \\ 0 & 0 & 0 & 1 \end{bmatrix}$$

(6.22)

4. The rotation about the arbitrary axis, now placed along the z axis, is finally obtained by

$$[T_R]_z^\theta = \begin{bmatrix} \cos \theta & \sin \theta & 0 & 0 \\ -\sin \theta & \cos \theta & 0 & 0 \\ 0 & 0 & 1 & 0 \\ 0 & 0 & 0 & 1 \end{bmatrix}$$

(6.23)

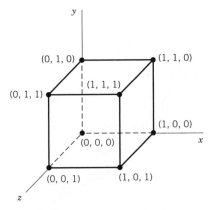

FIGURE 6.17 Geometry of unit cube.

The reverse transformation matrices are now applied to finish the problem.

Example 6.3

Find the new coordinates of a unit cube (shown in Figure 6.17) rotated about an axis defined by its endpoints $A(2, 1, 0)$ and $B(3, 3, 1)$. The angle of rotation should be 90° CCW.

Solution

The solution to this problem will follow the five steps outlined above.

1. Translate point A to the origin:

$$[T_{TR}] = \begin{bmatrix} 1 & 0 & 0 & 0 \\ 0 & 1 & 0 & 0 \\ 0 & 0 & 1 & 0 \\ -2 & -1 & 0 & 1 \end{bmatrix}$$

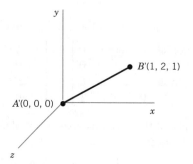

2. Rotate axis $A'B'$ about the x axis by an angle α, until it lies on the xz plane. From previous derivations

$$\sin \alpha = \frac{2}{\sqrt{2^2 + 1^2}} = \frac{2}{\sqrt{5}} = \frac{2\sqrt{5}}{5}$$

$$\cos \alpha = \frac{1}{\sqrt{5}} = \frac{\sqrt{5}}{5}$$

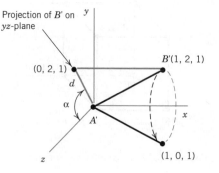

and

$$l = \sqrt{1^2 + 2^2 + 1^2} = \sqrt{6}$$

So

$$[T_R]_x^\alpha = \begin{bmatrix} 1 & 0 & 0 & 0 \\ 0 & \dfrac{\sqrt{5}}{5} & \dfrac{2\sqrt{5}}{5} & 0 \\ 0 & -\dfrac{2\sqrt{5}}{5} & \dfrac{\sqrt{5}}{5} & 0 \\ 0 & 0 & 0 & 1 \end{bmatrix}$$

3. Rotate axis $A'B''$ about the y axis by an angle ϕ until it coincides with the z axis.

$$\sin \phi = \frac{1}{\sqrt{6}} = \frac{\sqrt{6}}{6}$$

$$\cos \phi = \frac{\sqrt{5}}{\sqrt{6}} = \frac{\sqrt{30}}{6}$$

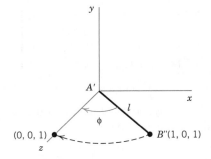

and

$$[T_R]_y^\phi = \begin{bmatrix} \dfrac{\sqrt{30}}{6} & 0 & \dfrac{\sqrt{6}}{6} & 0 \\ 0 & 1 & 0 & 0 \\ -\dfrac{\sqrt{6}}{6} & 0 & \dfrac{\sqrt{30}}{6} & 0 \\ 0 & 0 & 0 & 1 \end{bmatrix}$$

4. Rotate the cube 90° about the z axis.

$$[T_R]_z^{90°} = \begin{bmatrix} 0 & 1 & 0 & 0 \\ -1 & 0 & 0 & 0 \\ 0 & 0 & 1 & 0 \\ 0 & 0 & 0 & 1 \end{bmatrix}$$

5. Finally, the concatenated rotation matrix about the arbitrary axis AB becomes

$$
[T_R]_{AB} =
\begin{bmatrix}
1 & 0 & 0 & 0 \\
0 & 1 & 0 & 0 \\
0 & 0 & 1 & 0 \\
-2 & -1 & 0 & 1
\end{bmatrix}
\begin{bmatrix}
1 & 0 & 0 & 0 \\
0 & \dfrac{\sqrt{5}}{5} & \dfrac{2\sqrt{5}}{5} & 0 \\
0 & -\dfrac{2\sqrt{5}}{5} & \dfrac{\sqrt{5}}{5} & 0 \\
0 & 0 & 0 & 1
\end{bmatrix}
\begin{bmatrix}
\dfrac{\sqrt{30}}{6} & 0 & \dfrac{\sqrt{6}}{6} & 0 \\
0 & 1 & 0 & 0 \\
-\dfrac{\sqrt{6}}{6} & 0 & \dfrac{\sqrt{30}}{6} & 0 \\
0 & 0 & 0 & 1
\end{bmatrix}
$$

$$\quad [T_{TR}] \qquad\qquad [T_R]_x^{\alpha} \qquad\qquad [T_R]_y^{\phi}$$

$$
\begin{bmatrix}
0 & 1 & 0 & 0 \\
-1 & 0 & 0 & 0 \\
0 & 0 & 1 & 0 \\
0 & 0 & 0 & 1
\end{bmatrix}
\begin{bmatrix}
\dfrac{\sqrt{30}}{6} & 0 & -\dfrac{\sqrt{6}}{6} & 0 \\
0 & 1 & 0 & 0 \\
\dfrac{\sqrt{6}}{6} & 0 & \dfrac{\sqrt{30}}{6} & 0 \\
0 & 0 & 0 & 1
\end{bmatrix}
\begin{bmatrix}
1 & 0 & 0 & 0 \\
0 & \dfrac{\sqrt{5}}{5} & -\dfrac{2\sqrt{5}}{5} & 0 \\
0 & \dfrac{2\sqrt{5}}{5} & \dfrac{\sqrt{5}}{5} & 0 \\
0 & 0 & 0 & 1
\end{bmatrix}
\begin{bmatrix}
1 & 0 & 0 & 0 \\
0 & 1 & 0 & 0 \\
0 & 0 & 1 & 0 \\
2 & 1 & 0 & 1
\end{bmatrix}
$$

$$\quad [T_R]_z^{90°} \qquad\qquad ([T_R]_y^{-\phi}) \qquad\qquad ([T_R]_x^{-\alpha}) \qquad\qquad [T_{TR}]^{-1}$$

$$
= \begin{bmatrix}
0.166 & 0.742 & -0.650 & 0 \\
-0.075 & 0.667 & 0.741 & 0 \\
0.983 & 0.075 & 0.167 & 0 \\
1.742 & -1.151 & 0.560 & 1
\end{bmatrix}
$$

$$[T_R]_{AB}$$

Multiplying $[T_R]_{AB}$ by the point matrix of the original cube gives the transformed coordinates, that is,

$$[P^*] = [P][T_R]_{AB}$$

$$
[P^*] =
\begin{bmatrix}
0 & 1 & 1 & 1 \\
0 & 1 & 0 & 1 \\
1 & 1 & 0 & 1 \\
1 & 1 & 1 & 1 \\
0 & 0 & 1 & 1 \\
0 & 0 & 0 & 1 \\
1 & 0 & 0 & 1 \\
1 & 0 & 1 & 1
\end{bmatrix}
\begin{bmatrix}
0.166 & 0.742 & -0.650 & 0 \\
-0.075 & 0.667 & 0.741 & 0 \\
0.983 & 0.075 & 0.167 & 0 \\
1.742 & -1.151 & 0.560 & 1
\end{bmatrix}
$$

$$
[P^*] =
\begin{bmatrix}
2.650 & -0.558 & 1.467 & 1 \\
1.667 & -0.484 & 1.301 & 1 \\
1.834 & 0.258 & 0.650 & 1 \\
2.816 & 0.184 & 0.817 & 1 \\
2.725 & -1.225 & 0.726 & 1 \\
1.742 & -1.151 & 0.560 & 1 \\
1.909 & -0.409 & -0.091 & 1 \\
2.891 & -0.483 & 0.076 & 1
\end{bmatrix}
$$

6.3.3.2 Orthogonality Property of Rotation Matrices

The orthogonality property of the rotation matrix [3] is very useful in the solution of some types of engineering graphics problems. Consider Figure 6.18, showing three mutually orthogonal unit vectors, **u**, **v**, **w**.

Assume, for ease of explanation, that unit vectors **u** and **v** are located on the xy plane, so that:

$$\mathbf{u} = \cos \theta \, \mathbf{i} - \sin \theta \, \mathbf{j}$$
$$\mathbf{v} = \sin \theta \, \mathbf{i} + \cos \theta \, \mathbf{j} \qquad (6.24)$$
$$\mathbf{w} = \mathbf{k}$$

A 4×4 homogeneous matrix $[M]$ can be created by placing

- Unit vector **u** in the first column;
- Unit vector **v** in the second column;
- Unit vector **w** in the third column.

$$[M] = \begin{bmatrix} \cos\theta & \sin\theta & 0 & 0 \\ -\sin\theta & \cos\theta & 0 & 0 \\ 0 & 0 & 1 & 0 \\ 0 & 0 & 0 & 1 \end{bmatrix} \qquad (6.25)$$

Comparing Eq. 6.25 with Eq. 6.23 it can be seen that matrix $[M]$ represents a counterclockwise rotation about the z axis by an angle θ, or $[T_R]_z^\theta$. The columns of a rotation matrix are composed, therefore, of orthogonal unit vectors. Multiplying this orthogonal rotation matrix by the original unit vectors will locate their positions after rotation.

$$\begin{bmatrix} \cos\theta & -\sin\theta & 0 & 1 \\ \sin\theta & \cos\theta & 0 & 1 \\ 0 & 0 & 1 & 1 \end{bmatrix} \begin{bmatrix} \cos\theta & \sin\theta & 0 & 0 \\ -\sin\theta & \cos\theta & 0 & 0 \\ 0 & 0 & 1 & 0 \\ 0 & 0 & 0 & 1 \end{bmatrix}$$

$$\text{[coordinates of } \mathbf{u}, \mathbf{v}, \mathbf{w}] \qquad [M]$$

$$= \begin{bmatrix} (\cos^2\theta + \sin^2\theta) & (\sin\theta\cos\theta - \sin\theta\cos\theta) & 0 & 1 \\ (\sin\theta\cos\theta - \sin\theta\cos\theta) & (\sin^2\theta + \cos^2\theta) & 0 & 1 \\ 0 & 0 & 1 & 1 \end{bmatrix}$$

$$= \begin{bmatrix} 1 & 0 & 0 & 1 \\ 0 & 1 & 0 & 1 \\ 0 & 0 & 1 & 1 \end{bmatrix} \qquad (6.26)$$

After rotation, therefore, the unit vectors **u**, **v**, **w** became equal to **i**, **j**, **k**, that is, were rotated to the x, y, and z axes, respectively. Generalizing, it can be said that any three orthogonal unit vectors will be rotated to the x, y, and z axes by placing their components in the first, second, and third columns of a rotation matrix.

A simple example will show the usefulness of this property. Assume a plane in space defined by three points, V_1, V_2, V_3, as shown in Figure 6.19.

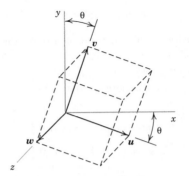

FIGURE 6.18 Orientation of three mutually orthogonal unit vectors.

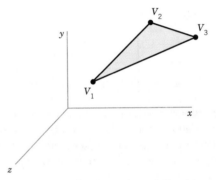

FIGURE 6.19 Plane in space defined by three points.

These three points are to be transformed, so that the inclined plane is forced to coincide with the xy principal plane. Using the orthogonality property of the rotation matrix, the problem can be solved in a few steps.

1. Translate V_1 to the origin.

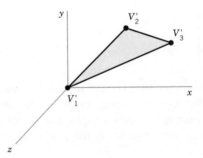

2. Calculate the unit vector along $V_1' V_2'$ and place it in the first column of the rotation matrix. This will rotate the unit vector, **u**, to the positive x axis.

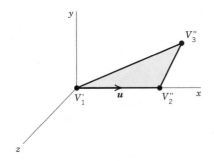

$$\mathbf{u} = R_{11}\mathbf{i} + R_{21}\mathbf{j} + R_{31}\mathbf{k} = \frac{\mathbf{V_1'V_2'}}{\|\mathbf{V_1'V_2'}\|}$$

$$= \left[\frac{(V_{2x}' - V_{1x}')\mathbf{i}}{\|\mathbf{V_1'V_2'}\|} + \frac{(V_{2y}' - V_{1y}')\mathbf{j}}{\|\mathbf{V_1'V_2'}\|} + \frac{(V_{2z}' - V_{1z}')\mathbf{k}}{\|\mathbf{V_1'V_2'}\|} \right.$$

(6.27)

where:

$$\|\mathbf{V_1'V_2'}\| = \sqrt{(V_{2x}' - V_{1x}')^2 + (V_{2y}' - V_{1y}')^2 + (V_{2z}' - V_{1z}')^2}$$

3. To make plane $V_1' V_2' V_3'$ lie on the xy plane, the unit vector perpendicular to it must be in the z direction. This unit vector **w** is found through the cross product of two vectors, $\mathbf{V_1'V_2'}$ and $\mathbf{V_1'V_3'}$, on the plane

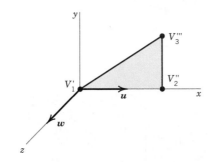

$$\mathbf{w} = R_{13}\mathbf{i} + R_{23}\mathbf{j} + R_{33}\mathbf{k} = \frac{\mathbf{V_1'V_2'} \times \mathbf{V_1'V_3'}}{\|\mathbf{V_1'V_2'} \times \mathbf{V_1'V_3'}\|} \qquad (6.28)$$

and should be placed in the third column of the rotation matrix.

4. Finally, for the three unit vectors to be perpendicular to each other, the third one, **v**, must be normal to the other two. Vector **v** is given as

$$\mathbf{v} = R_{12}\mathbf{i} + R_{22}\mathbf{j} + R_{32}\mathbf{k} = \mathbf{w} \times \mathbf{u} \qquad (6.29)$$

and placed on the second column of the rotation matrix. The final matrix is

$$[T_R] = \begin{bmatrix} R_{11} & R_{12} & R_{13} & 0 \\ R_{21} & R_{22} & R_{23} & 0 \\ R_{31} & R_{32} & R_{33} & 0 \\ 0 & 0 & 0 & 1 \end{bmatrix} \tag{6.30}$$

Example 6.4

A triangle DEF is defined by its vertices as follows: $D(1, 2, 2)$, $E(2, 4, 3)$, and $F(4, 3, 2)$—right-handed system. Use the orthogonality property of the rotation matrix to make

(a) Line DF coincide with the positive y axis.

(b) The triangle coincide with the yz plane.

Solution

The triangle DEF has the position shown in the accompanying figure. The first step in the solution is to translate the triangle so that D coincides with the origin. The translation matrix is

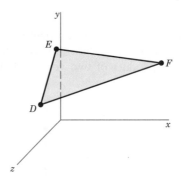

$$[T_{TR}] = \begin{bmatrix} 1 & 0 & 0 & 0 \\ 0 & 1 & 0 & 0 \\ 0 & 0 & 1 & 0 \\ -1 & -2 & -2 & 1 \end{bmatrix}$$

and the new location of the triangle is given by

$$\begin{bmatrix} 1 & 2 & 2 & 1 \\ 2 & 4 & 3 & 1 \\ 4 & 3 & 2 & 1 \end{bmatrix} \begin{bmatrix} 1 & 0 & 0 & 0 \\ 0 & 1 & 0 & 0 \\ 0 & 0 & 1 & 0 \\ -1 & -2 & -2 & 1 \end{bmatrix} = \begin{bmatrix} 0 & 0 & 0 & 1 \\ 1 & 2 & 1 & 1 \\ 3 & 1 & 0 & 1 \end{bmatrix} \begin{matrix} D \\ E \\ F \end{matrix}$$

To force line DF to coincide with the y axis, the unit vector along DF must be placed in the second column of the rotation matrix. A vector $\mathbf{DF}$ can be defined as

$$\mathbf{DF} = 3\mathbf{i} + \mathbf{j}$$

so that the unit vector along line *DF* becomes

$$\frac{\mathbf{DF}}{\|\mathbf{DF}\|} = \mathbf{v} = \frac{3}{\sqrt{10}}\mathbf{i} + \frac{1}{\sqrt{10}}\mathbf{j}$$

For the triangle to coincide with the *yz* plane, the unit vector perpendicular to plane *DEF* must be along the *x* axis. This unit vector, **u**, must therefore be placed in the first column of the rotation matrix. A vector perpendicular to plane *DEF* can be obtained by the cross product of two vectors on the plane. Choosing

$$\mathbf{DF} = 3\mathbf{i} + \mathbf{j} \qquad \text{and} \qquad \mathbf{DE} = \mathbf{i} + 2\mathbf{j} + \mathbf{k}$$

the cross product becomes

$$\mathbf{DF} \times \mathbf{DE} = \begin{bmatrix} \mathbf{i} & \mathbf{j} & \mathbf{k} \\ 3 & 1 & 0 \\ 1 & 2 & 1 \end{bmatrix} = \mathbf{i} - 3\mathbf{j} + 5\mathbf{k}$$

and the unit vector **u** is given by

$$\mathbf{u} = \frac{1}{\sqrt{35}}\mathbf{i} - \frac{3}{\sqrt{35}}\mathbf{j} + \frac{5}{\sqrt{35}}\mathbf{k}$$

The third column of the rotation matrix must contain a vector perpendicular to the other two, or

$$\mathbf{w} = \mathbf{u} \times \mathbf{v} \qquad \text{(lies on the } z \text{ axis)}$$

$$\mathbf{w} = \begin{bmatrix} \mathbf{i} & \mathbf{j} & \mathbf{k} \\ \dfrac{1}{\sqrt{35}} & \dfrac{-3}{\sqrt{35}} & \dfrac{5}{\sqrt{35}} \\ \dfrac{3}{\sqrt{10}} & \dfrac{1}{\sqrt{10}} & 0 \end{bmatrix} = \frac{-5}{\sqrt{350}}\mathbf{i} + \frac{15}{\sqrt{350}}\mathbf{j} + \frac{10}{\sqrt{350}}\mathbf{k}$$

The final rotation matrix is obtained by placing vectors **u**, **v**, and **w** in their appropriate locations, so that

$$[T_R] = \begin{bmatrix} \dfrac{1}{\sqrt{35}} & \dfrac{3}{\sqrt{10}} & \dfrac{-5}{\sqrt{350}} & 0 \\ \dfrac{-3}{\sqrt{35}} & \dfrac{1}{\sqrt{10}} & \dfrac{15}{\sqrt{350}} & 0 \\ \dfrac{5}{\sqrt{35}} & 0 & \dfrac{10}{\sqrt{350}} & 0 \\ 0 & 0 & 0 & 1 \end{bmatrix}$$

The final coordinates of the triangle can now be calculated.

$$[P^*] = \begin{bmatrix} 0 & 0 & 0 & 1 \\ 1 & 2 & 1 & 1 \\ 3 & 1 & 0 & 1 \end{bmatrix} \begin{bmatrix} \dfrac{1}{\sqrt{35}} & \dfrac{3}{\sqrt{10}} & \dfrac{-5}{\sqrt{350}} & 0 \\ \dfrac{-3}{\sqrt{35}} & \dfrac{1}{\sqrt{10}} & \dfrac{15}{\sqrt{350}} & 0 \\ \dfrac{5}{\sqrt{35}} & 0 & \dfrac{10}{\sqrt{350}} & 0 \\ 0 & 0 & 0 & 1 \end{bmatrix}$$

$$= \begin{bmatrix} 0 & 0 & 0 & 1 \\ 0 & \dfrac{5}{\sqrt{10}} & \dfrac{35}{\sqrt{350}} & 1 \\ 0 & \dfrac{10}{\sqrt{10}} & 0 & 1 \end{bmatrix}$$

The coordinates after the transformations are

$$D^* \ (0,0,0)$$

$$E^* \left(0, \frac{5}{\sqrt{10}}, \frac{35}{\sqrt{350}}\right) \cong (0, \sqrt{2.5}, \sqrt{3.5})$$

$$F^* \ (0, \sqrt{10}, 0)$$

6.3.4 Other Transformations

As in the case of two-dimensional transformations, additional three-dimensional transformations are needed in engineering applications. These include reflection, shearing, and change of coordinate system.

6.3.4.1 Reflection

Three-dimensional reflections (mirroring) are usually obtained by coordinate transformations about specified reflection planes, as shown in Figure 6.20. The two-dimensional case described in Section 4.4.1 is a subset of three-dimensional reflection. The two-dimensional axis of reflection is the edge of a three-dimensional reflection plane.

Figure 6.21 shows the matrices that produce reflection about the planes $x = 0$, $y = 0$, $z = 0$, and a central reflection about the origin.

To reflect objects about any arbitrary plane, combined transformations involving rotation and mirroring will have to be performed, events similar to the two-dimensional reflections about an arbitrary line. It may be convenient to use again the orthogonality property of the rotation matrix, as shown in the following example.

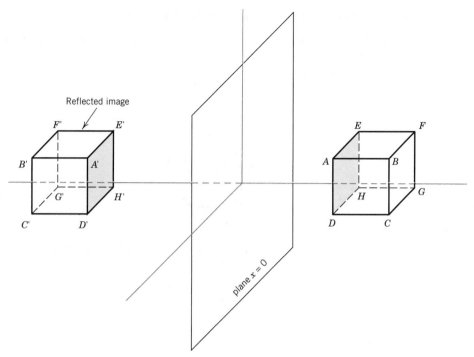

FIGURE 6.20 Reflection of a block about plane $x = 0$.

Example 6.5

Given a point $P(2, 2, -1)$, mirror it about the plane defined by the vertices $A(0,0,0)$, $B(0,3,0)$ and $C(3,1,1)$. Assume a right-handed system.

Solution

Two approaches will be used in the solution of this problem:

    (a) A sequence of transformations

    (b) Employing the orthogonality property of the rotation matrix

Plane	$x = 0$	$y = 0$	$z = 0$	Point $(0,0,0)$
$[T]_{\text{RFL}}$	$\begin{bmatrix} -1 & 0 & 0 & 0 \\ 0 & 1 & 0 & 0 \\ 0 & 0 & 1 & 0 \\ 0 & 0 & 0 & 1 \end{bmatrix}$	$\begin{bmatrix} 1 & 0 & 0 & 0 \\ 0 & -1 & 0 & 0 \\ 0 & 0 & 1 & 0 \\ 0 & 0 & 0 & 1 \end{bmatrix}$	$\begin{bmatrix} 1 & 0 & 0 & 0 \\ 0 & 1 & 0 & 0 \\ 0 & 0 & -1 & 0 \\ 0 & 0 & 0 & 1 \end{bmatrix}$	$\begin{bmatrix} -1 & 0 & 0 & 0 \\ 0 & -1 & 0 & 0 \\ 0 & 0 & -1 & 0 \\ 0 & 0 & 0 & 1 \end{bmatrix}$

FIGURE 6.21 Reflection matrices.

For solution (a), the following sequence of transformations will be used:

1. Rotation by θ about the y axis to make plane ABC coincide with the xy plane (see accompanying figure).

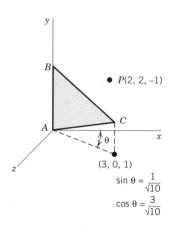

$$\sin \theta = \frac{1}{\sqrt{10}}$$

$$\cos \theta = \frac{3}{\sqrt{10}}$$

2. Mirror about the xy plane.

3. Rotation of ABC back to its original position.

The transformation matrix is given by

$$[T_{\text{RFL}}] = \begin{bmatrix} \cos \theta & 0 & -\sin \theta & 0 \\ 0 & 1 & 0 & 0 \\ \sin \theta & 0 & \cos \theta & 0 \\ 0 & 0 & 0 & 1 \end{bmatrix} \begin{bmatrix} 1 & 0 & 0 & 0 \\ 0 & 1 & 0 & 0 \\ 0 & 0 & -1 & 0 \\ 0 & 0 & 0 & 1 \end{bmatrix} \begin{bmatrix} \cos \theta & 0 & \sin \theta & 0 \\ 0 & 1 & 0 & 0 \\ -\sin \theta & 0 & \cos \theta & 0 \\ 0 & 0 & 0 & 1 \end{bmatrix}$$

$$\begin{pmatrix} \text{Rotation by } \theta \\ \text{about } y \text{ axis} \end{pmatrix} \qquad \begin{pmatrix} \text{Mirror} \\ \text{about } xy \\ \text{plane} \end{pmatrix} \qquad \begin{pmatrix} \text{Inverse} \\ \text{rotation} \\ \text{by } \theta \end{pmatrix}$$

$$= \begin{bmatrix} \dfrac{3}{\sqrt{10}} & 0 & \dfrac{-1}{\sqrt{10}} & 0 \\ 0 & 1 & 0 & 0 \\ \dfrac{1}{\sqrt{10}} & 0 & \dfrac{3}{\sqrt{10}} & 0 \\ 0 & 0 & 0 & 1 \end{bmatrix} \begin{bmatrix} 1 & 0 & 0 & 0 \\ 0 & 1 & 0 & 0 \\ 0 & 0 & -1 & 0 \\ 0 & 0 & 0 & 1 \end{bmatrix} \begin{bmatrix} \dfrac{3}{\sqrt{10}} & 0 & \dfrac{1}{\sqrt{10}} & 0 \\ 0 & 1 & 0 & 0 \\ -\dfrac{1}{\sqrt{10}} & 0 & \dfrac{3}{\sqrt{10}} & 0 \\ 0 & 0 & 0 & 1 \end{bmatrix}$$

$$= \begin{bmatrix} 0.8 & 0 & 0.6 & 0 \\ 0 & 1 & 0 & 0 \\ 0.6 & 0 & -0.8 & 0 \\ 0 & 0 & 0 & 1 \end{bmatrix}$$

The mirror image of point P is:

$$P^* = [2 \quad 2 \quad -1 \quad 1] \begin{bmatrix} 0.8 & 0 & 0.6 & 0 \\ 0 & 1 & 0 & 0 \\ 0.6 & 0 & -0.8 & 0 \\ 0 & 0 & 0 & 1 \end{bmatrix}$$

$$= [1 \quad 2 \quad 2 \quad 1]$$

For solution (b), using the orthogonality property of the rotation matrix, the three columns are defined by the unit vectors **u**, **v**, **w**. Two vectors on plane ABC are initially defined:

$$\mathbf{AB} = 3\mathbf{j}$$

$$\mathbf{AC} = 3\mathbf{i} + \mathbf{j} + \mathbf{k}$$

The unit vector perpendicular to the plane is given by

$$\mathbf{u} = \frac{\mathbf{AB} \times \mathbf{AC}}{\|\mathbf{AB} \times \mathbf{AC}\|} = \frac{3\mathbf{i} - 9\mathbf{k}}{\sqrt{90}} = \frac{3\mathbf{i}}{\sqrt{90}} - \frac{9\mathbf{k}}{\sqrt{90}}$$

and is placed on the first column of the general rotation matrix, so that plane ABC lies on the yz plane.

Since **AB** is located on the positive y axis:

$$\mathbf{v} = \mathbf{j}$$

The unit vector **w** is given by:

$$\mathbf{w} = \mathbf{u} \times \mathbf{v} = \begin{vmatrix} \mathbf{i} & \mathbf{j} & \mathbf{k} \\ \dfrac{3}{\sqrt{90}} & 0 & \dfrac{-9}{\sqrt{90}} \\ 0 & 1 & 0 \end{vmatrix} = \frac{9}{\sqrt{90}}\mathbf{i} + \frac{3}{\sqrt{90}}\mathbf{k}$$

The rotation matrix can now be expressed as

$$[T_R] = \begin{bmatrix} \dfrac{3}{\sqrt{90}} & 0 & \dfrac{9}{\sqrt{90}} & 0 \\ 0 & 1 & 0 & 0 \\ \dfrac{-9}{\sqrt{90}} & 0 & \dfrac{3}{\sqrt{90}} & 0 \\ 0 & 0 & 0 & 1 \end{bmatrix}$$

The reflection about the yz plane is given by the matrix

$$[T_{RFL}] = \begin{bmatrix} -1 & 0 & 0 & 0 \\ 0 & 1 & 0 & 0 \\ 0 & 0 & 1 & 0 \\ 0 & 0 & 0 & 1 \end{bmatrix}$$

The final reflection of point P about plane ABC becomes:

$$P^* = [2 \quad 2 \quad -1 \quad 1] \begin{bmatrix} \dfrac{3}{\sqrt{90}} & 0 & \dfrac{9}{\sqrt{90}} & 0 \\ 0 & 1 & 0 & 0 \\ \dfrac{-9}{\sqrt{90}} & 0 & \dfrac{3}{\sqrt{90}} & 0 \\ 0 & 0 & 0 & 1 \end{bmatrix}$$

$$\begin{bmatrix} -1 & 0 & 0 & 0 \\ 0 & 1 & 0 & 0 \\ 0 & 0 & 1 & 0 \\ 0 & 0 & 0 & 1 \end{bmatrix} \begin{bmatrix} \dfrac{3}{\sqrt{90}} & 0 & \dfrac{-9}{\sqrt{90}} & 0 \\ 0 & 1 & 0 & 0 \\ \dfrac{9}{\sqrt{90}} & 0 & \dfrac{3}{\sqrt{90}} & 0 \\ 0 & 0 & 0 & 1 \end{bmatrix}$$

$$P^* = [1 \quad 2 \quad 2 \quad 1]$$

6.3.4.2 Shearing

Three-dimensional shearing transformations cause distortions in objects by altering the values of one or more coordinates by an amount proportional to the third. This means that shear along any pair of axes is controlled by a third axis. Off-diagonal terms in the upper 3×3 submatrix of the general transformation matrix produce the effect of shearing:

$$[T_{\text{SH}}] = \begin{bmatrix} 1 & S_{xy} & S_{xz} & 0 \\ S_{yx} & 1 & S_{yz} & 0 \\ S_{zx} & S_{zy} & 1 & 0 \\ 0 & 0 & 0 & 1 \end{bmatrix} \tag{6.31}$$

The "S" terms can be interpreted as follows: S_{xy} is the amount of shear due to x along y; S_{yx} is the amount of shear due to y along x, and so forth. Figure 6.22 gives the shearing matrices along the x, y, and z axes, and their effect on a point $P(P_x, P_y, P_z)$. Figure 6.23 shows the effect of each individual shearing factor S on the shape of a unit cube.

6.3.5 Coordinate System Transformation

Until now all geometric transformations have been performed within the same reference frame. In many engineering applications, however, there is a need to switch from one coordinate system to another. Figure 6.24 shows the use of multiple coordinate systems, simulating the movements of a robot.

The robot translates in the x and z directions in the world coordinate system. The arms and grip, however, have rotational movement with respect to coordinate frames fixed at A, B, and C. Coordinate transformations can be applied by determining how one set of coordinates is related to another set

Shear Control Axis	x	y	z
Shearing matrix	$\begin{bmatrix} 1 & S_{xy} & S_{xz} & 0 \\ 0 & 1 & 0 & 0 \\ 0 & 0 & 1 & 0 \\ 0 & 0 & 0 & 1 \end{bmatrix}$	$\begin{bmatrix} 1 & 0 & 0 & 0 \\ S_{yx} & 1 & S_{yz} & 0 \\ 0 & 0 & 1 & 0 \\ 0 & 0 & 0 & 1 \end{bmatrix}$	$\begin{bmatrix} 1 & 0 & 0 & 0 \\ 0 & 1 & 0 & 0 \\ S_{zx} & S_{zy} & 1 & 0 \\ 0 & 0 & 0 & 1 \end{bmatrix}$
Effect on a point P	$P_x^* = [P_x, (S_{xy}P_x + P_y), (S_{xz}P_x + P_z)]$	$P_y^* = [(P_x + S_{yx}P_y), P_y, (S_{yz}P_y + P_z)]$	$P_z^* = [(P_x + S_{zx}P_z), (P_y + S_{zy}P_z), P_z]$

FIGURE 6.22 Shearing matrices and their effect on a point.

FIGURE 6.23 Effect of *shearing factors S on the shape of a cube.*

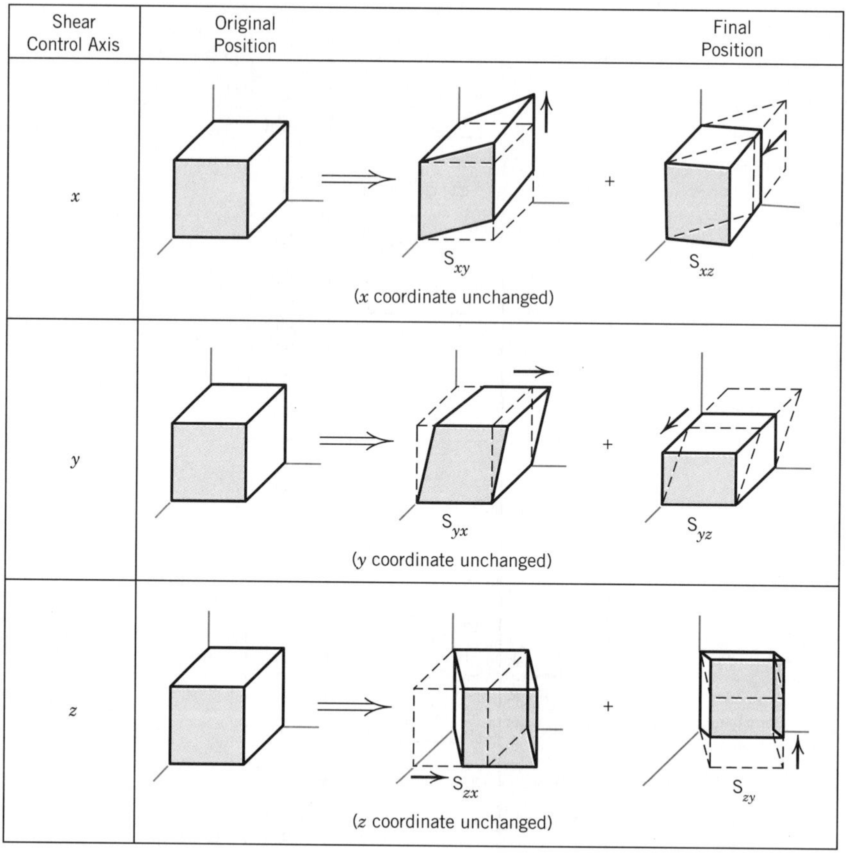

Shear Control Axis	Original Position	Final Position
x	S_{xy} (*x* coordinate unchanged)	$+$ S_{xz}
y	S_{yx} (*y* coordinate unchanged)	$+$ S_{yz}
z	S_{zx} (*z* coordinate unchanged)	$+$ S_{zy}

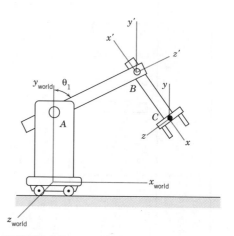

FIGURE 6.24 Use of multiple coordinate systems.

for the same object. This is accomplished by a series of translations, rotations, and scalings that superimpose the two coordinate systems.

The following example illustrates this process.

Example 6.6

The origin of the coordinate system for the wrist of a robotic arm is located at (15, 10, 10) with respect to the world coordinate system (WC) and undergoes a 30° CW rotation about the z axis, as shown in the accompanying figure. After this rotation, the tip of the wrist has coordinates (2, 1, 4) with respect to its own frame. The wrist is to be rotated about the x' axis by 45° clockwise. Obtain the final coordinates of the tip of the wrist with respect to the WC system.

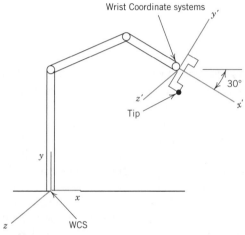

Wrist Coordinate systems

Solution

The solution is obtained by first performing the 45° CW rotation of the wrist about its own axis. Next, the coordinate system of the wrist is superimposed on the WC system by a translation of the origin and a counterclockwise rotation of 30° about the z axis. The transformed coordinates of point [2 1 4 1] representing the wrist are obtained as follows:

$$[x \quad y \quad z \quad 1] = [2 \quad 1 \quad 4 \quad 1] \begin{bmatrix} \cos 45° & -\sin 45° & 0 & 0 \\ \sin 45° & \cos 45° & 0 & 0 \\ 0 & 0 & 1 & 0 \\ 0 & 0 & 0 & 1 \end{bmatrix}$$

$$\begin{bmatrix} \cos 30° & \sin 30° & 0 & 0 \\ -\sin 30° & \cos 30° & 0 & 0 \\ 0 & 0 & 1 & 0 \\ 0 & 0 & 0 & 1 \end{bmatrix} \begin{bmatrix} 1 & 0 & 0 & 0 \\ 0 & 1 & 0 & 0 \\ 0 & 0 & 1 & 0 \\ 15 & 10 & 10 & 1 \end{bmatrix}$$

$$= [17.2 \quad 10.5 \quad 14 \quad 1]$$

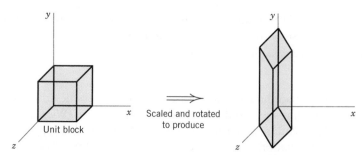

FIGURE 6.25 Transformations used to modify basic shapes in geometric modeling systems.

SUMMARY

This chapter describes three-dimensional geometric transformations as important tools in the creation and manipulation of models. These geometric transformations can be combined to produce a desired effect, with a single composite transformation represented by a single matrix.

Three-dimensional transformations may be harder to visualize than their two-dimensional counterparts, but are important and useful in various engineering applications. For example, many engineering objects can be described as a combination of simple volumes. These volumes vary in shape, size, and orientation in space. If a graphics system provides the user/designer with a few fixed volumes such as unit cubes, cylinders, and the like, the appropriate geometric transformations can be applied to the unit volume to produce the final desired shape and size, as shown in Figure 6.25. This approach reduces the number of basic shapes that a geometric modeling system must provide.

EXERCISES

1. Rotate the straight line joining A(1,1,1) and B(4, 3, 2) 30° about the x axis and 60° about the y axis, both in a counterclockwise direction. Repeat the process in the reverse order, rotation about y followed by rotation about x, and compare the final coordinates of the line.

2. Consider the cube shown in the accompanying figure, with sides of length 4 in. Rotate the cube by an angle of 45° CCW about the diagonal OA. Knowing that point E is the midpoint of AB, find the coordinates of E, B, and C before and after the rotation.

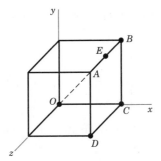

3. Prove that, given a line and its midpoint, the transformed midpoint will still be the midpoint of the transformed line.

4. Three points in space are represented by A, B, C. Given three other points, Q, R, S, find the transformation matrices needed to

   (a) Transform A into Q.
   (b) Transform the plane of ABC into the plane of QRS.

5. In the accompanying figure, use the orthogonality property of the rotation matrix to place triangle AOB on the xz plane.

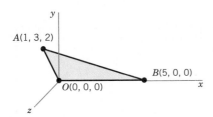

6. Consider a rectangular box with its top side open, represented by the following coordinates:

$$\begin{bmatrix} 6 & 9 & 13 & 1 \\ 10 & 9 & 16 & 1 \\ 7 & 9 & 20 & 1 \\ 3 & 9 & 17 & 1 \\ 6 & 14 & 13 & 1 \\ 10 & 14 & 16 & 1 \\ 7 & 14 & 20 & 1 \\ 3 & 14 & 17 & 1 \end{bmatrix}$$

A plate is available on a conveyor belt and its coordinates, when the conveyor belt stops, are:

$$\begin{bmatrix} -2.5 & -2.5 & 0 & 1 \\ 2.5 & -2.5 & 0 & 1 \\ 2.5 & 2.5 & 0 & 1 \\ -2.5 & 2.5 & 0 & 1 \end{bmatrix}$$

Obtain the concatenated transformation matrix needed to place the plate on top of the box correctly.

7. Any angle formed by two intersecting planes is called a *dihedral angle*. Calculate this angle for the two planes defined as follows:

   Plane 1 $(-1, 1, -1), (0, -1, -2), (4, 0, 2)$
   Plane 2 $(-1, 1, 1), (4, -3, -1), (6, -1, 2)$

8. Rotate the point $P(1, -1, -1)$ 45° clockwise about the axis given by the points $A(1, 2, 1)$ and $B(2, 1, 4)$.

9. Establish in matrix form the series of transformations needed to transform the unit cube shown in Figure 6.26(*a*) into the solid shown in Figure 6.26(*b*).

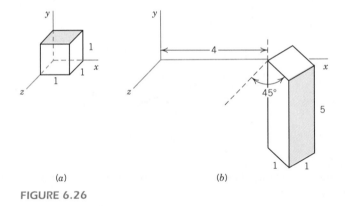

(*a*)   (*b*)

FIGURE 6.26

10. Implement an algorithm that will scale and rotate the object in Figure 6.10. Solve the same problem by using an interactive CAD system.

Chapter 7

Data Structures for Computer Graphics

Although the study of data structures falls more into the realm of computer science than engineering, it is important to know how the geometric data used in computer graphics should be organized for more efficient utilization and output.

Any computer model of an object must comprise three different types of entities: data, algorithm, and structure. The data are the most basic elements in the model description and may consist of numerical values, characters, instructions, or any other representation of attributes defined in a formalized language. Algorithms indicate how the data should be manipulated, and structure indicates how the data are organized. If the data are highly structured, the need for algorithm structuring decreases.

Structuring of data is a very important aspect of a *database*, which is a "bank" of the information to be processed and of the results, stored for future use. This is especially true in graphics and design systems where large amounts of data must be processed at very high speeds. A major portion of the database in CAD applications comprises geometric information. Thus, proper representation of geometric data is both integral and imperative for an efficient CAD database.

This chapter presents a description of data structures that are relevant to computer graphics applications. A brief description of elementary data structures is included for completeness.

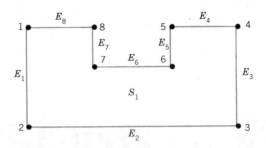

FIGURE 7.1 Object to be described using various types of database.

7.1   GENERAL DATABASES

Before going into specific data structures and their use for computer graphics purposes, a brief description of popular database systems and how they relate to object modeling will be given. The three most popular database models are relational, hierarchical, and network. All three will be viewed in the context of the object shown in Figure 7.1.

1. A *relational database* contains data representing relations stored in files usually accessed in a sequential form. The object shown in Figure 7.1, for example, would be described by three relations:

Points indicate Cartesian coordinates of the vertices;

Lines show which vertices are at the endpoints of edges;

Surfaces show which edges bound a surface.

The relational database for the object in Figure 7.1 is shown in Figure 7.2. This type of database has the advantage of being always consistent and very flexible with respect to user manipulation of relations and data. However, it requires a substantial amount of sorting in its implementation.

FIGURE 7.2 Example of a relational database.

Point	x	y	Line	Beginning Point	Ending Point	Surface	Line
1	x_1	y_1	E_1	1	2		E_1
2	x_2	y_2	E_2	2	3		E_2
3	x_3	y_3	E_3	3	4		E_3
4	x_4	y_4	E_4	4	5	S_1	E_4
5	x_5	y_5	E_5	5	6		E_5
6	x_6	y_6	E_6	6	7		E_6
7	x_7	y_7	E_7	7	8		E_7
8	x_8	y_8	E_8	8	1		E_8

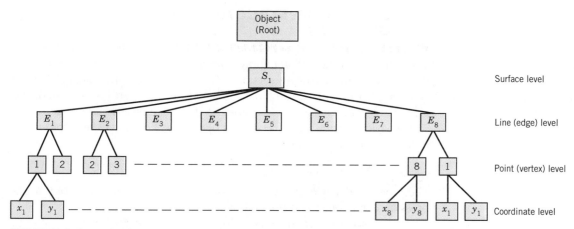

FIGURE 7.3 Example of a hierarchical database.

2. A *hierarchical database* is a *tree* structure composed of a hierarchy of elements called nodes. The top of the tree is the *root* node, and the hierarchy, showing the different levels of the tree with respect to each other, moves down from this node. More information on the tree structure will be given in Section 7.2.7. A hierarchical structure for the object in Figure 7.1 requires four levels for complete description (Figure 7.3). Notice that each level's elements connect to only one element of the level above. Hierarchical models are usually simple and fast, but have the disadvantage that few relations in the real world are purely hierarchical. In addition, the hierarchical implementation usually creates redundancy and a danger of inconsistency.

3. A *network database* has a "many-to-many" relationship among its elements; in other words, elements at each level can be connected to many elements of the level above. Figure 7.4 shows a network model for the object in Figure 7.1. This type of database often becomes unduly complex in both structure and amount of programming needed to implement it.

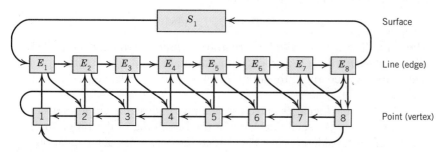

FIGURE 7.4 Example of a network database.

7.2 BASIC DATA STRUCTURES FOR GRAPHICS

The databases discussed in the previous section are built by basic structures described in the following sections. These structures are essential for the creation and organization of data; but before they can be evaluated, the elementary data elements to be structured must themselves be understood. These basic elements can be classified by means of primitive data types given in most computer languages as

INTEGER, REAL, BOOLEAN (LOGICAL), CHARACTER

The types of data determine the value, or set of values, a variable or expression can assume and operate on.

The primary reason to structure a set of data values is to be able to manipulate it. The type of structure will depend on how the manipulation is to be accomplished. In general, data structures can be classified as static or dynamic.

Static structures assume fixed, predefined values and have fixed memory locations. In many problems, however, not only do the values change during computation but the structure as well. This gives rise to the need for data structures that support dynamic storage allocation. Data structures of this type are called dynamic.

7.2.1 Static Arrays

The most common example of a static data structure is the array, which is widely used in computer graphics. It consists of components of the same basic type and is thus called a homogeneous data structure. Arrays also have a random access structure, since their components can be selected individually. The selection process is done through a subscripting operation and can be used either as a destination in which to store a value or as a source from which to obtain a value. The elements of an array R are given by a parenthesis notation in FORTRAN

R(1), R(2), . . . , R(N)

or by a bracket notation in C or PASCAL

R[1], R[2], . . . , R[N]

The value K in R(K) is called the *index* or *subscript* of the array; and R(K) is a *subscripted variable*, regardless of the language used. These subscripts give access to any element of the array by referencing its relative position inside the array.

High-level languages make use of arrays to describe graphics data. The size of the array is usually declared at the beginning of the program. They are therefore considered static data structures. Examples of the creation process for various computer languages are

DIMENSION REALARRAY(100)   (FORTRAN)

a = array [1. .100] of real   (PASCAL)

float a[100];   (C)

Arrays are commonly used to describe objects that do not change their shape. Consider, for example, a data structure based on the use of arrays to describe a line from point P_1 to points P_2, P_3, P_4, as shown in Figure 7.5. An array containing the coordinates (x, y) of these points would be given as:

COORD

1	x_1	y_1
2	x_2	y_2
3	x_3	y_3
4	x_4	y_4

Since this is a two-dimensional array, the program must create it with two subscripts. In FORTRAN, for example, the dimension statement would be

DIMENSION COORD(4,2)

Arrays are said to be linear because all their elements form a sequence. Several operations can be performed on any linear data structure, or linear list, such as an array. From the point of view of computer graphics, the kinds of operations needed can be reduced to the following:

Traversal Accessing and processing each element of the array exactly once. This is also called *visiting* each element of the list. Traversing a linear array is a simple process because of the indexing operation, which allows each element to be located independently.

Insertion Adding a new element to an existing list. This can be accomplished easily if the new element is to be inserted at the end of the existing list. However, if the insertion is to occur in the middle, all subsequent elements must be moved one location to accommodate the new one. This process can be relatively expensive from the computational point of view.

Deletion Removing an element from an existing list. The same considerations used in the insertion process apply.

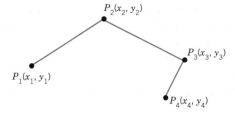

FIGURE 7.5 Geometric definition of a polyline.

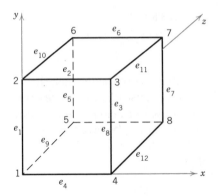

	Edges	Vertices
Face 1	1, 2, 3, 4	1, 2, 3, 4
Face 2	1, 9, 5, 10	1, 5, 6, 2
Face 3	8, 7, 6, 5	5, 8, 7, 6
Face 4	3, 11, 7, 12	3, 7, 8, 4
Face 5	4, 9, 8, 12	1, 5, 8, 4
Face 6	2, 10, 6, 11	2, 6, 7, 3

FIGURE 7.6 Representation of a unit cube.

7.2.2 Representation of Polyhedral Objects Using Static Arrays

Given an array of coordinate values like those of the previous section, a variable *I* can be made to point to any element of the coordinate array. If an array of these pointing indices is created, it is referred to as a *pointer array*. This type of array helps the processing of information and a common example of its use in computer graphics is the representation of polyhedral objects. If, for example, the unit cube shown in Figure 7.6 is to be described by means of a data structure based on the use of arrays, pointer arrays facilitate the process.

The three arrays used in the description of the cube are:

1. A vertex array listing the *x*, *y*, *z* coordinates of each vertex
2. An edge array, pointing to the vertex array, indicating the two vertices at the end of each edge
3. A face array, pointing to the edge array, listing the edges that form each face

Figure 7.7 shows the values of the arrays used in the description of the unit cube and also shows how these arrays can be accessed through FORTRAN programs. Subprogram I creates the model as a series of connected edges, using the vertex and edge arrays. Subprogram II represents the model as a series of faces, and utilizes the vertex and face arrays. Subroutines MOVE and DRAW in subprogram I and INSERT_POLYGON in subprogram II are assumed to be part of a graphics library available to the programmer. These calls may vary in syntax, depending on the graphics library used.

Note that, in the representation of objects with arrays of this type, there are two kinds of information given—numerical data defining the *x*, *y*, *z* coordinates of the vertices, and pointing indices defining the "connectivity" between edges and faces. The model can be altered by subsequent transformations that change the numerical data or the indices, or both. For ex-

Vertex (8 × 3)

	x	y	z
1	0.0	0.0	0.0
2	0.0	1.0	0.0
3	1.0	1.0	0.0
4	1.0	0.0	0.0
5	0.0	0.0	1.0
6	0.0	1.0	1.0
7	1.0	1.0	1.0
8	1.0	0.0	1.0

Edge (12 × 2)

	Vertices	
1	1	2
2	2	3
3	3	4
4	4	1
5	5	6
6	6	7
7	7	8
8	8	5
9	1	5
10	2	6
11	3	7
12	4	8

Face (6 × 4)

	Edges			
1	1	2	3	4
2	1	9	5	10
3	8	7	6	5
4	3	11	7	12
5	4	9	8	12
6	2	10	6	11

Face (6 × 4)

	Vertices			
1	1	2	3	4
2	1	5	6	2
3	5	8	7	6
4	3	7	8	4
5	1	5	8	4
6	2	6	7	3

FIGURE 7.7 Arrays used in the description of the unit cube in Figure 7.6.

Arrays: Face ⇒ Edge ⇒ Vertex

```
      FORTRAN Subprogram I
C     Declaration of arrays

C     NV=total number of vertices
C     NEDG=total number of edges
      READ(1,*) NV
         DO 10 I=1,NV
         READ(1,*) X(I),Y(I),Z(I)
10       CONTINUE
      READ(1,*) NEDG
         DO 20 I=1,NEDG
         READ(1,*) INI(I),IFIN(I)
20       CONTINUE
         DO 30 I=1,NEDG
         CALL MOVE(X(INI(I)),Y(INI(I)),Z(INI(I)))
         CALL DRAW(X(IFIN(I)),Y(IFIN(I)),Z(IFIN(I)))
30       CONTINUE

FORTRAN Subprogram II
C     Declaration of arrays

nv=total number of vertices in the figure
ns=number of surfaces to be connected each time
nvc=number of vertices connected each time

      READ(1, *) NV

      DO 10 I=1,NV
          READ(1,*) X(I),Y(I),Z(I)
```

(continued)

FIGURE 7.7 (Continued).

```
10   CONTINUE

     READ(1,*)NS

     DO 20 I=1,NS
               READ(1,*)NVC,(V(L),L=1,NVC)
                    DO 30 J=1,NVC
                              A(1,J)=X(V(J))
                              A(2,J)=Y(V(J))
                              A(3,J)=Z(V(J))
30   CONTINUE
     CALL INSERT_POLYGON(NVC,A)
20   CONTINUE
```

ample, rigid-body transformations such as translations or rotations are accomplished by changing the numerical data and leaving the pointing relationships unaltered. This type of representation is also referred to as a *graph-based model.*

A more concise way of representing polyhedral objects such as the cube in Figure 7.6 is to list the vertices with their coordinates in one array and their connectivity in a connectivity matrix as shown in Figure 7.8. This connectivity matrix can still be considered a pointer array and contains only two types of elements:

zero-valued, indicating absence of connectivity

one-valued, indicating presence of connectivity

The connectivity matrix can be used for various elements in a model, as shown in Figure 7.8, where it is described for both vertices and faces. Additional savings in computational time can be achieved by noticing that this is a sparse matrix, consisting mostly of zeros. The efficient storage of large sparse matrices has been studied for a long time and is well documented [23].

Vertex Connectivity Matrix

	1	2	3	4	5	6	7	8
1	0	1	0	1	1	0	0	0
2	1	0	1	0	0	1	0	0
3	0	1	0	1	0	0	1	0
4	1	0	1	0	0	0	0	1
5	1	0	0	0	0	1	0	0
6	0	1	0	0	1	0	1	0
7	0	0	1	0	0	1	0	1
8	0	0	0	1	1	0	1	0

Face Connectivity Matrix

	1	2	3	4	5	6
1	0	1	0	1	1	1
2	1	0	1	0	1	1
3	0	1	0	1	1	1
4	1	0	1	0	1	1
5	1	1	1	1	0	0
6	1	1	1	1	0	0

FIGURE 7.8 Connectivity matrices for the unit cube of Figure 7.6.

7.2.3 Structured Data Types

A structure is a basic data type created by combining other data types, such
as arrays. The general form of a structure is

```
struct    A
    {
        data_type1    var1;
        data_type2    var2;
        data_type3    var3;
        . . . . . . . . . . . . . . . . .
        . . . . . . . . . . . . . . . . .
        . . . . . . . . . . . . . . . . .
        data_typen    varn;
    }
```

Each component is called a *field* of the structure, and its name is the *field
identifier*. Examples of this type of data structure in high-level languages are

STRUCT   (C)

RECORD   (PASCAL)

Both C and PASCAL can create structures through facilities built into the
language. FORTRAN, on the other hand, does not have this capability at this
time, although the upcoming FORTRAN 90 will include it. But, since each
field of the structure has data elements of the same type, the entire structure
can be created by means of parallel arrays, where elements with the same
subscript belong to the same structure. This approach was used in the FOR-
TRAN subprograms shown in Figure 7.7.

The unit cube of Figure 7.6 can be defined as a structure in a computer
language such as C or PASCAL, making use of arrays. The advantage of such
a representation is that all the information required to define the cube is
contained in one structure. Figure 7.9 shows the use of a structure in PASCAL
and C for the representation of the unit cube. Notice the arrays embedded
in the description of the data.

In the C implementation, for example, if information is needed about
the fifth face of the cube, which is declared to be of type object, this information can be obtained from the field faces [5][i], i — ranging from
1......NUM_EDGES. The edge information will in turn be obtained from the
field edges which indicate the starting and ending vertices. It should be noted
that the field edges could alternatively be defined as:

```
int  edges[NUM_VERTS][2];
```

Here, the second dimension would contain the vertex numbers that
form each edge.

FIGURE 7.9 Use of C and PASCAL to represent a structure.

PASCAL Implementation of a Structure

```
Object =    RECORD

              no_of_edges, no_of_vertices, ⎫
              no_of_faces                  ⎭ : integer ;

              vertices : array [1.. NOVERTS] of

                         ⎡ RECORD
                         ⎢    x,y,z : real
                         ⎣ END;


              edges : array [1.. NOEDGES] of

                      ⎡ RECORD
                      ⎢    x₁, y₁, z₁ : real
                      ⎢    x₂, y₂, z₂ : real
                      ⎣ END;


              face : array [1.. NOFACES] of array
              [1.. NOEDGES] of integer;


            END;
```

C Implementation of a Structure

```
struct   point
         {
              float   x,y,z;
         };

struct   edge
         {
              struct point v1 , v2 ;
         };

struct   object
         {
              int no_of_edges,no_of_vertices,
              no_of_faces;
              struct   point   vertices[NUM_VERTS];
              struct   edge    edges[NUM_EDGES];
              int  faces[NUM_FACES][NUM_EDGES];
         };
```

(continued)

NOTE:
1. NUM_VERTS - maximum number of vertices.
2. NUM_EDGES - maximum number of edges .
3. NUM_FACES - maximum number of faces .

FIGURE 7.9 (Continued).

7.2.4 Pointers

Pointers are used to effectively represent complex data structures and to deal more concisely with arrays. Pointers are not data entities, but an "attribute" of some data entity. A particular data type can be indirectly accessed through a pointer. In more simple terms, a pointer provides a reference or an address where a particular data item is being stored.

A more compact representation of the structure "edge" in Figure 7.9 makes use of the concept of pointers, as follows:

```
struct edge
        {
            struct  point  *pv1, *pv2;
            . . . . . . . . . . . . . . . . . . . . .
        };
```

Note that in the above implementation, the edge structure points to two vertices rather than referring to the vertices themselves. In the C-language, for example, the operator * is used to define a pointer to an object. If an edge e1 is formed by joining the two vertices v1 and v2, the vertex fields of the edge structure are initialized as follows:

```
e1.pv1 = & v1 ;
e1.pv2 = & v2 ;
```

where & is the address operator providing the means to access the actual storage location. Many high-level languages such as C, PASCAL, and the upcoming FORTRAN 90 provide a facility to create pointers.

7.2.5 Linked Lists

The data structures discussed in the previous sections are fundamental building blocks out of which more complex structures are made. They have predefined values and fixed memory locations. The cube representation in Figure 7.9, for example, has limitations due to the fact that the arrays are dimensioned in each field to a maximum size, much of which may not be needed in the description of various objects. The storage for the array of vertices, which is of size NUM_VERTS, was statically allocated at the compile time. However, the capability of dynamically allocating this value by means of dynamic arrays is present in C, PASCAL, and the upcoming FORTRAN 90.

In C, a vertex array of variable size n can be dynamically allocated as

```
vertex_header = (struct point *) calloc (n,sizeof
                       (struct point));
```

where vertex_header is a pointer to the first element in the vertex array.

As stated in Section 7.2, many situations arise in the geometric representation of objects where not only the data values but also the data structure must change during computation. Of these dynamic data structures perhaps the most common one is the *linked list*. This type of structure can grow or shrink, depending on its usage.

A linked list is a collection of data elements or nodes placed in a linear order by pointers. In our discussion of pointer arrays, the geometric data and the pointing index information were located in different structures. In the example given in Figure 7.7, one array contained the (x, y, z) coordinates and another the pointing information. In a linked list this information is integrated, each node containing both the geometric data and the pointer. The node is divided into two parts, one with only the data information and the other containing the address of the next node in the list.

Consider, for example, a triangle specified by three vertices P_1, P_2, and P_3. Figure 7.10 is a schematic diagram of a linked list representing this triangle. The data information is stored in the left part of each node, under cells labeled x and y. The last cell contains the pointer which is represented by the arrow. The pointer field of the last node contains a special value, called the "null" pointer, indicating that the end of the list is reached. The linked list must also contain a "list pointer variable," pointing to the beginning of the list and labeled START in Figure 7.10. In FORTRAN, parallel arrays can be used to represent in memory the elements of the linked list. In the case of the triangle these parallel arrays, carrying the same index values, could be represented as X(K), Y(K), and LINK(K).

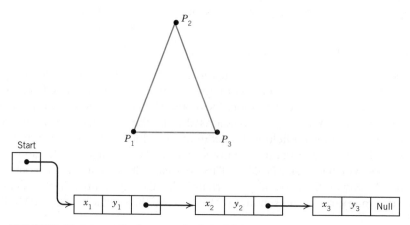

FIGURE 7.10 Schematic diagram of a linked list.

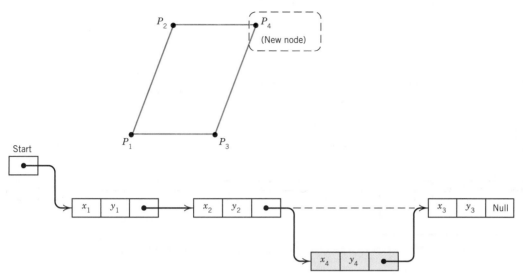

FIGURE 7.11 Node insertion in a linked list.

Operations on linked lists follow the same pattern described for arrays. Insertion, for example, is a common operation in computer graphics applications. Suppose there was a need to add another vertex to the triangle of Figure 7.10 in order to create a closed polygon as shown in Figure 7.11. The original list would have to be expanded by the insertion of the new node through three operations:

- Creation of the new node
- Linking P2 to the new node
- Linking the new node to the node P2 was originally pointing to

This operation can be described by the schematic diagram shown in Figure 7.11. The insertion of nodes requires access to an availability list from which nodes can be obtained, formed by unused memory cells in the arrays that describe the nodes. These unused memory cells would also be linked to form a linked list of available nodes called AVAIL, which uses AVAIL as its list pointer variable. The schematic diagram in Figure 7.12 shows the use of this availability list to create the additional vertex.

A simple FORTRAN implementation of this process is shown below. The original linked list is maintained in memory in the form

LIST (XDATA, YDATA, LINK, START, AVAIL)

where AVAIL is an integer variable indicating which node is currently available in the availability list. Assuming that the new node data are X=XNEW and Y=YNEW to be linked to a new LINK=NLINK, the FORTRAN code could be constructed as

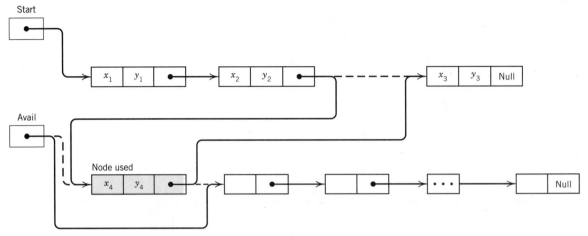

FIGURE 7.12 Use of an availability list for node insertion.

```
AVAIL=NLINK     |*Initialize*|
IF (AVAIL.GT.0)THEN
   X(AVAIL) = XNEW
   Y(AVAIL) = YNEW
   LINK (AVAIL) = NLINK
   AVAIL = AVAIL-1
ELSE
   WRITE (*,*) "NO NODE IS AVAILABLE"
ENDIF
```

In C, the implementation could be as follows:

```
struct  node
        {
          int  x , y ;
          struct node  * next_link;
        } ;

struct  node * temp , *nlink ;
```

and, to create the new node , the predeclared routine 'malloc' could be used:

```
temp = (struct node *) malloc (sizeof(struct node));
temp->x = XNEW;
temp->y = YNEW;
temp->next_link = NLINK;
NLINK  =  temp ;
```

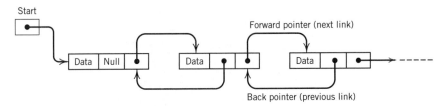

Start

Forward pointer (next link)

Data | Null   Data   Data

Back pointer (previous link)

FIGURE 7.13 Double linked list.

A linked list with a single link is often too restrictive. For instance, when node i is reached, there is no way to move back to node $(i\text{-}1)$ unless the list is traversed again from nodes 1 to $(i\text{-}1)$. Therefore, for applications where movement in either direction is necessary, a *double linked* list is useful. Here a node typically has three fields: data, previous link, and next link, as shown in the schematic diagram of Figure 7.13.

The representation of polyhedral objects through double linked lists can be used to demonstrate their utilization [24]. Assume that in Figure 7.14 F_1 and F_2 are faces of a polyhedral object. These faces are created through three lists: vertices (P), edges (e), and faces (F), as shown in Figure 7.14. In the list of edges, elist is a pointer to the first edge. The nodes in the edge list include:

- A counter, representing the number of faces to which the edge belongs;
- Pointers to the vertices (P) at the end of the edges;
- Pointers to the faces (F) containing the edge. A null field is used if the edge belongs to only one face;
- A pointer to the next edge.

In the list of faces Flist is itself a list pointing to all faces forming the object. The null field indicates the end of the list. The faces are represented by:

- Pointers to the edges (e) bounding the face, taken in CCW order. The orientation of the edges on the face helps in future calculations;
- A null field indicating the end of the list.

A schematic representation of the structure for this problem is given in Figure 7.15. Notice the use of double links in the description of the edges, which point to a face and a vertex.

A more general representation of a structure of this type is given in Figure 7.16. Here, each face, edge and vertex is a double linked list pointing to a "previous" and "next" entity, and

- Each face points to both the lists of its bounding edges and vertices;
- Each edge points to its parent faces and to its three-dimensional endpoints;
- Each vertex points to its parent faces and edges.

FIGURE 7.14 Linked lists describing faces of a polyhedral object.

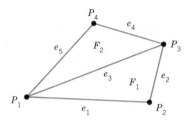

List of vertices:

$$P_1 (x_1, y_1, z_1)$$
$$P_2 (x_2, y_2, z_2)$$
$$P_3 (x_3, y_3, z_3)$$
$$P_4 (x_4, y_4, z_4)$$

List of edges:
elist $= $ ptre_1

$$e_1 = (1, \text{ptr}P_1, \text{ptr}P_2, \text{ptr}F_1, \text{null}, \text{ptr}e_2)$$
$$e_2 = (1, \text{ptr}P_2, \text{ptr}P_3, \text{ptr}F_1, \text{null}, \text{ptr}e_3)$$
$$e_3 = (2, \text{ptr}P_1, \text{ptr}P_3, \text{ptr}F_1, \text{ptr}F_2, \text{ptr}e_4)$$
$$e_4 = (1, \text{ptr}P_3, \text{ptr}P_4, \text{ptr}F_2, \text{null}, \text{ptr}e_5)$$
$$e_5 = (1, \text{ptr}P_1, \text{ptr}P_4, \text{ptr}F_2, \text{null}, \text{null})$$

List of faces:
Flist $= (\text{ptr}F_1, \text{ptr}F_2, \text{null})$ $F_1 = (\text{ptr}e_1, \text{ptr}e_2, \text{ptr}e_3, \text{null})$
$$F_2 = (\text{ptr}e_3, \text{ptr}e_4, \text{ptr}e_5, \text{null})$$

In addition to their use in the representation of geometry, linked lists, whether single or double linked, have other uses in computer graphics and image processing. They could, for example, contain a set of commands to be used by a display processor, or a set of transformations to be applied to the image of an object.

FIGURE 7.15 Schematic representation of the structure of Figure 7.14.

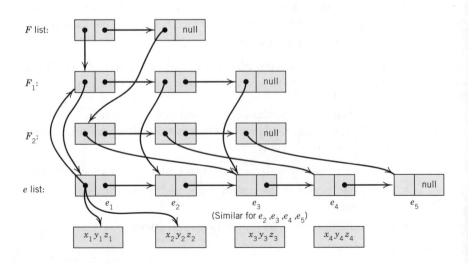

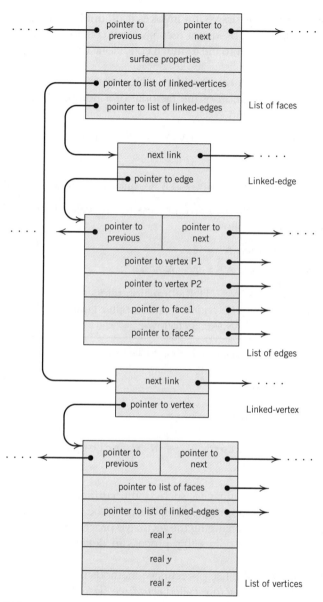

FIGURE 7.16 A more general hierarchical linked data structure for polyhedral geometry.

7.2.6 A Note on Recursion

Recursion is a fundamental and powerful programming technique, yielding an efficient and intuitive approach to the solution of many problems in computer graphics and geometric modeling. For this reason it will be described here, though it is not necessarily a "data structure" but more a "programming procedure."

A procedure is recursive if it invokes itself until a terminal condition is satisfied. Each time a subsequent recursive call is made, it should bring the recursive program closer to the terminal condition. The recursion is then said to be "well-defined."

A simple example of a problem where recursion can be used to advantage is the computation of the factorial of a number. The factorial of a positive integer N is defined as

$$N! = 1 \cdot 2 \cdot 3 \dots (N - 1) \cdot N \quad \text{and} \quad 0! = 1 \qquad \text{(I)}$$

or

$$N! = N \cdot (N - 1)! \quad \text{and} \quad 0! = 1 \qquad \text{(II)}$$

Equation (II) indicates a recursive process for the calculation of $N!$ through a function defined as follows:

(a) If $N = 0$, then $N! = 1$.

(b) If $N > 0$, then $N! = N \cdot (N - 1)!$

Note that when using $(N - 1)!$ the function refers to itself and the terminal value is zero. This may be coded in a computer language that supports recursion, such as C or PASCAL, as follows:

```
Function factorial (N : integer) ; integer;
Begin
     if (N = 0)
     then
         factorial := 1
     else
         factorial := N * factorial (N - 1);
End
```

Some programming languages, such as the current FORTRAN 77, do not allow such recursive subprograms. In this case, the programmer must set up the necessary steps by changing the recursive procedure into a nonrecursive one. Reference [25] describes this process in detail. FORTRAN 90 should correct this problem.

An example of the use of recursive methods in computer graphics applications is the data structure called *quadtree*, described in detail in Section 12.7. We will simply say here that the quadtree is a procedure that allows for the recursive subdivision of two-dimensional regions into variably sized squares, as shown in Figure 7.17. The object to be modeled is enclosed inside a square. If not uniformly covering the object, the square is subdivided into quadrants. When any of these quadrants are completely inside or outside the object, no further subdivision is performed. Any quadrant partially full, that is, partially inside and partially outside the object, is further subdivided. The process is continued until the final resolution needed for object definition is reached.

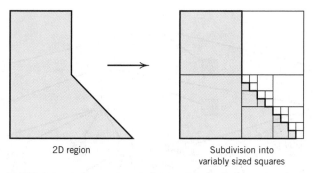

2D region · Subdivision into variably sized squares

FIGURE 7.17 Recursive subdivision of a two-dimensional region.

The recursive nature of this problem can be seen in the following general code.

```
Procedure subdivide (Quadrant)
Begin
     If (Quadrant = full) or (Quadrant = empty)
     then
          Return
     else
          subdivide (Quadrant)
     end; procedure
```

7.2.7   Trees

All the data structures studied so far in this chapter, such as arrays and linked lists, are linear in nature. *Trees* are nonlinear data structures used to represent data having a hierarchical relationship.

A tree structure is defined by a finite number of elements called *nodes*, described in Section 7.1. The tree contains one distinguishable node called the *root*; all the remaining nodes form an ordered collection of subtrees, as shown in Figure 7.18. Family terminology is commonly used to describe the

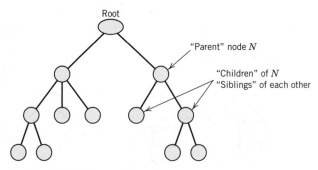

FIGURE 7.18 A general tree structure.

FIGURE 7.19 Tree
structure for a quadtree.

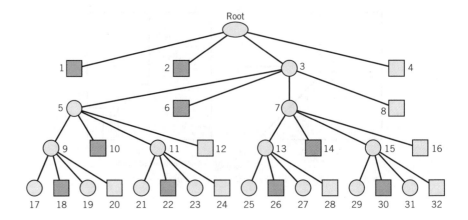

relationships among tree elements. For example, if *N* is a node with various successors, as shown in Figure 7.18, it is called the "parent" node. Its successors are the "children" nodes. The successors of a single node on a particular level are called "siblings."

Section 7.2.6 described one such tree structure—the quadtree. In this case the root node is the square or quadrant that encloses the entire object. The root node has at most four children, each of which can have up to four other children. Figure 7.19 shows the tree structure for the quadtree in Figure 7.17.

Each node in a tree contains some specific information, in addition to pointers to its parent and children. In the quadtree example, the specific information in the node might have been the limiting coordinates ($X_{\min}$, $X_{\max}$, $Y_{\min}$, $Y_{\max}$) of the quadrant.

In general, a node is defined by the number of branches converging to it. The quadtree example has many nodes of degree four. If each node of the tree has at most two children the tree is called a *binary tree*. This type of tree is widely used in geometric modeling applications. For example, a physical object is often modeled as a combination of simple volumes, such as blocks, cylinders, cones, and the like. These volumes are combined in

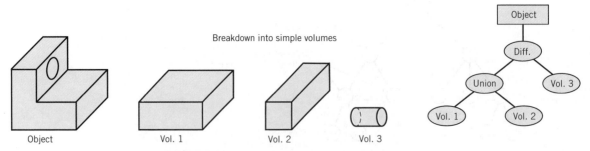

FIGURE 7.20 Binary tree representation.

different ways, perhaps by joining them (union operation) or extracting one from the other (difference operation). This type of representation is named *constructive solid geometry* (CSG) and will be studied in detail in Section 12.3. Suffice it to say here that a binary tree is used in this representation of solids. Figure 7.20 shows a physical object and its binary tree representation. The nodes in a binary tree are usually created by linked lists with pointers to its two children.

Many important operations, such as traversal, node insertion, and deletion, are performed in trees. Details on these operations are beyond the scope of this text but can be found in the literature [25].

SUMMARY

This chapter describes the structuring of geometric data for computer graphics and geometric modeling applications. Static (arrays) and dynamic (linked lists) data structures are compared, and their use in the creation of geometric

FIGURE 7.21

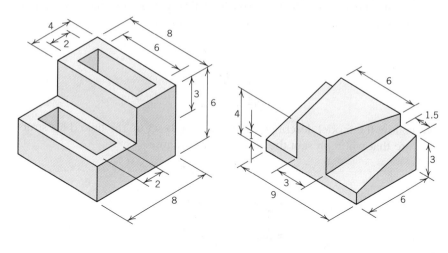

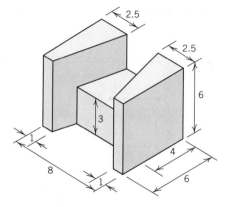

models is explained. Polyhedral objects are represented by point and connectivity arrays and by linked lists. Hierarchical data structures, such as trees, are shown to be of considerable use in the description of graphics data.

EXERCISES

1. For the objects shown in Figure 7.21, establish the vertex, edge and face arrays needed for their representation using parallel arrays. Write a FORTRAN program that will output an image of these objects

   (a) As a collection of edges
   (b) As a collection of faces

2. Establish a vertex connectivity matrix and a face connectivity matrix for the objects shown in Figure 7.21. Orient the faces so that their normals point outward in a right-handed system.

3. Use the linked list structure to schematically represent the two-dimensional object shown in the accompanying figure.

4. Follow the model described in Figure 7.14 to set up the linked list structure that will represent the accompanying figure.

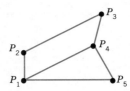

5. Develop a FORTRAN program that will insert or delete a node in a linked list.

6. Establish the tree structure that implements a quadtree for the accompanying figure.

Chapter 8

Three-Dimensional Viewing Operations

Three-dimensional viewing operations are more complex than their two-dimensional counterparts not only because of the additional dimension, but also because the three-dimensional model must be represented on a two-dimensional display surface. In two dimensions, a simple mapping produces an image. In three dimensions, there are many more options depending on how the model is to be viewed—front, side, and so on. In addition, to account for the mismatch between the three-dimensional model and the two-dimensional image, projections must be used that map the three-dimensional model to a two-dimensional projection plane. Various projection types generate various views of a model. Since the mechanics of projections are at the heart of the three-dimensional viewing process, they will be discussed first.

8.1 PROJECTIONS

The problem of projecting a three-dimensional object onto a two-dimensional surface has been studied by engineers, architects, and artists for

FIGURE 8.1 Classification of planar geometric projections.

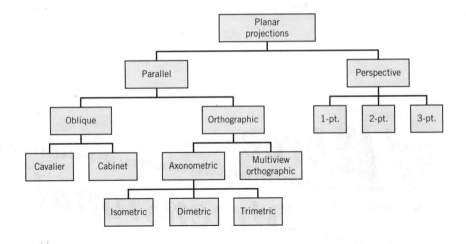

centuries. Computer graphics systems also address problems related to projections.

Planar geometric projections are the ones of most interest to engineers. They can be classified by the tree structure of Figure 8.1 [26]. In planar projections as shown in Figure 8.2, a viewing direction is established from the observer to the object by means of projector lines that cut through a plane where the projection appears.

Each of the planar projections listed in Figure 8.1 can be further explained.

(1) *Parallel projections*—The center of projection is located at infinity, so that all projectors are parallel to each other.

(a) *Oblique:* The projectors are inclined with respect to the plane of projection. In addition, one of the faces of the object is kept parallel to the projection plane, as shown in Figure 8.3.

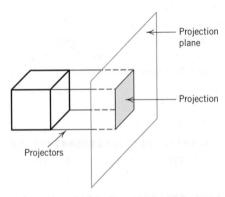

FIGURE 8.2 Example of planar projection.

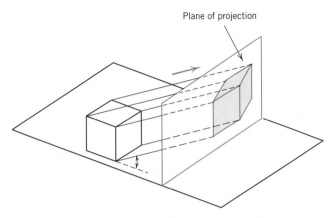

FIGURE 8.3 Parallel-oblique projection.

(b) *Orthographic:* The projectors are perpendicular to the plane of projection:

 (i) *Multiview orthographic:* The planes of the object remain parallel to the principal planes of projection, as shown in Figure 8.4.

 (ii) *Axonometric:* The planes of the object are inclined with respect to the projection plane, as shown in Figure 8.5.

(2) *Perspective projections*—The center of projection is located at a finite distance from the projection plane, as shown in Figure 8.6.

Parallel projections have traditionally been used in engineering practice. In some cases, they preserve the true dimensions of an object but do not produce a realistic picture. The perspective projection gives the exact opposite effect: realistic image but loss of true dimensions.

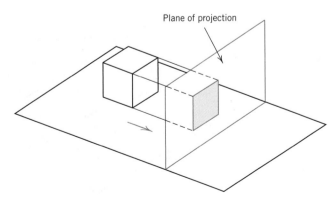

FIGURE 8.4 Orthographic projection.

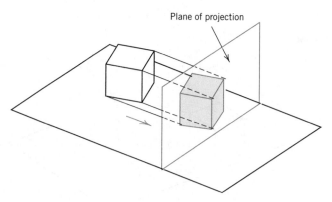

FIGURE 8.5 Axonometric projection.

When applying computerized methods, both systems of projection can be used with relative ease, and both will therefore be described in this chapter.

8.1.1 Multiview Orthographic Projections

This type of projection, usually simply labeled *orthographic projection*, is commonly used in engineering and produces multiple views of an object as shown in Figure 8.7.

In Figure 8.8, consider point $P(x, y, z)$, projected onto the xy plane. The projection of point P is $P^*(x^*, y^*, 0)$, and the transformation that produces

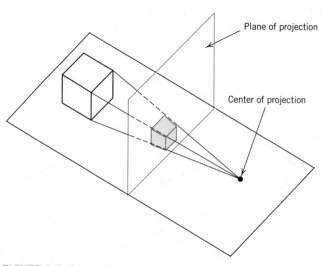

FIGURE 8.6 Perspective projection.

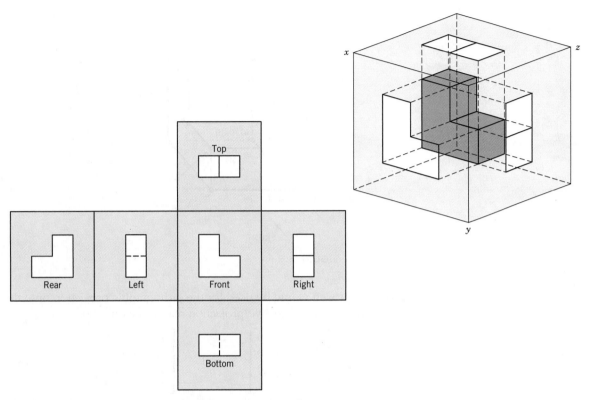

FIGURE 8.7 Multiview orthographic projection representation.

this projection can be written as:

$$[x^* \quad y^* \quad 0 \quad 1] = [x \quad y \quad z \quad 1]\begin{bmatrix} 1 & 0 & 0 & 0 \\ 0 & 1 & 0 & 0 \\ 0 & 0 & 0 & 0 \\ 0 & 0 & 0 & 1 \end{bmatrix} \quad\quad (8.1)$$

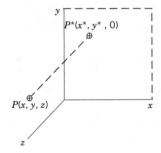

FIGURE 8.8 Orthographic projection of a point on the *xy* plane.

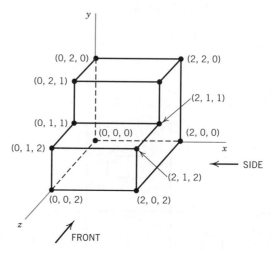

FIGURE 8.9

The same approach would be used for the orthographic projection onto the xz or yz planes. The respective projection matrices would be:

$$\begin{bmatrix} 1 & 0 & 0 & 0 \\ 0 & 0 & 0 & 0 \\ 0 & 0 & 1 & 0 \\ 0 & 0 & 0 & 1 \end{bmatrix} \quad \text{and} \quad \begin{bmatrix} 0 & 0 & 0 & 0 \\ 0 & 1 & 0 & 0 \\ 0 & 0 & 1 & 0 \\ 0 & 0 & 0 & 1 \end{bmatrix} \quad (8.2)$$

This type of projection can also be obtained by simply ignoring the appropriate coordinate component, instead of actually performing the matrix operation.

Example 8.1

Given an object as shown in Figure 8.9, find its front and side orthographic projections in the directions indicated by the arrows.

Solution

(a) The indicated front view is a projection on the xy plane. Based on Eq. 8.1, the matrix of points becomes

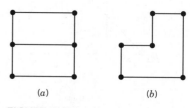

(a)   (b)

FIGURE 8.10

$$[P^*]_{xy} = \begin{bmatrix} 0 & 2 & 0 & 1 \\ 2 & 2 & 0 & 1 \\ 2 & 0 & 0 & 1 \\ 0 & 0 & 0 & 1 \\ 0 & 2 & 0 & 1 \\ 2 & 2 & 0 & 1 \\ 2 & 1 & 0 & 1 \\ 2 & 1 & 0 & 1 \\ 2 & 0 & 0 & 1 \\ 0 & 0 & 0 & 1 \\ 0 & 1 & 0 & 1 \\ 0 & 1 & 0 & 1 \end{bmatrix}$$

The projection is as shown in Figure 8.10*a*.

(b) The side view is obtained through an orthographic projection onto the *yz* plane. Based on Eq. 8.2, the matrix of points becomes

$$[P^*]_{yz} = \begin{bmatrix} 0 & 2 & 0 & 1 \\ 0 & 2 & 0 & 1 \\ 0 & 0 & 0 & 1 \\ 0 & 0 & 0 & 1 \\ 0 & 2 & 1 & 1 \\ 0 & 2 & 1 & 1 \\ 0 & 1 & 1 & 1 \\ 0 & 1 & 2 & 1 \\ 0 & 0 & 2 & 1 \\ 0 & 0 & 2 & 1 \\ 0 & 1 & 2 & 1 \\ 0 & 1 & 1 & 1 \end{bmatrix}$$

The projection is as shown in Figure 8.10*b*.

Orthographic projections can be used to solve other types of problems. For example, in Figure 8.11, it may be necessary to have the inclined surface projected on the *xy* plane in its exact shape, without distortion. This can be accomplished by following the steps outlined below.

1. Establish vectors $\mathbf{V}_1$ and $\mathbf{V}_2$ on the plane of the inclined surface. These vectors can easily be identified, since all vertices of the object have known coordinate values.

2. The cross product of $\mathbf{V}_1$ and $\mathbf{V}_2$ determines the normal vector to the surface.

3. Rotate the normal vector until it coincides with one of the coordinate axis. This can be done by any of the methods described in Chapter

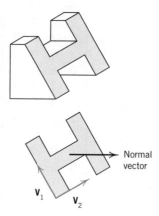

FIGURE 8.11

6, with the option of using the orthogonality property of the rotation matrix.

4. Project orthographically onto the plane perpendicular to the normal.

8.1.2 Axonometric Projections

Of the axonometric projections, the most commonly used in engineering is the isometric projection. In this type of projection, the angles between the principal axes are all equal to 120°, as shown in Figure 8.12.

To obtain an isometric projection using computational methods, a series of rotations, translations, or both, are performed on the object. After these transformations, an orthographic projection, usually to the $z = 0$ plane, is performed, with the constraint that parallel lines on the object are *equally* foreshortened. The foreshortening factor is given by the ratio of the projected length of each line to its true length.

Assuming a projection to the xy plane, the necessary rotations can be defined as a θ_y rotation about the y axis first, followed by a θ_x rotation about the x axis, as shown in Figure 8.13. This sequence will maintain the verticality

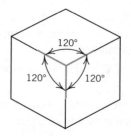

FIGURE 8.12 Isometric axes.

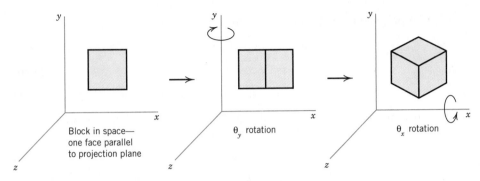

FIGURE 8.13 Transformations required to obtain an isometric projection.

of lines in the projection, a standard technique for showing isometric drawings in engineering. The total operation can be referred to as "tilting." The appropriate rotation matrices that cause this tilt are written as

$$[M_{TILT}] = [T_R]_y^\theta [T_R]_x^\theta$$

$$= \begin{bmatrix} \cos\theta_y & 0 & -\sin\theta_y & 0 \\ 0 & 1 & 0 & 0 \\ \sin\theta_y & 0 & \cos\theta_y & 0 \\ 0 & 0 & 0 & 1 \end{bmatrix} \begin{bmatrix} 1 & 0 & 0 & 0 \\ 0 & \cos\theta_x & \sin\theta_x & 0 \\ 0 & -\sin\theta_x & \cos\theta_x & 0 \\ 0 & 0 & 0 & 1 \end{bmatrix} \quad (8.3)$$

$$= \begin{bmatrix} \cos\theta_y & \sin\theta_y\sin\theta_x & -\sin\theta_y\cos\theta_x & 0 \\ 0 & \cos\theta_x & \sin\theta_x & 0 \\ \sin\theta_y & -\sin\theta_x\cos\theta_y & \cos\theta_x\cos\theta_y & 0 \\ 0 & 0 & 0 & 1 \end{bmatrix} \quad (8.4)$$

To finalize the isometric view, an orthographic projection onto the xy plane is obtained by:

$$[M_{ISO}] = [M_{TILT}] \begin{bmatrix} 1 & 0 & 0 & 0 \\ 0 & 1 & 0 & 0 \\ 0 & 0 & 0 & 0 \\ 0 & 0 & 0 & 1 \end{bmatrix} = \begin{bmatrix} \cos\theta_y & \sin\theta_y\sin\theta_x & 0 & 0 \\ 0 & \cos\theta_x & 0 & 0 \\ \sin\theta_y & -\sin\theta_x\cos\theta_y & 0 & 0 \\ 0 & 0 & 0 & 1 \end{bmatrix} \quad (8.5)$$

The specific values for θ_y and θ_x that produce an isometric projection must now be found. Consider three unit vectors along the x, y, and z axes, transformed by matrix $[M_{ISO}]$ to x^*, y^*, z^*. The equal ratio of the projected length to the original length needed for the isometric projection can be obtained through these unit vectors. The projections of the unit vectors are found as follows:

$$x^* = [1 \quad 0 \quad 0 \quad 1][M_{ISO}] = [\cos\theta_y \quad \sin\theta_y\sin\theta_x \quad 0 \quad 1] \quad (8.6)$$

$$y^* = [0 \quad 1 \quad 0 \quad 1][M_{ISO}] = [0 \quad \cos\theta_x \quad 0 \quad 1] \quad (8.7)$$

$$z^* = [0 \quad 0 \quad 1 \quad 1][M_{ISO}] = [\sin\theta_y \quad -\sin\theta_x\cos\theta_y \quad 0 \quad 1] \quad (8.8)$$

The projected length of each unit vector is

$$|x^*| = \sqrt{\cos^2\theta_y + \sin^2\theta_y \sin^2\theta_x} \qquad (8.9)$$

$$|y^*| = \sqrt{\cos^2\theta_x} \qquad (8.10)$$

$$|z^*| = \sqrt{\sin^2\theta_y + \sin^2\theta_x \cos^2\theta_y} \qquad (8.11)$$

Since the original lengths are all equal to one, the equal ratio of projected to original lengths can be written as follows:

1.
$$|x^*| = |y^*| \qquad (8.12)$$

$$\cos^2\theta_y + \sin^2\theta_y \sin^2\theta_x = \cos^2\theta_x$$

$$1 - \sin^2\theta_y + \sin^2\theta_y \sin^2\theta_x = 1 - \sin^2\theta_x$$

$$\sin^2\theta_y (\sin^2\theta_x - 1) = -\sin^2\theta_x$$

$$\sin^2\theta_y = \frac{\sin^2\theta_x}{1 - \sin^2\theta_x} \qquad (8.13)$$

2.
$$|z^*| = |y^*| \qquad (8.14)$$

$$\sin^2\theta_y + \sin^2\theta_x \cos^2\theta_y = \cos^2\theta_x$$

$$\sin^2\theta_y + \sin^2\theta_x (1 - \sin^2\theta_y) = 1 - \sin^2\theta_x$$

$$\sin^2\theta_y = \frac{1 - 2\sin^2\theta_x}{1 - \sin^2\theta_x} \qquad (8.15)$$

So that

$$\frac{\sin^2\theta_x}{1 - \sin^2\theta_x} = \frac{1 - 2\sin^2\theta_x}{1 - \sin^2\theta_x} \qquad (8.16)$$

And

$$\sin^2\theta_x = 1 - 2\sin^2\theta_x$$

$$\sin^2\theta_x = \tfrac{1}{3} \qquad (8.17)$$

$$\theta_x = \pm 35.26°$$

Substitution of the value of θ_x into Eqs. 8.13 or 8.15 yields

$$\sin^2\theta_y = \tfrac{1}{2} \qquad (8.18)$$

$$\theta_y = \pm 45°$$

FIGURE 8.14

In general engineering practice, the angle usually measured in an isometric projection is the angle A shown in Figure 8.14. This angle can be found by checking the x^* or the z^* matrices in Eqs. 8.6 or 8.8. Using Eq. 8.6, which gives the transformation of the unit vector along the x axis, the angle A can be found through the ratio of x and y components, as follows:

$$\tan A = \frac{x_y^*}{x_x^*} = \frac{\sin \theta_y \sin \theta_x}{\cos \theta_y} \tag{8.19}$$

Since

$$\theta_y = 45°, \sin \theta_y = \cos \theta_y,$$

and

$$\tan A = \pm \sin \theta_x = \pm \sin (35.26)°$$

so that

$$A = \pm 30° \tag{8.20}$$

It can also be seen that the ratio between the length of the projection and the original length of the unit vector or, in other words, the foreshortening factor for an isometric projection, is given by any of Eqs. 8.9, 8.10, 8.11 as

$$F = \frac{|y^*|}{1} = \sqrt{\cos^2 \theta_x} = \sqrt{\tfrac{2}{3}} = 0.8165 \tag{8.21}$$

This foreshortening is very often ignored in manual drawing practice, where it is conventional to use the full dimension along the receding isometric lines, or $F = 1$ (see Figure 8.15).

Example 8.2

Determine the isometric projection of the block described in Figure 8.9, for $\theta_y = 45°$ and $\theta_x = 35.26°$.

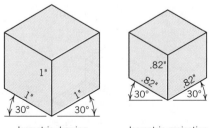

Isometric drawing   Isometric projection

FIGURE 8.15 Conventions used in isometric representation.

Solution

The solution is obtained with Eq. 8.5.

$$[P^*] = [P][M_{ISO}] = [P]\begin{bmatrix} \cos\theta_y & \sin\theta_y\sin\theta_x & 0 & 0 \\ 0 & \cos\theta_x & 0 & 0 \\ \sin\theta_y & -\sin\theta_x\cos\theta_y & 0 & 0 \\ 0 & 0 & 0 & 1 \end{bmatrix}$$

For the given values of θ_x and θ_y, this becomes:

$$[P^*] = \begin{bmatrix} 0 & 2 & 0 & 1 \\ 2 & 2 & 0 & 1 \\ 2 & 0 & 0 & 1 \\ 0 & 0 & 0 & 1 \\ 0 & 2 & 1 & 1 \\ 2 & 2 & 1 & 1 \\ 2 & 1 & 1 & 1 \\ 2 & 1 & 2 & 1 \\ 2 & 0 & 2 & 1 \\ 0 & 0 & 2 & 1 \\ 0 & 1 & 2 & 1 \\ 0 & 1 & 1 & 1 \end{bmatrix} \begin{bmatrix} 0.707 & 0.408 & 0 & 0 \\ 0 & 0.816 & 0 & 0 \\ 0.707 & -0.408 & 0 & 0 \\ 0 & 0 & 0 & 1 \end{bmatrix}$$

$$[P^*] = \begin{bmatrix} 0.0 & 1.632 & 0.0 & 1.0 \\ 1.414 & 2.448 & 0.0 & 1.0 \\ 1.414 & 0.816 & 0.0 & 1.0 \\ 0.0 & 0.0 & 0.0 & 1.0 \\ 0.707 & 1.224 & 0.0 & 1.0 \\ 2.121 & 2.040 & 0.0 & 1.0 \\ 2.12 & 1.224 & 0.0 & 1.0 \\ 2.828 & 0.816 & 0.0 & 1.0 \\ 2.828 & 0.0 & 0.0 & 1.0 \\ 1.414 & -0.816 & 0.0 & 1.0 \\ 1.414 & 0.0 & 0.0 & 1.0 \\ 0.707 & 0.408 & 0.0 & 1.0 \end{bmatrix}$$

Figure 8.16 shows the result of this projection.

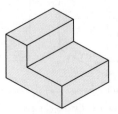

FIGURE 8.16

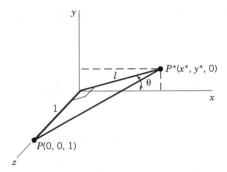

FIGURE 8.17 Oblique projection of a point on the *xy* plane.

8.1.3 Oblique Projections

Both the multiview orthographic and the axonometric projections are created with the projectors perpendicular to the plane of projection. An oblique projection has the projectors at an angle with the plane of projection as shown in Figure 8.3. The general formulation for the oblique projection will be derived by considering a unit vector in the z direction, as shown in Figure 8.17.

The distance l gives the foreshortening ratio of any line perpendicular to the $z = 0$ plane, after projection. If θ is the angle between the projection and the horizontal axis,

$$x^* = l \cos \theta$$
$$y^* = l \sin \theta$$

(8.22)

and the oblique projection matrix becomes

$$[M_{OBL}] = \begin{bmatrix} 1 & 0 & 0 & 0 \\ 0 & 1 & 0 & 0 \\ l \cos \theta & l \sin \theta & 0 & 0 \\ 0 & 0 & 0 & 1 \end{bmatrix}$$

(8.23)

If l, the foreshortening ratio, is equal to 1, lines perpendicular to the projection plane preserve their original length. This is usually referred to as a *cavalier* projection. If $l = \frac{1}{2}$, then the projection length of lines perpendicular to the projection plane is half their original length. This is known as a *cabinet* projection. The value of θ is not dependent on l. The most commonly used values for θ are 30° to 45°.

It is important to notice that the oblique projection matrix is also a shearing matrix, as described in Section 6.3.4.2, Eq. 6.31. In fact, application of the oblique projection matrix causes shearing of the object in space. The oblique projection can be thought of as the result of the following transformations:

1. Shearing of the object in space in a direction parallel to the plane of projection
2. Orthographic projection onto the plane of projection

So

$$[M_{\text{OBL}}] = \begin{bmatrix} 1 & 0 & 0 & 0 \\ 0 & 1 & 0 & 0 \\ l\cos\theta & l\sin\theta & 1 & 0 \\ 0 & 0 & 0 & 1 \end{bmatrix} \begin{bmatrix} 1 & 0 & 0 & 0 \\ 0 & 1 & 0 & 0 \\ 0 & 0 & 0 & 0 \\ 0 & 0 & 0 & 1 \end{bmatrix} \qquad (8.24)$$

$$= \begin{bmatrix} 1 & 0 & 0 & 0 \\ 0 & 1 & 0 & 0 \\ l\cos\theta & l\sin\theta & 0 & 0 \\ 0 & 0 & 0 & 1 \end{bmatrix}$$

In traditional engineering drawing, oblique projections have been useful in representing objects with curved features that can be placed on the plane of projection parallel to the observer. In computer graphics their use is not apparent, since isometric projections are easy to calculate and more pleasing to the eye.

Example 8.3

A tetrahedron is defined by the coordinates of its vertices, as follows:

$$P_1(3,4,0),\ P_2(1,0,4),\ P_3(2,0,5),\ P_4(4,0,3)$$

Find the oblique cavalier projection onto a viewing surface in the $z = 0$ plane. The angle between the z axis and the horizontal should be $45°$ in the projection.

Solution

The oblique matrix is given in Eq. 8.23. For cavalier projections, $l = 1$, and the matrix, with $\theta = 45°$, becomes

$$[M_{\text{OBL}}] = \begin{bmatrix} 1 & 0 & 0 & 0 \\ 0 & 1 & 0 & 0 \\ \dfrac{\sqrt{2}}{2} & \dfrac{\sqrt{2}}{2} & 0 & 0 \\ 0 & 0 & 0 & 1 \end{bmatrix}$$

The transformed coordinates of the original tetrahedron are

$$[P^*] = [P][M_{\text{OBL}}] = \begin{bmatrix} 3 & 4 & 0 & 1 \\ 1 & 0 & 4 & 1 \\ 2 & 0 & 5 & 1 \\ 4 & 0 & 3 & 1 \end{bmatrix} \begin{bmatrix} 1 & 0 & 0 & 0 \\ 0 & 1 & 0 & 0 \\ \dfrac{\sqrt{2}}{2} & \dfrac{\sqrt{2}}{2} & 0 & 0 \\ 0 & 0 & 0 & 1 \end{bmatrix}$$

$$[P^*] = \begin{bmatrix} 3 & 4 & 0 & 1 \\ 3.83 & 2.83 & 0 & 1 \\ 5.54 & 3.54 & 0 & 1 \\ 6.12 & 2.12 & 0 & 1 \end{bmatrix}$$

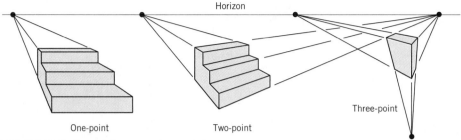

FIGURE 8.18 Types of perspective projections.

One-point   Two-point   Three-point   Horizon

8.1.4 Perspective Projections

Perspective projections, as mentioned before, are obtained when all projectors emanate from a center of projection, so that the size of the object changes as the projection plane moves away from the center of projection. Examples of perspective projection are shown in Figure 8.18. These types of projections are realistic but do not preserve the exact dimensions of the object.

As indicated in Figure 8.18, there are three types of perspective projections: 1-point, 2-point, and 3-point, so-called depending on how many finite centers of projection there are. The simplest of these is the 1-point perspective, where the center of projection is located along one of the three coordinate axes. The other two centers are at infinity, so horizontal lines remain horizontal and vertical lines remain vertical.

Consider, for example, a point $P(x, y, z)$ in space, as shown in Figure 8.19. The perspective projection of P onto the xy plane, $P^*(x^*, y^*, 0)$, with the center of projection a distance z_{cp} along the z axis, can be found as follows:

(a) Looking along the y axis toward the origin (Figure 8.20):

$$\frac{x^*}{x} = \frac{z_{cp}}{z_{cp} - z}$$

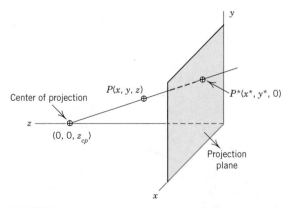

FIGURE 8.19 Perspective projection of point P on the xy plane.

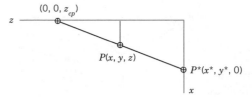

FIGURE 8.20 View along y axis.

or

$$x^* = \frac{x}{1 - \dfrac{z}{z_{cp}}} \tag{8.25}$$

(b) Looking along the x axis toward the origin (Figure 8.21):

$$\frac{y^*}{y} = \frac{z_{cp}}{(z_{cp} - z)}$$

or

$$y^* = \frac{y}{1 - \dfrac{z}{z_{cp}}} \tag{8.26}$$

Based on the relationships in Eqs. 8.25 and 8.26, the projected point becomes

$$
\begin{aligned}
P^* = [x^* \quad y^* \quad 0 \quad 1] &= \left[\frac{x}{\left(1 - \dfrac{z}{z_{cp}}\right)} \quad \frac{y}{\left(1 - \dfrac{z}{z_{cp}}\right)} \quad 0 \quad 1 \right] \\
&= \left[x \quad y \quad 0 \quad \left(1 - \frac{z}{z_{cp}}\right) \right] \tag{8.27}
\end{aligned}
$$

$$
= [x \quad y \quad z \quad 1]
\begin{bmatrix}
1 & 0 & 0 & 0 \\
0 & 1 & 0 & 0 \\
0 & 0 & 0 & -\dfrac{1}{z_{cp}} \\
0 & 0 & 0 & 1
\end{bmatrix}
$$

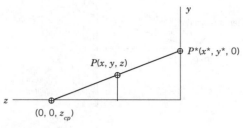

FIGURE 8.21 View along x axis.

The matrix

$$[M_{PER}] = \begin{bmatrix} 1 & 0 & 0 & 0 \\ 0 & 1 & 0 & 0 \\ 0 & 0 & 0 & -\dfrac{1}{z_{cp}} \\ 0 & 0 & 0 & 1 \end{bmatrix} \tag{8.28}$$

is the perspective matrix. It can be considered the concatenation of a simple 1-point perspective "transformation" matrix and an orthographic projection onto the $z = 0$ plane, shown as follows.

$$[M_{PER}] = \begin{bmatrix} 1 & 0 & 0 & 0 \\ 0 & 1 & 0 & 0 \\ 0 & 0 & 1 & \dfrac{-1}{z_{cp}} \\ 0 & 0 & 0 & 1 \end{bmatrix} \begin{bmatrix} 1 & 0 & 0 & 0 \\ 0 & 1 & 0 & 0 \\ 0 & 0 & 0 & 0 \\ 0 & 0 & 0 & 1 \end{bmatrix}$$

$$\qquad\qquad \text{perspective} \qquad \text{orthographic}$$
$$\qquad\qquad \text{transformation} \qquad \text{projection} \tag{8.29}$$

$$= \begin{bmatrix} 1 & 0 & 0 & 0 \\ 0 & 1 & 0 & 0 \\ 0 & 0 & 0 & \dfrac{-1}{z_{cp}} \\ 0 & 0 & 0 & 1 \end{bmatrix}$$

$$\text{perspective projection}$$

The perspective transformation matrix is obtained by giving specific values to the (3×1) submatrix elements of the (4×4) homogeneous coordinates transformation matrix, given as Eq. 6.3. In this case, since a 1-point projection with the center of projection on the z axis was used, only the third element of the fourth column in the matrix is given a value.

If the center of projection is located along the x or y axis, and the projection plane is $x = 0$ or $y = 0$, similar matrices are obtained for the 1-point perspective projection:

$$\text{Center of projection on the } x \text{ axis: } [M_{PER}] = \begin{bmatrix} 0 & 0 & 0 & \dfrac{-1}{x_{cp}} \\ 0 & 1 & 0 & 0 \\ 0 & 0 & 1 & 0 \\ 0 & 0 & 0 & 1 \end{bmatrix} \tag{8.30}$$

$$\text{Center of projection on the } y \text{ axis: } [M_{PER}] = \begin{bmatrix} 1 & 0 & 0 & 0 \\ 0 & 0 & 0 & \dfrac{-1}{y_{cp}} \\ 0 & 0 & 1 & 0 \\ 0 & 0 & 0 & 1 \end{bmatrix}$$

To obtain the 2-point or 3-point perspective projections one must create a (4 × 4) homogeneous coordinate transformation matrix with two or three of the top three elements on the fourth column having nonzero values. This matrix should then be multiplied by an appropriate orthographic projection matrix.

The perspective transformation matrix can be written, for example, as follows:

For 2-point perspective:

$$\begin{bmatrix} 1 & 0 & 0 & r \\ 0 & 1 & 0 & s \\ 0 & 0 & 1 & 0 \\ 0 & 0 & 0 & 1 \end{bmatrix} \quad \text{or} \quad \begin{bmatrix} 1 & 0 & 0 & 0 \\ 0 & 1 & 0 & s \\ 0 & 0 & 1 & t \\ 0 & 0 & 0 & 1 \end{bmatrix} \tag{8.31}$$

For 3-point perspective:

$$\begin{bmatrix} 1 & 0 & 0 & r \\ 0 & 1 & 0 & s \\ 0 & 0 & 1 & t \\ 0 & 0 & 0 & 1 \end{bmatrix} \tag{8.32}$$

These matrices can also be obtained by concatenation of the appropriate 1-point perspective transformation matrices, such as

$$\begin{bmatrix} 1 & 0 & 0 & r \\ 0 & 1 & 0 & 0 \\ 0 & 0 & 1 & 0 \\ 0 & 0 & 0 & 1 \end{bmatrix} \begin{bmatrix} 1 & 0 & 0 & 0 \\ 0 & 1 & 0 & s \\ 0 & 0 & 1 & 0 \\ 0 & 0 & 0 & 1 \end{bmatrix} = \begin{bmatrix} 1 & 0 & 0 & r \\ 0 & 1 & 0 & s \\ 0 & 0 & 1 & 0 \\ 0 & 0 & 0 & 1 \end{bmatrix} \tag{8.33}$$

which gives the 2-point perspective transformation.

Example 8.4

Find the perspective projection of the tetrahedron given in Example 8.3 onto a projection plane at $z = 0$. The center of projection should be located at $z_{cp} = -5$.

Solution

Equation 8.28 is used in the solution of this problem. The projected points are

$$[P^*] = [P][M_{\text{PER}}] = \begin{bmatrix} 3 & 4 & 0 & 1 \\ 1 & 0 & 4 & 1 \\ 2 & 0 & 5 & 1 \\ 4 & 0 & 3 & 1 \end{bmatrix} \begin{bmatrix} 1 & 0 & 0 & 0 \\ 0 & 1 & 0 & 0 \\ 0 & 0 & 0 & \frac{1}{5} \\ 0 & 0 & 0 & 1 \end{bmatrix}$$

$$[P^*] = \begin{bmatrix} 3 & 4 & 0 & 1 \\ 1 & 0 & 0 & 1.8 \\ 2 & 0 & 0 & 2 \\ 4 & 0 & 0 & 1.6 \end{bmatrix} = \begin{bmatrix} 3 & 4 & 0 & 1 \\ \frac{5}{9} & 0 & 0 & 1 \\ 1 & 0 & 0 & 1 \\ \frac{5}{2} & 0 & 0 & 1 \end{bmatrix}$$

Figure 8.22 shows the result of this projection.

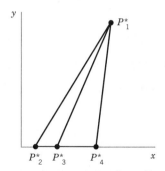

FIGURE 8.22 Perspective projection of tetrahedron on *xy* plane.

8.1.4.1 Vanishing Points

Whenever the 1-point, 2-point, or 3-point perspective views discussed in the previous section are obtained, lines originally parallel to the coordinate axes converge in the perspective view to a point usually referred to as the vanishing point (see Figure 8.18). To establish the location of these points, consider, for example, the perspective transformation of a point located at infinity on the z axis. This point can be represented in homogeneous coordinates as [0 0 1 0]. The zero value in the fourth column changes the standard cartesian (x,y,z) coordinates to infinity [5].

Applying the perspective transformation to this point yields

$$[0 \quad 0 \quad 1 \quad 0] \begin{bmatrix} 1 & 0 & 0 & 0 \\ 0 & 1 & 0 & 0 \\ 0 & 0 & 1 & t \\ 0 & 0 & 0 & 1 \end{bmatrix} = [0 \quad 0 \quad 1 \quad t] \tag{8.34}$$

and the transformed point becomes

$$[x^* \quad y^* \quad z^* \quad 1] = [0 \quad 0 \quad 1/t \quad 1] \tag{8.35}$$

which is the vanishing point, a finite point on the z axis.

For a 2-point perspective transformation given by

$$\begin{bmatrix} 1 & 0 & 0 & r \\ 0 & 1 & 0 & s \\ 0 & 0 & 1 & 0 \\ 0 & 0 & 0 & 1 \end{bmatrix}$$

the two vanishing points are located on the x axis at $[1/r \quad 0 \quad 0 \quad 1]$ and on the y axis at $[0 \quad 1/s \quad 0 \quad 1]$.

For the 3-point perspective transformation

$$\begin{bmatrix} 1 & 0 & 0 & r \\ 0 & 1 & 0 & s \\ 0 & 0 & 1 & t \\ 0 & 0 & 0 & 1 \end{bmatrix}$$

the 3 vanishing points are:

$$
\begin{aligned}
\text{on the } x \text{ axis: } & [1/r \quad 0 \quad 0 \quad 1] \\
\text{on the } y \text{ axis: } & [0 \quad 1/s \quad 0 \quad 1] \\
\text{on the } z \text{ axis: } & [0 \quad 0 \quad 1/t \quad 1]
\end{aligned}
\tag{8.36}
$$

8.1.4.2 Special Techniques for Producing Perspective Views

The perspective projections obtained from the application of the matrices found in the previous section do not usually supply an appropriate view of the object, as seen in Figure 8.23. In general, several faces of an object must be seen to give a clear understanding of the object's shape. If the 1-point perspective projection is preceded by translations or rotations of the object, a better view is obtained.

Assume, for example, a unit cube with the lower back corner at the origin, as shown in Figure 8.24. This cube is rotated by θ about the y axis and translated by $[0 \quad m \quad n]$, before a 1-point perspective projection onto the $z = 0$ plane, with center of projection along the z axis, is applied.

The vertex coordinates of the cube will therefore undergo the following transformations:

$$[T_R]_y^\theta \, [T_{TR}]_{(0,m,n)} [M_{PER}]$$

or

$$
\begin{bmatrix}
\cos\theta & 0 & -\sin\theta & 0 \\
0 & 1 & 0 & 0 \\
\sin\theta & 0 & \cos\theta & 0 \\
0 & 0 & 0 & 1
\end{bmatrix}
\begin{bmatrix}
1 & 0 & 0 & 0 \\
0 & 1 & 0 & 0 \\
0 & 0 & 1 & 0 \\
0 & m & n & 1
\end{bmatrix}
\begin{bmatrix}
1 & 0 & 0 & 0 \\
0 & 1 & 0 & 0 \\
0 & 0 & 0 & \dfrac{-1}{z_{cp}} \\
0 & 0 & 0 & 1
\end{bmatrix}
$$

$$
=
\begin{bmatrix}
\cos\theta & 0 & 0 & \dfrac{\sin\theta}{z_{cp}} \\
0 & 1 & 0 & 0 \\
\sin\theta & 0 & 0 & \dfrac{-\cos\theta}{z_{cp}} \\
0 & m & 0 & \left(1 - \dfrac{n}{z_{cp}}\right)
\end{bmatrix}
\tag{8.37}
$$

Equation 8.37 now represents a 2-point perspective projection, with two nonzero values in the (3×1) perspective submatrix.

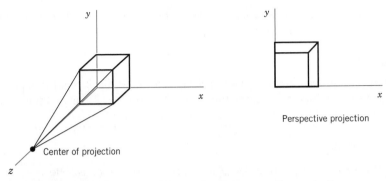

FIGURE 8.23 Results obtained from a 1-point perspective projection may not be easy to interpret.

If the cube is instead first rotated about the y axis and then about the x axis, before applying the same perspective projection, the following concatenated matrix will be obtained:

$$[T_R]_y^\theta \ [T_R]_x^\phi \ [M_{PER}]$$

or

$$
\begin{bmatrix}
\cos\theta & 0 & -\sin\theta & 0 \\
0 & 1 & 0 & 0 \\
\sin\theta & 0 & \cos\theta & 0 \\
0 & 0 & 0 & 1
\end{bmatrix}
\begin{bmatrix}
1 & 0 & 0 & 0 \\
0 & \cos\phi & \sin\phi & 0 \\
0 & -\sin\phi & \cos\phi & 0 \\
0 & 0 & 0 & 1
\end{bmatrix}
\begin{bmatrix}
1 & 0 & 0 & 0 \\
0 & 1 & 0 & 0 \\
0 & 0 & 0 & \dfrac{-1}{z_{cp}} \\
0 & 0 & 0 & 1
\end{bmatrix}
$$

$$
=
\begin{bmatrix}
\cos\theta & \sin\theta\sin\phi & 0 & \sin\theta\cos\phi/z_{cp} \\
0 & \cos\phi & 0 & -\sin\phi/z_{cp} \\
\sin\theta & -\cos\theta\sin\phi & 0 & -\cos\theta\cos\phi/z_{cp} \\
0 & 0 & 0 & 1
\end{bmatrix}
\quad (8.38)
$$

In this case, therefore, a 3-point perspective projection occurs.

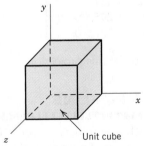

FIGURE 8.24 Representation of a unit cube.

Vanishing points for these cases can be found by calculating the intersection point of a pair of projected parallel lines.

Example 8.5

For the unit cube shown in Figure 8.24, determine the 2-point perspective projection obtained by rotating the cube 30° about the y axis and translating it by $(0,3,-3)$. The center of projection is at $(0,0,2)$.

Solution

Equation 8.37 is applied to the point matrix of the cube, as follows:

$$[P^*] = \begin{bmatrix} 0 & 0 & 0 & 1 \\ 1 & 0 & 0 & 1 \\ 1 & 1 & 0 & 1 \\ 0 & 1 & 0 & 1 \\ 0 & 1 & 1 & 1 \\ 0 & 0 & 1 & 1 \\ 1 & 0 & 1 & 1 \\ 1 & 1 & 1 & 1 \end{bmatrix} \begin{bmatrix} 0.866 & 0 & 0 & 0.250 \\ 0 & 1 & 0 & 0 \\ 0.5 & 0 & 0 & -0.433 \\ 0 & 3 & 0 & 2.5 \end{bmatrix}$$

$$[P^*] = \begin{bmatrix} 0 & 3.0 & 0 & 2.5 \\ 0.866 & 3.0 & 0 & 2.75 \\ 0.866 & 4.0 & 0 & 2.75 \\ 0 & 4.0 & 0 & 2.5 \\ 0.5 & 4.0 & 0 & 2.07 \\ 0.5 & 3.0 & 0 & 2.07 \\ 1.37 & 3.0 & 0 & 2.32 \\ 1.37 & 4.0 & 0 & 2.32 \end{bmatrix}$$

$$[P^*] = \begin{bmatrix} 0 & 1.2 & 0 & 1 \\ 0.315 & 1.1 & 0 & 1 \\ 0.315 & 1.455 & 0 & 1 \\ 0 & 1.6 & 0 & 1 \\ 0.242 & 1.935 & 0 & 1 \\ 0.242 & 1.451 & 0 & 1 \\ 0.59 & 1.295 & 0 & 1 \\ 0.59 & 1.727 & 0 & 1 \end{bmatrix}$$

Figure 8.25 shows the result of this projection.

8.2   THE VIEWING PIPELINE

A three-dimensional model must undergo a series of transformations before its image appears on the screen of a physical display device. As seen in the previous sections, these may be geometric or projection transformations, and can also relate to various directions for viewing.

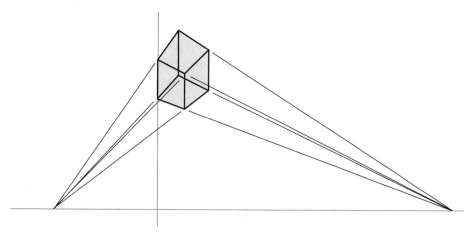

FIGURE 8.25 Two-point perspective projection of unit cube, obtained through a combined transformation.

Three-dimensional modeling transformations were discussed in Chapter 6. Here, the emphasis will fall on the different steps needed to perform the viewing operations shown in the PHIGS transformation pipeline of Figure 8.26.

8.3 THREE-DIMENSIONAL VIEWING PARAMETERS

The viewing process for three-dimensional models is analogous to a camera taking pictures from different positions in space and in various orientations. The parts of the object seen through the viewfinder of the camera will appear on the film, as shown in Figure 8.27.

The viewfinder of the camera corresponds to the window in the computer graphics system. The object is assumed to be stationary in the world coordinate system—the camera is moved around it. As the camera moves, different views of the object appear in the viewfinder. The position of the camera in three-dimensional space must be defined to determine what view of the object will be captured and mapped onto the display (see Figure 8.28).

To define the position of the camera in space (and its viewfinder or window), it is necessary to establish a new coordinate system, the Viewing Reference Coordinate (VRC) system, which will be centered at the window. This new coordinate system simplifies the positioning of the window. The axes in the VRC are defined with respect to the WC system. They uniquely define the plane that contains the window, usually referred to as the view plane. Figure 8.29 shows their relative positions with respect to the WC system.

Three parameters are necessary to define the VRC. The first is the View Reference Point (VRP), defined in world coordinates as a point in the direction of which the camera is looking. It can be used as the origin of the VRC, as indicated in Figure 8.29.

The second parameter is the View Plane Normal (VPN) in the normal direction to the view plane, defining its orientation. The VPN is represented by a vector **N**, and establishes the z direction in the VRC, as shown in Figure 8.29.

The third parameter is the "up" direction for the camera. The VPN and the camera's location on it define the position of the camera in space. How-

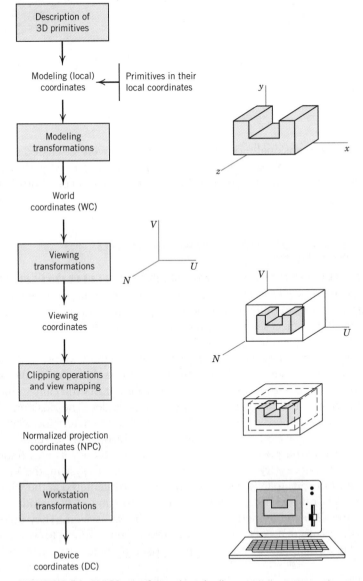

FIGURE 8.26 PHiGS transformation pipeline.

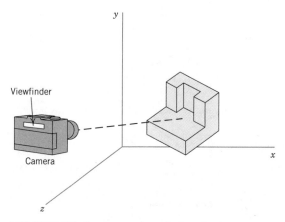

FIGURE 8.27 Camera analogy to the viewing process.

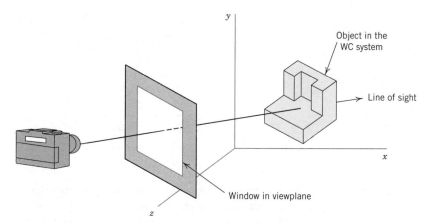

FIGURE 8.28 Viewfinder of camera corresponds to the graphics window.

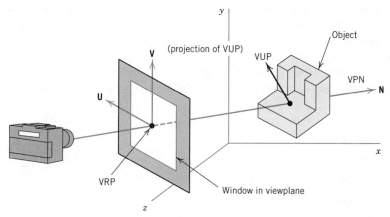

FIGURE 8.29 Establishing the Viewing Reference Coordinate (VRC) system.

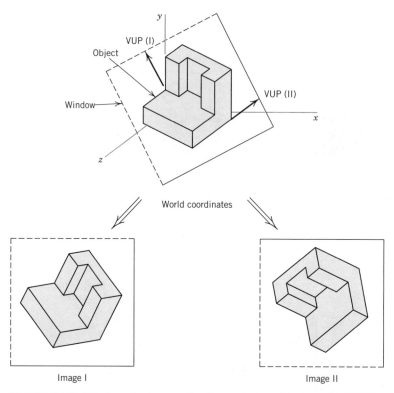

FIGURE 8.30 Effect on the image of a change in the direction of the VUP.

ever, the camera can still rotate around the normal while keeping its original position. The up direction orients the camera around the VPN. A View-Up Vector (VUP) is defined with respect to the object, in world coordinates, and its projection on the view plane establishes the y direction in the VRC system, represented by a vector **V**, as shown in Figure 8.29. The effect on the image of a change in the direction of the view-up vector is shown in Figure 8.30.

To indicate the x direction of the VRC a vector **U** is commonly used, perpendicular to **V** and **N**, causing the VRC to also be called the "UVN-system." The view plane in this system is the UV plane. The VRC can be left- or right-handed. Here, it will be assumed right-handed. PHIGS uses a set of default specifications to represent the viewing parameters, as follows:

	Value
VRP in WC	(0,0,0)
VPN in WC	(0,0,1)
VUP in WC	(0,1,0)
Window in VRC	(0,1,0,1)

These values are shown in Figure 8.31.

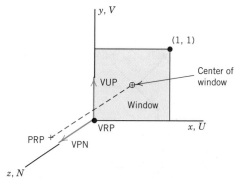

FIGURE 8.31 PHiGS default viewing parameters.

To create the view of an object as specified by the user, coordinates of the object defined in WC must be transformed to the VRC. A series of translations and rotations that convert the WC definition of the object to the VRC will accomplish this task.

The following steps describe this sequence of transformations (see accompanying figures):

1. Translate the view reference point to the WC origin.

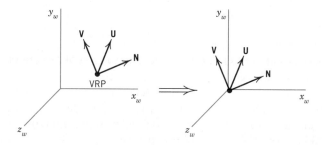

2. Rotate about the x_W axis so that $\mathbf{N}$ falls on the $x_W z_W$ plane.

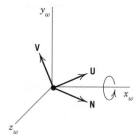

3. Rotate about the y_W axis, so that $\mathbf{N}$ coincides with z_W.

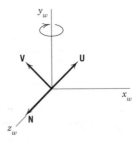

4. Rotate about z_W so that all axes coincide.

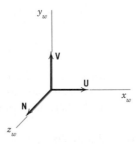

This procedure is similar to the one used when rotating an object about an arbitrary axis (Section 6.3.3.1). The appropriate matrices can also be taken from Section 6.3.3.1.

8.4 VIEW VOLUMES

A three-dimensional viewing transformation must also specify the type of projection to be used. As described in Section 8.1, the types of projection depend on the position of the center of projection. The lines of projection define the image of an object by projecting all its points onto the view plane.

PHIGS establishes a Projection Reference Point (PRP) as part of a projection transformation (see Figure 8.31). For parallel projections, the PRP determines the direction of projection. The projectors are parallel to a vector extending from the PRP to the center of the window. For perspective projections, the PRP defines the center of projection. PHIGS default value for the PRP is (0.5,0.5,1), defined in the VRC system.

The position of the window in the view plane and the type of projection—parallel or perspective—determine a *view volume*. As shown in Figure 8.32, for parallel projections the view volume is an infinite parallelepiped, and for perspective projections it is a pyramid. Only the parts of the object inside the view volume are projected onto the view plane.

For parallel projections, the position of the view plane (window) along the VPN does not change the projected image. For perspective projections,

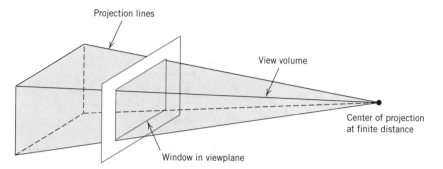

FIGURE 8.32 View volumes for perspective and parallel projections.

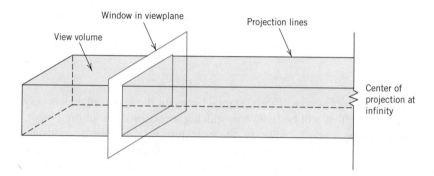

however, since the lines of projection emanate from the center of projection, the position of the view plane along the VPN alters the image.

In general, two additional planes are used to define a finite section of the view volume. These two planes are always parallel to the view plane and are a "front (hither) plane" and a "back (yon) plane." Figure 8.33 shows one possible position for these planes. Any parts of the model lying outside this finite section of the view volume are clipped. The hither plane cuts parts that are behind the observer or in front but too close. The yon plane clips away

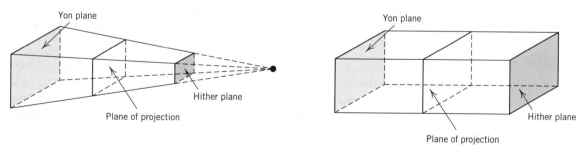

FIGURE 8.33 Front (hither) and back (yon) planes defining a finite section of the view volumes.

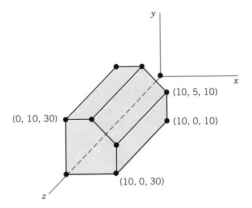

FIGURE 8.34 Chamfered block described in WC.

parts far from the observer. If the distance between these two planes is very small, the final effect will be that of producing a section view of the object.

When using a graphics library, the user must establish the appropriate viewing parameters that will produce the desired results. The following example was solved using the parameters of PHIGS—VRP, VPN, VUP, PRP, Window (x_{min}, x_{max}, y_{min}, y_{max}), and the type of projection.

Example 8.6

Consider the chamfered block in Figure 8.34, described in world coordinates. Establish the viewing parameters (PHIGS) needed to produce

(a) An orthographic front view

(b) An orthographic top view

Solution

The viewing parameter values that will produce the desired projections are not unique. Various possible combinations can be found. The important thing to remember is the coordinate system in which the parameter is established, WC or VRC.

(a) *Front View.* Figure 8.35 gives one solution to this problem. Notice that the PRP, in the VRC, establishes the direction of viewing as it connects to the center of the window. As seen in Figure 8.35, this line passes through the approximate center of the front face and is parallel to the *z* axis.

(b) *Top View.* Figure 8.36 shows one possible solution. Notice the rotation of the UVN system with respect to the WC system. The PRP is set to (10,5,25) in this new orientation of the UVN.

Front View

PHIGS Viewing Parameters	Values	Coordinate System
VRP	(0,0,0)	WC
VPN	(0,0,1)	WC
VUP	(0,1,0)	WC
PRP	(5,5,75)	VRC
Window	(−1, 11, −1, 11)	VRC
Projection	Parallel	

FIGURE 8.35 PHiGS parameters for definition of the front view.

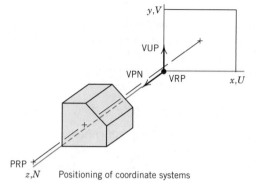

Positioning of coordinate systems

Projection image

Top View

PHIGS Viewing Parameters	Values	Coordinate System
VRP	(10,0,30)	WC
VPN	(0,1,0)	WC
VUP	(−1,0,0)	WC
PRP	(10,5,25)	VRC
Window	(−1, 21, −5, 15)	VRC
Projection	Parallel	

FIGURE 8.36 PHiGS parameters for definition of the top view.

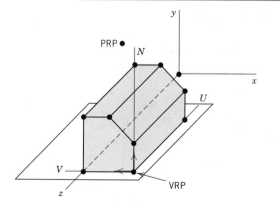

Positioning of coordinate systems

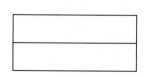

Projection image

8.5 CLIPPING IN THREE DIMENSIONS

Three-dimensional clipping occurs against the planes of the view volume and is controlled by the size and position of the window on the view plane, the front and back planes, and the type of projection. The lines being checked for clipping are tested against the equations of the planes bounding the view volume, defined for the six planes as:

$$a_i x + b_i y + c_i z + d_i = 0 \quad i = 1, \dots, 6 \quad (8.39)$$

Except for the front and back planes, which are parallel to the view plane, all other planes of the view volume can have any orientation. Figure 8.37 shows some possible cases. If the complete view volume is used, clipping would require the calculation of the equations of these planes. However, if the view volume is converted to a unit cube defined by

$$x = 0, \, x = 1, \, y = 0, \, y = 1, \, z = 0, \, z = 1 \quad (8.40)$$

the clipping operation will be greatly simplified. This unit cube is referred to as the *normalized* or *canonical view volume*.

The conversion to the canonical representation of the three types of view volumes can be accomplished as follows:

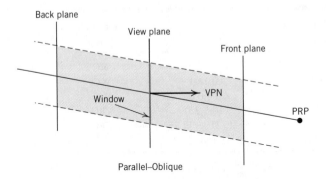

Parallel–Oblique

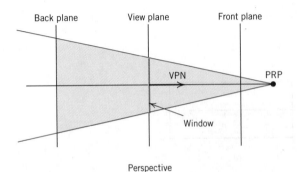

Perspective

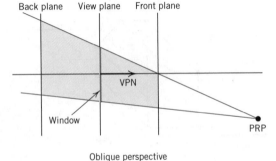

Oblique perspective

FIGURE 8.37 Examples of PHiGS projection systems.

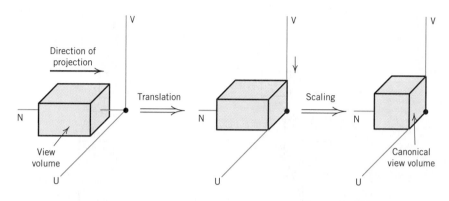

FIGURE 8.38 Establishing the canonical view volume for an orthographic projection.

1. View volume produced by an orthographic projection—The view volume is a rectangular parallelepiped. To obtain the canonical view volume a translation and a scaling transformation must be performed, as shown in Figure 8.38.

2. View volume produced by an oblique projection—The view volume must first be sheared to align the view plane normal with the projectors, as shown in Figure 8.39. This is followed by translation and scaling as for case 1, to obtain the unit cube.

3. View volume produced by a perspective projection—The view volume must be sheared in the x and y directions to locate the center of projection on the normal to the window or view plane, as shown in Figure 8.40. A scaling transformation must now be applied to change the truncated pyramid into a parallelepiped. Figure 8.41 shows this process. All points on the truncated pyramid are scaled an amount inversely proportional to their distance from the window. The parallelepiped thus obtained undergoes the same translation and scaling used for cases 1 and 2, which convert it to the canonical view volume (unit cube).

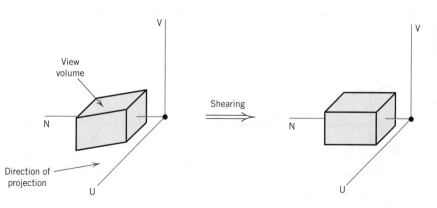

FIGURE 8.39 Establishing the canonical view volume for an oblique projection.

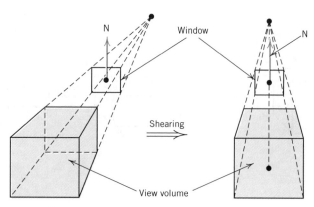

FIGURE 8.40 Shearing of the perspective projection view volume to locate the center of projection on the normal to the window.

For a more general and rigorous description of the approaches to obtain the canonical view volume, see reference [3].

Once the canonical view volume is obtained, clipping is performed against its faces. Extensions of the algorithms used in two-dimensional clipping are applicable. The Cohen–Sutherland algorithm, for example, can be used with a six-bit region code instead of the four used in two-dimensions, to account for the additional depth dimension (Figure 8.42). Bit positions are assigned as follows:

$$\text{bit } 1 = 1 \longrightarrow \text{above}$$
$$\text{bit } 2 = 1 \longrightarrow \text{below}$$
$$\text{bit } 3 = 1 \longrightarrow \text{right}$$
$$\text{bit } 4 = 1 \longrightarrow \text{left}$$
$$\text{bit } 5 = 1 \longrightarrow \text{back}$$
$$\text{bit } 6 = 1 \longrightarrow \text{front}$$

The same bitwise logical AND calculation described in Section 5.2.2.1 is used to identify the lines as visible, invisible, or indeterminate. Intersection calculations are found by representing the three-dimensional line in parametric form as:

FIGURE 8.41 Scaling transformation needed to change truncated pyramid into a parallelepiped.

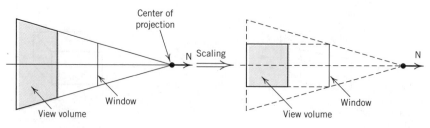

Side view of truncated pyramid

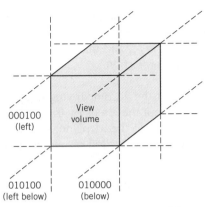

FIGURE 8.42 Six-bit regions used for three-dimensional clipping.

$$x = x_1 + t(x_2 - x_1)$$
$$y = y_1 + t(y_2 - y_1) \qquad 0 \leq t \leq 1 \qquad (8.41)$$
$$z = z_1 + t(z_2 - z_1)$$

The value $t = 0$ produces one endpoint of the line, $P_1(x_1, y_1, z_1)$, and $t = 1$ produces the other endpoint, $P_2(x_2, y_2, z_2)$. Since the planes of the canonical view volume are defined by Eq. 8.40, these constant values can be substituted into the parametric equations to yield the value of t. If t is not within the limits zero and one, the intersection is outside the cube. Otherwise, substitute t back into the appropriate parametric equations to find the points of intersection.

SUMMARY

The transformation pipeline for a three-dimensional model shown in Figure 8.26 can now be revisited. The three-dimensional viewing process has been found to be more complex than the two-dimensional, with projections filling the gap between the three-dimensional model and the two-dimensional display. Viewing is accomplished by specifying a viewing coordinate system used to define a view volume. This volume is then normalized to the coordinate system of the parallel or perspective canonical view volumes, and finally to the device coordinates. The viewing pipeline used in PHIGS was described in detail in this chapter.

EXERCISES

1. A *dimetric* projection is an axonometric projection with two of the three foreshortening factors equal and the third arbitrary. It is constructed by

a rotation about the y axis by ϕ followed by a rotation about the x axis by θ and an orthographic projection. Knowing that the foreshortening factor along the z axis is f_z, and that $f_x = f_y$, find the angles ϕ and θ needed for a dimetric projection.

2. Given the unit cube of the accompanying figure, rotate it about the y axis by $\phi = -45°$, about the x axis by $\theta = 30°$ and perform a 1-point perspective projection onto the xy plane, with the center of projection at $z = 2.0$. What kind of projection results from these transformations? Plot your results.

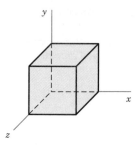

3. The unit cube of Exercise 2 is translated by five units in the negative z direction, and a cavalier projection is obtained with an angle of inclination of 45°. Calculate the final coordinates of the projection and sketch the view.

4. Use a graphics library to implement the four steps described in association with Figure 8.11. Any set of values that maintains the proportions of the object can be used to create the geometric data structure.

5. For the object in Figure 8.34, establish the viewing parameters (PHIGS) to obtain the following:

   - An orthographic side view
   - A one-point perspective with center of projection along the z axis

6. Check the viewing parameters needed for the graphics library available to you, and find their default values. Use these parameters to output the views stated in Exercise 5 (Figure 8.34).

7. Using a CAD system, choose one of the objects in Figure 7.21 and create its front, top, and side orthographic views in three different viewports. Verify how the viewing process is performed in the CAD system, and compare the viewing parameters used with those of PHIGS.

8. Use a graphics library to create an interactive program that displays wireframe models of polyhedral objects, as described in section 7.2.2.

User input should include the VRP, VPN, VUP and the window boundaries.

9. Use a graphics library to develop an interactive, menu-driven program that accepts data representing a polyhedral object, as described in section 7.2.2, and displays the object. The menu structure should give the user the choice of orthographic (front, top, side), isometric, or perspective projections.

10. Find information on the GKS-3D standard and compare its default viewing parameters with those of PHIGS. Create a table summarizing the viewing procedures of the two standards, highlighting differences and similarities.

Chapter 9

Visual Realism

The visual impact of a display image on its users is one of the most important results of a computer graphics operation. Visualization can be considered from two different points of view: as a tool for better understanding the image presented on the computer screen or as a means of representing graphically complex multidimensional data sets. Both types have applications in the engineering disciplines and were illustrated in Chapter 1.

Many approaches can be used in the quest for visual realism. All take into account the need to project a three-dimensional model on a two-dimensional display. Among these approaches are parallel and perspective projections, studied in Chapter 8. In addition, and to improve the appearance of the visual model, lines or surfaces that are not visible to the observer can be removed through hidden line/surface algorithms, and shaded images of models can be created. The latter represents the highest level of visual realism that can be attained.

For many engineering applications full realism is not necessarily desirable. Ideally, images should provide just the amount of information needed by the viewer since an increase in the level of realism comes at the expense of added complexity to the model. The storage and retrieval of such models can be slow. Very realistic pictures are generally produced by powerful graphics systems, and most of the shading algorithms are embedded into the hardware. Section 9.4 describes the architecture of such systems. This chapter studies the most common approaches to visual realism:

- Hidden line/surface removal
- Shading
- Color models

9.1   HIDDEN LINE/SURFACE REMOVAL

Objects to be represented by computer graphics systems are composed of bounded (constrained) surfaces assumed to be opaque. To capture the image of the object realistically, edges and faces that are hidden as the observer looks from a particular direction must be removed. The task of deciding which edges or faces (or portions thereof) must be removed is referred to as the hidden line/surface removal problem. In general, this process requires substantial computer time and memory, and various techniques have been developed to optimize the solution.

A wide range of procedures for performing hidden line/surface removal have been developed, their use depending in large part on the type of display to be used—vector or raster (see Chapter 2). When vector displays were predominant, the problem was constrained to the removal of hidden lines, since the display was capable of producing only line drawings. With the increased use of raster displays, capable of showing shaded surfaces, the need to remove not only hidden edges but also faces of objects became of primary importance. The hidden surface removal algorithms were developed only for raster displays, though hidden line removal algorithms apply to both vector and raster devices.

Three general approaches can be used in the visible line and surface determination:

Object space determines which parts of any object are visible by using spatial and geometrical relationships. It operates with object database precision.

Image space determines what is visible at each image pixel, concentrating therefore on the final image to determine visibility. It operates with image resolution precision. This type of algorithm is very adaptable for use in raster displays.

Hybrid approach uses a combination of both types described above.

Object space algorithms are more accurate than image space because they do not depend on the resolution of the display and perform calculations based on the precision of the CPU used. Image space algorithms were first used to take advantage of the finite resolution of the raster display, where visibility tests are usually performed. In this case, no advantage is gained by going below the limit of resolution of the display, as it will not be possible to represent the calculated details with sufficient precision. Modern algorithms use a combination of the two approaches, resulting in more accuracy (object space) and speed (image space).

9.1.1 Visibility of Objects–Depth Comparison

When checking the visibility of an object or group of objects, viewing parameters and the type of projection (Chapter 8) must be established first. A depth comparison of points (or their projections) located in various edges or faces of an object is the basic check used in hidden line/surface removal. The type of projection used—orthographic or perspective—may add to the complexity of the solution. If an orthographic projection is used, the depth comparison between two points, $P_1(x_1, y_1, z_1)$ and $P_2(x_2, y_2, z_2)$ is obtained by checking if the two points lie on the same projector, as shown in Figure 9.1. If this condition is satisfied, the projections of the two points (P_1^* and P_2^*) coincide and the z coordinate values can be compared to determine which point is closer to the viewer. The larger z value will be the closest point. Point P_1, therefore, obscures point P_2 in Figure 9.1.

When using a perspective projection, projectors in various directions emanate from the eye of the observer, as shown in Figure 9.2, so the viewing transformation distorts the image of objects. To take advantage of the simple depth comparison operation inherent in the orthographic projection, the *perspective transformation* is instead applied, as previously shown in Eq. 8.29, followed by an orthographic projection. This can be interpreted as follows:

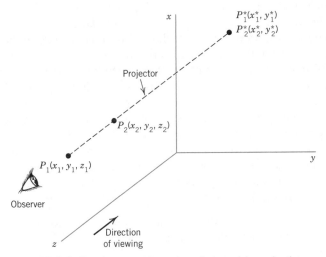

FIGURE 9.1 Depth comparisons in orthographic projection.

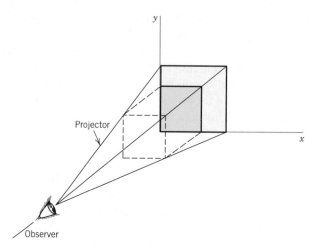

FIGURE 9.2 *Perspective projections do not permit the simple depth comparisons possible with orthographic projections.*

The orthographic projection of a transformed view (perspective) of an object is equivalent to the perspective projection of the "untransformed" object.

Figure 9.3 illustrates this process.

9.1.2 Visibility Techniques

The sole use of depth comparisons in hidden line/surface algorithms is very CPU-intensive. To reduce the number of calculations and optimize the process, visibility techniques have been developed which establish relationships among edges and faces projected in the viewing plane.

Back-face culling is a simple technique to remove faces in the back of an object, away from the viewer. It is limited to convex polyhedra, but it is a powerful first step in the solution of many hidden line/surface removal problems for more complex objects. Back-face culling operates in object space.

The technique makes use of the outward normal to each face of the object in consideration, as shown in Figure 9.4. To find whether a normal vector is directed outward, a simple check can be performed. First, choose a vector $\mathbf{I}$ directed to a point inside the object. Find the normal vector $\mathbf{n}$ by using the cross product of two vectors located on the face. Finally, use the dot product of $\mathbf{n}$ and $\mathbf{I}$ to verify the direction of the normal:

> If $\mathbf{n} \cdot \mathbf{I} > 0$, the normal is pointing inward;
> otherwise, the normal is pointing outward.

This check is unnecessary if all faces have been described by vertices placed

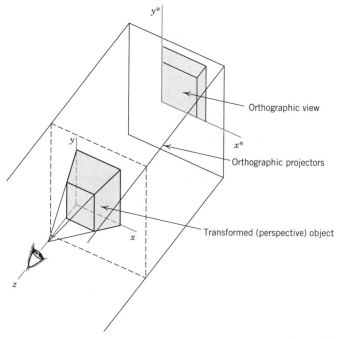

y*

Orthographic view

y

x*

Orthographic projectors

Transformed (perspective) object

x

z

FIGURE 9.3 Perspective transformation followed by orthographic projection.

in order, following the right-hand rule (CCW). The normal in this case is automatically pointing outward.

Example 9.1

Compute the outward normal to face *AED* in the rectangular pyramid shown in the accompanying figure.

Solution

The normal can be found by the cross product of vectors

$$\mathbf{AE} = -\mathbf{i} + \mathbf{j}$$

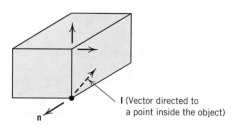

l (Vector directed to a point inside the object)

n

FIGURE 9.4 Determining the direction of a normal vector to a surface.

and

$$\mathbf{AD} = -\mathbf{i} + \mathbf{k}$$

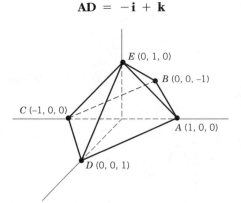

and is given by:

$$\mathbf{n} = \mathbf{AE} \times \mathbf{AD} = \begin{bmatrix} \mathbf{i} & \mathbf{j} & \mathbf{k} \\ -1 & 1 & 0 \\ -1 & 0 & 1 \end{bmatrix} = (\mathbf{i} + \mathbf{j} + \mathbf{k})$$

Choosing a point inside the pyramid, such as

$$P(0, 0.5, 0)$$

the vector **AP** can be established as

$$\mathbf{AP} = -\mathbf{i} + 0.5\mathbf{j}$$

The dot product of this vector and the normal will indicate the normal's orientation:

$$\mathbf{n} \cdot \mathbf{AP} = (\mathbf{i} + \mathbf{j} + \mathbf{k}) \cdot (-\mathbf{i} + 0.5\mathbf{j}) = -0.5$$

Since this value is negative, the normal is pointing outward, as needed.

Once the outward normal vectors for all faces have been found, the process of removing the back faces can start. The following data are needed from the object database description:

- Coordinates of all vertices
- Description of all faces—for example, vertex connectivity for each face
- Outward normal vectors for each face

To check for face visibility, a view vector, **V**, is constructed from any point on the surface to the viewpoint, as shown in Figure 9.5. The dot product of this vector and the normal, **n**, indicates visible faces as follows:

If $\mathbf{V} \cdot \mathbf{n} > 0$, the face is visible;
otherwise, the face is hidden.

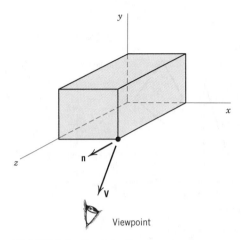

FIGURE 9.5 Check for face visibility.

Example 9.2

Refer back to Example 9.1. Find the faces visible to an observer located at point $P(5,5,5)$.

Solution

Face *AED* will be considered first. In Example 9.1, the normal to this surface was found to be:

$$\mathbf{n} = \mathbf{i} + \mathbf{j} + \mathbf{k}$$

A vector $\mathbf{V}_1$ is established from the viewpoint $P(5, 5, 5)$ to a point in *AED*, such as point $A(1, 0, 0)$:

$$\mathbf{V}_1 = 4\mathbf{i} + 5\mathbf{j} + 5\mathbf{k}$$

The dot product of $\mathbf{n}$ and $\mathbf{V}_1$ is next found:

$$\mathbf{n} \cdot \mathbf{V}_1 = (1.0)(4.0) + (1.0)(5.0) + (1.0)(5.0) = 14 > 0$$

Face *AED* is thus visible.

Similar visibility operations are performed for the remaining faces, with the following results:

Face	Visibility
AED	Visible
BEA	Visible
DEC	Visible
CEB	Invisible
ABCD	Invisible

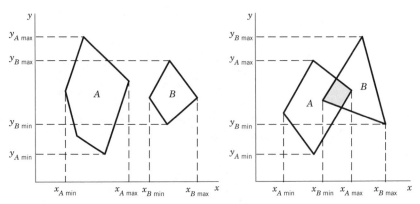

FIGURE 9.6 Minimax test.

Extents and bounding boxes (minimax test) is a technique that checks whether a point is in a given bounded surface or volume. It can be applied to object or image space and provides a simple method of determining whether two edges or faces overlap. If the minimax test is passed (two surfaces or volumes do not intersect), the edges or faces under scrutiny also do not intersect.

As an example of the application of the minimax test, consider the polygons shown in Figure 9.6. The maximum and minimum values of both *x* and *y* coordinates are found and compared through the following inequalities:

$$x_{A_{\max}} < x_{B_{\min}}$$
$$x_{B_{\max}} < x_{A_{\min}}$$
$$y_{A_{\max}} < y_{B_{\min}}$$
$$y_{B_{\max}} < y_{A_{\min}}$$

(9.1)

If any one of these inequalities is true, the two polygons do not overlap.

When applying this test, the extents in the *x* and *y* directions are found on the vertex list of each polygon. If working with volumes, the minimax test is applied by comparing *x*, *y*, and *z* coordinates, and the inequalities shown in Eq. 9.1 are extended to include the *z* values.

Containment test checks the vertices of one polygon for containment in the other. If the minimax test fails for a pair of polygonal entities, the possibility exists that one of them completely surrounds the other. Elementary geometry can be used to solve this problem by checking the sum of the angles subtended by each edge of a polygon as seen from the point being tested. Figure 9.7 illustrates this process. Point *P* is the point to be tested against polygon *ABCDE* (case *a*) or *ABCD* (case *b*). As shown in Figure 9.7, this point can be inside or outside the polygon. Lines are drawn from *P* to every vertex of the polygons, which should be ordered in a clockwise or

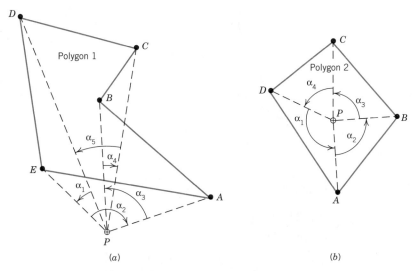

FIGURE 9.7 Containment test.

counterclockwise direction. The angles that these imaginary lines form with each other are measured, changing the sign ($+$ or $-$) assigned to the angle if the direction in which the angle is measured changes. All the angles are added, and the check for containment proceeds as follows:

- If the sum of the angles is equal to zero, point P is outside the polygon.
- If the sum is equal to 360°, point P is inside the polygon.

The containment test is repeated for each vertex of a polygon against all the vertices of the other.

Example 9.3

Given the polygons

$$ABC \rightarrow A(0, 8),\ B(12, 15),\ C(6, 20)$$

$$PQRS \rightarrow P(15, 5),\ Q(25, 10),\ R(30, 20),\ S(15, 20)$$

run a check for possible containment.

Solution

The test is started by using vertex P and checking against all vertices of ABC. (See accompanying figure.)

$$\mathbf{PB} = -3\mathbf{i} + 10\mathbf{j}$$

$$\mathbf{PC} = -9\mathbf{i} + 15\mathbf{j}$$

$$\mathbf{PA} = -15\mathbf{i} + 3\mathbf{j}$$

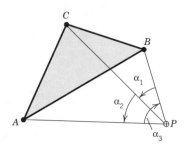

The angles α_1, α_2 and α_3 are calculated next:

$$\alpha_1 = \cos^{-1}\left(\frac{\mathbf{PB} \cdot \mathbf{PC}}{|\mathbf{PB}|\,|\mathbf{PC}|}\right)$$

$$= \cos^{-1}\left[\frac{(-3)(-9) + (10)(15)}{\sqrt{(-3)^2 + (10)^2}\,\sqrt{(-9)^2 + (15)^2}}\right] = 14.265°$$

$$\alpha_2 = \cos^{-1}\left(\frac{\mathbf{PC} \cdot \mathbf{PA}}{|\mathbf{PC}|\,|\mathbf{PA}|}\right)$$

$$= \cos^{-1}\left[\frac{(-9)(-15) + (15)(3)}{\sqrt{(-9)^2 + (15)^2}\,\sqrt{(-15)^2 + (3)^2}}\right] = 47.726°$$

$$\alpha_3 = \cos^{-1}\left(\frac{\mathbf{PA} \cdot \mathbf{PB}}{|\mathbf{PA}|\,|\mathbf{PB}|}\right)$$

$$= \cos^{-1}\left[\frac{(-15)(-3) + (3)(10)}{\sqrt{(-15)^2 + (3)^2}\,\sqrt{(-3)^2 + (10)^2}}\right] = -61.991°$$

Adding all these angles and keeping track of the appropriate sign;

$$\Sigma\,\alpha_i = 14.265° + 47.726° - 61.991° = 0$$

Point P is, therefore, outside triangle ABC. Similarly, points Q, R, and S are found to be outside ABC. Therefore, either $PQRS$ surrounds ABC or there is no overlapping.

   If the same test is repeated, checking each vertex of ABC against $PQRS$, that is, the reverse of the operation previously described, an unambiguous conclusion can be reached.

   Silhouettes are formed by the edges that separate visible from invisible faces in an object, as shown in Figure 9.8. The back-face culling technique checks for face visibility by using the dot product between the view vector and the normal to the face. If an edge belongs to two visible faces, it is visible but not a part of the silhouette. In Figure 9.8, edges between the following faces form the silhouette:

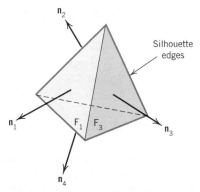

FIGURE 9.8 Establishing the silhouette of an object.

F_1 (visible) and F_2 (invisible)
F_1 (visible) and F_4 (invisible)
F_3 (visible) and F_2 (invisible)
F_3 (visible) and F_4 (invisible)

The edge between faces F_1 and F_3 is not a part of the silhouette.

Other visibility techniques, such as segment comparisons, homogeneity tests, sorting, and coherence, can be used in the development of hidden line/surface algorithms. The reader is directed to the list of references at the end of the text for additional information on these topics.

9.1.3 Examples of Hidden Line/Surface Removal Algorithms

As mentioned in the previous section, the back-face culling technique can be used as a hidden line removal algorithm for convex polyhedra. Many other algorithms for this purpose have been developed throughout the years, both in object and image space. It is left to the reader to check the appropriate literature [21,22] for details on all these algorithms. This section will describe a few.

A simple algorithm called *priority fill* or *painter's* algorithm establishes a priority list based on the depth of parts of (an) object(s), so the parts farthest from the viewer are rendered first. The algorithm continues in reverse priority, just as an artist would create a painting starting with the background, then add elements located at an intermediate distance, and finally elements in the foreground. Where flat polygonal faces are used to describe an object, the polygons are displayed from back to front. When one polygon obscures another no intersections need be calculated. The easiest sorting of the polygons is by the mean depth of each which, for orthographic projections onto the xy plane, requires only the mean depth of the z coordinates of the vertices:

$$z_{\text{mean}} = \frac{1}{n} \sum_{i=1}^{n} z_i$$

where n = number of vertices.

This simple sort may not work for all cases. For a more complete form of this algorithm, check [22].

The z *buffer* algorithm is one of the simplest hidden surface removal algorithms and is often implemented at the hardware level. It uses the idea of the frame buffer described in Section 2.1.4, but instead of storing pixel intensities it stores the z coordinate or depth of every pixel in the image. The algorithm initializes the z buffer to the lowest z value and then compares the z coordinates of image points placed at all pixel locations with the existing value on the buffer. If the new z has a larger value than the existing one, that is, if the polygon being examined is closer to the viewer, the z buffer is updated to this new value. Once all the polygons in image space have been checked, the z buffer will contain the solution to the hidden surface problem.

Ray tracing algorithms are based on a "brute-force" technique that has gained much popularity because of its simplicity and reliability. They work on the principle that an observer sees an object by having light from a source strike it and then reach the observer. In the algorithm, the light is usually traced back from the observer to the object as the image of the object is created. The ray travels through the center of all pixels on the raster grid, as shown in Figure 9.9. A determination is then made of which part(s) of the object are intersected by the ray, and all intersections are calculated and sorted in depth. The most important part of the algorithm is the intersection routine. Section 12.11.5 describes an application of the method for hidden line removal in solid modeling.

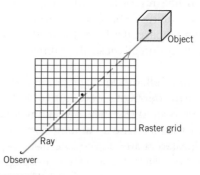

FIGURE 9.9 Ray-tracing technique.

9.2   SHADING

Although line drawings are still commonly used in engineering applications, they lack the ability to represent objects in a realistic way. Shaded color images fulfill this purpose and are capable of conveying information not found in a line drawing, such as surface texture. Their use became relatively common in the 1970s, as the decrease in memory cost made raster technology predominant for graphics displays.

When rendering a surface, the shade of any point on it is determined by the following:

- A description of the light sources available
- Characteristics of the surface itself
- Relative position of the light sources with respect to the surface

Lighting description should include details on the light sources, such as where they are placed, their intensity, where they are pointing, and so forth. In general, two types of light sources are considered, point light and ambient light. Point lights distribute the light from a single point in specific directions. Their effect can be somewhat harsh, since the object is illuminated from a single specified direction. Ambient light is distributed uniformly in all directions, without regard to location. It can be seen as an overall sort of illumination, originating from the surroundings of the object.

In developing shading models, a relationship between the light source and the surface to be rendered must be found. The effect of all point light sources is considered, with ambient light adding a constant intensity value to the calculation. The way in which light is reflected off a surface is an important factor in shading. Diffuse reflection occurs when light is scattered equally in all directions so the surface's brightness appears the same when viewed from different angles. It produces a dull, mattelike finish, such as created by flat paint on a real surface. Specular reflection, on the other hand, reflects light in only one direction, producing a shiny effect like that of a mirror. Real surfaces, as expected, reflect light by a combination of these two effects. Because it is easier to calculate, diffuse reflection is incorporated in most engineering modeling systems.

The output of a shading model is the intensity value for a point (or series of points) on the image of an object. To find this intensity value, an incident ray from the light source is cast on the surface, as shown in Figure 9.10. The angle θ this ray forms with the unit normal vector **n** to the surface is used to calculate the intensity value at the point.

Faceted (Lambert) shading uses Lambert's law, which relates the intensity of light reflected from a perfect diffuser to the angle of incidence θ. It assumes that the intensity of the reflected light is independent of the view-

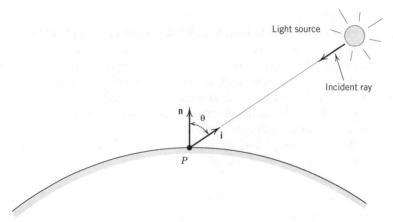

FIGURE 9.10 Determination of angle θ needed for the calculation of intensity values.

er's position. This intensity value is given by

$$I = I_s k_d \cos\theta \qquad (9.2)$$

where I_s is the intensity of the point source itself and k_d is a coefficient indicating the reflectivity of the surface, set to a constant value between zero and one. The cosine of the angle θ can also be expressed by the dot product of unit vector **n** and **i**, as shown in Figure 9.10, so:

$$I = I_s k_d (\mathbf{n} \cdot \mathbf{i}) \qquad (9.3)$$

If several light sources and ambient light are incorporated in the model, Lambert's law is modified as follows:

$$I = I_a + \sum_{j=1}^{m} I_j k_d \cos\theta = I_a + \sum_{j=1}^{m} I_j k_d (\mathbf{i}_j \cdot \mathbf{n}) \qquad (9.4)$$

where

$$I_a = \text{contribution from ambient light}$$

$$I_j = \text{intensities of all individual light sources}$$

The smaller the value of the angle θ between vectors **n** and **i**, the more the surface under study will be directed toward the light source. This will cause the surface to appear brighter on the screen. For polygonal models, this shading assigns the same light intensity to all points on a facet, creating a banded appearance, as shown in Figure 9.11. It is, however, the quickest shading algorithm to execute, and is commonly used as a preliminary check for a design, when a lot of realism is not needed.

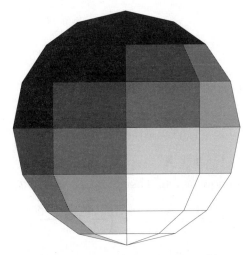

FIGURE 9.11 Banded appearance resulting from faceted shading.

Example 9.4

Given three points:

$$A(0, 0, 1)$$
$$B(1, 0, 0)$$
$$C(0, 1, 0)$$

and an illumination source of intensity 9 located at a far distance in the direction

$$(\sqrt{2}\mathbf{i} + 3\mathbf{j} + 4\mathbf{k})$$

determine the shaded intensity for a reflectivity of 0.25.

Solution

Equation 9.3 will be used to solve this problem. Given values are:

$$I_s = 9$$

$$\mathbf{i} = \frac{\sqrt{2}\mathbf{i} + 3\mathbf{j} + 4\mathbf{k}}{3\sqrt{3}} \quad \text{(unit vector)}$$

$$k_d = 0.25$$

The unit normal to surface ABC must be calculated by

$$\mathbf{n} = \frac{\mathbf{AB} \times \mathbf{AC}}{\|\mathbf{AB} \times \mathbf{AC}\|}$$

Knowing that:

$$\mathbf{AB} = \mathbf{i} - \mathbf{k}$$

$$\mathbf{AC} = \mathbf{j} - \mathbf{k}$$

the cross product becomes

$$\mathbf{AB} \times \mathbf{AC} = [(0)(-1) - (1)(-1)]\,\mathbf{i} + [(0)\,(-1) - (1)(-1)]\,\mathbf{j}$$
$$+ [(1)(1) - (0)\,(0)]\mathbf{k}$$
$$= \mathbf{i} + \mathbf{j} + \mathbf{k}$$

The value of $\mathbf{n}$ can now be found as

$$\mathbf{n} = \frac{\mathbf{i} + \mathbf{j} + \mathbf{k}}{\sqrt{(1)^2 + (1)^2 + (1)^2}} = \left(\frac{\sqrt{3}}{3}\,\mathbf{i} + \frac{\sqrt{3}}{3}\,\mathbf{j} + \frac{\sqrt{3}}{3}\,\mathbf{k}\right)$$

The shade intensity given by Eq. 9.3 is

$$I = (9)(0.25)\left[\left(\frac{\sqrt{3}}{3}\,\mathbf{i} + \frac{\sqrt{3}}{3}\,\mathbf{j} + \frac{\sqrt{3}}{3}\,\mathbf{k}\right) \cdot \left(\frac{\sqrt{2}\mathbf{i} + 3\mathbf{j} + 4\mathbf{k}}{3\sqrt{3}}\right)\right]$$

$$I = 2.1$$

The comparison of the normal to a surface and the direction of the incident ray from a light source is at the heart of all shading techniques. However, to avoid the faceted appearance of Lambert-shaded objects, other shading techniques try to smooth the surface of the object to be rendered.

Gouraud (smooth) shading involves every vertex of a polygonal surface. In Gouraud shading, light intensities are computed at each vertex, and the intensities at the vertices are smoothed and blended across the overall surface. To compute the intensity at a vertex shared by more than one polygon, the normals to all these polygons are averaged before intensity calculations, as follows:

$$\mathbf{n}_{\text{ave}} = \frac{\Sigma\,\mathbf{n}_i}{|\Sigma\,\mathbf{n}_i|} \tag{9.5}$$

where $\mathbf{n}_i$ = unit normals of surfaces sharing a vertex (see Figure 9.12).

Once the intensitities at the vertices are obtained, linear interpolation of vertex intensities, as shown in Figure 9.13, provides the shade of each polygon. When used in concurrence with a scan-line algorithm this provides a very efficient shading model.

Example 9.5

For the trapezoid shown in the accompanying figure, find the intensity at the point $P(5, 2)$, using Gouraud shading and scan lines parallel to *BC*. The

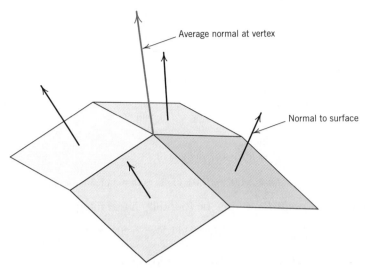

FIGURE 9.12 Normals to polygons sharing a vertex are averaged and used to calculate the intensity at the vertex.

averaged intensities at the four vertices are:

$$I_A = 5.0$$

$$I_B = 6.0$$

$$I_C = 4.0$$

$$I_D = 9.0$$

A(2, 4)   D(8, 4)

P(5,2)
⊕

B(0, 0)   C(10, 0)

Solution

Linear interpolation is first used along *AB* and *CD* to find the intensity values at points *x* and *y* on a scan line passing through *P*:

$$I_x = (I_B - I_A)(\tfrac{1}{2}) + I_A$$

$$I_x = \frac{(6.0 - 5.0)}{2} + 5.0 = 5.5$$

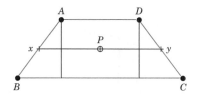

And

$$I_y = (I_C - I_D)(\tfrac{1}{2}) + I_D$$

$$I_y = (4.0 - 9.0)(\tfrac{1}{2}) + 9.0 = 11.5$$

The intensity at point P can now be found by linear interpolation along xy:

$$I_P = (I_y - I_x)(\tfrac{1}{2}) + I_x = (11.5 - 5.5)\tfrac{1}{2} + 5.5 = 8.5$$

Phong (normal interpolating) shading avoids some of the problems of Gouraud shading. Although Gouraud shading is an improvement over faceted shading and produces relatively smooth images, it has some disadvantages. For example, highlights can be shown only at the vertices with this shading algorithm and even then can be distorted. In addition, Mach bands (an effect resulting when, on a scene with smoothly shaded colors, the eye searches for areas of rapid brightness change) can occasionally be produced.

Phong shading avoids these problems and adds more realism to an image. It differs from Gouraud shading in that it interpolates normal vectors instead of shade intensities. It finds the surface normal at each vertex, and then blends this normal over the face of the polygon, as shown in Figure 9.14. It next compares the normal with the light vector at each point, computing a new shade for each pixel location. It is a much slower process than Gouraud shading, but can create very realistic pictures.

All shading models described, with their various degrees of realism, share some common problems because of the interpolated shading calculation. For example, unless the number of polygons is considerably increased

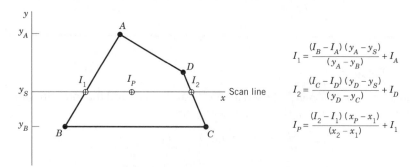

FIGURE 9.13 Linear interpolation of vertex intensities provides the shade of each polygon—Gouraud shading.

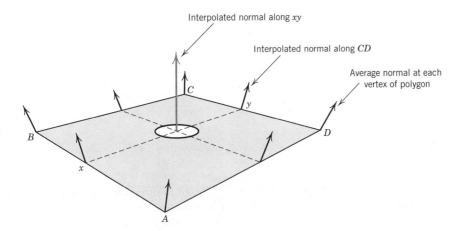

Interpolated normal along xy

Interpolated normal along CD

Average normal at each vertex of polygon

FIGURE 9.14 *Averaged normals at the vertices are interpolated over the face of the polygons—Phong shading.*

at the cost of CPU time, silhouettes of curved surfaces are always shown in a polygonal form, which is not very realistic. However, the shading models based on the interpolation technique are easy to process and, in spite of these problems, still constitute the core of most rendering systems. A variety of methods can add texture, shadows, transparency, and the like, to the shaded surfaces. The reader is guided to the list of references at the end of the text for additional information. More complex illumination models, such as physically based models, can also be found in the literature.

9.3   COLOR MODELS

Coloring is used extensively in computer graphics systems, to help in the understanding of geometric entities. It is one of the primary ingredients of shaded images, and can also be used effectively in many engineering applications, such as the display of contour lines.

Chromatic colors are used in color graphics displays. They follow the tri-stimulus theory of the human brain, which states that the color of light is perceived by the brain as a combination of the three primary colors: red, green, blue. As stated in Chapter 2, color displays create a color image by using electron guns of different colors, and mixing them through shadow-mask technology. The description of color generally includes three properties, namely hue, saturation and brightness, defining a position in the color spectrum, purity, and the intensity value of a color.

A wide variety of methods have been developed through the years to specify color models for use in computer graphics systems [28,29]. In this section, a few color models will be described in general terms, to help in the process of understanding how application programs can choose color appropriately. It is left to the reader, if interested, to search the literature for information on the theory of color models.

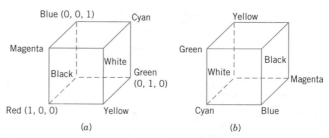

FIGURE 9.15 Representation of color models: (a) RGB; (b) CMY.

The RGB Model represents color as a point in three-dimensional space (Figure 9.15a) obtained from the three RGB primaries, red, green, blue. The color black is located at the origin (0,0,0) of the RGB model and white is at the point (1,1,1). All other colors are represented by points inside the cube.

The CMY Model uses the colors cyan, magenta and yellow, which are the complement of the RGB colors. In the cube representation of Figure 9.15b, the white is located at the origin (0,0,0) and black at point (1,1,1), which is the opposite of the RGB model. This is described as a subtractive model and is popular in hard-copy devices which work with pigments.

The HSV Model allows the user to specify the Hue, Saturation and Value of a color. It follows the process used by artists to produce colors. Its representation is given in Figure 9.16 from which the following are specified:

- Hue, as an angle between 0° and 360° at the base of the hexpyramid (see Figure 9.16a), and described for any point on or inside the hexpyramid;

- Saturation, as a number between 0 and 1, represented by a specific position on a line joining vertices of the hexpyramid's base (see Figure 9.16b);

- Value, as a number between 0 and 1, found on the intersection of a vertical half-plane and the hexpyramid (see Figure 9.16c).

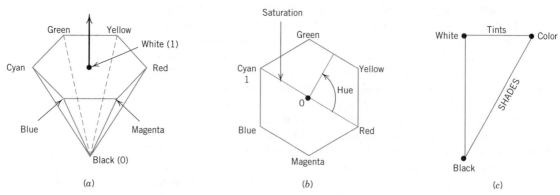

FIGURE 9.16 Representation of (a) the HSV model, (b) hue and saturation, and (c) tints.

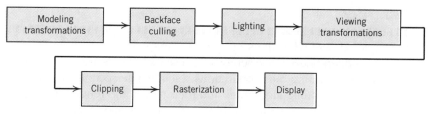

FIGURE 9.17 *Rendering pipeline using the z-buffer algorithm and Gouraud shading.*

9.4 THE RENDERING PIPELINE

How and where to add all the visibility enhancements described in this chapter into the viewing pipeline of Chapter 8 is the subject of this section. There are a variety of ways to accomplish this task in a polygonal environment, some of them with hardware implementations. The simplest may be a combination of the z-buffer algorithm and Gouraud shading. Figure 9.17 shows this rendering pipeline. As seen in the previous sections, most rendering algorithms require a description of the normals to the polygonal surfaces. These normals may be available from the database or may be created during the rendering process. After modeling transformations are performed in the world coordinate system, all primitives located outside the window are discarded and back-face culling is performed on all faces of the object contained in the window. This eliminates unnecessary computations during the lighting/shading step. In preparation for Gouraud shading, intensities are now found at each polygonal vertex in the world coordinate system which preserves distances from the light source to the surface. Viewing transformations are then performed and objects are clipped against the view volume. The clipped primitive is then sent to the z-buffer, which conducts rasterization while checking the z value and color intensity of each pixel.

This rendering pipeline can be implemented in both hardware or software. In hardware implementations, high-performance graphics systems are commonly needed because of their multiprocessing capabilities. Figure 9.18 shows how the front end of the graphics system can be accelerated with a geometry subsystem consisting of several processors. Special-purpose geometry processors have been developed, most notably Clark's "Geometry Engine," capable of performing modeling and viewing transformations, clipping, and shading [27].

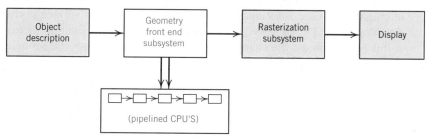

FIGURE 9.18 *Multiprocessing used to accelerate the front end of graphics systems.*

SUMMARY

|||||||||||||||||||||||||||||||||||||||||||||||||||||||||||||||||||||||||||||||||

This chapter described various visibility techniques used to optimize the process of hidden line/surface removal. These techniques are also found to be useful in performing other operations, such as intersection calculations. A description of shading algorithms and their role in the rendering process was given. New and powerful graphics systems have specialized CPUs that permit the efficient execution of rendering algorithms at the hardware level. PHIGS+, the extension of the PHIGS standard, includes facilities for lighting and shading control.

EXERCISES

|||||||||||||||||||||||||||||||||||||||||||||||||||||||||||||||||||||||||||||||||

1. For the unit cube shown in the accompanying figure, find the visibility of all faces when viewed from a point $V(0.5, 0.5, 2.0)$.

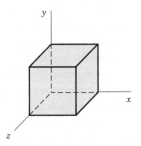

2. Consider a plane defined by $A(1,0,1)$, $B(4,0,1)$, $C(2,4,2)$. If it were to undergo a minimax test, what would be the dimensions of the bounding box? Run a minimax test to check the visibility of this plane against another defined by $D(3,0,2)$, $E(2,0,0)$, and $F(1,6,0)$.

3. Given the polygons

$$ABCD: A(2,2), B(6,3), C(4,8), D(3,6)$$
$$PQRS: P(8,10), Q(16,2), R(12,18), S(8,18)$$

run a check for possible containment.

4. A surface is defined by three points, $A(1,0,1)$, $B(1,0,0)$, and $C(1,1,1)$. An illumination source is located at a large distance from this surface in the direction $(\mathbf{i} + 5\mathbf{j} + 8\mathbf{k})/3\sqrt{10}$. Determine the intensity of light necessary at this light source if the shaded intensity for the surface is to be set at 2. The reflectivity of the surface is 0.3.

5. For the rectangular plane defined by points $A(0,0)$, $B(1,0)$, $C(1,1)$, and $D(0,1)$, find the reflected intensity at point $P(0.5, 0.5)$ using the Gouraud

shading technique. The average intensities of reflected illumination at the four vertices are:

$$I_A = 8, I_B = 9, I_C = 2, I_D = 4$$

6. For the painter's algorithm described in Section 9.1.3, design a data structure (refer to Chapter 7) that will store the depth values of the model's faces.

7. Check your graphics library for availability of hidden line/surface removal procedures and shading. What are the specific algorithms used?

Chapter 10

Curves

Curves used in geometric modeling can be as simple as a line or a circle. However, more complex curves are required for some applications, such as the design of automobiles, ships, and airplanes, where various shape constraints must be met. Figure 10.1 shows some of these curves, usually referred to as "freeform curves." This chapter will cover both freeform curves and the more common conics—lines, circles, ellipses.

10.1 GEOMETRIC CURVE DESCRIPTION

Any curve can be described by an array of points, as shown in previous sections on the representation of polyhedral objects. This requires excessive storage, however, and the exact shape of the curve becomes unknown, causing difficulty in finding, for example, its integral properties. Analytic equations are usually preferred, giving the designer better control over the shape and behavior of the curves. One class of mathematical function is particularly suitable for this purpose—the polynomial function.

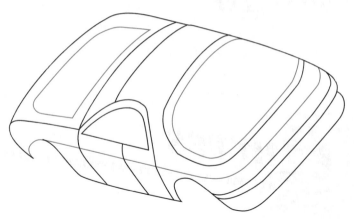

FIGURE 10.1 Examples of freeform curves in the design of automobile bodies.

The general form of a polynomial function is:

$$p(x) = a_n x^n + a_{n-1} x^{n-1} + \cdots + a_1 x + a_0 = \sum_{i=0}^{n} a_i x^i \quad (10.1)$$

where n is a nonnegative integer and $a_0, a_1, \ldots, a_n$ are real numbers. The polynomial $p(x)$ is said to be of degree n if it has this representation and $a_n \neq 0$.

Polynomials are popular mostly because they are very convenient for computational purposes. To evaluate a polynomial at a point simply requires the multiplication and addition of real values a finite number of times. In addition, computer graphics applications require the determination of tangents, normals, and so forth, for specific curves, so a differentiation of the function used should be easily accomplished. Polynomial functions are an obvious good choice. They will be used extensively in this text to represent various types of curves.

10.2 PARAMETRIC AND IMPLICIT FORMULATIONS

Curves can be represented in two forms: parametric and implicit. The parametric representation

$$x = x(t) \qquad y = y(t) \qquad z = z(t) \tag{10.2}$$

where all functions of the parameter t are polynomials, describes a space curve directly. This representation permits a quick computation of the x, y, z coordinates of all points on the curve, with each point coordinate defined separately.

The parametric form can be used to define a curve segment by constraining the parameter to the interval [0,1]. Because curves are usually bounded in computer graphics, this characteristic is of considerable importance.

The implicit representation of a planar curve takes the form

$$f(x, y) = 0 \qquad (10.3)$$

A three-dimensional curve is described in implicit form by the intersection of two surface equations

$$s_1(x, y, z) = 0$$

$$s_2(x, y, z) = 0$$

These implicit equations must be solved simultaneously to determine points on the curve, a lengthy and inconvenient process.

It is easy to determine, in the implicit representation, whether a specific point lies on the curve, or if not on the curve, on which side it lies. This is useful in many applications, solid modeling, for example, where points must be defined inside and outside the boundaries of an object.

In geometric modeling, the most common form of curve representation has been the parametric form, because of its ease of programming and computability. This representation will be largely used throughout this text. However, since, as mentioned above, the implicit form may be required in some instances, a simple method of conversion from the parametric to the implicit representation will be described.

10.2.1 Implicitization

The method for conversion of a parametric equation of a curve into an implicit equation is called *implicitization*. For ease of explanation, the two-dimensional case will be described; the implicit representation in three dimensions requires two equations.

Assume that a parametric equation for a curve segment in the form

$$x = x(t) \qquad y = y(t)$$

is to be transformed into the implicit equation $f(x, y) = 0$. For some types of curves, a "brute force" approach can be used to obtain the implicitization. For example, given the line

$$x = t + 1 \qquad y = 2t + 1 \qquad (10.4)$$

the implicit equation can be found by solving for t as a function of x and substituting into the equation for y:

$$t = x - 1$$

$$y = 2(x - 1) + 1 \qquad (10.5)$$

or

$$2x - y - 1 = 0$$

This implicit equation represents "exactly" the same curve as the parametric equation. This approach to implicitization works well for linear and quadratic equations. However, when applied to curves of higher degrees, problems begin to occur. Cubic (3rd degree) and quartic (4th degree) curves can be changed, but the resulting expressions are very complex. In addition, for higher degree curves it is impossible to use the brute force implicitization, and special techniques had to be developed. One of them uses the concept of a *resultant* of two polynomials [30].

Consider two polynomials of the form

$$x(t) = \sum_{i=0}^{n} a_i t^i \qquad y(t) = \sum_{i=0}^{n} b_i t^i \tag{10.6}$$

The resultant of $x(t)$ and $y(t)$ is called $R(x,y)$, and is an expression in terms of the coefficients $a_i b_i$ such that there is a common root of $x(t)$ and $y(t)$ if and only if $R(x,y) = 0$. The expression for the resultant of quadratic and cubic polynomials is given as follows, in determinant form.

For quadratic curves:

$$\begin{bmatrix} (a_2 b_1) & (a_2 b_0) \\ (a_2 b_0) & (a_1 b_0) \end{bmatrix} \tag{10.7}$$

For cubic curves:

$$\begin{bmatrix} (a_3 b_2) & (a_3 b_1) & (a_3 b_0) \\ (a_3 b_1) & (a_3 b_0) + (a_2 b_1) & (a_2 b_0) \\ (a_3 b_0) & (a_2 b_0) & (a_1 b_0) \end{bmatrix} \tag{10.8}$$

In both determinants, $(a_i b_j) \equiv (a_i b_j - a_j b_i)$. An algorithm for forming the elements of the determinant for any polynomial degree is given in [31].

To apply these concepts of implicitization of a curve segment from a parametric form $x = x(t)$, $y = y(t)$ for $0 \le t \le 1$ into an implicit form $f(x,y) = 0$ the first step is to create two auxiliary polynomials:

$$r(x, t) = x - x(t)$$
$$s(y, t) = y - y(t) \tag{10.9}$$

The values of $r(x,t)$ and $s(y,t)$ are zero only when x, y satisfy the relationships $x = x(t)$, $y = y(t)$. Since $x(t)$ and $y(t)$ are polynomial expressions, they can be written as shown in Eq. 10.6.

The resultant of $r(x,t)$ and $s(y,t)$ can be computed based on the expressions given in Eqs. 10.7 and 10.8. Instead of a numerical value, a polynomial expression $f(x,y)$ in x and y is found. Any (x,y) pair for which

$f(x,y) = 0$ also causes the resultant of $r(x,t)$ and $s(y,t)$ to be zero. If the resultant is zero, then all (x,y) pairs lie on the parametric curve and the resulting $f(x,y)$ is, by definition, the implicit equation of that curve. Note that the degree of the implicit equations resulting from this process is at most equal to the degree of the parametric equations.

Example 10.1

Consider the planar quadratic curve given by

$$x = t^2 - 1 \qquad y = t^2 - 2t + 2$$

Determine its implicit equation.

Solution

The brute-force approach applied to this case yields the following results:

From the x equation: $t = \pm\sqrt{x + 1}$

Substituting in y: $y = (\sqrt{x + 1})^2 \mp 2\sqrt{x + 1} + 2$

Isolating the radicals and squaring both sides:

$$[y - (x + 1) - 2]^2 = (\pm 2\sqrt{x + 1})^2$$

or

$$x^2 - 2xy + y^2 + 2x - 6y + 5 = 0$$

The same results are obtained using the general resultant method.

$$x = t^2 - 1$$
$$y = t^2 - 2t + 2$$

From Eq. 10.9, the auxiliary polynomials are:

$$r(x,t) = -t^2 + (x + 1)$$
$$s(y,t) = -t^2 + 2t + (y - 2)$$

The resultant is given by the determinant:

$$\begin{bmatrix} -2 & (x - y + 3) \\ (x - y + 3) & -2(x + 1) \end{bmatrix}$$

$$= x^2 - 2xy + y^2 + 2x - 6y + 5 = 0$$

This general procedure is valid for cases where the brute-force approach does not apply, that is, cases where the curve is represented by cubic or higher-degree polynomials. The cubic representation is one of the most commonly used in geometric modeling and computer-aided design; this general implicitization method can therefore be of great value.

FIGURE 10.2 Conic
representations.

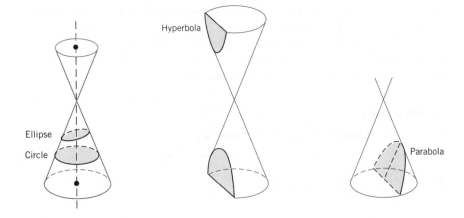

FIGURE 10.2 Conic
representations.

10.3 CONICS

Conics are curves obtained by the intersection of a plane and a cone, as
shown in Figure 10.2.

These curves are commonly described in implicit form by the general
quadratic equation

$$ax^2 + by^2 + 2hxy + 2ux + 2vy + d = 0 \qquad (10.10)$$

In matrix form, this equation can be written as

$$[P][R][P]^T = 0 \qquad (10.11)$$

where $[P] = [x \quad y \quad 1]$ and

$$[R] = \begin{bmatrix} a & b & u \\ b & b & v \\ u & v & d \end{bmatrix} \qquad (10.12)$$

All conics can be expressed by assigning specific values to the coefficients
of Eq. 10.10. The flowchart in Figure 10.3 gives specific conditions producing
the different types of conics [32], including degenerate forms such as a pair
of intersecting or parallel lines.

Conic curves are used extensively in computer graphics and geometric
modeling. They lend themselves in a relatively easy way to computation and
storage. These curves are commonly used to fit a set of data values or to
satisfy some specified design criteria. One of their most important characteristics is a lack of inflection points. At least five independent coefficient
values are needed to define a specific conic curve from the general implicit
Eq. 10.10. Conics can also be approximated by cubic polynomials or represented exactly by rational quadratic expressions, described in the next section. Only the two most common conic curves in engineering design—circles
and ellipses—will be studied here in detail.

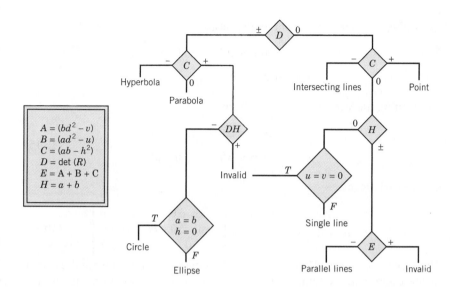

FIGURE 10.3 Flowchart for conic classification.

$A = (bd^2 - v)$
$B = (ad^2 - u)$
$C = (ab - h^2)$
$D = \det (R)$
$E = A + B + C$
$H = a + b$

10.3.1 Circles

Circles and arcs are used extensively in engineering design, in particular the design of mechanical parts, and can be well represented by parametric equations. The variables x and y are given in terms of the angle θ, as shown in Figure 10.4.

Therefore

$$x_i = r \cos \theta \qquad y_i = r \sin \theta \qquad (10.13)$$

and

$$x_{i+1} = r \cos (\theta + \Delta\theta)$$

$$y_{i+1} = r \sin (\theta + \Delta\theta)$$

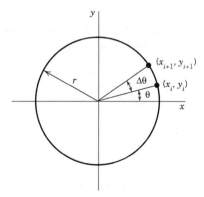

FIGURE 10.4 Parametric representation of a circle.

Expanding the sine and cosine expressions:

$$x_{i+1} = r \cos \theta \cos \Delta\theta - r \sin \theta \sin \Delta\theta$$
$$y_{i+1} = r \sin \theta \cos \Delta\theta + r \cos \theta \sin \Delta\theta \tag{10.14}$$

Substituting the values of x_i and y_i from Eq. 10.13:

$$x_{i+1} = x_i \cos \Delta\theta - y_i \sin \Delta\theta$$
$$y_{i+1} = y_i \cos \Delta\theta + x_i \sin \Delta\theta \tag{10.15}$$

or, in matrix form,

$$[x_{i+1}, y_{i+1}, 1] = [x_i, y_i, 1] \begin{bmatrix} \cos \Delta\theta & \sin \Delta\theta & 0 \\ -\sin \Delta\theta & \cos \Delta\theta & 0 \\ 0 & 0 & 1 \end{bmatrix} \tag{10.16}$$

These parametric equations are valid for a circle with the center at the origin of the coordinate system. To place the center of the circle (x_c, y_c) in any position in the plane, the following sequence of two-dimensional transformations should be performed.

$$[x_{i+1}, y_{i+1}, 1] = [x_i, y_i, 1] \begin{bmatrix} \cos \Delta\theta & \sin \Delta\theta & 0 \\ -\sin \Delta\theta & \cos \Delta\theta & 0 \\ 0 & 0 & 1 \end{bmatrix} \begin{bmatrix} 1 & 0 & 0 \\ 0 & 1 & 0 \\ x_c & y_c & 1 \end{bmatrix} \tag{10.17}$$

Expanding yields the parametric equations:

$$x_{i+1} = x_c + x_i \cos \Delta\theta - y_i \sin \Delta\theta$$
$$y_{i+1} = y_c + x_i \sin \Delta\theta + y_i \cos \Delta\theta \tag{10.18}$$

Appendix 10.1 at the end of this chapter shows an implementation of this approach.

10.3.2 Ellipses

An ellipse is simply a variation of a circle. The parametric equations of an ellipse centered at the coordinate axes and stretched along these axes are

$$x_i = a \cos \theta$$
$$y_i = b \sin \theta$$

with θ varying from 0 to 2π.

For a point x_{i+1}, y_{i+1}, the equations become (see accompanying figure):

$$x_{i+1} = a \cos (\theta + \Delta\theta)$$
$$y_{i+1} = b \sin (\theta + \Delta\theta) \tag{10.19}$$

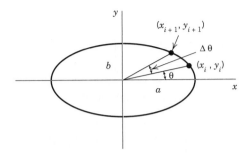

and the expansion yields

$$x_{i+1} = a \cos \theta \cos \Delta\theta - a \sin \theta \sin \Delta\theta$$

$$y_{i+1} = b \sin \theta \cos \Delta\theta + b \cos \theta \sin \Delta\theta$$

(10.20)

Or

$$x_{i+1} = x_i \cos \Delta\theta - \left(\frac{a}{b}\right) y_i \sin \Delta\theta$$

$$y_{i+1} = y_i \cos \Delta\theta + \left(\frac{b}{a}\right) x_i \sin \Delta\theta$$

(10.21)

A more general relationship can be developed for the case when the axes of the ellipse are not parallel to the coordinate axes, and the center of the ellipse is at a distance x_c, y_c from the origin.

Assume that the major axis a of the ellipse makes an angle α with the horizontal, as shown in Figure 10.5. The following relationships can be derived from the figure:

$$x_i = x_c + x'_i \cos \alpha - y'_i \sin \alpha \qquad (10.22)$$

$$y_i = y_c + x'_i \sin \alpha - y'_i \cos \alpha \qquad (10.23)$$

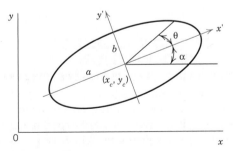

FIGURE 10.5 A general position for an ellipse.

Or, in matrix form,

$$[x_i \quad y_i \quad 1] = [x_i' \quad y_i' \quad 1] \begin{bmatrix} \cos \alpha & \sin \alpha & 0 \\ -\sin \alpha & \cos \alpha & 0 \\ x_c & y_c & 1 \end{bmatrix} \qquad (10.24)$$

Assuming a right-handed coordinate system, the matrix

$$\begin{bmatrix} \cos \alpha & \sin \alpha & 0 \\ -\sin \alpha & \cos \alpha & 0 \\ x_c & y_c & 1 \end{bmatrix}$$

represents a CCW rotation by an angle α, and a translation of the origin of the coordinate system by (x_c, y_c). This matrix, when used in conjunction with Eq. 10.21, describes points in the general ellipse of Figure 10.5. To describe the full ellipse with the best distribution of points the angle θ should vary from 0 to 2π by increments of $2\pi/(n - 1)$, where n equals the number of points used [5]. Appendix 10.2 at the end of this chapter implements the iteration formulas for the representation of an ellipse.

Table 10.1 presents some standard conics in both parametric and implicit forms.

TABLE 10.1

	Parametric	Implicit
Circle	$x = r \cos \theta$ $y = r \sin \theta$	$x^2 + y^2 = r^2$
Ellipse	$x = a \cos \theta$ $y = b \sin \theta$	$\dfrac{x^2}{a^2} + \dfrac{y^2}{b^2} = 1$
Parabola	$x = a\theta^2$ $y = 2a\theta$	$y^2 = 4ax$
Hyperbola	$x = a \cosh (\theta)$ $y = b \sinh (\theta)$	$\dfrac{x^2}{a^2} - \dfrac{y^2}{b^2} = 1$

10.4 INTERPOLATION TECHNIQUES FOR CURVE DEFINITION

Engineering students are commonly faced with the problem of finding an arbitrary curve that fits a set of data values. This problem is encountered, for example, when trying to fit a curve to a set of experimental values. A popular solution method is the least squares fit, which provides a curve that best describes a sequence of observations. Interpolation problems for scattered data are also common in engineering. When using numerical methods to

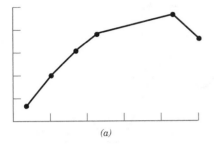 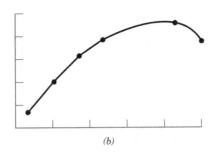

(a) (b)

FIGURE 10.6 (a) Piecewise linear interpolation. (b) Third order Lagrange interpolation.

solve differential equations it is frequently necessary to find function values that do not lie on the actual points used for the computations. Interpolating schemes are then used to find these values utilizing neighboring points. Examples of data interpolation are shown in Figure 10.6.

If accuracy is not a major consideration, piecewise linear interpolation may be an appropriate solution. The linear interpolation formula (Eq. 10.25) evaluates function $f(x)$ for any value of x between two arbitrary points, x_i and x_{i+1}.

$$f(x) = f(x_i) + [f(x_{i+1}) - f(x_i)][(x - x_i)/d] \qquad (10.25)$$

where $d = x_{i+1} - x_i$.

Another popular interpolation scheme uses polynomial functions. The Lagrange polynomials are among the simplest of these interpolating polynomials.

10.4.1 Lagrange Polynomial

Consider a sequence of planar points defined by (x_0, y_0), (x_1, y_1), ... (x_n, y_n) where $x_i < x_j$ for $i < j$. The interpolating polynomial of nth degree can be calculated as

$$f_n(x) = \sum_{i=0}^{n} y_i L_{i,n}(x)$$

where $\qquad (10.26)$

$$L_{i,n}(x) = \frac{(x - x_0) \cdots (x - x_{i-1})(x - x_{i+1}) \cdots (x - x_n)}{(x_i - x_0) \cdots (x_i - x_{i-1})(x_i - x_{i+1}) \cdots (x_i - x_n)}$$

A short notation for this formula is

$$f_n(x) = \sum_{i=0}^{n} y_i \prod_{\substack{j=0 \\ j \neq i}}^{n} \left(\frac{x - x_j}{x_i - x_j} \right) \qquad (10.27)$$

where Π denotes multiplication of the n factors obtained by varying j from 0 to n, excluding $j = i$. It can be observed that the fraction multiplying y_i is

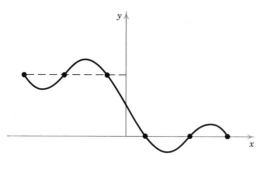 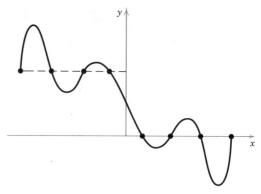

FIGURE 10.7 Excessive oscillations for Lagrange interpolation, resulting from an increase in the number of points used.

equal to unity when $x = x_i$ but becomes zero when x equals any of the other coordinates. The equation of a line between two points is obtained by setting $n = 1$:

$$
f_1(x) = \frac{x - x_1}{x_0 - x_1} \cdot y_0 - \frac{x - x_0}{x_1 - x_0} \cdot y_1
$$

$$
= y_0 + (y_1 - y_0)\left(\frac{x_0 - x}{x_0 - x_1}\right)
$$

(10.28)

The Lagrange polynomial has the disadvantage of having the degree of the polynomial tied to the number of points used. If, in search of greater accuracy, the number of points used is increased, the result is a polynomial of higher degree subject to excessive oscillations, as shown in Figure 10.7. In most engineering applications, these oscillations are unacceptable.

Example 10.2

Use a Lagrangian polynomial to interpolate the points

$P_1(1,1)$	$P_2(2,2)$	$P_3(3,3)$	$P_4(4,2)$	$P_5(5,1)$

Solution

Equation 10.26 is used to solve this problem, as follows.

$$
f(x) = \left[\frac{(x - 2)(x - 3)(x - 4)(x - 5)}{(1 - 2)(1 - 3)(1 - 4)(1 - 5)}\right](1) + \left[\frac{(x - 1)(x - 3)(x - 4)(x - 5)}{(2 - 1)(2 - 3)(2 - 4)(2 - 5)}\right](2)
$$

$$
+ \left[\frac{(x - 1)(x - 2)(x - 4)(x - 5)}{(3 - 1)(3 - 2)(3 - 4)(3 - 5)}\right](3) + \left[\frac{(x - 1)(x - 2)(x - 3)(x - 5)}{(4 - 1)(4 - 2)(4 - 3)(4 - 5)}\right](4)
$$

$$
+ \left[\frac{(x - 1)(x - 2)(x - 3)(x - 4)}{(5 - 1)(5 - 2)(5 - 3)(5 - 4)}\right](1)
$$

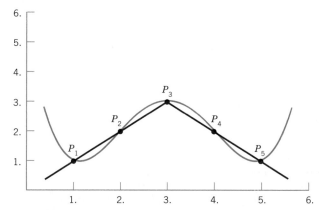

FIGURE 10.8 Plot showing linear and Lagrange interpolation for a given set of points.

The graph of this function interpolating the given points is shown in Figure 10.8. A straight line is also passed through all the points, describing the results more accurately. It is evident that the Lagrange interpolation function oscillates about the plot of correct values.

10.4.2 Parametric Cubic

A parametric cubic curve is defined as

$$P(t) = \sum_{i=0}^{3} a_i t^i \qquad 0 \le t \le 1 \tag{10.29}$$

where $P(t)$ is a point on the curve, as shown in Figure 10.9.

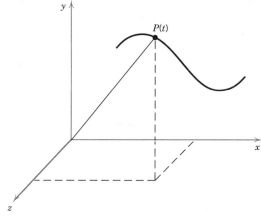

FIGURE 10.9 Point on a parametric cubic curve.

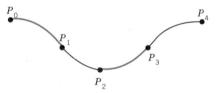

FIGURE 10.10 Piecewise parametric cubic interpolation.

Expansion of Eq. 10.29 yields

$$P(t) = a_3 t^3 + a_2 t^2 + a_1 t + a_0 \tag{10.30}$$

This equation can be separated into the three components of $P(t)$, such that

$$
\begin{aligned}
x(t) &= a_{3x} t^3 + a_{2x} t^2 + a_{1x} t + a_{0x} \\
y(t) &= a_{3y} t^3 + a_{2y} t^2 + a_{1y} t + a_{0y} \\
z(t) &= a_{3z} t^3 + a_{2z} t^2 + a_{1z} t + a_{0z}
\end{aligned}
\tag{10.31}
$$

To be able to solve Eqs. 10.31, the twelve unknown coefficients a_{ij}, known as the algebraic coefficients, must be specified.

Controlling the shape of a curve by varying the a_{ij} values is difficult. A more intuitive approach is to establish appropriate boundary conditions satisfying geometric constraints. The boundary conditions must allow the setting of the twelve equations necessary for the calculation of the twelve algebraic coefficients. Since the problem being solved is one of interpolation, it is logical to assume that the coordinates of the points are known. One possible solution performs the interpolation in a piecewise fashion; that is, two points are interpolated at a time by a parametric cubic curve, as shown in Figure 10.10.

From the known endpoint coordinates of each segment, six of the twelve needed equations are obtained. The other six equations are found by using tangent vectors at the two ends of each segment, as shown in Figure 10.11. The direction of the tangent vectors establishes the slopes (direction cosines) of the curve at the endpoints, and changes in the magnitude of the vectors allow modification of the shape of the curve. For example, for a

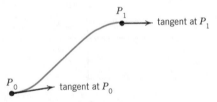

FIGURE 10.11 Tangent vectors at the end of a segment.

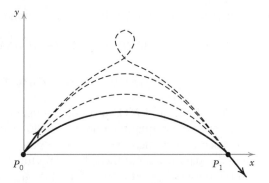

FIGURE 10.12 Changes in the magnitude of tangent vectors cause variations on the shape of a parametric cubic curve.

constant slope at the endpoints, an increase in the magnitude of the tangent vectors would cause variations on the curve as shown in Figure 10.12.

This procedure for defining a cubic curve, using endpoints and tangent vectors, is one form of *Hermite* interpolation. Each cubic curve segment is parameterized from 0 to 1, so that the two known endpoints correspond to the limit values of the parametric variable t, that is, $P(0)$ and $P(1)$. Substituting $t = 0$ and $t = 1$ into Eq. 10.30, the relationships between the two endpoint vectors and the algebraic coefficients are found:

$$P(0) = a_0$$
$$P(1) = a_3 + a_2 + a_1 + a_0$$

(10.32)

To find the tangent vectors, Eq. 10.30 must be differentiated with respect to t, yielding:

$$P'(t) = 3a_3 t^2 + 2a_2 t + a_1$$

(10.33)

The tangent vectors at the two endpoints are found by substituting $t = 0$ and $t = 1$ in this equation:

$$P'(0) = a_1$$
$$P'(1) = 3a_3 + 2a_2 + a_1$$

(10.34)

The algebraic coefficients a_i in Eq. 10.30 can now be written explicitly in terms of the boundary conditions—endpoints and tangent vectors—as follows:

$$a_0 = P(0)$$
$$a_1 = P'(0)$$
$$a_2 = -3P(0) + 3P(1) - 2P'(0) - P'(1)$$
$$a_3 = 2P(0) - 2P(1) + P'(0) + P'(1)$$

(10.35)

Substituting these values of a_i into Eq. 10.30 and rearranging terms yields

$$P(t) = (2t^3 - 3t^2 + 1)P(0) + (-2t^3 + 3t^2)P(1)$$

$$+ (t^3 - 2t^2 + t)P'(0) + (t^3 - t^2)P'(1)$$

(10.36)

The values of $P(0)$, $P(1)$, $P'(0)$, and $P'(1)$ are called geometric coefficients and represent the known vector quantities in Eq. 10.36. The polynomial coefficients of these vector quantities are commonly known as *blending functions*. By varying the parameter t in these blending functions from 0 to 1, several points on the curve segment can be found. Notice that Eq. 10.36 is valid for each parametric cubic segment of the set of segments in Figure 10.10.

10.4.3 Matrix Approach

Eqs. 10.30 and 10.36 can be rewritten in matrix form as follows:

$$P(t) = [t^3 \quad t^2 \quad t \quad 1] \begin{bmatrix} a_3 \\ a_2 \\ a_1 \\ a_0 \end{bmatrix}$$

(10.37)

and

$$P(t) = [t^3 \quad t^2 \quad t \quad 1] \begin{bmatrix} 2 & -2 & 1 & 1 \\ -3 & 3 & -2 & -1 \\ 0 & 0 & 1 & 0 \\ 1 & 0 & 0 & 0 \end{bmatrix} \begin{bmatrix} P(0) \\ P(1) \\ P'(0) \\ P'(1) \end{bmatrix}$$

(10.38)

Or, in more compact form

$$P(t) = [t][A] \qquad \text{algebraic form}$$
$$P(t) = [t][M][G] \quad \text{geometric form}$$

(10.39)

In geometric modeling, the second equation is the one that is normally used. Matrices $[t]$ and $[M]$ are invariant for any cubic curve. Only matrix $[G]$, specifying the endpoints and tangent vectors, is modified to produce a new parametric cubic curve. The 4×4 matrix $[M]$ is known as the "Hermite matrix." To differentiate the Hermite geometric form from others to be introduced later in this chapter, this matrix will be referred to as $[M]_H$ and $[G]$ will become $[G]_H$.

In Eq. 10.39

$$[A] = \text{algebraic coefficients matrix}$$

and

$$[G]_H = \text{geometric coefficients matrix}$$

A direct comparison of the two Eqs. 10.39 yields

$$[A] = [M]_H[G]_H \tag{10.40}$$

and conversely

$$[G]_H = [M]_H^{-1}[A] \tag{10.41}$$

where

$$[M]_H^{-1} = \begin{bmatrix} 0 & 0 & 0 & 1 \\ 1 & 1 & 1 & 1 \\ 0 & 0 & 1 & 0 \\ 3 & 2 & 1 & 0 \end{bmatrix} \tag{10.42}$$

An algorithm for the generation of Hermite curves is given in Appendix 10.3.

Example 10.3

Find the matrix of geometric coefficients for a parametric cubic curve, knowing that

for $t = 0$ → (2, 20, 2) is a point on the curve and $P'(0) = (x_1, 0, 4x_1)$

for $t = 1$ → (10, 20, 2) is a point on the curve and $P'(1) = (x_2, 0, -2x_2)$

for $t = 0.5$ → (6, 20, 6) is a point on the curve

Solution

The matrix of geometric coefficients is given as

$$\begin{bmatrix} P(0) \\ P(1) \\ P'(0) \\ P'(1) \end{bmatrix}$$

For this problem, $P(0)$ and $P(1)$ are given as (2, 20, 2) and (10, 20, 2), respectively. To obtain the values of $P'(0)$ and $P'(1)$, the unknowns x_1 and x_2 must be calculated. For $t = 0.5$, the following expression can be used based on Eq. 10.38:

$$P(0.5) = \begin{bmatrix} 6 & 20 & 6 \end{bmatrix}$$

$$= \begin{bmatrix} (0.5)^3 & (0.5)^2 & 0.5 & 1 \end{bmatrix} \begin{bmatrix} 2 & -2 & 1 & 1 \\ -3 & 3 & -2 & -1 \\ 0 & 0 & 1 & 0 \\ 1 & 0 & 0 & 0 \end{bmatrix} \begin{bmatrix} 2 & 20 & 2 \\ 10 & 20 & 2 \\ x_1 & 0 & 4x_1 \\ x_2 & 0 & -2x_2 \end{bmatrix}$$

which, when expanded, yields:

$$6 = 6 + 0.125x_1 - 0.125x_2 \tag{I}$$

and

$$6 = 2 + 0.5x_1 + 0.25x_2 \tag{II}$$

From (I)

$$x_1 = x_2$$

Substituting in (II)

$$x_1 = x_2 = \tfrac{16}{3}$$

The geometric coefficients matrix is therefore

$$\begin{bmatrix} 2 & 20 & 2 \\ 10 & 20 & 2 \\ \tfrac{16}{3} & 0 & \tfrac{64}{3} \\ \tfrac{16}{3} & 0 & -\tfrac{32}{3} \end{bmatrix}$$

10.4.4 Cubic Spline

Interpolation problems in CAD can also be solved conveniently by means of spline functions. The idea of splines is based on the use of the "drafting spline," a thin, flexible strip used to draw a smooth curve through a given series of points. The physical spline is shaped by attaching appropriate lead weights to the flexible strip, as shown in Figure 10.13. It may be considered a thin elastic beam to which the Bernoulli–Euler equation applies. In this case, if small deflections are considered, the curvature is approximated by the second derivative of the assumed curve. If the weights in the physical spline act as simple supports, the curve becomes a piecewise cubic polynomial, continuous up to its second derivative at each support, that is, continuous with respect to position, tangent, and curvature.

Piecewise cubic splines can be used advantageously in engineering problems, particularly when the data values are relatively accurate and large in number. Standard polynomial interpolation—Lagrange's, for example— yields polynomials of high order, causing possible oscillations on the interpolated curve, as described in Section 10.4.1. Cubic spline interpolation is

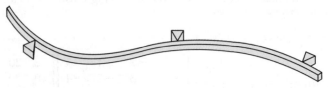

FIGURE 10.13 Physical spline.

satisfactory in many engineering applications which deal with large sets of very accurate values, such as measurements of material properties (density, modulus of elasticity, and so forth), or results obtained from the simulation of various engineering systems.

The term "spline" in computer graphics and geometric modeling refers to the general piecewise parametric representation of geometry with a specified level of parametric continuity. The cubic spline is represented by a piecewise cubic polynomial with second order derivative continuity at the common joints between segments.

The idea of parametric continuity will be explained here in more detail. It can be symbolically represented by a capital C with a numerical superscript. The simplest form of continuity, referred to as C^0 continuity, ensures that there will be no gaps or jumps in a curve. If an additional level of continuity, C^1, is required, then the curve will be slope or first derivative continuous. A C^2 continuity implies curvature or second derivative continuity, and so on. Figure 10.14 shows examples of these various cases. Note that these continuity requirements relate to the parametric formulation. In this text the term continuity will always refer to parametric continuity. More general continuity requirements, such as *geometric continuity* which is a parameterization independent measure of continuity, are described in the literature [33].

If the segments of the cubic spline are parameterized separately, so that the parameter t varies between 0 and 1 for all segments, then this normalized cubic spline is simply a special case of Hermite interpolation, which ensures first derivative continuity between segments. In the cubic spline, first derivative values are chosen that also match the second derivatives.

The blending function matrix for the normalized cubic spline $(0 \leq t \leq 1)$ is in this case the same as the one used in Hermite interpolation:

$$[t^3 \quad t^2 \quad t \quad 1] \begin{bmatrix} 2 & -2 & 1 & 1 \\ -3 & 3 & -2 & -1 \\ 0 & 0 & 1 & 0 \\ 1 & 0 & 0 & 0 \end{bmatrix} \qquad (10.43)$$

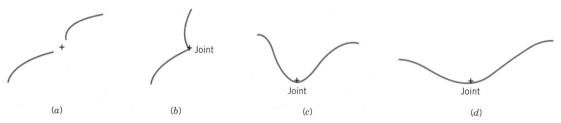

FIGURE 10.14 Examples of parametric continuity: (a) Discontinuous; (b) C^0; (c) C^1; (d) C^2.

The cubic spline function for each segment is defined by Eq. 10.38, repeated below:

$$P(t) = [t^3 \quad t^2 \quad t \quad 1] \begin{bmatrix} 2 & -2 & 1 & 1 \\ -3 & 3 & -2 & -1 \\ 0 & 0 & 1 & 0 \\ 1 & 0 & 0 & 0 \end{bmatrix} \begin{bmatrix} P(0) \\ P(1) \\ P'(0) \\ P'(1) \end{bmatrix}$$

or

$$P(t) = [t][M]_H[G]_H \qquad (10.44)$$

As with the parametric cubic formulation, matrices $[t]$ and $[M]$ are invariant for all cubic spline segments. Variations occur only in the geometric matrix $[G]_H$, which varies from one segment to another. In matrix $[G]_H$ the endpoint vectors are known for each cubic segment, but the tangent vectors must be found, as stated before, so that second derivative continuity is enforced. At each point of a curve segment, P_i, therefore, values must be chosen so that the second derivative at the endpoint of one curve segment coincides with the second derivative of the starting point of the following segment. Mathematically,

$$P''_{i-1}(1) = P''_i(0) \qquad (10.45)$$

For the cubic polynomial expressed as

$$P_i(t) = a_{3i}t^3 + a_{2i}t^2 + a_{1i}t + a_{0i} \qquad (10.46)$$

the second derivative is

$$P''_i(t) = 6a_{3i}t + 2a_{2i} \qquad (10.47)$$

Substituting this expression into Eq. 10.45 for the appropriate parameter values yields

$$\underbrace{6a_{3(i-1)} + 2a_{2(i-1)}}_{t=1 \text{ for segment } (i-1)} = \underbrace{2a_{2i}}_{t=0 \text{ for segment } i} \qquad (10.48)$$

Values of a_2 and a_3 from Eq. 10.35 can be substituted into Eq. 10.48. Before performing this substitution, however, and in order to simplify the notation, let P_i represent $P_i(0)$ and P'_i represent $P'_i(0)$ for all values of i. Also, from the position continuity C^0

$$P_i(1) = P_{i+1}(0)$$

for all i, as shown in Figure 10.15. Keeping the above in mind, the substitution of the appropriate expressions for a_2 and a_3 from Eq. 10.35 into Eq. 10.48 can now be performed, changing all occurrences of $P_i(1)$ to $P_{i+1}(0)$:

$$2[3(P_i - P_{i-1}) - 2P'_{i-1} - P'_i] + 6[2(P_{i-1} - P_i) + P'_{i-1} + P'_i]$$
$$= 2[3(P_{i+1} - P_i) - 2P'_i - P'_{i+1}] \qquad (10.49)$$

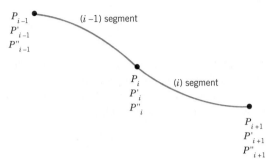

FIGURE 10.15 Two cubic spline segments

Simplification yields

$$P'_{i-1} + 4P'_i + P'_{i+1} = 3(P_{i+1} - P_{i-1}) \qquad (10.50)$$

In Eq. 10.50, the parameter value $t = 0$ is implied in all terms and was dropped, as stated before, to simplify the notation.

The iterative application of Eq. 10.50 over all cubic spline segments allows the calculation of all internal tangent vectors. Assume that the cubic spline has $m - 1$ segments interpolating m points, P_0 to P_{m-1}. In this case, $m - 2$ internal joints are present, leading to $m - 2$ equations such as 10.50. Since m tangent vectors are needed, additional constraints must be imposed on the cubic spline. Two commonly used constraints are

(a) Known end tangent vectors, P'_0 and P'_{m-1}

(b) Second derivatives at the endpoints P_0 and P_{m-1} both made equal to zero; this is referred to as a *natural cubic spline*

Case (a)—Recursive use of Eq. 10.50 over all spline segments and known tangent vectors at the two ends of the cubic spline can be represented in matrix form as:

$$
\begin{bmatrix}
1 & 0 & \cdot & \cdot & \cdot & \cdot \\
1 & 4 & 1 & 0 & \cdot & \cdot \\
0 & 1 & 4 & 1 & 0 & \cdot \\
\cdot & \cdot & \cdot & \cdot & \cdot & \cdot \\
\cdot & \cdot & 0 & 1 & 4 & 1 \\
\cdot & \cdot & \cdot & \cdot & 0 & 1
\end{bmatrix}
\begin{bmatrix}
P'_0 \\
P'_1 \\
\cdot \\
\cdot \\
\cdot \\
P'_{m-1}
\end{bmatrix}
=
\begin{bmatrix}
P'_0 \\
3(P_2 - P_0) \\
\cdot \\
\cdot \\
3(P_{m-1} - P_{m-3}) \\
P'_{m-1}
\end{bmatrix}
\qquad (10.51)
$$

Solution of this matrix equation yields the values of all tangent vectors:

$$
\begin{bmatrix}
P'_0 \\
P'_1 \\
\cdot \\
\cdot \\
P'_{m-1}
\end{bmatrix}
=
\begin{bmatrix}
1 & 0 & \cdot & \cdot & \cdot & \cdot \\
1 & 4 & 1 & 0 & \cdot & \cdot \\
0 & 1 & 4 & 1 & 0 & \cdot \\
\cdot & \cdot & \cdot & \cdot & \cdot & \cdot \\
\cdot & \cdot & 0 & 1 & 4 & 1 \\
\cdot & \cdot & \cdot & \cdot & 0 & 1
\end{bmatrix}^{-1}
\begin{bmatrix}
P'_0 \\
3(P_2 - P_0) \\
\cdot \\
\cdot \\
3(P_{m-1} - P_{m-3}) \\
P'_{m-1}
\end{bmatrix}
\qquad (10.52)
$$

or

$$[P'_i] = [M]_{Cs}^{-1}[G]_{Cs} \qquad (10.53)$$

Note that the matrix $[M]_{Cs}$ is tridiagonal, that is, nonzero values appear only on the main, first upper, and first lower diagonals. Inversion of this matrix is therefore computationally less intensive. Solution of this system of m equations in m unknowns can be obtained by Gaussian elimination.

Example 10.4

Consider four two-dimensional point vectors

$$P_0[0 \quad 0] \qquad P_1[2 \quad 1] \qquad P_2[4 \quad 4] \qquad P_3[6 \quad 0]$$

with given tangent vectors $P'_0[1 \quad 1]$ and $P'_3[-1 \quad 1]$. Determine the values of the tangent vectors at P_1 and P_2 needed for a cubic spline interpolation.

Solution

The tangent vectors are found through Eq. 10.51.

$$
\begin{bmatrix} 1 & 0 & 0 & 0 \\ 1 & 4 & 1 & 0 \\ 0 & 1 & 4 & 1 \\ 0 & 0 & 0 & 1 \end{bmatrix}
\begin{bmatrix} P'_0 \\ P'_1 \\ P'_2 \\ P'_3 \end{bmatrix}
=
\begin{bmatrix} (1 & 1) \\ 3[(4-0) & (4-0)] \\ 3[(6-2) & (0-1)] \\ (-1 & 1) \end{bmatrix}
=
\begin{bmatrix} 1 & 1 \\ 12 & 12 \\ 12 & -3 \\ -1 & 1 \end{bmatrix}
$$

or

$$
\begin{bmatrix} P'_0 \\ P'_1 \\ P'_2 \\ P'_3 \end{bmatrix}
=
\begin{bmatrix} 1 & 0 & 0 & 0 \\ 1 & 4 & 1 & 0 \\ 0 & 1 & 4 & 1 \\ 0 & 0 & 0 & 1 \end{bmatrix}^{-1}
\begin{bmatrix} 1 & 1 \\ 12 & 12 \\ 12 & -3 \\ -1 & 1 \end{bmatrix}
$$

$$
\begin{bmatrix} P'_0 \\ P'_1 \\ P'_2 \\ P'_3 \end{bmatrix}
=
\frac{1}{15}
\begin{bmatrix} 15 & 0 & 0 & 0 \\ -4 & 4 & -1 & 1 \\ 1 & -1 & 4 & -4 \\ 0 & 0 & 0 & 15 \end{bmatrix}
\begin{bmatrix} 1 & 1 \\ 12 & 12 \\ 12 & -3 \\ -1 & 1 \end{bmatrix}
=
\begin{bmatrix} 1 & 1 \\ \frac{31}{15} & \frac{48}{15} \\ \frac{41}{15} & \frac{27}{15} \\ -1 & 1 \end{bmatrix}
$$

Case (b)—Eq. 10.51 is again used, and second derivatives are set to zero at the first and last points of the cubic spline. At the first point, P_0 (parameter $t = 0$), the second derivative constraint forces Eq. 10.47 to become:

$$2a_{2i} = 0$$

or

$$a_{2i} = 0 \qquad (10.54)$$

Substituting this value of a_{2i} into Eq. 10.35 yields

$$3(P_1 - P_0) - 2P'_0 - P'_1 = 0 \qquad (10.55)$$

or

$$2P'_0 + P'_1 = 3(P_1 - P_0)$$

Forcing the second derivative at the endpoint, P_{m-1} (parameter $t = 1$), also to be equal to zero yields, after substitution into Eq. 10.47 and simplification,

$$P'_{m-2} + 2P'_{m-1} = 3(P_{m-1} - P_{m-2}) \qquad (10.56)$$

The m equations in m unknowns can be represented in matrix form as follows:

$$
\begin{bmatrix}
2 & 1 & \cdot & \cdot & \cdot & \cdot & \cdot \\
1 & 4 & 1 & \cdot & \cdot & \cdot & \cdot \\
\cdot & 1 & 4 & 1 & \cdot & \cdot & \cdot \\
\cdot & \cdot & \cdot & \cdot & \cdot & \cdot & \cdot \\
\cdot & \cdot & \cdot & \cdot & 1 & 4 & 1 \\
\cdot & \cdot & \cdot & \cdot & \cdot & 1 & 2
\end{bmatrix}
\begin{bmatrix}
P'_0 \\
\cdot \\
\cdot \\
\cdot \\
\cdot \\
P'_{m-1}
\end{bmatrix}
=
\begin{bmatrix}
3(P_1 - P_0) \\
3(P_2 - P_0) \\
3(P_3 - P_1) \\
\cdot \\
3(P_{m-1} - P_{m-3}) \\
3(P_{m-1} - P_{m-2})
\end{bmatrix}
\qquad (10.57)
$$

Once the P'_i values are obtained by either case (a) or case (b), Eq. 10.44 supplies the points on the cubic spline.

Example 10.5

Solve the problem in Example 10.4, using a natural cubic spline. Calculate cubic spline values at $t = \frac{1}{3}$ and $t = \frac{2}{3}$ for each spline segment.

Solution

Eq. 10.57 is used in this problem to calculate the tangent vectors.

$$
\begin{bmatrix}
2 & 1 & 0 & 0 \\
1 & 4 & 1 & 0 \\
0 & 1 & 4 & 1 \\
0 & 0 & 1 & 2
\end{bmatrix}
\begin{bmatrix}
P'_0 \\
P'_1 \\
P'_2 \\
P'_3
\end{bmatrix}
=
\begin{bmatrix}
6 & 3 \\
12 & 12 \\
12 & -3 \\
6 & -12
\end{bmatrix}
$$

$$
\begin{bmatrix}
P'_0 \\
P'_1 \\
P'_2 \\
P'_3
\end{bmatrix}
=
\frac{1}{45}
\begin{bmatrix}
26 & -7 & 2 & -1 \\
-7 & 14 & -4 & 2 \\
2 & -4 & 14 & -7 \\
-1 & 2 & -7 & 26
\end{bmatrix}
\begin{bmatrix}
6 & 3 \\
12 & 12 \\
12 & -3 \\
6 & -12
\end{bmatrix}
$$

$$
\begin{bmatrix}
P'_0 \\
P'_1 \\
P'_2 \\
P'_3
\end{bmatrix}
=
\begin{bmatrix}
2 & 0 \\
2 & 3 \\
2 & 0 \\
2 & -6
\end{bmatrix}
$$

To find points on the curve at $t = \frac{1}{3}$ and $t = \frac{2}{3}$ in the first segment, Eqs. 10.43 and 10.44 are used.

At $t = \frac{1}{3}$

$$P(\tfrac{1}{3}) = [(\tfrac{1}{3})^3 \quad (\tfrac{1}{3})^2 \quad \tfrac{1}{3} \quad 1] \begin{bmatrix} 2 & -2 & 1 & 1 \\ -3 & 3 & -2 & -1 \\ 0 & 0 & 1 & 0 \\ 1 & 0 & 0 & 0 \end{bmatrix} \begin{bmatrix} 0 & 0 \\ 2 & 1 \\ 2 & 0 \\ 2 & 3 \end{bmatrix}$$

(for 1st segment)

$P(\tfrac{1}{3}) = [0.666 \quad 0.0372]$
(for 1st segment)

At $t = \frac{2}{3}$

$$P(\tfrac{2}{3}) = [(\tfrac{2}{3})^3 \quad (\tfrac{2}{3})^2 \quad \tfrac{2}{3} \quad 1] \begin{bmatrix} 2 & -2 & 1 & 1 \\ -3 & 3 & -2 & -1 \\ 0 & 0 & 1 & 0 \\ 1 & 0 & 0 & 0 \end{bmatrix} \begin{bmatrix} 0 & 0 \\ 2 & 1 \\ 2 & 0 \\ 2 & 3 \end{bmatrix}$$

(for 1st segment)

$P(\tfrac{2}{3}) = [1.332 \quad 0.2964]$
(for 1st segment)

The same Eqs. 11.43 and 11.44 are applied to the second and third segments. In both cases only the geometry matrix varies, the first two matrices remaining the same for each parametric value.

For the second segment:

$$[G]_H = \begin{bmatrix} 2 & 1 \\ 4 & 4 \\ 2 & 3 \\ 2 & 0 \end{bmatrix}$$

and the curve values are:

$P(\tfrac{1}{3}) = [2.666 \quad 2.223]$
(for 2nd segment)

$P(\tfrac{2}{3}) = [3.333 \quad 3.444]$
(for 2nd segment)

For the third segment:

$$[G]_H = \begin{bmatrix} 4 & 4 \\ 6 & 0 \\ 2 & 0 \\ 2 & -6 \end{bmatrix}$$

and

$P(\tfrac{1}{3}) = [4.666 \quad 3.407]$
(for 3rd segment)

$P(\tfrac{2}{3}) = [5.333 \quad 1.925]$
(for 3rd segment)

10.4.5 **Summary of Interpolation Functions**

This section summarizes the various interpolation techniques described in the previous sections.

1. *Linear Interpolation*

$$f(x) = f(x_i) + [f(x_{i+1}) - f(x_i)][(x - x_i)/d] \quad (10.25)$$

in which $d = x_{i+1} - x_i$

2. *Lagrange Polynomial*

$$f_n(x) = \sum_{i=0}^{n} y_i \prod_{\substack{j=0 \\ j \neq i}}^{n} \left(\frac{x - x_j}{x_i - x_j} \right) \quad (10.27)$$

3. *Parametric Cubic (Hermite)*

     Parametric cubic curves are represented by piecewise cubic polynomials with position and slope continuity. The parameter value varies from zero to one for each segment.

$$P(t) = [t^3 \quad t^2 \quad t \quad 1] \begin{bmatrix} 2 & -2 & 1 & 1 \\ -3 & 3 & -2 & -1 \\ 0 & 0 & 1 & 0 \\ 1 & 0 & 0 & 0 \end{bmatrix} \begin{bmatrix} P(0) \\ P(1) \\ P'(0) \\ P'(1) \end{bmatrix} \quad (10.38)$$

4. *Cubic Spline*

     Cubic splines are represented by piecewise cubic polynomials with second derivative continuity at the common joints between segments. With the parameter normalized between zero and one, the cubic spline is just a special case of the Hermite interpolation where first derivative values at the ends of each segment are so chosen as to ensure second derivative continuity.

Case (a)—Tangent vectors known at the ends:

$$P(t) = [t][M]_H[G]_H \quad (10.44)$$

and

$$\begin{bmatrix} P'_0 \\ P'_1 \\ \vdots \\ P'_{m-1} \end{bmatrix} = \begin{bmatrix} 1 & 0 & \cdot & \cdot & \cdot & \cdot \\ 1 & 4 & 1 & 0 & \cdot & \cdot \\ 0 & 1 & 4 & 1 & 0 & \cdot \\ \cdot & \cdot & \cdot & \cdot & \cdot & \cdot \\ \cdot & \cdot & 0 & 1 & 4 & 1 \\ \cdot & \cdot & \cdot & \cdot & 0 & 1 \end{bmatrix}^{-1} \begin{bmatrix} P'_0 \\ 3(P_2 - P_0) \\ \vdots \\ \vdots \\ 3(P_{m-1} - P_{m-3}) \\ P'_{m-1} \end{bmatrix} \quad (10.52)$$

Case (b)—Natural Cubic Splines, second derivatives equal to zero at the end points:

$$P(t) = [t][M]_H[G]_H \quad (10.44)$$

and

$$
\begin{bmatrix} P'_0 \\ P'_1 \\ \cdot \\ \cdot \\ P'_{m-1} \end{bmatrix} = \begin{bmatrix} 2 & 1 & \cdot & \cdot & \cdot & \cdot \\ 1 & 4 & 1 & 0 & \cdot & \cdot \\ 0 & 1 & 4 & 1 & 0 & \cdot \\ \cdot & \cdot & \cdot & \cdot & \cdot & \cdot \\ \cdot & \cdot & 0 & 1 & 4 & 1 \\ \cdot & \cdot & \cdot & \cdot & 1 & 2 \end{bmatrix}^{-1} \begin{bmatrix} 3(P_1 - P_0) \\ 3(P_2 - P_0) \\ \cdot \\ \cdot \\ 3(P_{m-1} - P_{m-3}) \\ 3(P_{m-1} - P_{m-2}) \end{bmatrix} \tag{10.57}
$$

10.5 INTERPOLATION VERSUS APPROXIMATION

Mathematical approaches to the representation of curves in CAD can be based on either interpolation or approximation theories. If the problem of curve design is a problem of data fitting, the classic interpolation solutions are used, as described in the previous sections. Other types of problems, however, cannot use these solutions. The fender of a car, the transition between the wing and the fuselage of an airplane, the hull of a ship, the handle of a coffee mug, the femur in a human leg—these apparently unrelated objects share a common feature: They are described by freeform shapes that cannot be represented in terms of analytic surfaces such as planar, cylindrical, or spherical surfaces. Figure 10.16 shows some examples. The design of freeform curves and surfaces is of utmost importance in engineering problems of this type.

Traditionally, these design problems have been dealt with by means of descriptive geometry methods. Car bodies, for example, have their outer

FIGURE 10.16 Examples of freeform shapes.

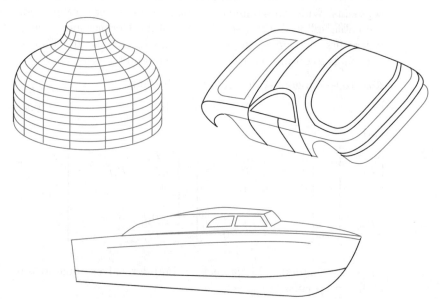

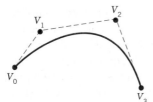

FIGURE 10.17 Curve approximates the given points, without necessarily passing through all of them.

surfaces defined by planar sections and some characteristic lines. With this information, master models are created from which the final stamps and dies are produced by means of milling machines.

The advent of the computer changed this process entirely. To begin with, milling machines driven by computer instructions were developed, leading to computerized models created by a digitizing process from existing curve and surface definitions. Soon it was possible to use a computer, instead of a master model or drawing, to design the freeform shape conceptually. The era of CAD had arrived!

In computer-aided design, particularly design problems as previously described, the most important criteria relate to the smoothness of a curve or surface. Essential to the success of a design is that the appearance of the model be acceptable to the designer's judgment, without consideration of the quality of the interpolation. It is also important that any changes in the design be localized, so modifications implemented in restricted areas do not affect the shape of the curve or surface as a whole. Approximation methods were therefore designed to satisfy these requirements at least partially. These approaches to the representation of curves provide a smooth shape that approximates the original points, without exactly passing through all of them, as shown in Figure 10.17.

Two approximation methods have become the most commonly used in present-day CAD systems—Bezier and B-spline.

10.6 BEZIER CURVES

Interpolating techniques using the parametric cubic curves described in Section 10.4 were familiar to P. Bezier of the French car company Renault. In the early 1960s, Bezier started working on a mathematical formulation to give the designer greater flexibility than the interpolating techniques. It is interesting to note that this mathematical formulation was concurrently and independently developed by P. de Casteljau of the Citroen car company. Because accounts of Bezier's work soon appeared in several publications, the theory is now known by his name.

Bezier curves employ *control points* or *control vertices*, that is, an ordered set of points $(V_0, \ldots, V_n)$ that approximate the curve (see Figure 10.17). These points can be represented on a graphics screen, and allow the user to control the shape of the curve in a predictable fashion. Bezier curves are based on polynomial functions, which are typical in the representation of freeform curves. A Bezier curve of degree n, specified by $n + 1$ control vertices, is a parametric function of the following form:

$$Q(t) = \sum_{i=0}^{n} V_i B_{i,n}(t) \tag{10.58}$$

where the vectors V_i represent the $n + 1$ control points [34]. The function $B_{i,n}(t)$ is the blending function for the Bezier representation, and is described by Bernstein polynomials as follows:

$$B_{i,n}(t) = \binom{n}{i}(t)^i(1 - t)^{n-i} \qquad 0 \le t \le 1 \tag{10.59}$$

where n is the degree of the polynomial and

$$\binom{n}{i} = \frac{n!}{i!(n - i)!} \qquad i = 0, \cdots, n \tag{10.60}$$

is the binomial coefficient.

These blending functions satisfy the following conditions:

$$B_{i,n}(t) \ge 0 \qquad \text{for all } i, \qquad 0 \le t \le 1$$
$$\sum_{i=0}^{n} B_{i,n}(t) = 1, \qquad 0 \le t \le 1 \tag{10.61}$$

The second of Eqs. 10.61 is called the "normalizing property". These conditions force the curve to lie entirely within the convex figure set by the extreme points of the polygon formed by the control points, called the *convex hull*, as shown in Figure 10.18. The convex hull can be thought of as equivalent to the polygon that would be obtained if a rubber band were stretched around all control points.

Bezier's blending functions produce an nth degree polynomial for $n + 1$ control points and, in general, force the Bezier curve to interpolate the first and last control points. This can be verified in Figure 10.18. The

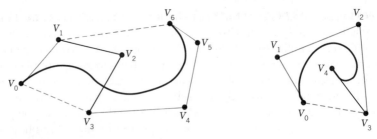

FIGURE 10.18 Bezier curves satisfy the convex hull property.

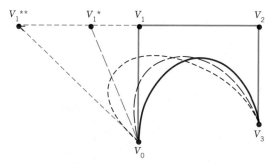

FIGURE 10.19 Changes on a Bezier curve caused by repositioning of one control point.

intermediate control points merely pull the curve toward them, and can be used to adjust the curve to the desired shape. Figure 10.19 shows the effect on the final shape of a Bezier curve of moving one control point.

As an example of the use of blending functions, consider the case of four control points V_0, V_1, V_2, V_3. Since $n + 1 = 4$, the degree n of the polynomial is 3. Expanding Eq. 10.58 yields

$$Q(t) = V_0 B_{0,3} + V_1 B_{1,3} + V_2 B_{2,3} + V_3 B_{3,3} \qquad (10.62)$$

Four blending functions must be found based on the Bernstein polynomial given in Eq. 10.59.

$$B_{0,3} = \frac{3!}{0!\ 3!}\ t^0(1 - t)^3 = (1 - t)^3$$

$$B_{1,3} = \frac{3!}{1!\ 2!}\ t^1(1 - t)^2 = 3t(1 - t)^2$$

$$\qquad (10.63)$$

$$B_{2,3} = \frac{3!}{2!\ 1!}\ t^2(1 - t) = 3t^2(1 - t)$$

$$B_{3,3} = \frac{3!}{3!\ 0!}\ t^3(1 - t)^0 = t^3$$

Note that the normalizing property applies to the blending functions, which means that they add to one.

$$[(1 - t)^3] + [3t(1 - t)^2] + [3t^2(1 - t)] + t^3 = 1 \qquad (10.64)$$

Substituting these functions into Eq. 10.62 yields

$$Q(t) = (1 - t)^3 V_0 + 3t(1 - t)^2 V_1 + 3t^2(1 - t)V_2 + t^3 V_3 \qquad (10.65)$$

Note that at

$$t = 0, \qquad Q(0) = V_0$$

$$t = 1, \qquad Q(1) = V_3$$

$$\qquad (10.66)$$

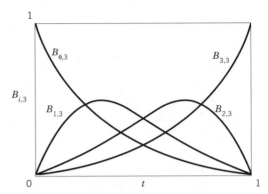

FIGURE 10.20 Plot of blending functions for a cubic Bezier curve.

which shows that the Bezier curve passes through the first and last control points, as previously stated. The blending functions at these values of the parametric variable are:

$$\text{At } t = 0, \qquad B_{0,3} = 1$$
$$\text{At } t = 1, \qquad B_{3,3} = 1 \tag{10.67}$$

and $B_{1,3} = B_{2,3} = 0$ for both cases.

A plot of the blending functions for a cubic Bezier curve is shown in Figure 10.20. Each control point is weighted by the blending function associated with it, and the influence of each point is shifted as the parametric variable increases from 0 to 1. The blending functions also force the Bezier curve to be tangent to the lines joining the first two and last two control points. Closed curves can be produced by making the first and last points of the control polygon coincide, as shown in Figure 10.21.

The Bernstein polynomials used as blending functions for Bezier curves approximate an array of control points with a single polynomial curve. The degree of the resulting shape, therefore, depends on the number of control

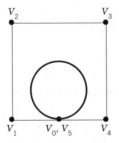

FIGURE 10.21 Closed curves are obtained by making the first and last control points coincide.

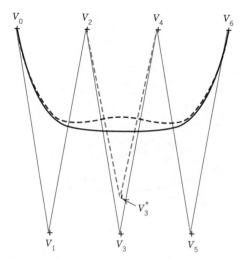

FIGURE 10.22 Bezier curves lack local control.

points. These curves are said to lack local control; that is, moving the position of one control point alters the shape of the entire curve segment. Figure 10.22 shows one such example.

For improved design flexibility a large number of control points is necessary, resulting in a high-degree polynomial that can be difficult to handle. To keep the degree of the curve low and still obtain the required design flexibility, curves with a large number of control points are generated by connecting several segments of lower degree, as shown in Figure 10.23. Here, two segments—V_0 V_1 V_2 V_3 V_4 and V_0^* V_1^* V_2^* V_3^* V_4^*—were used. C^1 continuity is usually applied to piecewise Bezier curves, which also implies C^0 continuity. To ensure this condition, control polygon sides converging at a joint between segments must form a straight line. In other words, the control point joining two segments and the points immediately before and after it must be colinear. Figure 10.23 shows these conditions—the connecting control point V_4, which is also V_0^*, joins V_3 and V_1^* in a straight line.

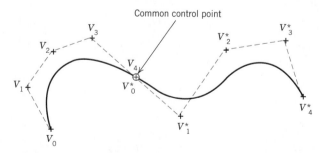

FIGURE 10.23 Piecewise Bezier curve.

FIGURE 10.24 (*a*) Curve traces representing an airfoil, created by joining two Bezier segments with C^0 continuity. The control polygons for the segments are: V_0, V_1, V_2, V_3 and V_0, V_4, V_5, V_3. (*b*) Curve traces simulating the shape of a car body, formed by several cubic Bezier segments joined with C^1 continuity.

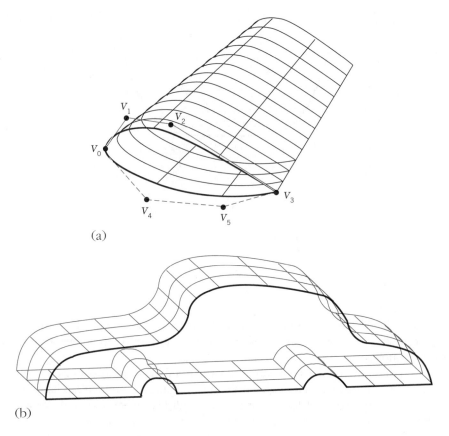

(a)

(b)

Applications of the Bezier formulation are shown in Figure 10.24a and b. An algorithm for the generation of three-dimensional Bezier curves with *n* control points is given in Appendix 10.4.

10.6.1 Matrix Form

Bezier curves can be conveniently expressed in matrix form. Consider, for example, the cubic Bezier curve given in Eq. 10.65. It can be rewritten in matrix form as

$$Q(t) = [(1-t)^3 \quad 3t(1-t)^2 \quad 3t^2(1-t) \quad t^3] \begin{bmatrix} V_0 \\ V_1 \\ V_2 \\ V_3 \end{bmatrix} \quad (10.68)$$

or

$$Q(t) = [(1 - 3t + 3t^2 - t^3) \ (3t - 6t^2 + 3t^3) \ (3t^2 - 3t^3) \ t^3] \begin{bmatrix} V_0 \\ V_1 \\ V_2 \\ V_3 \end{bmatrix} \quad (10.69)$$

which can be reduced to

$$Q(t) = [t^3 \quad t^2 \quad t \quad 1] \begin{bmatrix} -1 & 3 & -3 & 1 \\ 3 & -6 & 3 & 0 \\ -3 & 3 & 0 & 0 \\ 1 & 0 & 0 & 0 \end{bmatrix} \begin{bmatrix} V_0 \\ V_1 \\ V_2 \\ V_3 \end{bmatrix} \qquad (10.70)$$

In more compact form,

$$Q(t) = \underset{(1 \times 4)}{[t]} \quad \underset{(4 \times 4)}{[M]_\text{B}} \quad \underset{(4 \times 1)}{[V]_\text{B}} \qquad (10.71)$$

Example 10.6

The slope continuity (C^1) requirement of Bezier curves forces two curves to share the same parametric slope at the common point. Given two Bezier curves defined by the following sequence of control points,

1st curve: $A(2,3,4)$ $B(3,1,5)$ $C(x,y,z)$ $D(3,4,3)$

2nd curve: $D(3,4,3)$ $E(2,6,0)$ $F(5,7,5)$ $G(5,2,3)$

establish the algebraic conditions that x, y, z must satisfy to ensure C^1 continuity.

Solution:

Eq. 10.68 can be differentiated with respect to t to find the tangent vectors:

$$Q'(t) = [-3(1 - t)^2 \quad 3(3t^2 - 4t + 1) \quad -3t(3t - 2) \quad 3t^2] \begin{bmatrix} V_0 \\ V_1 \\ V_2 \\ V_3 \end{bmatrix}$$

To ensure C^1 continuity at the joint between segments, $Q'(t)$ at $t = 1$ for the first segment should equal $Q'(t)$ at $t = 0$ for the second segment.
First segment ($t = 1$):

$$Q'_1(1) = [0 \quad 0 \quad -3 \quad 3] \begin{bmatrix} A \\ B \\ C \\ D \end{bmatrix} = 3(D - C)$$

Second segment ($t = 0$):

$$Q'_2(0) = [-3 \quad 3 \quad 0 \quad 0] \begin{bmatrix} D \\ E \\ F \\ G \end{bmatrix} = 3(E - D)$$

As previously stated:

$$Q'_1(1) = Q'_2(0)$$

To take into account variable magnitudes for the tangent vector (slope remains constant), this equality can be written as:

$$Q_1'(1) = kQ_2'(0)$$

where k is a constant.
Substituting appropriate values:

$$3(D - C) = 3k(E - D)$$

$$3[(3 \quad 4 \quad 3) - (x \quad y \quad z)] = 3k[(2 \quad 6 \quad 0) - (3 \quad 4 \quad 3)]$$

or

$$3[(3 - x)(4 - y)(3 - z)] = 3k[-1 \quad 2 \quad -3]$$

And the algebraic conditions are

$$\begin{aligned} 3 - x &= -k \rightarrow x = 3 + k \\ 4 - y &= 2k \;\; \rightarrow y = 4 - 2k \\ 3 - z &= -3k \rightarrow z = 3 + 3k \end{aligned}$$

10.7 B-SPLINE CURVES

As seen in the previous section, Bezier blending functions make use of Bernstein polynomials which depend on the number of control points available. These curves possess what is called global control—the movement of a single control vertex affects the entire curve. To avoid high-degree polynomials and reduce the global effect, Bezier curves are frequently built by connecting several segments of lower degree. This permits local control and the freedom to alter the degree at the expense of continuity. Each segment of the resulting Bezier curve has the properties previously mentioned, but the composite curve has different properties. The method chosen for piecing together the individual segments depends on the desired degree of continuity. If the pieces simply share end vertices, C^0 continuity occurs. Higher order continuity is obtained only by imposing geometric constraints on the placement of vertices (see Figure 10.23).

An alternative to Bernstein polynomials is the use of B-spline blending functions which generate a single piecewise parametric polynomial curve through any number of control points. The degree of the polynomial can be selected by the designer independently of the number of control points. It is the degree of the blending or basis function that controls the degree of the resulting B-spline curve [35,36,37]. B-spline curves exhibit local control, that is, if one vertex is moved only some curve segments are affected and the rest of the curve remains invariant. Continuity among B-spline segments is a function of the degree of the basis function. Continuity is, therefore, a major factor in narrowing down the choices of degree available to the designer. For applications such as the design of freeform curves, where the smoothness is a critical factor, the curvature continuity, C^2, guaranteed by cubic B-splines is preferred.

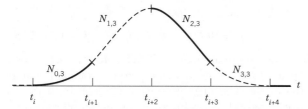

FIGURE 10.25 Uniform cubic B-spline basis functions, $N_i(t)$.

10.7.1 Uniform Cubic B-splines

As a starting point in the study of B-splines, and to simplify the problem, a particularly useful type called *uniform cubic* B-spline will be studied first. The uniform cubic B-spline, $N_i(t)$, is a cubic C^2 basis function as shown in Figure 10.25. The parametric intervals or *knots*, t, within which the basis function is defined, are equal, and that is why they are called uniform or periodic.

The knots form a vector of real numbers called the *knot vector*, in nondecreasing order. The function is centered at t_{i+2} and has a zero value for $t < t_i$ and for $t > t_{i+4}$. The nonzero portion of the function is composed of four cubic polynomials, $N_{0,3}$ $N_{1,3}$ $N_{2,3}$ $N_{3,3}$. A B-spline curve is obtained by multiplying this approximation function by a subset of four control points in the vicinity of the curve, and can be represented by the following equation:

$$P_i(t) = N_{0,3}(t)V_i + N_{1,3}(t)V_{i+1} + N_{2,3}(t)V_{i+2} + N_{3,3}(t)V_{i+3} \quad (10.72)$$

Figure 10.26 shows a uniform cubic B-spline curve through six control vertices. In Eq. 10.72 the control vertices are indicated by the V values. To determine the basis function, we first define each of the four segments by a

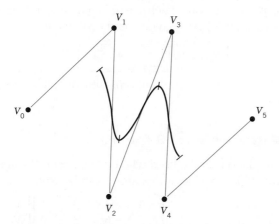

FIGURE 10.26 Uniform cubic B-spline curve with six control points.

general cubic polynomial of the form

$$N_{j,3}(t) = a_j + b_j t + c_j t^2 + d_j t^3 \qquad j = 0, 1, 2, 3 \qquad (10.73)$$

The sixteen unknown polynomial coefficients, four for each segment of the basis function, are found from sixteen equations obtained by imposing constraints on the curve. The first six equations result from the fact that the function and its first and second derivatives are identically zero at the left and right endpoints, such that

$$N_{0,3}(0) = N'_{0,3}(0) = N''_{0,3}(0) = 0 \qquad \text{at the left end}$$

$$N_{3,3}(1) = N'_{3,3}(1) = N''_{3,3}(1) = 0 \qquad \text{at the right end}$$

C^0, C^1, and C^2 continuity requirements at the three internal knots of the basis function give rise to nine more equations. These equations can be obtained by locally parameterizing the B-spline segments from $t = 0$ to $t = 1$. Fifteen equations have now been established, and the last one is obtained by imposing the normalizing condition previously defined in Section 10.6. Thus

$$N_{0,3}(t) + N_{1,3}(t) + N_{2,3}(t) + N_{3,3}(t) = 1 \qquad 0 \le t \le 1$$

Solving this set of sixteen simultaneous equations yields the following four polynomial segments comprising the B-spline basis function:

$$
\begin{aligned}
N_{0,3}(t) &= \tfrac{1}{6}t^3 \qquad [0 \le t \le 1] \\
N_{1,3}(t) &= \tfrac{1}{6}(-3t^3 + 3t^2 + 3t + 1) \\
N_{2,3}(t) &= \tfrac{1}{6}(3t^3 - 6t^2 + 4) \\
N_{3,3}(t) &= \tfrac{1}{6}(-t^3 + 3t^2 - 3t + 1)
\end{aligned}
\qquad (10.74)
$$

To generate a uniform cubic B-spline curve, four control vertices are multiplied at a time with the basis functions given in Eqs. 10.74. The curve is generated in a piecewise fashion, using four new consecutive control vertices and the same basis functions. Each curve segment shares three common control vertices with the next segment, as shown below:

| V_0 | V_1 | V_2 | V_3 | V_4 | V_5 | $\cdots$ |

An algorithm for the generation of uniform cubic B-spline curves is given in Appendix 10.5.

10.7.2   Matrix Form for B-splines

The matrix formulation can be used when dealing with B-splines. Eq. 10.74 for the uniform cubic B-spline, for example, can be written as:

$$P_i(t) = \tfrac{1}{6}[t^3 \quad t^2 \quad t \quad 1]
\begin{bmatrix}
-1 & 3 & -3 & 1 \\
3 & -6 & 3 & 0 \\
-3 & 0 & 3 & 0 \\
1 & 4 & 1 & 0
\end{bmatrix}
\begin{bmatrix}
V_{i-1} \\
V_i \\
V_{i+1} \\
V_{i+2}
\end{bmatrix}
\qquad (10.75)$$

or, in more concise form,

$$P(t) = \tfrac{1}{6}[t][M]_{Bs}[V]_{Bs} \tag{10.76}$$

Note that uniform B-splines of other degrees can also be represented in matrix form. The uniform quadratic B-spline, for example, can be formulated like the cubic, starting from a quadratic polynomial. Its representation in matrix form is

$$P_i(t) = \tfrac{1}{2}[t^2 \quad t \quad 1]\begin{bmatrix} 1 & -2 & 1 \\ -2 & 2 & 0 \\ 1 & 1 & 0 \end{bmatrix}\begin{bmatrix} V_{i-1} \\ V_i \\ V_{i+1} \end{bmatrix} \tag{10.77}$$

In this case only three control vertices are used, as shown in Figure 10.27.

Uniform B-splines are well suited to represent closed curves. All that is needed is a change in the number of segments used. Consider Figure 10.28, representing a closed quadratic B-spline curve produced by six control points. The B-spline has six segments, created as follows:

Segment	Control Vertices		
1	V_0	V_1	V_2
2	V_1	V_2	V_3
3	V_2	V_3	V_4
4	V_3	V_4	V_5
5	V_4	V_5	V_0
6	V_5	V_0	V_1

A more general discussion of B-splines is given in Section 10.9.

Example 10.7

Find the starting and ending locations for a uniform quadratic B-spline segment.

Solution

Eq. 10.77 will be used in the solution of this problem. Knowing that the segment starts at $t = 0$ and ends at $t = 1$, substitution into Eq. 10.77 yields:

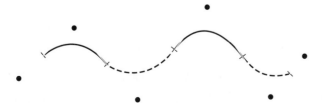

FIGURE 10.27 Uniform quadratic B-spline curve.

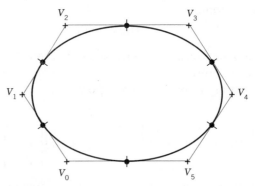

FIGURE 10.28 Closed quadratic uniform B-spline curve.

For $t = 0$

$$P_i(0) = \tfrac{1}{2}[0 \quad 0 \quad 1]\begin{bmatrix} 1 & -2 & 1 \\ -2 & 2 & 0 \\ 1 & 1 & 0 \end{bmatrix}\begin{bmatrix} V_{i-1} \\ V_i \\ V_{i+1} \end{bmatrix}$$

$$P_i(0) = \tfrac{1}{2}(V_{i-1} + V_i)$$

For $t = 1$

$$P_i(1) = \tfrac{1}{2}[1 \quad 1 \quad 1]\begin{bmatrix} 1 & -2 & 1 \\ -2 & 2 & 0 \\ 1 & 1 & 0 \end{bmatrix}\begin{bmatrix} V_{i-1} \\ V_i \\ V_{i+1} \end{bmatrix}$$

$$P_i(1) = \tfrac{1}{2}(V_i + V_{i+1})$$

Thus, for uniform quadratic B-splines, the joints between segments are located halfway between the control vertices, as shown in Figure 10.29.

Example 10.8

Use four control vertices to approximate a circle by a closed, uniform, quadratic B-spline. Check the error incurred in the approximation at $t = 0.5$ in the first segment.

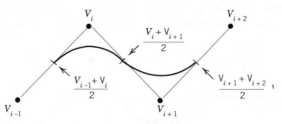

FIGURE 10.29 Location of joints between uniform quadratic B-spline segments.

Solution

In this solution the circle is assumed to have its center at the origin of the coordinate axis (see accompanying figure). Since this is a quadratic B-spline approximation, each of the four segments—I, II, III, IV—will be formed by three control vertices, as follows:

$$\begin{array}{llll}
\text{Segment} & \text{I—} & V_0 & V_1 & V_2 \\
\text{Segment} & \text{II—} & V_1 & V_2 & V_3 \\
\text{Segment} & \text{III—} & V_2 & V_3 & V_0 \\
\text{Segment} & \text{IV—} & V_3 & V_0 & V_1
\end{array}$$

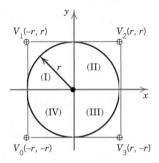

Each segment is obtained using equation 10.77. Segment I, for example, will be as follows:

$$P(t) = \tfrac{1}{2}[t^2 \quad t \quad 1]\begin{bmatrix} 1 & -2 & 1 \\ -2 & 2 & 0 \\ 1 & 1 & 0 \end{bmatrix}\begin{bmatrix} -r & -r \\ -r & r \\ r & r \end{bmatrix}$$

To find the error incurred in this formulation, calculate the value of P for $t = \tfrac{1}{2}$. If the exact circle had been generated, this value should be equal to the radius, r. Substituting $t = \tfrac{1}{2}$ into the equation above yields

$$P(\tfrac{1}{2}) = [\tfrac{1}{8} \quad \tfrac{3}{4} \quad \tfrac{1}{8}]\begin{bmatrix} -r & -r \\ -r & r \\ r & r \end{bmatrix}$$

$$P(\tfrac{1}{2}) = [-\tfrac{3}{4}r \quad \tfrac{3}{4}r]$$

And the radius becomes $\left(\dfrac{3\sqrt{2}}{4}\right)r$

or

$$1.061r$$

The error is approximately 6.1%, at $t = 0.5$ in the first segment.

10.8 CONVERSION BETWEEN REPRESENTATIONS

As seen in earlier sections, a freeform cubic curve is described by equations of the form:

$$x = [t^3 \quad t^2 \quad t \quad 1][M][V] \tag{10.78}$$

where $[V]$ is the matrix of control points (or geometric coefficients) and $[M]$ is the basis matrix. Corresponding values of y and z can be similarly found.

A summary of the basis matrices $[M]$ is given in Table 10.2 for cubic curves parameterized in the interval $0 \leq t \leq 1$ [38]. To change from one type of curve to another, the following expression can be used:

$$x = [t^3 \quad t^2 \quad t \quad 1][M_{\text{from}}[V]_{\text{from}} = [t^3 \quad t^2 \quad t \quad 1][M]_{\text{to}}[V]_{\text{to}} \tag{10.79}$$

which yields

$$[M]_{\text{from}}[V]_{\text{from}} = [M]_{\text{to}}[V]_{\text{to}} \tag{10.80}$$

and

$$[V]_{\text{to}} = [M]_{\text{to}}^{-1}[M]_{\text{from}}[V]_{\text{from}}$$

Table 10.3 shows the conversion matrices $\{[M]_{\text{to}}^{-1}[M]_{\text{from}}\}$ for the various types of freeform cubic curves.

Example 10.9

Given a cubic Bezier curve represented by the control points $P_1(-6,0,0)$, $P_2(-3, 4, 0)$, $P_3(3, -4,0)$ and $P_4(6, 0, 0)$, find:

(a) The control points that would reproduce this curve as a uniform cubic B-spline.

(b) The geometric coefficient matrix that would reproduce this curve as a Hermite.

TABLE 10.2

Hermite				Bezier				B-Spline			
2	−2	1	1	−1	3	−3	1	−1	3	−3	1
−3	3	−2	−1	3	−6	3	0	3	−6	3	0
0	0	1	0	−3	3	0	0	−3	0	3	0
1	0	0	0	1	0	0	0	1	4	1	0

(B-Spline matrix multiplied by $\frac{1}{6}$)

TABLE 10.3

From → To ↓	Hermite	Bezier	B-Spline
Hermite	$\begin{bmatrix} 1 & 0 & 0 & 0 \\ 0 & 1 & 0 & 0 \\ 0 & 0 & 1 & 0 \\ 0 & 0 & 0 & 1 \end{bmatrix}$	$\begin{bmatrix} 1 & 0 & 0 & 0 \\ 0 & 0 & 0 & 1 \\ -3 & 3 & 0 & 0 \\ 0 & 0 & -3 & 3 \end{bmatrix}$	$\frac{1}{6}\begin{bmatrix} 1 & 4 & 1 & 0 \\ 0 & 1 & 4 & 1 \\ -3 & 0 & 3 & 0 \\ 0 & -3 & 0 & 3 \end{bmatrix}$
Bezier	$\frac{1}{3}\begin{bmatrix} 3 & 0 & 0 & 0 \\ 3 & 0 & 1 & 0 \\ 0 & 3 & 0 & -1 \\ 0 & 3 & 0 & 0 \end{bmatrix}$	$\begin{bmatrix} 1 & 0 & 0 & 0 \\ 0 & 1 & 0 & 0 \\ 0 & 0 & 1 & 0 \\ 0 & 0 & 0 & 1 \end{bmatrix}$	$\frac{1}{6}\begin{bmatrix} 1 & 4 & 1 & 0 \\ 0 & 4 & 2 & 0 \\ 0 & 2 & 4 & 0 \\ 0 & 1 & 4 & 1 \end{bmatrix}$
B-Spline	$\frac{1}{3}\begin{bmatrix} -3 & 6 & -7 & -2 \\ 6 & -3 & 2 & 1 \\ -3 & 6 & -1 & -2 \\ 6 & -3 & 2 & 7 \end{bmatrix}$	$\begin{bmatrix} 6 & -7 & 2 & 0 \\ 0 & 2 & -1 & 0 \\ 0 & -1 & 2 & 0 \\ 0 & 2 & -7 & 6 \end{bmatrix}$	$\begin{bmatrix} 1 & 0 & 0 & 0 \\ 0 & 1 & 0 & 0 \\ 0 & 0 & 1 & 0 \\ 0 & 0 & 0 & 1 \end{bmatrix}$

Solution

(a) From Table 10.3 the conversion from a cubic Bezier representation to a cubic uniform B-spline is obtained, so that

$$[V]_{Bs} = \begin{bmatrix} 6 & -7 & 2 & 0 \\ 0 & 2 & -1 & 0 \\ 0 & -1 & 2 & 0 \\ 0 & 2 & -7 & 6 \end{bmatrix} \begin{bmatrix} -6 & 0 & 0 & 1 \\ -3 & 4 & 0 & 1 \\ 3 & -4 & 0 & 1 \\ 6 & 0 & 0 & 1 \end{bmatrix}$$

and

$$[V]_{Bs} = \begin{bmatrix} -9 & -36 & 0 & 1 \\ -9 & 12 & 0 & 1 \\ 9 & -12 & 0 & 1 \\ 9 & 36 & 0 & 1 \end{bmatrix}$$

(b) Again from Table 10.3, the conversion is given by

$$[V]_{H} = [G]_{H} = \begin{bmatrix} 1 & 0 & 0 & 0 \\ 0 & 0 & 0 & 1 \\ -3 & 3 & 0 & 0 \\ 0 & 0 & -3 & 3 \end{bmatrix} \begin{bmatrix} -6 & 0 & 0 & 1 \\ -3 & 4 & 0 & 1 \\ 3 & -4 & 0 & 1 \\ 6 & 0 & 0 & 1 \end{bmatrix}$$

and

$$[V]_{\mathrm{H}} = \begin{bmatrix} -6 & 0 & 0 & 1 \\ 6 & 0 & 0 & 1 \\ 9 & 12 & 0 & 1 \\ 9 & 12 & 0 & 1 \end{bmatrix}$$

10.9 GENERAL B-SPLINE REPRESENTATION

In a more general form, B-spline curves can be represented in terms of their blending functions, as was done for the Bezier curves.

$$P(t) = \sum_{i=0}^{n} N_{i,k}(t) V_i \qquad (10.81)$$

where V_i is the set of control points and $N_{i,k}$ represents the appropriate blending functions of degree $(k - 1)$. A spline is said to be of order k or degree $(k - 1)$ when defined mathematically as a piecewise $(k - 1)$st degree polynomial that is C^{k-2} continuous. In other words

(a) The degree of the polynomial does not exceed $(k - 1)$ inside each $[t_i, t_{i+1}]$ interval;

(b) The position and $[1$ to $(k - 2)]$ derivatives are continuous.

For the case of the cubic B-spline described in the previous section:

- $k = 4$
- Degree $= (k - 1) = 3$
- Second degree continuity is satisfied

The ith blending function $N_{i,k}(t)$ is defined by the following recursive equation:

$$N_{i,1}(t) = \begin{bmatrix} 1 & \text{for } t_i \le t \le t_{i+1} \\ 0 & \text{otherwise} \end{bmatrix}$$

and $\qquad (10.82)$

$$N_{i,k}(t) = \frac{(t - t_i)}{(t_{i+k-1} - t_i)} N_{i,k-1}(t) + \frac{(t_{i+k} - t)}{(t_{i+k} - t_{i+1})} N_{i+1,\,k-1}(t)$$

where the knot vector is $[t_i, \ldots, t_{i+k}]$.

Equation 10.82 can be expressed in words as "a B-spline of order k in the ith span is the weighted average of the B-splines of order $(k - 1)$ in the ith and $(i + 1)$st spans." The weights are given by the expressions within parentheses in Eq. 10.82. The only constraints imposed on the knot vector are:

- It must be of nondecreasing order, that is, the values of the elements t_i of the knot vector must satisfy the relationship

$$t_i \leq t_{i+1}$$

- The same value should not appear more than k times, that is, no more times than the order of the spline. These same value knots are usually referred to as *multiple knots*.

The knot vector has a significant influence on the blending functions $N_{i,k}(t)$ and thereby on the B-spline curve itself.

Like Bezier curves, B-splines satisfy the convex-hull property and the normalizing property. The last one insures that

$$\sum_{i=0}^{n} N_{i,k}(t) \equiv 1$$

In any B-spline curve, the degree $(k - 1)$, the number of control points, and the number of knots are related to each other. Assuming a knot vector $[t_0, \ldots, t_m]$, this relationship becomes

$$
\begin{array}{ccccc}
(m + 1) & = & (n + 1) & + & k \\
\downarrow & & \downarrow & & \downarrow \\
\text{no. of knots} & & \text{no. of control} & & \text{order} \\
 & & \text{points} & & \text{of curve}
\end{array}
\tag{10.83}
$$

or

$$m = n + k \tag{10.84}$$

The knot vector is, therefore, $[t_0, \ldots, t_{n+k}]$. These knot vectors can be classified as:

- Uniform/periodic
- Nonperiodic
- Nonuniform

Since the knot vectors influence the shape of the B-spline, it can be said, in general, that B-spline curves have this classification.

10.9.1 Uniform/Periodic

A uniform knot vector has equispaced t_i values, so that $[(t_i - t_{i-1}) = a]$ for all intervals, and a is a real number. For example,

$$[0 \quad 1 \quad 2 \quad 3 \quad 4] \quad \text{with } a = 1$$

$$[-0.5 \quad 0.0 \quad 0.5 \quad 1.0 \quad 1.5] \quad \text{with } a = 0.5$$

In most practical applications, the knot sequence starts at zero and often is

TABLE 10.4

Degree $(k - 1)$	Order (k)	Knot Vector $(m = n + k)$	Parameter Range $(k - 1) \leq t \leq (n + 1)$
1	2	[0 1 2 3 4 5 6 7]	$1 \leq t \leq 6$
2	3	[0 1 2 3 4 5 6 7 8]	$2 \leq t \leq 6$
3	4	[0 1 2 3 4 5 6 7 8 9]	$3 \leq t \leq 6$

normalized in the range [0 to 1]; for example,

$$[0 \quad \tfrac{1}{4} \quad \tfrac{1}{2} \quad \tfrac{3}{4} \quad 1]$$

Frequently, too, each segment of the B-spline curve is locally normalized as done in the case of the uniform cubic B-spline described earlier (Section 10.7.1).

Uniform knot vectors are also periodic, that is, the B-spline functions for each segment are all translates of each other. The influence of each basis function is limited to k (order of the curve) intervals. Therefore, if a cubic curve is used, the "local basis" of the function spreads over four intervals, as shown in Section 10.7.1 on the uniform cubic B-spline. Note that a periodic B-spline does not interpolate the first and last control polygon vertices, except for $k = 2$, that is, linear curves. Figure 10.30 shows examples of periodic B-splines of various degrees, calculated within the same control polygon. For $k = 2$ (degree 1) the curve coincides with the control polygon. For $k = 3$ (degree 2), the B-spline starts at the midpoint of the first polygon side and ends at the midpoint of the last. There is, therefore, a loss of parameter range for the curve (visually shown as a reduction in the curve size in Figure 10.32) as the degree increases. This is represented by the expression $(k - 1) \leq t \leq (n + 1)$. Table 10.4 shows the variation of the parameter range and knot vector for the B-spline curves shown in Figure 10.30. Remember that the number of knot vectors is controlled by the expression $m = n + k$ (Eq. 10.84). For the cases shown in Table 10.4, the number of control points $(n + 1)$ is equal to 6.

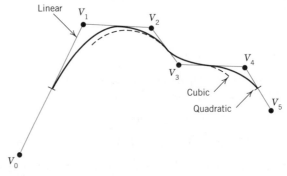

FIGURE 10.30 Uniform B-splines of various degrees.

10.9.2 Nonperiodic

A nonperiodic or open knot vector has repeated knot values at the ends with multiplicity equal to the order of the function k and internal knots equally spaced. For example, assuming a control polygon with four vertices:

Order (k)	No. of knots (m = n + k)	Nonperiodic knot vector
2	6	[0 0 1 2 3 3]
3	7	[0 0 0 1 2 2 2]
4	8	[0 0 0 0 1 1 1 1]

These curves are shown in Figure 10.31. In general terms, the following expressions must be satisfied for a knot t_i in a nonperiodic knot vector starting at t_0:

$$t_i = 0 \rightarrow i < k$$

$$t_i = i - k + 1 \rightarrow k \le i \le n \tag{10.85}$$

$$t_i = n - k + 2 \rightarrow i > n$$

The list of nonperiodic knot vectors given previously in this section can be seen to satisfy these expressions. Note that the nonperiodic knot vector provides basis functions defined in the complete parameter range. No loss occurs, as seen on the periodic formulation, and the curve always interpolates the first and last control vertices. Figure 10.32 shows a cubic ($k = 4$) nonperiodic B-spline over seven control points and the local variation of the curve when one of the control points is moved.

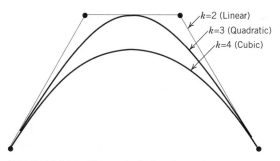

k=2 (Linear)
k=3 (Quadratic)
k=4 (Cubic)

FIGURE 10.31 Nonperiodic B-splines of various degrees (or order).

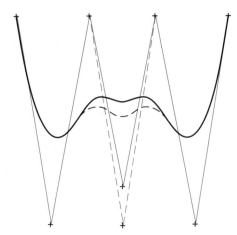

FIGURE 10.32 Cubic nonperiodic B-spline exhibiting local control.

The Bezier representation described in Section 10.6 is a special case of a nonperiodic B-spline, where the number of vertices used equals the order of the curve. The knot vector, in this case, becomes

$$[\underbrace{0 \quad 0 \quad \cdots \quad 0}_{k} \quad \underbrace{1 \quad 1 \quad \cdots \quad 1}_{k}]$$

In Figure 10.31, the cubic B-spline curve with four control points and a nonperiodic knot vector [0 0 0 0 1 1 1 1] is also a Bezier curve.

10.9.3 Nonuniform

In the nonperiodic knot vector, multiplicity of knot values occurred at the ends and the internal knots were equispaced. If either or both of these conditions is not satisfied, the knot vector is said to be nonuniform.

A nonuniform knot sequence can be obtained by the introduction of multiple interior knot values, such as

$$[0 \quad 1 \quad 2 \quad 3 \quad 3 \quad 4]$$

or by unequal spacing between the knots

$$[0.0 \quad 0.20 \quad 0.55 \quad 0.75 \quad 1.0]$$

Although a uniform knot spacing is easy to use, there are advantages to the availability of nonuniform spacing for shape control in the design process. For example, undesirable oscillations may occur when using a uniform B-spline curve with highly unevenly spaced data points. Figure 10.33 shows examples of nonuniform B-splines.

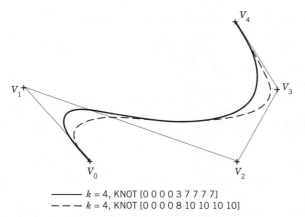

$$\text{——— } k = 4, \text{ KNOT } [0\ 0\ 0\ 0\ 3\ 7\ 7\ 7\ 7]$$
$$\text{– – – } k = 4, \text{ KNOT } [0\ 0\ 0\ 0\ 8\ 10\ 10\ 10\ 10]$$

FIGURE 10.33 Nonuniform cubic B-splines.

10.9.4 B-spline Recursive Formulation

The general recursive formulation given in Eq. 10.82 is used in this section to find a series of lower degree B-splines. The knot vectors in these splines can themselves vary, according to the classifications described in sections 10.9.1, 10.9.2, and 10.9.3. In the following derivation, the blending functions *N* for B-splines of order 1 (constant), 2 (linear), 3 (quadratic), and 4 (cubic) are described as a function of the knot vector, using Eq. 10.82.

$k = 1$—Constant

$$N_{i,1}(t) = \begin{cases} 1 & t_i \leq t < t_{i+1} \\ 0 & \text{otherwise} \end{cases} \tag{10.86}$$

$k = 2$—Linear

$$N_{i,2}(t) = \frac{(t - t_i)}{(t_{i+1} - t_i)} N_{i,1}(t) + \frac{(t_{i+2} - t)}{(t_{i+2} - t_{i+1})} N_{i+1,1}(t) \tag{10.87}$$

which can be written as:

$$N_{i,2}(t) = \begin{cases} \dfrac{(t - t_i)}{(t_{i+1} - t_i)} & t_i \leq t < t_{i+1} \\[2mm] \dfrac{(t_{i+2} - t)}{(t_{i+2} - t_{i+1})} & t_{i+1} \leq t \leq t_{i+2} \end{cases} \tag{10.88}$$

$k = 3$—Quadratic

$$N_{i,3}(t) = \frac{(t - t_i)}{(t_{i+2} - t_i)} N_{i,2}(t) + \frac{(t_{i+3} - t)}{(t_{i+3} - t_{i+1})} N_{i+1,2}(t) \tag{10.89}$$

From Eq. 10.88 the value of $N_{i+1,2}(t)$ can be found:

$$N_{i+1,2}(t) = \begin{cases} \dfrac{(t - t_{i+1})}{(t_{i+2} - t_{i+1})} & t_{i+1} \leq t < t_{i+2} \\[3mm] \dfrac{(t_{i+3} - t)}{(t_{i+3} - t_{i+2})} & t_{i+2} \leq t \leq t_{i+3} \end{cases} \tag{10.90}$$

Substituting Eqs. 10.90 and 10.88 into Eq. 10.89 yields the expression for $N_{i,3}(t)$:

$$N_{i,3}(t) = \frac{(t - t_i)^2}{(t_{i+2} - t_i)(t_{i+1} - t_i)} \qquad t_i \leq t < t_{i+1} \tag{10.91}$$

$$\left. N_{i,3}(t) = \begin{aligned} &\frac{(t_{i+2} - t)(t - t_i)}{(t_{i+2} - t_{i+1})(t_{i+2} - t_i)} \\[2mm] +\, &\frac{(t_{i+3} - t)(t - t_{i+1})}{(t_{i+3} - t_{i+1})(t_{i+2} - t_{i+1})} \end{aligned} \right\} \quad t_{i+1} \leq t < t_{i+2} \tag{10.92}$$

$$N_{i,3}(t) = \frac{(t_{i+3} - t)^2}{(t_{i+3} - t_{i+1})(t_{i+3} - t_{i+2})} \qquad t_{i+2} \leq t \leq t_{i+3} \tag{10.93}$$

$k = 4$—Cubic

$$N_{i,4}(t) = \frac{(t - t_i)}{(t_{i+3} - t_i)} N_{i,3}(t) + \frac{(t_{i+4} - t)}{(t_{i+4} - t_{i+1})} N_{i+1,3}(t) \tag{10.94}$$

From Eqs. 10.91, 10.92, and 10.93 the value of $N_{i+1,3}$ can be found. Following a procedure similar to the one used for the quadratic blending functions, the cubics can be written as

$$N_{i,4}(t) = \frac{(t - t_i)^3}{(t_{i+1} - t_i)(t_{i+2} - t_i)(t_{i+3} - t_i)} \qquad t_i \leq t < t_{i+1} \tag{10.95}$$

$$\left. N_{i,4}(t) = \begin{aligned} &\frac{(t - t_i)^2(t_{i+2} - t)}{(t_{i+3} - t_i)(t_{i+2} - t_i)(t_{i+2} - t_{i+1})} \\[2mm] +\, &\frac{(t - t_i)(t_{i+3} - t)(t - t_{i+1})}{(t_{i+3} - t_i)(t_{i+3} - t_{i+1})(t_{i+2} - t_{i+1})} \\[2mm] +\, &\frac{(t_{i+4} - t)(t - t_{i+1})^2}{(t_{i+4} - t_{i+1})(t_{i+3} - t_{i+1})(t_{i+2} - t_{i+1})} \end{aligned} \right\} \quad t_{i+1} \leq t < t_{i+2} \tag{10.96}$$

$$\left. N_{i,4}(t) = \begin{aligned} &\frac{(t - t_i)(t_{i+3} - t)^2}{(t_{i+3} - t_i)(t_{i+3} - t_{i+1})(t_{i+3} - t_{i+2})} \\[2mm] +\, &\frac{(t_{i+4} - t)(t - t_{i+1})(t_{i+3} - t)}{(t_{i+4} - t_{i+1})(t_{i+3} - t_{i+1})(t_{i+3} - t_{i+2})} \\[2mm] +\, &\frac{(t_{i+4} - t)^2(t - t_{i+2})}{(t_{i+4} - t_{i+1})(t_{i+4} - t_{i+2})(t_{i+3} - t_{i+2})} \end{aligned} \right\} \quad t_{i+2} \leq t < t_{i+3} \tag{10.97}$$

$$N_{i,4}(t) = \frac{(t_{i+4} - t)^3}{(t_{i+4} - t_{i+1})(t_{i+4} - t_{i+2})(t_{i+4} - t_{i+3})} \qquad t_{i+3} \leq t \leq t_{i+4} \tag{10.98}$$

Example 10.10

Apply Eqs. 10.87 to 10.98 to a uniform/periodic B-spline which has the variable t modified as follows:

(a) t is reparameterized so that it varies within equal subintervals: $0 \le t \le 1, 1 \le t \le 2$, and so forth.

(b) t is locally reparameterized so that, for each B-spline segment, the parameter t ranges from zero to one. Do this for quadratic and cubic B-splines.

Solution

(a) With t reparameterized within the equal intervals given, the blending functions become

$k = 2$—Linear
$$N_{i,2}(t) = \begin{cases} t & 0 \le t < 1 \\ 2 - t & 1 \le t \le 2 \end{cases} \tag{10.99}$$

$k = 3$—Quadratic
$$N_{i,3}(t) = \begin{cases} \frac{1}{2}t^2 & 0 \le t < 1 \\ \frac{3}{4} - (t - \frac{3}{2})^2 & 1 \le t < 2 \\ \frac{1}{2}(3 - t)^2 & 2 \le t \le 3 \end{cases} \tag{10.100}$$

$k = 4$—Cubic
$$N_{i,4}(t) = \begin{cases} \frac{1}{6}t^3 & 0 \le t < 1 \\ \frac{2}{3} - \frac{1}{2}(t - 2)^3 - (t - 2)^2 & 1 \le t < 2 \\ \frac{2}{3} + \frac{1}{2}(t - 2)^3 - (t - 2)^2 & 2 \le t < 3 \\ \frac{1}{6}(4 - t)^3 & 3 \le t \le 4 \end{cases} \tag{10.101}$$

Figure 10.34 shows a plot of these blending functions.

(b) In this case t is replaced by $(t + i)$ in each individual interval in Eqs. 10.99 to 10.101.

For the quadratic and cubic B-splines (Eqs. 10.100 and 10.101), this local reparameterization yields

Quadratic
$$N_{i,3}(t) = \begin{cases} \frac{1}{2}t^2 \\ \frac{1}{2}(-2t^2 + 2t + 1) \\ \frac{1}{2}(t^2 - 2t + 1) \end{cases}$$

Cubic
$$N_{i,4}(t) = \begin{cases} \frac{1}{6}t^3 \\ \frac{1}{6}(-3t^3 + 3t^2 + 3t + 1) \\ \frac{1}{6}(3t^3 - 6t^2 + 4) \\ \frac{1}{6}(-t^3 + 3t^2 - 3t + 1) \end{cases}$$
$$\tag{10.102}$$

The blending functions for the uniform cubic B-spline in this equation are identical to the ones listed in Eq. 10.74.

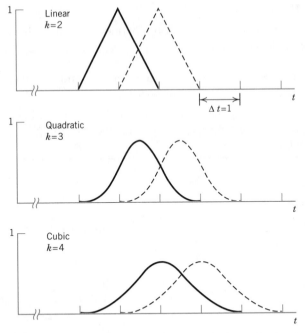

FIGURE 10.34 Plots of blending functions for uniform B-splines of various degrees (or order).

Example 10.11

Find the blending functions for a nonperiodic quadratic B-spline curve, defined over five control points.

Solution

For this B-spline: $k = 3 \rightarrow$ (order)
$n = 4 \rightarrow$ (no. of control vertices $= n + 1 = 5$)
$m = 7 \rightarrow (n + k)$

We have a series of eight knots varying from t_0 to t_7, with multiplicity of $k = 3$ at the ends. A knot vector $[t] = \{0,0,0,1,2,3,3,3\}$ will be used.

Eq. 10.82 is applied recursively in the definition of the blending functions. Individual knots are

$$t_0 = t_1 = t_2 = 0$$

$$t_3 = 1$$

$$t_4 = 2$$

$$t_5 = t_6 = t_7 = 3$$

For $k = 1$

$$N_{0,1} = 1 \qquad \text{if } t = 0 \text{ and } 0 \text{ elsewhere}$$

$$N_{1,1} = 1 \qquad \text{if } t = 0 \text{ and } 0 \text{ elsewhere}$$

$$N_{2,1} = 1 \qquad \text{if } 0 \le t < 1 \text{ and } 0 \text{ elsewhere}$$

$$N_{3,1} = 1 \qquad \text{if } 1 \le t < 2 \text{ and } 0 \text{ elsewhere}$$

$$N_{4,1} = 1 \qquad \text{if } 2 \le t < 3 \text{ and } 0 \text{ elsewhere}$$

$$N_{5,1} = 1 \qquad \text{if } t = 3 \text{ and } 0 \text{ elsewhere}$$

$$N_{6,1} = 1 \qquad \text{if } t = 3 \text{ and } 0 \text{ elsewhere}$$

For $k = 2$

$$N_{0,2} = \frac{(t - t_0)}{(t_1 - t_0)} N_{0,1} + \frac{(t_2 - t)}{(t_2 - t_1)} N_{1,1} = 0 + 0 = 0$$

$$N_{1,2} = \frac{(t - t_1)}{t_2 - t_1} N_{1,1} + \frac{(t_3 - t)}{(t_3 - t_2)} N_{2,1} = 0 + (1 - t)$$

$$= (1 - t) \qquad \text{for } 0 \le t < 1$$

$$N_{2,2} = \frac{(t - t_2)}{(t_3 - t_2)} N_{2,1} + \frac{(t_4 - t)}{(t_4 - t_3)} N_{3,1}$$

$$= \begin{cases} t & \text{for } 0 \le t < 1 \\ (2 - t) & \text{for } 1 \le t < 2 \end{cases}$$

$$N_{3,2} = \frac{(t - t_3)}{(t_4 - t_3)} N_{3,1} + \frac{(t_5 - t)}{(t_5 - t_4)} N_{4,1}$$

$$= \begin{cases} (t - 1) & \text{for } 1 \le t < 2 \\ (3 - t) & \text{for } 2 \le t < 3 \end{cases}$$

$$N_{4,2} = \frac{(t - t_4)}{(t_5 - t_4)} N_{4,1} + \frac{(t_6 - t)}{(t_6 - t_5)} N_{5,1}$$

$$= (t - 2) \qquad \text{for } 2 \le t < 3$$

For $k = 3$

$$N_{0,3} = \frac{(t - t_0)}{(t_2 - t_0)} N_{0,2} + \frac{(t_3 - t)}{(t_3 - t_1)} N_{1,2}$$

$$= (1 - t)^2 \qquad \text{for } 0 \le t < 1$$

$$N_{1,3} = \frac{(t - t_1)}{(t_3 - t_1)} N_{1,2} + \frac{(t_4 - t)}{(t_4 - t_2)} N_{2,2}$$

$$= \begin{cases} t(1 - t) + \dfrac{t}{2}(2 - t) & \text{for } 0 \le t < 1 \\ \frac{1}{2}(2 - t)^2 & \text{for } 1 \le t < 2 \end{cases}$$

$$N_{2,3} = \frac{(t - t_2)}{(t_4 - t_2)} N_{2,2} + \frac{(t_5 - t)}{(t_5 - t_3)} N_{3,2}$$

$$= \begin{cases} \frac{1}{2}t^2 & \text{for } 0 \le t < 1 \\ \frac{1}{2}t(2 - t) + \frac{1}{2}(3 - t)(t - 1) & \text{for } 1 \le t < 2 \\ \frac{1}{2}(3 - t)^2 & \text{for } 2 \le t < 3 \end{cases}$$

$$N_{3,3} = \frac{(t - t_3)}{(t_5 - t_3)} N_{3,2} + \frac{(t_6 - t)}{(t_6 - t_4)} N_{4,2}$$

$$= \begin{cases} \frac{1}{2}(t - 1)^2 & \text{for } 1 \le t < 2 \\ \frac{1}{2}(t - 1)(3 - t) + (3 - t)(t - 2) & \text{for } 2 \le t < 3 \end{cases}$$

$$N_{4,3} = \frac{(t - t_4)}{(t_6 - t_4)} N_{4,2} + \frac{(t_7 - t)}{(t_7 - t_5)} N_{5,2}$$

$$= (t - 2)^2 \qquad \text{for } 2 \le t < 3$$

A plot of these blending functions is shown in Figure 10.35.

B-splines can also be defined with a multiplicity of control points. The result will be similar to that obtained for Bezier curves, that is, a pull towards the respective control point. Figure 10.36 shows the effect of this multiplicity. Appendix 10.6, at the end of this chapter, gives an algorithm for the evaluation of B-spline curves.

The theory of splines for use in computer-aided geometric design has been studied extensively and new forms have been developed, allowing better control of shape and continuity. As an example, β-splines maintain geometric instead of the parametric continuity inherent in Bezier and B-

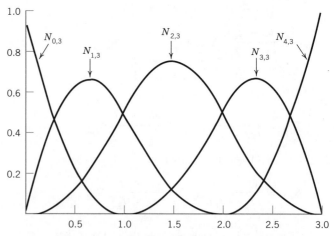

FIGURE 10.35 Plot of blending functions for a nonperiodic quadratic B-spline over five control points.

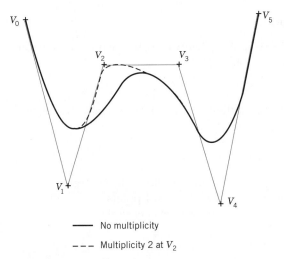

— No multiplicity

--- Multiplicity 2 at V_2

FIGURE 10.36 Effect of multiplicity of control points on the shape of B-spline curves.

splines. For better shape control, they introduce two new parameters, called *bias* and *tension*. A wealth of information on various kinds of splines can be found in the literature [39,40].

10.9.5   B-Spline Formulation—Highlights

This section summarizes the many important relationships and definitions used in the previous sections for formulating B-splines.

B-Spline General Form

$$P(t) = \sum_{i=0}^{n} N_{i,k}(t) V_i$$

defining a point on the curve

where i indicates position: $V_i \rightarrow$ control point i

$t_i \rightarrow$ knot i

k is order of curve

$(n + 1)$ is number of control points

$N_{i,k}(t)$ are blending functions given by Eq. 10.82

V_i are control points

Continuity

Continuity of position, C°

[1 to $(k - 2)$] derivatives are continuous

Knot Vectors

These are the parametric intervals within which the blending functions are defined. For example:

$$[t_0 \ldots \ldots t_m]$$

The elements "t_i" of the knot vector must satisfy the relation:

$$t_i \leq t_{i+1}$$

The relationship among

> degree of the curve $(k - 1)$
> no. of control points $(n + 1)$
> no. of knots $(m + 1)$

is given by

$$m = n + k$$

Classification of Knot Vectors:
I. Uniform/Periodic

> $(t_i - t_{i-1}) =$ constant
> Influence of each basis function is limited to k (see Figure 10.34).
> Parameter range: $(k - 1) \leq t \leq (n + 1)$
>
> Example: [0   1   2   3   4]

II. Nonperiodic

> Satisfies the following equations:
> $t_i = 0$ for $i < k$
>
> $t_i = i - k + 1$ for $k \leq i \leq n$
>
> $t_i = n - k + 2$ for $i > 0$
> for a knot vector starting at $i = 0$ and $(n + 1)$ control points.
> No loss of parameter range, so that the curve interpolates the first and last control points.
>
> Example: [0   0   1   2   2   2]

III. Nonuniform

> Knot vector is not equispaced.
>
> Example: [0   1   2   3   3   4]

Bezier Representation

It is simply a special case of the general B-spline formulation when the following conditions are satisfied:

- The number of defining polygon vertices is equal to the order of the B-spline basis.
- A nonperiodic knot vector is used.

For example:

    No. of control points $= 4$ (i.e., $n = 3$)

    Order of the curve, $k = 4$

    Open periodic knot vector: [0 0 0 0 1 1 1 1]

10.10 RATIONAL CURVES

The curve generation schemes described in the previous sections are commonly used in the design of freeform curves. However, engineering design often requires the use of standard analytic shapes such as lines, circles, and conics. A procedure that allows the incorporation of both types of curves (freeform and conics) is the use of rational polynomial functions.

    The term "rational" means these functions are obtained by the "ratio" of two polynomials. They are invariant under projective transformations. For example, the perspective projection of a rational curve is itself a rational curve, which is not true for the nonrational or integral curves. CAD applications of this representation make use of the concept of homogeneous coordinates, that is, the idea of representing points of $(n - 1)$ space as projections of points in n space [41,42,43]. This concept was previously explained in Chapter 3. A point defined in three-dimensional Euclidean space as $P(x,y,z)$ has a corresponding representation in four-dimensional homogeneous space as $Q^w = (wx, wy, wz, w)$, where $w \geq 0$. The value of w is the homogeneous coordinate, often referred to as the *weight*.

    Both Bezier and B-spline curves possess a rational form. Table 10.5 shows the appropriate expressions.

TABLE 10.5

	Bezier	B-Spline
Nonrational (Integral)	$Q(t) = \sum\limits_{i=0}^{n} B_{i,n}(t) V_i$	$P(t) = \sum\limits_{i=0}^{n} N_{i,k}(t) V_i$
Rational	$Q(t) = \dfrac{\sum\limits_{i=0}^{n} B_{i,n}(t) w_i V_i}{\sum\limits_{i=0}^{n} B_{i,n}(t) w_i}$	$P(t) = \dfrac{\sum\limits_{i=0}^{n} N_{i,k}(t) w_i V_i}{\sum\limits_{i=0}^{n} N_{i,k}(t) w_i}$

In both cases, we start by expressing a general nonrational curve in four-dimensional homogeneous space. Considering the Bezier formulation as an example, this would result in the expression

$$Q^w(t) = \sum_{i=0}^{n} B_{in}(t) V_i^w \tag{10.103}$$

where

$Q^w(t)$ = points on the curve in four-dimensional homogeneous space—coordinates $(w_x(t), w_y(t), w_z(t), w)$

$B_{i,n}(t)$ = standard Bezier blending function

V_i^w = control points in four-dimensional homogeneous space

The set of three-dimensional points formed by the projection of $Q^w(t)$ into three-dimensional space is obtained by dividing the first three coordinates of $Q^w(t)$ by its homogeneous coordinate. The result is the rational Bezier curve. The three dimensional projection of the four-dimensional control points V_i^w is

$$V_i = \frac{V_i^w}{w_i} \tag{10.104}$$

so that

$$V_i^w = w_i V_i \tag{10.105}$$

Analogously, the points $Q(t)$ on the curve can be written in rational form as the projection from four-dimensional to three-dimensional space:

$$Q(t) = \frac{Q^w(t)}{w(t)} = \frac{\sum_{i=0}^{n} B_{in}(t) w_i V_i}{\sum_{i=0}^{n} B_{in}(t) w_i} \tag{10.106}$$

In the rational expression above, if all w_i are equal to 1 the expression reverts back to its nonrational counterpart. The weights, therefore, give an added degree of freedom to the design of curves. All the properties that apply to the nonrational expression are still valid when working with rational curves, for example, convex hull, variation diminishing, and the like. The only constraint necessary is that $w_i \geq 0$. If w_{i-1} and w_{i+1} are fixed, an increase in the value of w_i will pull the curve toward V_i. Figure 10.37 demonstrates this property.

Rational curves have been gaining popularity in CAD, and today many commercial systems use these representations which include Bezier and all forms of B-splines (uniform/periodic, nonperiodic and nonuniform). Figure 10.38 shows an example of a nonperiodic cubic rational B-spline.

The most common scheme, however, appears to be the nonuniform rational B-spline, commonly referred to as NURB, popular because the NURB

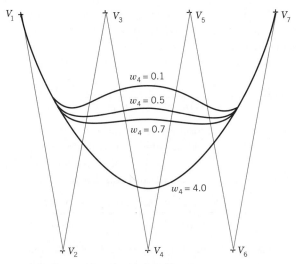

FIGURE 10.37 Rational curves, with varying weight values at V_4.

representation includes all B-splines and Bezier curves. It has the capability of representing a wide range of shapes, including conics, using one canonical form [41]. NURBs have actually become a part of the Initial Graphics Exchange Standard (IGES) for curve (or surface) definition. The general rational B-spline equation given in Table 10.5 is used for the NURB curve. The only constraint is that the knot vector be nonuniform. Figure 10.39 shows examples of cubic NURBs for various knot vectors and weights.

Appendices 10.7 and 10.8, at the end of this chapter, give algorithms for the evaluation of rational Bezier and B-spline curves.

When representing conic sections, rational B-splines provide a unique representation that merges the conics with freeform curves [43]. For computational efficiency, rational quadratic B-splines ($n = 2$, $k = 3$) are best

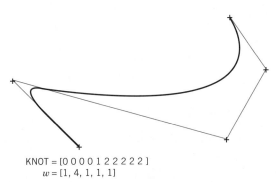

KNOT = [0 0 0 0 1 2 2 2 2 2]
$w = [1, 4, 1, 1, 1]$

FIGURE 10.38 Nonperiodic cubic rational B-spline.

suited to represent the conics, since they provide the lowest order possible. The knot vector can be determined by the order and the number of control points. Defining the quadratic rational B-spline by three control points, with $0 \leq t \geq 1$ and a knot vector $[t] = [0 \quad 0 \quad 0 \quad 1 \quad 1 \quad 1]$, yields:

$$P(t) = \frac{N_{0,3}(t)w_0 V_0 + N_{1,3}(t)w_1 V_1 + N_{2,3}(t)w_2 V_2}{N_{0,3}(t)w_0 + N_{1,3}(t)w_1 + N_{2,3}(t)w_2}$$

This equation defines a one-parameter family of conics, with each conic passing through V_0 and V_2, and tangent to the chords $[V_0 \; V_1]$ and $[V_1 \; V_2]$, as shown in Figure 10.40. Included in this family are ellipses, parabolas, and hyperbolas. If $w_0 = w_2 = 1$, the equation reduces to

$$P(t) = \frac{N_{0,3}(t) V_0 + N_{1,3}(t)w_1 V_1 + N_{2,3}(t)}{N_{0,3}(t) + N_{1,3}(t)w_1 + N_{2,3}(t)}$$

The various conics are obtained by adjusting V_0, V_1, V_2, and w_1. The value of w_1 determines what conic type will be obtained, such that

$$w_1 = 0 \qquad \text{straight line}$$
$$0 < w_1 < 1 \qquad \text{elliptic segment}$$
$$w_1 = 1 \qquad \text{parabolic segment}$$
$$w_1 > 1 \qquad \text{hyperbolic segment}$$

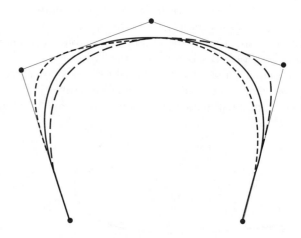

$$w = [.1,.5,1,.5,.1]$$

——— KNOT = [0 0 0 0 1 2 2 2 2]

- - - KNOT = [0 0 0 0 1 7 7 7 7]

– – KNOT = [0 0 0 0 7 8 8 8 8]

FIGURE 10.39 *Examples of cubic NURBs.*

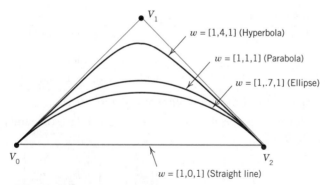

FIGURE 10.40 Nonuniform rational quadratic B-spline representation of conics.

10.11 APPLICATION PROBLEMS

A number of techniques were described in this chapter, specifically applied to two types of problems:

(a) Interpolation of scattered data points, using Lagrange polynomial, parametric cubics, and cubic splines.

(b) Approximation for shape design, using Bezier and B-spline curves.

This section will present some general application problems that use these various techniques.

Example 10.12

This problem will compare the shape of curves resulting from the use of various curve-defining techniques. Given the data points $P_0(0,0)$, $P_1(1,1)$, $P_2(2,-1)$, $P_3(3,1)$ and $P_4(4,2)$, describe a curve that will interpolate them using the following techniques:

(a) Lagrange polynomial

(b) Natural cubic spline

(c) Bezier representation—in this case the Bezier control polygon that forces the curve to pass through the given points will have to be found.

(d) Nonperiodic, quadratic B-spline representation—in this case the control polygon will also have to be defined.

Solution

(a) *Lagrange polynomial.* The Lagrangian interpolation formula is given in Eq. 10.26. For this problem it becomes

$$f(x) = 0 + \frac{x(x - 2)(x - 3)(x - 4)}{(1 - 0)(1 - 2)(1 - 3)(1 - 4)} \cdot (1) + \frac{x(x - 1)(x - 3)(x - 4)}{(2 - 0)(2 - 1)(2 - 3)(2 - 4)} \cdot (-1)$$

$$+ \frac{x(x - 1)(x - 2)(x - 4)}{(3 - 0)(3 - 1)(3 - 2)(3 - 4)} \cdot (1) + \frac{x(x - 1)(x - 2)(x - 3)}{(4 - 0)(4 - 1)(4 - 2)(4 - 3)} \cdot (2)$$

A plot of this function is shown in Figure 10.41.

(b) *Natural cubic spline.* Equation 10.57 is used to solve the problem, as follows:

$$\begin{bmatrix} 2 & 1 & 0 & 0 & 0 \\ 1 & 4 & 1 & 0 & 0 \\ 0 & 1 & 4 & 1 & 0 \\ 0 & 0 & 1 & 4 & 1 \\ 0 & 0 & 0 & 1 & 2 \end{bmatrix} \begin{bmatrix} P_0' \\ P_1' \\ P_2' \\ P_3' \\ P_4' \end{bmatrix} = \begin{bmatrix} 3(P_1 - P_0) \\ 3(P_2 - P_0) \\ 3(P_3 - P_1) \\ 3(P_4 - P_2) \\ 3(P_4 - P_3) \end{bmatrix}$$

and

$$\begin{bmatrix} P_0' \\ P_1' \\ P_2' \\ P_3' \\ P_4' \end{bmatrix} = \begin{bmatrix} -.167 & .94 \\ 1.33 & -.881 \\ .833 & -.42 \\ 1.33 & 2.55 \\ -.167 & -0.77 \end{bmatrix}$$

A plot of the natural cubic curve obtained from the application of these tangent vectors to the given points is shown in Figure 10.41.

FIGURE 10.41

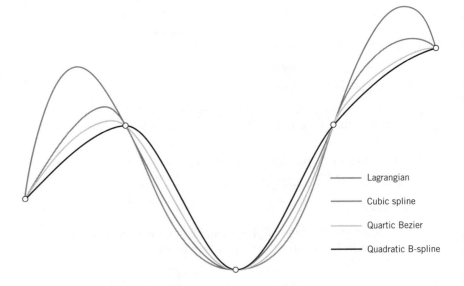

Lagrangian

Cubic spline

Quartic Bezier

Quadratic B-spline

(c) *Bezier curve.* Five control vertices are to be found, describing a fourth degree Bezier curve (order = 5). The blending functions for this Bezier curve are obtained from Eq. 10.59, as follows:

$$B_{0,4} = (1 - t)^4$$

$$B_{1,4} = 4t(1 - t)^3$$

$$B_{2,4} = 6t^2(1 - t)^2$$

$$B_{3,4} = 4(1 - t)t^3$$

$$B_{4,4} = t^4$$

or, in matrix form:

$$[t^4 \quad t^3 \quad t^2 \quad t \quad 1]\begin{bmatrix} 1 & -4 & 6 & -4 & 1 \\ -4 & 12 & -12 & 4 & 0 \\ 6 & -12 & 6 & 0 & 0 \\ -4 & 4 & 0 & 0 & 0 \\ 1 & 0 & 0 & 0 & 0 \end{bmatrix}$$

The parameter values t along the Bezier curve corresponding to the data points can be found as an approximation to the chord length between each two data points [5]:

$$L_{21} = |P_2 - P_1| = \sqrt{(1 - 0)^2 + (1 - 0)^2} \quad = \sqrt{2}$$

$$L_{32} = |P_3 - P_2| = \sqrt{(2 - 1)^2 + (-1 - 1)^2} = \sqrt{5}$$

$$L_{43} = |P_4 - P_3| = \sqrt{(3 - 2)^2 + (1 + 1)^2} \quad = \sqrt{5}$$

$$L_{54} = |P_5 - P_4| = \sqrt{(4 - 3)^2 + (2 - 1)^2} \quad = \sqrt{2}$$

The total chord length is

$$L_{51} = L_{21} + L_{32} + L_{43} + L_{54} = 7.3$$

and the parameter values become

$$t_1 = 0$$

$$\frac{t_2}{t_{max}} = \frac{L_{21}}{L_{51}} = \frac{\sqrt{2}}{7.3} = 0.19$$

$$\frac{t_3}{t_{max}} = \frac{L_{31}}{L_{51}} = \frac{\sqrt{5} + \sqrt{2}}{7.3} = 0.5$$

$$\frac{t_4}{t_{max}} = \frac{L_{41}}{L_{51}} = \frac{\sqrt{5} + \sqrt{2} + \sqrt{5}}{7.3} = 0.81$$

$$\frac{t_5}{t_{max}} = \frac{L_{51}}{L_{51}} = 1$$

where t_{max} is the maximum parameter value, equal to one in the Bezier formulation.

Substituting these t values into the blending function equations for the quartic Bezier curve yields:

$$[B] = \begin{bmatrix} 1 & 0 & 0 & 0 & 0 \\ .4305 & .4039 & .1421 & .0222 & .0013 \\ .0625 & .25 & .375 & .25 & .0625 \\ .0013 & .0222 & .1421 & .4039 & .4 \\ 0 & 0 & 0 & 0 & 1 \end{bmatrix}$$

The control vertices are found from:

$$[V]_B = [B]^{-1}[P]_B$$

$$= \begin{bmatrix} 1 & 0 & 0 & 0 & 0 \\ -1.375 & 3.423 & -1.601 & .803 & -.25 \\ .916 & -2.817 & 4.802 & -2.817 & .916 \\ -.25 & .803 & -1.602 & 3.423 & -1.375 \\ 0 & 0 & 0 & 0 & 1 \end{bmatrix} \begin{bmatrix} 0 & 0 \\ 1 & 1 \\ 2 & -1 \\ 3 & 1 \\ 4 & 2 \end{bmatrix}$$

$$= \begin{bmatrix} 0 & 0 \\ 1.629 & 5.327 \\ 2 & -8.604 \\ 2.37 & 3.078 \\ 4 & 2 \end{bmatrix}$$

Figure 10.41 shows a plot of this curve.

(d) *Nonperiodic, quadratic B-spline.* For this problem, five control vertices are used, and the order of the curve is $k = 3$. The knot vector, based on Eq. 10.85, is

$$[0 \quad 0 \quad 0 \quad 1 \quad 2 \quad 3 \quad 3 \quad 3]$$

with maximum knot value equal to 3. The same chord approximation used in the Bezier case is applied, knowing that t_{max} here is equal to 3, so that

$$t_1 = 0$$

$$t_2 = 0.57$$

$$t_3 = 1.5$$

$$t_4 = 2.43$$

$$t_5 = 3$$

For $k = 3$ and five control points, the blending functions N were derived in Example 10.11 and, for the values of t found in this problem, become for $t_1 = 0$

$N_{0,3} = 1$ and all others are zero.

for $t_2 = 0.57, \quad 0 \le t < 1$

$N_{0,3} = (1 - t)^2 = 0.1849$

$N_{1,3} = t(1 - t) + \dfrac{t}{2}(2 - t) = 0.6527$

$N_{2,3} = \dfrac{t^2}{2} = 0.1625$

for $t_3 = 1.5, \quad 1 \le t < 2$

$N_{1,3} = \dfrac{(2 - t)^2}{2} = 0.125$

$N_{2,3} = \dfrac{t(2 - t)}{2} + \dfrac{(3 - t)(t - 1)}{2} = 0.75$

$N_{3,3} = \dfrac{(t - 1)^2}{2} = 0.125$

for $t_4 = 2.43, \quad 2 \le t < 3$

$N_{2,3} = \dfrac{(3 - t)^2}{2} = 0.1625$

$N_{3,3} = \dfrac{(t - 1)(3 - t)}{2} + (3 - t)(t - 2) = 0.6527$

$N_{4,3} = (t - 2)^2 = 0.1849$

for $t_5 = 3$

$N_{4,3} = 1$ and all others are zero.

In matrix form:

$$[N] = \begin{bmatrix} 1 & 0 & 0 & 0 & 0 \\ .1849 & .6527 & .1625 & 0 & 0 \\ 0 & .125 & .75 & .125 & 0 \\ 0 & 0 & .1625 & .6527 & .1849 \\ 0 & 0 & 0 & 0 & 1 \end{bmatrix}$$

The control vertices are given by:

$$[V]_{\text{Bs}} = [N]^{-1}[P]_{\text{Bs}}$$

$$[V]_{\text{Bs}} = [N]^{-1} \begin{bmatrix} 0 & 0 \\ 1 & 1 \\ 2 & -1 \\ 3 & 1 \\ 4 & 2 \end{bmatrix}$$

$$[V]_{\text{Bs}} = \begin{bmatrix} 0 & 0 \\ 1.034 & 2.007 \\ 2.000 & -1.908 \\ 2.965 & 1.440 \\ 4 & 2 \end{bmatrix}$$

A plot of this curve is also shown in Figure 10.41.

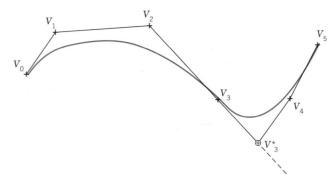

FIGURE 10.42

The curves resulting from the four interpolating techniques can now be compared in Figure 10.41.

Example 10.13

The Bezier representation was used to create the airfoil shown in Figure 10.24a, using a CAD system. Two control polygons—V_0, V_1, V_2, V_3, and V_0, V_4, V_5, V_3—gave shape to two cubic Bezier curves, connected with C^0 continuity. The curves were then translated and scaled to form additional sectional curves on the airfoil.

When shaping Bezier curves, it is often necessary to use more than four control vertices. CAD systems usually keep the degree of the curve low (cubic, for example) and deal in different ways with the problem of continuity. One way is to create "dummy" control points that enforce the continuity requirements.

Assume, for example, that the user chooses six control points and wants to create a cubic Bezier curve (see Figure 10.42). The system chooses the first four points—V_0, V_1, V_2, V_3—and shapes a cubic Bezier segment. Next, it selects another point along the line connecting V_2 and V_3, and uses V_3, V_3^*, V_4, V_5 to create the next segment, with C^1 continuity. As the user alters the position of the control points, the "dummy" points are also repositioned to enforce continuity.

SUMMARY

This chapter discussed a variety of curve representations, including the parametric representation for conics, interpolation (Lagrange, Hermite, cubic spline) and approximation (Bezier, B-spline) techniques. The focus throughout remained on the underlying analytical formulation of the various representations. A distinction was made between interpolation and approximation techniques, with approximation used for shape design in engineering applications, such as the design of automobile bodies and ship hulls. The use of piecewise continuous parametric curves was shown to be useful to represent curve-faced objects. Viewing and modeling transformations can be applied to the control polygon of Bezier and B-spline curves.

EXERCISES

1. Convert the given parametric form of a curve

$$x = 4t^3 - 3t + 6$$

$$y = t^3 + 2t^2 + 6t - 9$$

into an implicit form, using the implicitization method.

2. The equations for various conics are given below:

   (a) $x^2 + 4y^2 + 3xy + 6x + 6y + 2 = 0$
   (b) $2x^2 + 3y^2 + 6xy + 2x + 7y - 6 = 0$
   (c) $9x^2 + 4y^2 + 12xy + 5x - 6y + 9 = 0$

   Determine the type of curve represented by each equation.

3. Generate at least five points on a circle which is centered at (2,3) and has a radius of 3 units, using the parametric iteration formulas.

4. A parametric cubic curve passes through the points (0,0), (2,4), (4,3), (5,−2), which are parameterized at $t = 0, \frac{1}{4}, \frac{3}{4}$, and 1, respectively. Determine the geometric coefficient matrix and the slope of the curve when $t = 0.5$.

5. Fit a natural cubic spline through the points (0,0), (0,1), (3,2), (4,3) and (4,5). Determine the point on the third segment when $t = 0.4$.

6. A cubic Bezier curve is described by the four control points [0 0 0], [4 2 2], [8 6 4], [12 0 0]. Find the tangent to the curve at $t = \frac{1}{4}$.

7. Knowing that a uniform cubic B-spline does not interpolate the first and last control vertices, determine the position of its starting and ending points as a function of the four control vertices, V_0, V_1, V_2, V_3.

8. Use a uniform quadratic B-spline curve with four control points to describe an ellipse whose major axis has a length of four units and minor axis two units, as shown in the accompanying figure.

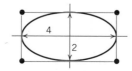

9. Derive the transformation needed to convert the Hermite control conditions into the Bezier control conditions.

10. Given a Bezier curve defined by the following control points: (0,0,0), (3,5,4), (6,3,2), determine the piecewise quadratic interpolating polynomial that would describe the same curve.

11. Derive the transformation needed to convert the control vertices of a periodic cubic B-spline curve into those of a cubic Bezier that represents the same curve.

12. The control points of a periodic cubic B-spline curve are (0,0), (2,2), (4,3), and (5,4). Determine the value of x when $y = 2$ for a point on the curve.

13. Given the control vertices for a Bezier curve $V_0(1,1)$, $V_1(2,3)$, $V_2(4,3)$, $V_3(3,1)$, determine the point on the curve at $t = 0.5$. For the same control vertices, use a fourth order, nonperiodic B-spline and determine the same point on the curve ($t = 0.5$). Compare the results.

14. Implement the algorithms given at the end of this chapter to output the various types of freeform curves. The geometric coefficients (or control points) should be defined by the user.

APPENDIX 10.1

```
subroutine Circle(xc,yc,radius,npts)
#module to draw a circle centered at (xc,yc) and of
#radius ''radius''
#npts—number of points along the circumference.

PI=3.14159

begin
      xn=xc+radius
      yn=yc
      delta=(2.0*PI)/npts
      cosc=cos(delta)
      sinc=sin(delta)

      Move_To(xn,yn)

      for i=1 to npts do
          xdif=xn-xc
          ydif=yn-yc
          xn=xc+xdif*cosc-ydif*sinc
          yn=yc+xdif*sinc+ydif*cosc

          Draw_To(xn,yn)
      next i
      return
end
```

APPENDIX 10.2

```
subroutine Ellipse(xc,yc,a,b,theta,npts)
#module to draw an ellipse with—
#xc,yc—center coordinates of ellipse
#a,b—length of the major and minor axes, respectively
#theta—inclination angle of major axis (in degrees)
#npts—number of points on ellipse

PI=3.14159
phi=theta*(PI/180.0)   # convert to radians

begin
        #compute sine and cosine of the inclination
        #angle of ellipse
        c1=cos(phi)
        s1=sin(phi)
        #calculate the increment in parameter
        par=(2.0*PI)/(npts-1)
        #compute sine and cosine of the parameter
        #increments
        c2=cos(par)
        s2=sin(par)
        #initialize accumulation variables
        c3=1
        s3=0
        for i=1 to npts do
            x1=a*c3
            y1=b*s3
            #compute new x,y
            xn=xc+x1*c1-y1*s1
            yn=yc+x1*s1+y1*c1
            #compute new angles
            temp=c3*c2-c3*s2
            s3=s3*c2+c3*s2
            c3=temp

            if (i=1)
                    then Move_To(xn,yn)
                    else Draw_To(xn,yn)
            endif
        next i

        return
    end
```

APPENDIX 10.3

```
subroutine Hermite_Curve()
#M4x4—Hermite Matrix
#G4x1—Geometric Coefficients Matrix
#t1x4—Matrix of parameters
#P—the calculated point on the curve

begin
      Initialize matrix M (Ref. equation 10.38)
      Read Hermite geometric coefficients; Endpoint
      coordinates and tangent vectors at end points.

      for t=0.0 to 1.0 insteps of 0.05 do
            Initialize the matrix [t] with current
            value of t
            P=t*M*G # standard matrix multiplication
            (Eq. 10.39)

            if P(t) is starting point
                  then
                        Move_To(P)
                  else
                        Draw_To(P)
            endif
      next t

      return

end
```

APPENDIX 10.4

```
subroutine Bezier_Curve()
#n+1—number of control points
#Pi—i'th control point having x,y,z coordinates as
(Pix,Piy,Piz)

begin
      for i=0 to n do
            Read control point Pi
      next i
      for t=0.0 to 1.0 insteps of 0.05 do
            x=y=z=0.0
            for i=0 to n do
                  B=Blend (i,n,t)
                  x=x+Pix*B
                  y=y+Piy*B
                  z=z+Piz*B
            next i
            if (x,y,z) is starting point
                  then
                          Move_To (x,y,z)
                  else
                          Draw_To (x,y,z)
            end if
      next t
      return
end

function Blend (i,n,t)

begin
      blend=Factorial(n)/(Factorial(i)*Factorial(n-i))
      blend=blend*(t)ⁱ*((1-t)ⁿ⁻ⁱ    )
      return (blend)
end
```

APPENDIX 10.5

```
subroutine Uniform_Cubic_B-spline()
#m+1—number of control points
#Pi—i'th control point, Pix, Piy, Piz are the x,y,z
coordinates of Pi
begin
      for i=0 to m do
            Read control point Pi
      next i

      for i=1 to (m-3) do
            for t=0.0 to 1.0 insteps of 0.05 do
                  x=Pix*N0(t)+Pi+1x*N1(t)+
                        Pi+2x*N2(t)+Pi+3x*N3(t)
                  y=Piy*N0(t)+Pi+1y*N1(t)+
                        Pi+2y*N2(t)+Pi+3y*N3(t)
                  z=Piz*N0(t)+Pi+1z*N1(t)+
                        Pi+2z*N2(t)+Pi+3z*N3(t)
                  #polynomials N0,N1,N2 and N3 are as
                  defined in equation 10.74.
                  if ((x,y,z) is starting point on curve
                        then
                              Move_To(x,y,z)
                        else
                              Draw_To(x,y,z)
                  endif
            next t
      next i

      return
end
```

APPENDIX 10.6

```
subroutine B-spline_Curve()
#n+1—number of control points
#Pi—i'th control point, Pix, Piy, Piz are the x,y,z
coordinates Pi

begin
      for i=0 to n do
            Read control point Pi
      next i
      Read the degree of the curve into DEGREE
      k=DEGREE+1      # order of the B-spline
      if ''nonperiodic B-spline curve''
            then
                  Calculate_Knots()
            else
                  begin
                        for i=0 to (n+k) do
                              Read knot(i) # for
                                          nonuniform B-splines
                        next i
                  end
      end if
      for t=0.0 to (n-k+2) insteps of 0.05 do
            for i=0 to n do
                  B=Blend(i,k,t)
                  x=x+Pix*B
                  y=y+Piy*B
                  z=z+Piz*B
            next i
            if (x,y,z) is starting point
                  then
                        Move_To(x,y,z)
                  else
                        Draw_To(x,y,z)
            end if
      next t

      return
end


function Calculate_Knots()
#this function is used only for nonperiodic B-spline
      curves.
```

```
#t,n and knot are global variables used in this
       function

begin
       for i=0 to (n+k) do
             if (i<k)
                   then
                             knot(i)=0
                   elseif (k<=i<n)
                         then
                                   knot(i)=i-k+1
                   elseif (i>n)
                         then
                                   knot(i)=n-k+2
             end if
       next i
       return
end

function blend(i,k,t)
#this function uses recursion to evaluate the B-spline
       blending function

begin
       if (k>1)
             then
                   begin
                         denom1=knot(i+k-1)-knot(i)
                         temp1=(t-knot(i))
                               *Blend(i,k-1,t))/denom1
                         denom2=knot(i+k)-knot(i+1)
                         temp2=(knot(i+k)-t)
                               *Blend(i+1,k-1,t)/denom2
                         blend=temp1+temp2
                   end
             else
                   begin
                         if(knot(i)<knot(i+1))
                               then
                                      blend=1
                               else
                                      blend=0
                         end if
                   end
       end if

       return (blend)
end
```

APPENDIX 10.7

```
subroutine Rational_Bezier_Curve()
#n+1—number of control points
#Pi—i'th control point <Pix,Piy,Piz,Pih>, Pih is the
      weight value of Pi.
#Blend is a function as described in Algorithm 10.4.

begin
      for i=0 to n do
            Read control points Pi
      next i

      for t=0.0 to 1.0 insteps of 0.05
            Initialize x,y,z, denom to 0
            #denom is the denominator of Bezier
                  formulation
            for i=0 to n do
                  B=Blend(i,k,t)
                  x=Pix*Pih*B+x
                  y=Piy*Pih*B+y
                  z=Piz*Pih*B+z
                  denom=denom+Pih
            next i
            x=x/denom
            y=y/denom
            z=z/denom

            if (x,y,z) is starting point
                  then
                        Move_To(x,y,z)
                  else
                        Draw_To(x,y,z)
            end if
      next t

      return
end
```

APPENDIX 10.8

```
subroutine Rational_B-spline_Curve()
#n+1—number of control points
#Pi—i'th control point having <Pix,Piy,Piz,Pih>, Pih
      is the weight value of Pi.
#Blend is a function as described in Algorithm 10.6.
#Calculate_Knots is a function as described in
      Algorithm 10.6.

begin
      for i=0 to n do
            Read control point Pi
      next i

      Read the degree of the curve into DEGREE
      k=DEGREE+1 #k being the order of curve
      if ''nonperiodic B-spline curve''
            then
                  Calculate_Knots()
            else
                  begin
                        for i=0 to (n+k) do
                              Read knot(i)
                        next i
                  end
            endif
      for t=0.0 to (n-k+2) insteps of 0.05
            Initialize x,y,z, denom to 0.0
            for i=0 to n do
                  B=Blend(i,k,t)
                  x=x+Pih*Pix*B
                  y=y+Pih*Piy*B
                  z=z+Pih*Piz*B
                  denom=denom+Pih*B
            next i
            x=x/denom
            y=y/denom
            z=z/denom
            if (x,y,z) is starting point
                  then
                        Move_To(x,y,z)
                  else
                        Draw_To(x,y,z)
            end if
      next t

      return
end
```

Chapter 11

Surfaces

S urfaces play a critical role in engineering design and manufacturing. Traditionally, surfaces were represented by multiple orthographic projections. With the advent of computer graphics and rapid developments in the area of computational geometry, surface modeling has taken a new dimension. A mathematical model can now be created, allowing relatively quick analysis of important surface characteristics, such as centroid, surface area, and so forth. From these surface models, information necessary for manufacture, such as numerical control codes, can also be extracted. Computer rendering of these surfaces simplifies the process of design verification.

The parametric representations used in Chapter 10 for curve design are also effective tools in the design of surfaces [36,94]. The parametric form of a curve was given by a vector-valued equation of the form:

$$P(t) = [x(t), y(t), z(t)] \qquad (11.1)$$

Only one parametric variable is needed, or one degree of freedom, for com-

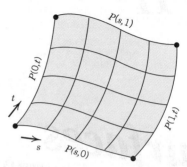

FIGURE 11.1 Surface created by a mesh of curves along the *s* and *t* parametric directions.

plete definition, which makes this equation a "univariate" vector-valued function.

Surface representation requires two parametric variables, and is still a vector-valued equation:

$$P(s,t) = [x(s,t), y(s,t), z(s,t)] \tag{11.2}$$

Curve traces representing the surface can be generated by keeping one parameter constant and varying the other. A series of curves is created along the *s* and *t* directions, as shown in Figure 11.1. Constraining the parameters *s* and *t* between zero and one, one set of curves along the *s* direction could be $P(0,t)$, $P(0.1,t)$, ..., $P(0.9,t)$, $P(1,t)$, and the other set of curves, along the *t* direction, $P(s,0)$, $P(s,0.1)$, ..., $P(s,0.9)$, $P(s,1)$. The creation of a surface, therefore, requires the creation of the multiple curves that constitute it. This concept can be applied to surfaces that have an analytic formulation or to freeform surfaces, as will be seen in the following sections.

11.1 SURFACES OF REVOLUTION

A very simple family of surfaces is obtained by rotating a plane curve around an axis. Figure 11.2 shows a circular cylinder formed by rotating a line segment parallel to the *z* axis through an angle of 2π radians (360°) around the same *z* axis. The line need not be parallel to the axis of rotation, as shown in Figure 11.3. Different types of surfaces are obtained for various specific conditions [5].

Any point on the surface of revolution is a function of two parameters, *t* and θ. The parameter *t* describes the entity to be rotated, and θ represents the angle of rotation. In Figure 11.3a and b, for example, *t* points in the direction of the line segment and θ is the angle of rotation around the *z* axis. A point on the line segment is represented by $[x(t), 0, z(t)]$ and, when rotated by θ radians, it becomes $[x(t)\cos \theta, x(t)\sin \theta, z(t)]$. In general, therefore, a

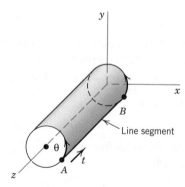

FIGURE 11.2 Circular cylinder obtained by revolution of line *AB* around the *z* axis.

point on the surface of revolution obtained by rotation around the z axis is given by

$$P(t, \theta) = [x(t)\cos \theta, x(t)\sin \theta, z(t)] \qquad (11.3a)$$

or, in matrix form,

$$P(t, \theta) = [x(t) \quad 0 \quad z(t) \quad 1] \begin{bmatrix} \cos \theta & \sin \theta & 0 & 0 \\ 0 & 0 & 0 & 0 \\ 0 & 0 & 1 & 0 \\ 0 & 0 & 0 & 1 \end{bmatrix} \qquad (11.3b)$$

Example 11.1

Generate the conical surface obtained by rotation of the line segment AB with $A = (1,0,1)$ and $B = (7,0,7)$ around the z axis.

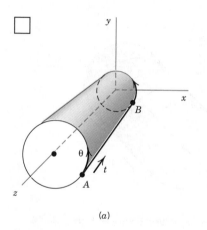

(a)

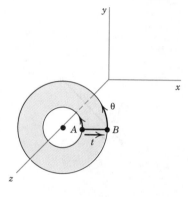

(b)

FIGURE 11.3 Surfaces of revolution, (a) Truncated cone. (b) Hollowed disc.

Solution

Line AB can be represented in parametric form as $L(t) = [x(t), y(t), z(t)] = A + (B - A)t$. Based on this, each component of the line is written as

$$x(t) = 1 + (7 - 1)t = 1 + 6t$$

$$y(t) = 0$$

$$z(t) = 1 + (7 - 1)t = 1 + 6t$$

Any point on the conical surface is found by using Eq. 11.3 a. For example, at $t = 0.4$ and $\theta = \pi/2$ radians,

$$P\left(0.4, \frac{\pi}{2}\right) = \left[(1 + 6(0.4))\cos\frac{\pi}{2}, (1 + 6(0.4))\sin\frac{\pi}{2}, 1 + 6(0.4)\right]$$

$$= [0 \quad 3.4 \quad 3.4]$$

Based on Eq. 11.3, a surface of revolution can be drawn by setting contours in the directions of t and θ. For each value of θ a rotated line or curve is drawn. In addition, for each chosen t value a circular contour is also drawn, as shown in Figure 11.4.

A simple torus can be generated by rotating a circle contained in the xz plane around the z axis, as shown in Figure 11.5. The center of the circle has coordinates $(a,0,0)$, and the circle, in parametric form, is given as $[(a + r\cos\phi), 0, a\sin\phi]$. The torus is represented by:

$$P(\phi, \theta) = [(a + r\cos\phi)\cos\theta], [(a + r\cos\phi)\sin\theta], a\sin\phi \quad (11.4)$$

In this case, the contours in the ϕ and θ directions are circles.

Surfaces of revolution can also be obtained by the rotation of a freeform curve, such as a Bezier or B-spline, around an axis. For the special case of a cubic curve, for example, the surface of revolution is represented in matrix form as

$$P(t,\theta) = [t][M][V][T_R]^\theta \quad (11.5)$$

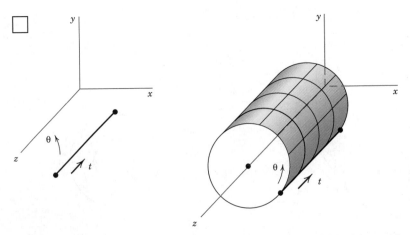

FIGURE 11.4 Surface of revolution obtained by setting contours in the t and θ directions of parameterization.

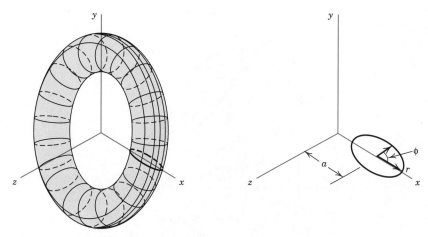

FIGURE 11.5 Torus generated by revolution of a circle around the z axis.

where $[t]$ = parameter matrix
$[M]$ = coefficients matrix
$[V]$ = geometry matrix
$[T_R]^\theta$ = rotation matrix about the axis of revolution

For the specific rotation around the z axis, as shown in Eq. 11.3b

$$[T_R]^\theta = \begin{bmatrix} \cos\theta & \sin\theta & 0 & 0 \\ 0 & 0 & 0 & 0 \\ 0 & 0 & 1 & 0 \\ 0 & 0 & 0 & 1 \end{bmatrix} \qquad (11.6)$$

Example 11.2

Consider the surface of revolution generated by a cubic Bezier curve defined by the control points $P_1 = (1,0,2)$ $P_2 = (3,0,4)$ $P_3 = (2,0,6)$ $P_4 = (5,0,7)$ rotating about the z axis. Calculate the point on the surface at $t = 0.5$, $\theta = \pi/4$ rad.

Solution

Applying Eq. 11.5,

$$P(0.5, \pi/4) = [(\tfrac{1}{2})^3 \quad (\tfrac{1}{2})^2 \quad (\tfrac{1}{2}) \quad 1] \begin{bmatrix} -1 & 3 & -3 & 1 \\ 3 & -6 & 3 & 0 \\ -3 & 3 & 0 & 0 \\ 1 & 0 & 0 & 0 \end{bmatrix} \begin{bmatrix} 1 & 0 & 2 & 1 \\ 3 & 0 & 4 & 1 \\ 2 & 0 & 6 & 1 \\ 5 & 0 & 7 & 1 \end{bmatrix} \begin{bmatrix} \dfrac{\sqrt{2}}{2} & \dfrac{\sqrt{2}}{2} & 0 & 0 \\ 0 & 0 & 0 & 0 \\ 0 & 0 & 1 & 0 \\ 0 & 0 & 0 & 1 \end{bmatrix}$$

$$= [1.86 \quad 1.86 \quad 4.88 \quad 1]$$

Figure 11.6 shows this surface.

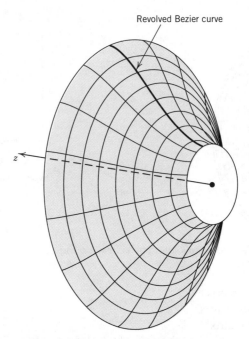

FIGURE 11.6 Surface of revolution generated by a cubic Bezier curve.

11.2 SWEEPING

Sweeping is a procedure by which a surface is generated through the movement of a line, segment of curve, polygon, and so forth, along or around a defined path. These types of surfaces are commonly found in geometric modeling and have various engineering applications, as shown in Figure 11.7. The paths followed in the sweeping operation can be straight lines or curves. The corresponding swept surface is represented in parametric form as

$$P(t,s) = Q(t)[T(s)] \qquad (11.7)$$

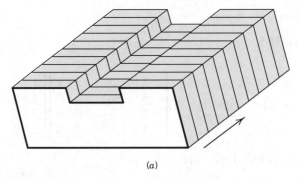

(a)

FIGURE 11.7 (a) Translational sweep.

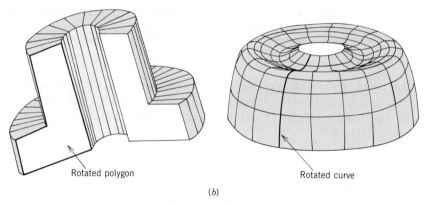

Rotated polygon

Rotated curve

(b)

FIGURE 11.7 (b) Rotational sweep.

where $Q(t)$ is the parametric equation of the line or curve and $[T(s)]$ is the sweep transformation based on the shape of the path.

The sweep transformation can contain translations, scalings, or rotations, as shown in Figure 11.7. It can also contain combinations of these transformations. For example, if the path is a straight line starting at the origin it can be represented in parametric form as

$$x(s) = as$$
$$y(s) = bs \qquad (11.8)$$
$$z(s) = cs$$

Then

$$[T(s)] = \begin{bmatrix} 1 & 0 & 0 & 0 \\ 0 & 1 & 0 & 0 \\ 0 & 0 & 1 & 0 \\ as & bs & cs & 1 \end{bmatrix} \quad 0 \le s \le 1 \qquad (11.9)$$

which is the equivalent of a three-dimensional translation, as described in Section 6.3.2.

If the path involves rotations about the coordinate axes, then the appropriate rotation angles should be included in the sweep transformation. When closed polygons are rotated or translated to generate swept surfaces, one of the ways to determine the final shape of the surface is to control the direction of the normal to the polygon. A common approach is to place the normal in the direction of the instantaneous tangent to the path. Example 11.3 shows how to implement this approach.

Example 11.3

Generate the swept surface obtained by moving a triangle located in the xy plane along the path $z = 8s$, $y = (\sin(\pi s) - 1)$. The vertices of the triangle are $P_1 = (-5,0,0)$, $P_2 = (0,5,0)$, $P_3 = (5,0,0)$. Keep the normal to the triangle in the direction of the instantaneous tangent to the path.

Solution

In this problem the path is contained on the yz plane, and the normal to the surface is rotated about the x axis to keep it aligned with the tangent to the path. The normal remains at all times parallel to the yz plane. (See accompanying figure.)

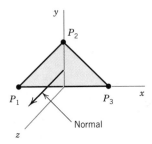

The first value to calculate is the instantaneous tangent to the path. This is given by:

$$\left[\frac{dx}{ds} \quad \frac{dy}{ds} \quad \frac{dz}{ds} \right] = [0, \ \pi \ \cos(\pi s), \ 8]$$

Next, the angle of rotation of the normal about the x-axis must be found at each instance, as follows:

$$\phi = \tan^{-1}\left(\frac{dy}{dz}\right) = \tan^{-1}\left[\frac{\pi \ \cos \ (\pi s)}{8}\right]$$

The complete sweep transformation involves a translation along the given path ($z = 8s, y = \sin \ (\pi s) - 1$) and a rotation by the angle ϕ around the x axis. Thus

$$[T(s)] = \begin{bmatrix} 1 & 0 & 0 & 0 \\ 0 & \cos \phi & \sin \phi & 0 \\ 0 & -\sin \phi & \cos \phi & 0 \\ 0 & \sin \ (\pi s) - 1 & 8s & 1 \end{bmatrix}$$

At a position along the path where $s = 0.25$, the rotation angle is (see accompanying figure)

$$\phi = \tan^{-1} y/z$$

$$\phi = \tan^{-1}\left(\frac{\pi \ \cos \ (\pi/4)}{8}\right) = 0.2708 \ \text{rad}$$

$$\phi = 15.52°$$

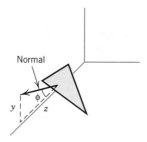

Substituting these values ($s = 0.25$ and $\phi = 15.52°$) into the sweep transformation matrix yields

$$
P(0.25, 15.52°) = \begin{bmatrix} -5 & 0 & 0 & 1 \\ 0 & 5 & 0 & 1 \\ 5 & 0 & 0 & 1 \end{bmatrix} \begin{bmatrix} 1 & 0 & 0 & 0 \\ 0 & 0.964 & 0.268 & 0 \\ 0 & -0.268 & 0.964 & 0 \\ 0 & -0.293 & 2.0 & 1 \end{bmatrix}
$$

$$
= \begin{bmatrix} -5.0 & -0.293 & 2.0 & 1 \\ 0 & 4.525 & 3.338 & 1 \\ 5.0 & -0.293 & 2.0 & 1 \end{bmatrix}
$$

The swept surface is shown in Figure 11.8. The cosine function described by vertex P_3 is highlighted in the figure. The triangle rotates as the surface is swept so that the normals remain parallel to the tangent to the path.

Sweeping of freeform curves can be performed in a similar manner. The surface equation will be defined by

$$
P(t,s) = [t][M][V][T(s)] \tag{11.10}
$$

where $T(s)$ represents the sweep operation.

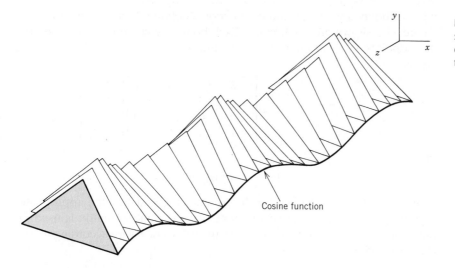

FIGURE 11.8 Swept surface obtained for a path combining rotations and translations.

Example 11.4

Consider the cubic B-spline curve defined by the control points $P_1 = (0,5,0)$, $P_2 = (3,4,0)$, $P_3 = (2,0,0)$, and $P_4 = (5,0,0)$. Translate this curve five units along the z axis to generate a swept surface.

Solution

Equation 11.10 can be represented as follows for the given conditions:

$$P(t,s) = [t^3 \quad t^2 \quad t \quad 1]\frac{1}{6}\begin{bmatrix} -1 & 3 & -3 & 1 \\ 3 & -6 & 3 & 0 \\ -3 & 0 & 3 & 0 \\ 1 & 4 & 1 & 0 \end{bmatrix}\begin{bmatrix} 0 & 5 & 0 & 1 \\ 3 & 4 & 0 & 1 \\ 2 & 0 & 0 & 1 \\ 5 & 0 & 0 & 1 \end{bmatrix}\begin{bmatrix} 1 & 0 & 0 & 0 \\ 0 & 1 & 0 & 0 \\ 0 & 0 & 1 & 0 \\ 0 & 0 & 5s & 0 \end{bmatrix}$$

If a particular position is chosen, for example, $t = 0.2$ and $s = 0.8$, then

$$P(0.2,0.8) = [2.464 \quad 2.949 \quad 4 \quad 1]$$

11.3 FREEFORM SURFACES

As in the case of curves, some surfaces cannot be totally described by the analytical representations mentioned in the previous sections. Among these are surfaces used in the design of automobile bodies, ship hulls, aircraft wings, and so forth. They are usually described by a series of "patches," in the same way that a patchwork quilt is put together. The basic formulations described in Chapter 10, Hermite, Bezier and B-spline, can be used in free-form surface design [45,46]

11.3.1 Parametric Cubic Surfaces

Parametric cubic surfaces are the extension of the Hermite curve formulation given in Section 10.4.2. The surface is formed by parametric cubics or Hermites as boundary curves, and the interior is defined by blending functions. Figure 11.9 shows one such patch. Each boundary curve is represented by its endpoints and end tangent vectors and is given by Eq. 10.38, rewritten below:

$$P(t) = [t^3 \quad t^2 \quad t \quad 1]\begin{bmatrix} 2 & -2 & 1 & 1 \\ -3 & 3 & -2 & -1 \\ 0 & 0 & 1 & 0 \\ 1 & 0 & 0 & 0 \end{bmatrix}\begin{bmatrix} P(0) \\ P(1) \\ P'(0) \\ P'(1) \end{bmatrix}$$

or

$$P(t) = [t][M]_H[G]_H$$

A similar equation is derived for the parameter s, to define the appropriate boundary curves in that direction. Note that the same M matrix is used in both parametric directions, s and t, and the values of P vary according to the curve's position.

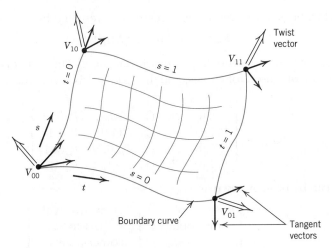

FIGURE 11.9 Parametric cubic surface and its defining parameters.

The definition of the boundary curves alone does not completely identify the surface. For the same boundary curves, various surfaces can be found by varying the interior shape, as shown in Figure 11.10. Therefore, to totally identify the surface, the interior shape in the vicinity of each corner is controlled by the cross derivative at the corner, also known as the *twist vector* (see Figure 11.9).

Since basis functions of two variables, s and t, are needed for the parametric cubic surface representation, it is logical that the surface basis be defined by the product of the single variable basis. This is called a surface or tensor product. Therefore, the parametric cubic surface, also known as

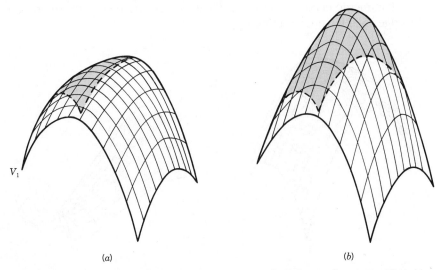

FIGURE 11.10 Variation of twist vectors causes the final shape of a parametric cubic surface to change.

Coons bicubic surface after its discoverer, is represented by

$$P(s,t) = [s][M]_H[G]_H[M]_H^T[t]^T \qquad (11.11)$$

which takes into account both parametric directions. The matrix $[M]_H$ is the same as the one used for curves, and the $[G]_H$ matrix represents the following:

$$[G]_H = \begin{bmatrix} P(0,0) & P(0,1) & P_t(0,0) & P_t(0,1) \\ P(1,0) & P(1,1) & P_t(1,0) & P_t(1,1) \\ P_s(0,0) & P_s(0,1) & P_{st}(0,0) & P_{st}(0,1) \\ P_s(1,0) & P_s(1,1) & P_{st}(1,0) & P_{st}(1,1) \end{bmatrix} \qquad (11.12)$$

which can be broken down as:

$$[G]_H = \begin{bmatrix} \begin{array}{c} \text{Position of} \\ \text{corner points} \end{array} & \begin{array}{c} \text{Derivative with} \\ \text{respect to } t \text{ at} \\ \text{corner points} \end{array} \\ \hline \begin{array}{c} \text{Derivative with} \\ \text{respect to } s \text{ at} \\ \text{corner points} \end{array} & \begin{array}{c} \text{Cross derivative} \\ \text{at corner points} \end{array} \end{bmatrix}$$

Variations on the surface are obtained by changing the corner points, tangent vectors, or twist vectors. Figure 11.11 shows examples of tangent vector variations for the same set of corner points. Variations of twist vectors were shown in Figure 11.10.

The parametric cubic surface can be simplified by setting all twist vectors to zero. This is called a Ferguson or *F-patch*. Although they simplify the surface formulation, F-patches are not commonly used in practice because they force the surface to flatten at the corners. For most engineering applications, nonzero twist vectors must be used.

Parametric cubic patches and *F*-patches can be pieced together, and the edges will have C^1 continuity.

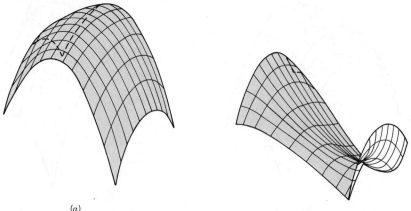

(a)

(b)

FIGURE 11.11 Variation of tangent vectors causes the final shape of a parametric cubic surface to change.

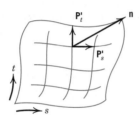

FIGURE 11.12 Representation of the normal to a parametric cubic surface.

The normal to a surface is also important in geometric modeling applications, such as numerical control calculations or interference detection for robotics. The normal to a parametric cubic curve at any specific point is found by the cross-product of the parametric derivatives at the point in question, as shown in Figure 11.12, so that

$$\mathbf{n} = \mathbf{P}'_s \times \mathbf{P}'_t \tag{11.13}$$

An algorithm for parametric cubic or Hermite surface generation is given at the end of the chapter as Appendix 11.1.

Example 11.5

A parametric bicubic surface is defined by its cartesian components as follows:

$$x(s,t) = [s^3 \quad s^2 \quad s \quad 1] \begin{bmatrix} 5 & 1 & 0 & 2 \\ 1 & 1 & 0 & 1 \\ 1 & 2 & 1 & 1 \\ 0 & 2 & 0 & -1 \end{bmatrix} \begin{bmatrix} t^3 \\ t^2 \\ t \\ 1 \end{bmatrix}$$

$$y(s,t) = [s^3 \quad s^2 \quad s \quad 1] \begin{bmatrix} 1 & 0 & 1 & 1 \\ 0 & 0 & 1 & 0 \\ 3 & 1 & 0 & 2 \\ 1 & 0 & 2 & 1 \end{bmatrix} \begin{bmatrix} t^3 \\ t^2 \\ t \\ 1 \end{bmatrix}$$

$$z(s,t) = [s^3 \quad s^2 \quad s \quad 1] \begin{bmatrix} 0 & 1 & 2 & 1 \\ 2 & 1 & 0 & 0 \\ 0 & 5 & 1 & 0 \\ 0 & 1 & 0 & 0 \end{bmatrix} \begin{bmatrix} t^3 \\ t^2 \\ t \\ 1 \end{bmatrix}$$

Calculate the tangent vectors in the parametric directions at the point $t = 1$, $s = \frac{1}{2}$.

Solution

Notice that the three numerical matrices given correspond to the product $[M]_H[G]_H[M]_H^T$ of the general parametric cubic surface in Eq. 11.11. To find the tangent vectors, derivatives with respect to s and t must be obtained as follows:

$$P'_s = [3s^2 \quad 2s \quad 1 \quad 0] \begin{bmatrix} \text{corresponding} \\ \text{matrix} \end{bmatrix} \begin{bmatrix} t^3 \\ t^2 \\ t \\ 1 \end{bmatrix}$$

and

$$P'_t = [s^3 \quad s^2 \quad s \quad 1] \begin{bmatrix} \text{corresponding} \\ \text{matrix} \end{bmatrix} \begin{bmatrix} 3t^2 \\ 2t \\ 1 \\ 0 \end{bmatrix}$$

So, at $s = \frac{1}{2}$ and $t = 1$,

$$x_s = [0.75 \quad 1 \quad 1 \quad 0] \begin{bmatrix} 5 & 1 & 0 & 2 \\ 1 & 1 & 0 & 1 \\ 1 & 2 & 1 & 1 \\ 0 & 2 & 0 & -1 \end{bmatrix} \begin{bmatrix} 1 \\ 1 \\ 1 \\ 1 \end{bmatrix} = 14$$

$$y_s = [0.75 \quad 1 \quad 1 \quad 0] \begin{bmatrix} 1 & 0 & 1 & 1 \\ 0 & 0 & 1 & 1 \\ 3 & 1 & 0 & 1 \\ 1 & 0 & 2 & 1 \end{bmatrix} \begin{bmatrix} 1 \\ 1 \\ 1 \\ 1 \end{bmatrix} = 9.25$$

$$z_s = [0.75 \quad 1 \quad 1 \quad 0] \begin{bmatrix} 0 & 1 & 2 & 1 \\ 2 & 1 & 0 & 0 \\ 0 & 5 & 1 & 0 \\ 0 & 1 & 0 & 0 \end{bmatrix} \begin{bmatrix} 1 \\ 1 \\ 1 \\ 1 \end{bmatrix} = 12$$

And

$$\mathbf{P}'_s = 14\mathbf{i} + 9.25\mathbf{j} + 12\mathbf{k}$$

In addition,

$$x_t = [0.125 \quad 0.25 \quad 0.50 \quad 1] \begin{bmatrix} 5 & 1 & 0 & 2 \\ 1 & 1 & 0 & 1 \\ 1 & 2 & 1 & 1 \\ 0 & 2 & 0 & -1 \end{bmatrix} \begin{bmatrix} 3 \\ 2 \\ 1 \\ 0 \end{bmatrix} = 11.375$$

$$y_t = [0.125 \quad 0.25 \quad 0.50 \quad 1] \begin{bmatrix} 1 & 0 & 1 & 1 \\ 0 & 0 & 1 & 0 \\ 3 & 1 & 0 & 2 \\ 1 & 0 & 2 & 1 \end{bmatrix} \begin{bmatrix} 3 \\ 2 \\ 1 \\ 0 \end{bmatrix} = 11.25$$

$$z_t = [0.125 \quad 0.25 \quad 0.50 \quad 1] \begin{bmatrix} 0 & 1 & 2 & 1 \\ 2 & 1 & 0 & 0 \\ 0 & 5 & 1 & 0 \\ 0 & 1 & 0 & 0 \end{bmatrix} \begin{bmatrix} 3 \\ 2 \\ 1 \\ 0 \end{bmatrix} = 10$$

And

$$\mathbf{P}'_t = 11.375\mathbf{i} + 11.25\mathbf{j} + 10\mathbf{k}$$

11.3.2 Bezier Surfaces

Parametric cubic surfaces, although effective design tools, have the disadvantage that no intuitive feel for the values of the tangent and twist vectors is available to the user. Bezier surfaces, on the other hand, are much easier to create and modify intuitively.

Bezier surfaces are defined by a simple generalization of the curve formulation. The tensor product approach used in the parametric cubic surface definition is again applied, with the same two directions of parameterization, s and t, as shown in Figure 11.13. Any point on the surface can be located for given values of the parametric pair by

$$Q(s,t) = \sum_{i=0}^{n} \sum_{j=0}^{m} V_{i,j}B_{i,n}(s)B_{j,m}(t) \qquad 0 \le s,t \le 1 \qquad (11.14)$$

As in the case of Bezier curves, the $V_{i,j}$ define the control vertices and the $B_{i,n}(s)$, $B_{j,m}(t)$ are the Bernstein blending functions in the s and t directions. Note that the degree of the blending functions does not have to be the same in the two parametric directions. It could, for example, be cubic in s and quadratic in t.

The properties of Bezier surfaces are controlled by the blending functions. For example:

- The surface takes the general shape of the control points.
- The surface is contained within the convex hull of the control points.
- The corners of the surface and the corner control vertices are coincident.

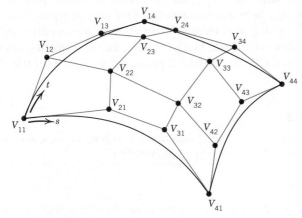

FIGURE 11.13 Control mesh for a bicubic Bezier surface.

The Bezier surface control points have the same function as the parameters used in the parametric cubic patch. The four corner points are on the surface itself, as stated above. The Hermite tangent vectors at the corners are determined by the location of adjacent Bezier control points on the boundary curves. In Figure 11.11, for example, the tangent vectors of the boundary curve at $s = 0$ are given by $V_{11}V_{12}$ and $V_{14}V_{13}$. The same is true for all other tangent vectors. The interior control points, V_{22}, V_{23}, V_{32}, V_{33}, define the interior shape of the surface as do the twist vectors in the parametric cubic. The user simply moves these points to modify the internal shape of the surface. This approach is much more intuitive than the one used in the parametric cubic definition, due to the difficulties in assigning proper values to the tangent and twist vectors. Figure 11.14 shows the effect of moving the control points at the boundary curves or on the interior part of the surface.

A Bezier surface can be represented in matrix form as

$$Q(s,t) = [s][M]_B[V]_B[M]_B^T[t]^T \qquad (11.15)$$

For a bicubic surface this reduces to:

$$Q(s,t) = [s^3 \quad s^2 \quad s \quad 1]\begin{bmatrix} -1 & 3 & -3 & 1 \\ 3 & -6 & 3 & 0 \\ -3 & 3 & 0 & 0 \\ 1 & 0 & 0 & 0 \end{bmatrix}$$

$$\begin{bmatrix} V_{0,0} & V_{0,1} & V_{0,2} & V_{0,3} \\ V_{1,0} & V_{1,1} & V_{1,2} & V_{1,3} \\ V_{2,0} & V_{2,1} & V_{2,2} & V_{2,3} \\ V_{3,0} & V_{3,1} & V_{3,2} & V_{3,3} \end{bmatrix}\begin{bmatrix} -1 & 3 & -3 & 1 \\ 3 & -6 & 3 & 0 \\ -3 & 3 & 0 & 0 \\ 1 & 0 & 0 & 0 \end{bmatrix}\begin{bmatrix} t^3 \\ t^2 \\ t \\ 1 \end{bmatrix} \qquad (11.16)$$

To represent a bicubic Bezier surface, therefore, sixteen control points must be specified. As with Bezier curves, an increase in the number of control points automatically increases the degree of the surface. Several Bezier patches are often necessary to create a specific surface of low degree. In the case of bicubic surfaces, first degree parametric continuity is enforced along the common edge between two patches. One way to ensure this condition is to force the polygon control sides meeting at the common edge to be collinear, as shown in Figure 11.15. An algorithm showing the logic used in the generation of a Bezier surface is presented at the end of the chapter as Appendix 11.2.

Example 11.6

A semicircular roof structure is described in Figure 11.16. Create the Bezier control net needed to approximate this surface.

Solution

The problem is solved by finding the control net that will recreate known points along the semicircular cross section, and then moving those points

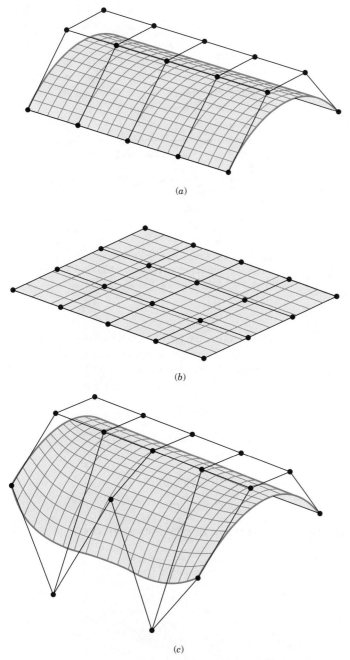

FIGURE 11.14 (a) Bezier surface. (b) Interior control points are changed, "flattening" the surface. (c) Boundary control points are changed.

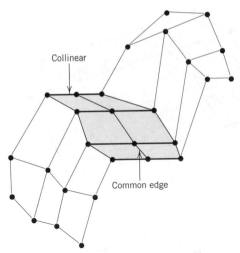

FIGURE 11.15 Enforcement of first-degree parametric continuity between two bicubic patches.

along the z axis at uniform intervals. It thus reduces to fitting a Bezier surface to a semicylindrical surface. The semicircular cross section at $z = 0$ will be fitted first, using five points on the arc as shown in Figure 11.17. The five points on the semicircular arc have the following coordinates:

$$P_0(20,0)$$

$$P_1(10\sqrt{2},10\sqrt{2})$$

$$P_2(0,20)$$

$$P_3(-10\sqrt{2},10\sqrt{2})$$

$$P_4(-20,0)$$

To interpolate these points five Bezier control vertices V_0, V_1, V_2, V_3, V_4 are

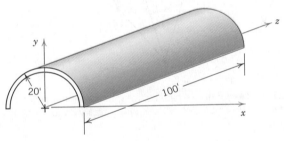

FIGURE 11.16 Semicircular roof structure to be described as a Bezier surface.

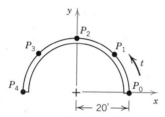

FIGURE 11.17

needed. Each V_i should satisfy the Bezier curve expression

$$P_i(t) = \sum_{i=0}^{4} B_{4,i}(t) V_i$$

The values of t, constrained within the limits $t = 0$ and $t = 1$, can be found as a ratio of the chord lengths as

$$t_1 = 0, \; t_2 = 0.25, \; t_3 = 0.5, \; t_4 = 0.75, \; t_5 = 1.0$$

In matrix form, and using homogeneous coordinates, the Bezier expression can be written as

$$[P]_{5\times3} = [B]_{5\times5}[V]_{5\times3}$$

$$
= \begin{bmatrix} B_{40}(t_1) & B_{41}(t_1) & \cdot\cdot & B_{44}(t_1) \\ \cdot & \cdot & \cdot\cdot & \cdot \\ \cdot & \cdot & \cdot\cdot & \cdot \\ \cdot & \cdot & \cdot\cdot & \cdot \\ B_{40}(t_5) & \cdot & \cdot\cdot & B_{44}(t_5) \end{bmatrix} \begin{bmatrix} V_0 \\ V_1 \\ V_2 \\ V_3 \\ V_4 \end{bmatrix}
$$

Each element of the $[B]$ matrix is evaluated through the expression given in Eq. 10.59:

$$B_{ni}(t) = \binom{n}{i} t^i (1 - t)^{n-i}$$

to yield

$$
\begin{bmatrix} V_0 \\ V_1 \\ V_2 \\ V_3 \\ V_4 \end{bmatrix} = \begin{bmatrix} 1 & 0 & 0 & 0 & 0 \\ 0.3164 & 0.4218 & 0.2109 & 0.0469 & 0.0039 \\ 0.0625 & 0.25 & 0.375 & 0.25 & 0.0625 \\ 0.0039 & 0.0469 & 0.2109 & 0.4218 & 0.3164 \\ 0 & 0 & 0 & 0 & 1 \end{bmatrix} \begin{bmatrix} 20 & 0 & 1 \\ 10\sqrt{2} & 10\sqrt{2} & 1 \\ 0 & 20 & 1 \\ -10\sqrt{2} & 10\sqrt{2} & 1 \\ -20 & 0 & 1 \end{bmatrix}
$$

$$
= \begin{bmatrix} 20 & 0 & 1 \\ 21.05 & 15.44 & 1 \\ -0.1 & 32.61 & 1 \\ -21.05 & 15.44 & 1 \\ -20 & 0 & 1 \end{bmatrix}
$$

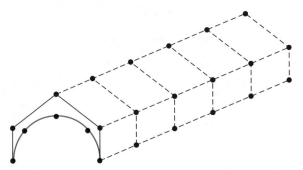

FIGURE 11.18 Mesh of control points for Example 11.6.

Figure 11.18 shows these control points and the curve interpolated. The additional control points on the Bezier net can be obtained by varying the z coordinates between 0 and 100 feet by uniform 20-foot intervals. The final 30-point Bezier control net becomes

$$
\begin{bmatrix}
(20,0,0) & (20,0,20) & (20,0,40) & \cdots \\
(21.05,15.44,0) & (21.05,15.44,20) & (21.05,15.44,40) & \cdots \\
(-0.1,32.61,0) & (-0.1,32.61,20) & (-0.1,32.61,40) & \cdots \\
(-21.05,15.44,0) & (-21.05,15.44,20) & (-21.05,15.44,40) & \cdots \\
(-20,0,0) & (-20,0,20) & (-20,0,40) & \cdots
\end{bmatrix}
$$

Example 11.7

Given the matrix of control points in Bezier form

$$
[V]_B = \begin{bmatrix}
V_{11} & V_{12} & V_{13} & V_{14} \\
V_{21} & V_{22} & V_{23} & V_{24} \\
V_{31} & V_{32} & V_{33} & V_{34} \\
V_{41} & V_{42} & V_{43} & V_{44}
\end{bmatrix}
$$

find the equivalent geometric coefficients matrix for the Hermite representation.

Solution

The bicubic Bezier patch is represented by Eq. 11.15:

$$
Q_B(s,t) = [s][M]_B[V]_B[M]_B^T[t]^T \tag{I}
$$

where

$$
[M]_B = \begin{bmatrix}
-1 & 3 & -3 & 1 \\
3 & -6 & 3 & 0 \\
-3 & 3 & 0 & 0 \\
1 & 0 & 0 & 0
\end{bmatrix}
$$

The Hermite patch is represented by Eq. 11.11:

$$Q_H(s,t) = [s][M]_H[G]_H[M]_H^T[t]^T \qquad \text{(II)}$$

where

$$[M]_H = \begin{bmatrix} 2 & -2 & 1 & 1 \\ -3 & 3 & -2 & -1 \\ 0 & 0 & 1 & 0 \\ 1 & 0 & 0 & 0 \end{bmatrix}$$

Equating I and II:

$$[s][M]_B[V]_B[M]_B^T[t]^T = [s][M]_H[G]_H[M]_H^T[t]^T$$

and

$$[G]_H = [M]_H^{-1}[M]_B[V]_B[M]_B^T([M]_H^T)^{-1}$$

$$= \begin{bmatrix} 1 & 0 & 0 & 0 \\ 0 & 0 & 0 & 1 \\ -3 & 3 & 0 & 0 \\ 0 & 0 & -3 & 3 \end{bmatrix}[V]_B \begin{bmatrix} 1 & 0 & -3 & 0 \\ 0 & 0 & 3 & 0 \\ 0 & 0 & 0 & -3 \\ 0 & 1 & 0 & 3 \end{bmatrix}$$

After substitution of the values in the $[V]_B$ matrix and multiplication, the Hermite geometric coefficients matrix becomes

$$[G]_H = \begin{bmatrix} V_{11} & V_{14} & 3(V_{12} - V_{11}) & 3(V_{14} - V_{13}) \\ V_{41} & V_{44} & 3(V_{42} - V_{41}) & 3(V_{44} - V_{43}) \\ 3(V_{21} - V_{11}) & 3(V_{24} - V_{14}) & 9(V_{11} - V_{21} - V_{12} + V_{22}) & 9(V_{13} - V_{23} - V_{14} + V_{24}) \\ 3(V_{41} - V_{31}) & 3(V_{44} - V_{34}) & 9(V_{31} - V_{41} - V_{32} + V_{42}) & 9(V_{33} - V_{43} - V_{34} + V_{44}) \end{bmatrix}$$

11.3.3 B-spline Surfaces

B-spline surfaces, like Bezier surfaces, can be represented by the tensor product:

$$P(s,t) = \sum_{i=0}^{n} \sum_{j=0}^{m} N_{i,k}(s)N_{j,l}(t)V_{i,j} \qquad (11.17)$$

where $V_{i,j}$ are the control points and $N_{i,k}(s)$, $N_{j,l}(t)$ are the B-spline blending functions, as defined in Section 10.9. The knot vectors in the two directions of parameterization can be classified as periodic/uniform, nonperiodic, and nonuniform, like the B-spline curves. The surface lies within the defining polyhedron formed by the control points. Figures 11.19 and 11.20 give examples of B-spline surfaces. They exhibit the same type of local control shown by B-spline curves: By varying one control point, only a small portion of the B-spline surface is affected.

FIGURE 11.19 (a) B-spline surface. (b) Surface exhibits local control when one control point is moved.

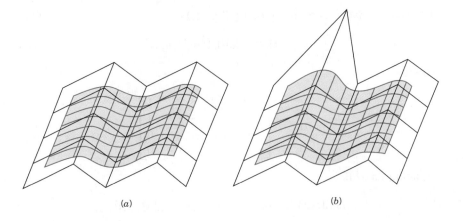

(a)   (b)

Periodic/uniform B-spline surfaces are generated by making use of uniform knot vectors and an array of control points. A bicubic surface, for example, would be represented by a 4×4 array of control points [47].

For bicubic periodic B-spline surfaces with C^2 continuity, of the sixteen control points needed for each segment, twelve are shared with the next

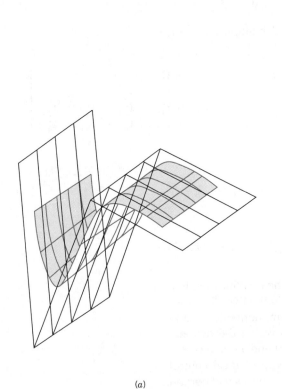

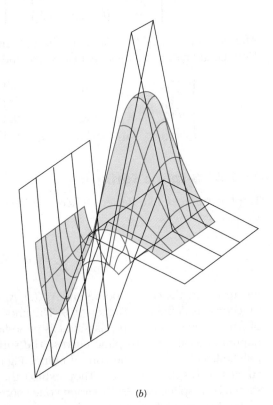

(a)   (b)

FIGURE 11.20 (a) B-spline surface. (b) Surface exhibits local control when two control points are moved.

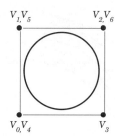

FIGURE 11.21 Closed periodic B-spline curve used in the approximation of a cylinder.

segment in developing the surface. The V arrays of control points are

$$
\begin{array}{|c|cccc|c}
V_{11} & V_{12} & V_{13} & V_{14} & V_{15} \\
V_{21} & V_{22} & V_{23} & V_{24} & V_{25} \\
V_{31} & V_{32} & V_{33} & V_{34} & V_{35} \\
V_{41} & V_{42} & V_{43} & V_{44} & V_{45} \\
\end{array} \quad \cdots
$$

Patch 1 ⌐→   Patch 2 ⌐→

Closed periodic B-spline surfaces can be obtained with the same approach used for closed periodic B-spline curves. Opposite edges of the surface are merged by repeating control graph vertices at the edges. An approximation of a cylinder, for example, can be obtained by using multiple control points as shown in Figure 11.21. First the circle is approximated by four cubic B-spline segments:

$$
\begin{array}{ll}
V_0 V_1 V_2 V_3 & \text{segment 1} \\
V_1 V_2 V_3 V_4 & \text{segment 2} \\
V_2 V_3 V_4 V_5 & \text{segment 3} \\
V_3 V_4 V_5 V_6 & \text{segment 4} \\
\end{array}
$$

By moving the control points in a direction perpendicular to the plane in which they lie, the control graph for the cylinder is obtained. Figure 11.22 shows the resulting surface. A torus approximation can also be created by

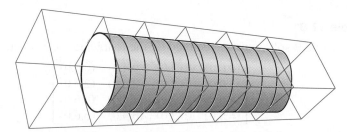

FIGURE 11.22 Cylindrical surface represented by B-spline patches.

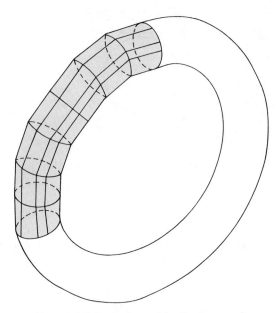

FIGURE 11.23 Torus formed by B-spline patches.

rotating the control points forming the circle around an axis located at a distance from their center. Figure 11.23 shows the result of these procedures.

Like periodic B-spline curves, the surfaces can be expressed in matrix form. In the case of bicubic surfaces, the matrix formulation takes the following form:

$$P(s,t) = [s][M]_{Bs}[V]_{Bs}[M]_{Bs}^{T}[t]^{T} \tag{11.18}$$

where $[M]_{Bs}$ is the same matrix used in the definition of cubic periodic B-spline curves:

$$[M]_{Bs} = (\tfrac{1}{6}) \begin{bmatrix} -1 & 3 & -3 & 1 \\ 3 & -6 & 3 & 0 \\ -3 & 0 & 3 & 0 \\ 1 & 4 & 1 & 0 \end{bmatrix} \tag{11.19}$$

and $[V]_{Bs}$ is a control graph with sixteen points.

An algorithm showing the generation of B-spline surfaces is given at the end of the chapter as Appendix 11.3.

Example 11.8

Given a cubic B-spline surface defined by the following control net:

$$[V]_{Bs} = \begin{bmatrix} (0,0,0) & (0,2,0) & (0,4,0) & (0,6,0) \\ (2,0,0) & (2,2,0) & (2,4,0) & (2,6,0) \\ (4,0,0) & (4,2,0) & (4,4,0) & (4,6,0) \\ (6,0,0) & (6,2,0) & (6,4,0) & (6,6,0) \end{bmatrix}$$

find the point on the surface at $s = 0.25$ and $t = 0.75$.

Solution

Using Eq. 11.18 to describe the surface, we obtain

$$
x = [0.0156 \quad 0.0625 \quad 0.25 \quad 1.0][M]_{\mathrm{Bs}}
\begin{bmatrix}
0 & 0 & 0 & 0 \\
2 & 2 & 2 & 2 \\
4 & 4 & 4 & 4 \\
6 & 6 & 6 & 6
\end{bmatrix}
[M]_{\mathrm{Bs}}^{T}
\begin{bmatrix}
0.4219 \\
0.563 \\
0.75 \\
1.0
\end{bmatrix}
$$

where $[M]_{\mathrm{Bs}}$ is given by Eq. 11.19. Multiplication of the appropriate matrices gives:

$$
x = 2.50
$$

Similarly:

$$
y = [0.0156 \quad 0.0625 \quad 0.25 \quad 1.0][M]_{\mathrm{Bs}}
\begin{bmatrix}
0 & 2 & 4 & 6 \\
0 & 2 & 4 & 6 \\
0 & 2 & 4 & 6 \\
0 & 2 & 4 & 6
\end{bmatrix}
[M]_{\mathrm{Bs}}^{T}
\begin{bmatrix}
0.4219 \\
0.5625 \\
0.75 \\
1.0
\end{bmatrix}
$$

$$
y = 3.5
$$

And

$$
z = 0.0
$$

The point on the surface at $s = 0.25$ and $t = 0.75$ is $P(2.5, 3.5, 0)$.

11.3.4 Conversion Between Cubic Surface Representations

The same approach used in the conversion of cubic curves can be used for surfaces [38]. In this case, the control points representing cubic Hermite, Bezier, or B-spline surfaces are related by the following expression, similar to Eq. 10.80.

$$
V_{\mathrm{to}} = [M_{\mathrm{to}}^{-1} M_{\mathrm{from}}] V_{\mathrm{from}} [M_{\mathrm{to}}^{-1} M_{\mathrm{from}}]^{T} \tag{11.20}
$$

The conversion matrices $[M_{\mathrm{to}}^{-1} M_{\mathrm{from}}]$ can be obtained from Table 10.3 and substituted into Eq. 11.20.

11.3.5 Rational Surfaces

The process for generating rational surfaces is an extension of the one used for rational curves. The concept of homogeneous coordinates is again applied. Table 11.1 shows the appropriate expressions for Bezier and B-spline surfaces.

The tensor product rational B-spline surface, for example, is given by the equation shown on the lower right corner of Table 11.1. The $N_{i,k}(s)$ and $N_{j,l}(t)$ are basis functions, $V_{i,j}$ is the control polyhedron and $w_{i,j}$ are the weights at each control point. The knot vector used can be periodic/uniform, nonperiodic, or nonuniform, and can vary in the two directions of parame-

TABLE 11.1

	Bezier	B-Spline
Non-ra-tional	$Q(s,t) = \sum\limits_{i=0}^{n} \sum\limits_{j=0}^{m} B_{i,n}(s) B_{j,m}(t) V_{i,j}$	$P(s,t) = \sum\limits_{i=0}^{n} \sum\limits_{j=0}^{m} N_{i,k}(s) N_{j,l}(t) V_{i,j}$
Ra-tional	$Q(s,t) = \dfrac{\sum\limits_{i=0}^{n} \sum\limits_{j=0}^{m} w_{i,j} B_{i,n}(s) B_{j,m}(t) V_{i,j}}{\sum\limits_{i=0}^{n} \sum\limits_{j=0}^{m} w_{i,j} B_{i,n}(s) B_{j,m}(t)}$	$P(s,t) = \dfrac{\sum\limits_{i=0}^{n} \sum\limits_{j=0}^{m} w_{i,j} N_{i,k}(s) N_{j,l}(t) V_{i,j}}{\sum\limits_{i=0}^{n} \sum\limits_{j=0}^{m} w_{i,j} N_{i,k}(s) N_{j,l}(t)}$

terization, s and t. As with rational curves, the weights provide an additional degree of freedom for the shaping of the surface. Figure 11.24 shows how variations on the value of the weights affect the shape of the surface.

Most properties of the nonrational surfaces extend to their rational counterparts. For example, rotations and translations are applied to the control points; the surface is contained within the convex hull of the enclosing

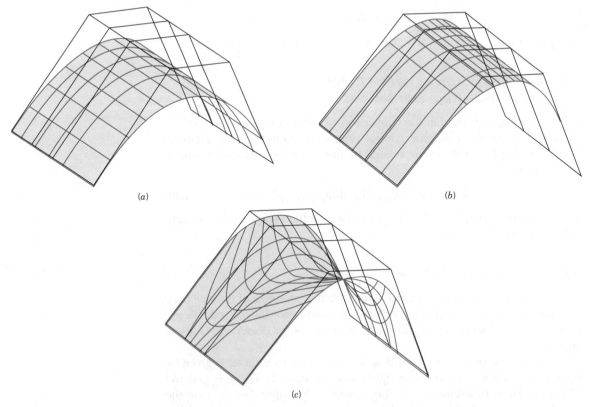

(a)

(b)

(c)

FIGURE 11.24 (a) Rational B-spline surface. (b) Larger values of weights at the interior control points. (c) Lower values of weights at the top interior control points.

polyhedron; if triangulated, the control net forms a planar approximation of the surface. Multiple vertices have the same effect on rational surfaces as on nonrational. In addition, the movement of one control vertex affects the surface only locally. Algorithms showing the logic in generating rational Bezier and B-spline surfaces are presented at the end of the chapter as Appendices 11.2 and 11.4.

11.3.6 NURBS (Nonuniform Rational B-spline Surfaces)

NURBS are rational B-spline surfaces obtained with a nonuniform knot vector. They are one of the most used surface representations in engineering design, largely because they encompass all other types of representations [41]. The general expression for NURBS is that given in Table 11.1 for rational B-spline, except that the knot vector used is nonuniform. They can easily reduce to the other types of representations, as shown below:

Nonrational B-splines	when all $w_{i,j} = 1$
Rational Bezier	when the number of defining control points is equal to the order in each parametric direction and no duplicate interior knot values exist
Nonrational Bezier	same as for rational Bezier, plus all $w_{i,j} = 1$

In addition, NURBS have the ability to represent quadric surfaces.

11.4 APPLICATION PROBLEMS

Many engineering application problems require the creation of surfaces of the type described in this chapter. This section gives one example solved with the help of a CAD system. The reader is encouraged to extrapolate this solution into other application areas of special interest.

Example 11.9

The airfoil of Figure 10.24a was developed in Example 10.13 as a series of sections formed by two cubic Bezier curves connected with C^0 continuity. The same problem could have been solved by means of a closed B-spline curve, ensuring a smoother transition through control vertices (such as V_0 in Figure 10.24a), as shown in Figure 11.25. Most CAD systems have a command that allows the creation of B-spline surfaces by connecting a series of B-spline curves. Such a procedure could be used to develop the skin of the airfoil. Since the CAD system will be using points on the various B-spline curves to create the surface, it is important that all curves have the same number of points and are connected in the same order, to avoid the possibility of twisting.

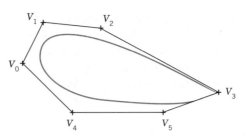

FIGURE 11.25

SUMMARY

This chapter described various methods for surface generation, including revolution, sweeping, Bezier and B-spline representations. The use of parametric geometry provides a systematic approach for the representation of surfaces. Bezier and B-spline surfaces can be manipulated through the use of modeling operations applied to their control polyhedra, and surface normals can be determined at various points and used for rendering purposes. Other geometric properties, such as surface area, are found by simple integration. The use of rational polynomials in surface definition was studied, and their use in geometric modeling emphasized.

EXERCISES

1. Generate a sphere by rotating a circle of radius 2 units placed on the xz plane with center at $(0,0,5)$.

2. Given a polygon described by its vertices

$$\begin{bmatrix} 0 & 0 & 0 \\ 0 & 8 & 0 \\ 2 & 8 & 0 \\ 2 & 4 & 0 \\ 6 & 4 & 0 \\ 6 & 8 & 0 \\ 8 & 8 & 0 \\ 8 & 0 & 0 \end{bmatrix}$$

sweep it along a straight line $z = 8s$ to describe a surface.

3. Generate a surface by rotating the polygon of Problem 2 about the x axis.

4. A bilinear patch is created by linear interpolation between four points which do not lie on the same plane, with parametric variables s and t ranging from zero to one. If the bilinear patch is described by the points

$$\begin{bmatrix} 0 & 0 & 0 \\ -2 & 0 & 1 \\ 1 & 1 & 3 \\ 4 & 2 & 3 \end{bmatrix}$$

determine the parametric equation of the curve which lies on this bilinear patch and has $y = 2$.

5. A parametric bicubic surface is defined by its cartesian components as follows

$$x(s,t) = [s^3 \quad s^2 \quad s \quad 1] \begin{bmatrix} 3 & 0 & 1 & 1 \\ 1 & 0 & 0 & 1 \\ 2 & 1 & 1 & 1 \\ 0 & 2 & -1 & 0 \end{bmatrix} \begin{bmatrix} t^3 \\ t^2 \\ t \\ 1 \end{bmatrix}$$

$$y(s,t) = [s^3 \quad s^2 \quad s \quad 1] \begin{bmatrix} 1 & 1 & 1 & 1 \\ 1 & 0 & 0 & 0 \\ 2 & 3 & 0 & 0 \\ 1 & 2 & 0 & 2 \end{bmatrix} \begin{bmatrix} t^3 \\ t^2 \\ t \\ 1 \end{bmatrix}$$

$$z(s,t) = [s^3 \quad s^2 \quad s \quad 1] \begin{bmatrix} 0 & 1 & 2 & 3 \\ 1 & 0 & 2 & 0 \\ 3 & 1 & 2 & 1 \\ 1 & 0 & 1 & 1 \end{bmatrix} \begin{bmatrix} t^3 \\ t^2 \\ t \\ 1 \end{bmatrix}$$

Obtain the normal vector at the point where $s = \frac{1}{2}, t = \frac{1}{2}$.

6. For the parametric bicubic surface of Problem 5, find the z coordinate of a point on the surface, when $x = 1.0$ and $y = 4.0$.

7. A cylinder is created by rotation of the straight line $A(1,0,1)$ $B(1,0,4)$ around the z axis. Define the lateral surface of the cylinder in terms of a Bezier surface.

8. A flat quadrilateral patch in the xy plane has its vertices as shown in the accompanying figure. Determine the $[G]_H$ matrix for this patch.

> *Hint:* The tangent vectors at each vertex are obtained by the difference of the point vectors in the corresponding parametric directions. The twist vectors are simply the difference between the slope vectors at the corresponding corners.

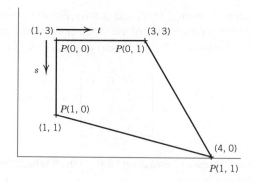

9. A bicubic Bezier patch is defined by the following control points:

$$[V]_B = \begin{bmatrix} (0,0,0) & (0,1,0) & (0,2,0) & (0,3,0) \\ (1,0,0) & (1,1,0) & (1,2,0) & (1,3,0) \\ (2,0,0) & (2,1,0) & (2,2,0) & (2,3,0) \\ (3,0,0) & (3,1,0) & (3,2,0) & (3,3,0) \end{bmatrix}$$

Find the final position of point $P(s = 1, t = 1)$ after the patch is translated along $x = 8s$, for $s = 0.5$, and rotated along the x axis by 360°.

10. Implement the algorithms given at the end of this chapter to output the various types of freeform surfaces. The geometric coefficients (or control points) should be defined by the user.

APPENDIX 11.1

||||||||||||||||||||||||||||||||||||||||||||||||||||||||||||||||||||||||||||||||||||||||||||||||||||||||

```
subroutine Hermite_Bicubic_Patch()
#s4x1—parametric matrix in s-direction
#t4x1—parametric matrix in t-direction
#G4x4—matrix to store geometry of the surface
#M4x4—Hermite matrix

#s^T,t^T,M^T —> transpose matrices of s, t and M,
     respectively

begin
     Read the geometry of the patch into matrix G
     Initialize matrix M

     Compute the transpose of matrix M and store
          in M^T

     ds=dt=0.05
     MOVE_FLAG=TRUE
     for s=0.0 to 1.0 insteps of 0.05 do
          Compute matrix s
          MOVE_FLAG=TRUE
          for t=0.0 to 1.0 insteps of 0.05 do
               Compute matrix t

               P(s,t)=s*M*G*M^T*t^T
               if MOVE_FLAG is TRUE
                    then
                         begin
                              Move(P(s,t))
                              MOVE_FLAG=FALSE
                         end
                    else
                         Draw(P(s,t))
               end if
          next t
```

(continued on next page)

```
next s
for t=0.0 to 1.0 insteps of 0.05 do
        Compute matrix t
        MOVE_FLAG=TRUE
        for s=0.0 to 1.0 insteps of 0.05 do
                Compute matrix s

                P(s,t)=t*M*B*M^T*s^T
                if MOVE_FLAG is TRUE
                        then
                                begin
                                        Move_To(P(s,t))
                                        MOVE_FLAG=FALSE
                                end
                        else
                                Draw_To(P(s,t))
                end if
        next s
next t

return

end
```

APPENDIX 11.2

```
subroutine Bezier_Surface()
#CPi,j -> is the (i,j)'th control point on the surface

begin
      for i=0 to n do
            for j=0 to m do
                  Read control point CPij
            next j
      next i

      for s=0.0 to 1.0 insteps of 0.05 do
            MOVE_Flag=TRUE
            for t=0.0 to 1.0 insteps of 0.05 do
```

$$P(s,t)=\sum_{i=0}^{n}\sum_{j=0}^{m}B_{n,i}(s)*B_{m,j}(t)*CP_{i,j}$$

```
                  if P(s,t) is starting point
                        then
                                    begin
                                          Move_To(P(s,t))
                                          MOVE_FLAG=FALSE
                                    end
                              else
                              Draw_To(P(s,t))
                  end if
            next t
      next s
```

(continued on next page)

```
for t=0.0 to 1.0 insteps of 0.05 do
     MOVE_FLAG=TRUE
     for s=0.0 to 1.0 insteps of 0.05 do
```

$$P(s,t)=\sum_{j=0}^{m}\sum_{i=0}^{n}B_{i,k}(s)*B_{j,k}(t)*CP_{i,j}$$

```
        if P(s,t) is starting point
             then
                     begin
                            Move_To(P(s,t))
                            MOVE_FLAG=FALSE
                     end
             else
                     Draw_To(P(s,t))
        endif
    next s
next t
return

end
```

Note: Details on the calculation of the blending functions B are given in Appendix 10.4. For rational Bezier surfaces refer to the appropriate equation in Table 11.1 and Appendix 10.7.

APPENDIX 11.3

```
subroutine B-spline_Surface()
#CPi,j -> is the (i,j)'th control point on the surface

begin
      for i=0 to n do
            for j=0 to m do
                  Read control point CPi,j
            next j
      next i
      Read degree of surface
      for s=0.0 to 1.0 insteps of 0.05 do
            MOVE_FLAG=TRUE
            for t=0.0 to 1.0 insteps of 0.05 do
```

$$P(s,t)=\sum_{i=0}^{n}\sum_{j=0}^{m}N_{i,k}(s)*N_{j,k}(t)*CP_{i,j}$$

```
                  if P(s,t) is starting point
                        then
                                    begin
                                          Move_To(P(s,t))
                                          MOVE_FLAG=FALSE
                                    end
                              else
                                    Draw_To(P(s,t))
                        end if
            next t
      next s
      for t=0.0 to 1.0 insteps of 0.05 do
            MOVE_FLAG=TRUE
            for s=0.0 to 1.0 insteps of 0.05 do
```

$$P(s,t)=\sum_{j=0}^{m}\sum_{i=0}^{n}N_{i,k}(s)*N_{j,k}(t)*CP_{i,j}$$

```
                  if P(s,t) is starting point
                        then
```

(continued on next page)

```
                              begin
                                    Move_To(P(s,t))
                                    MOVE_FLAG=FALSE
                              end
                        else
                              Draw_To(P(s,t))
                  end if
            next s
      next t

      return

end
```

Note: Details on the computation of the blending functions *N* and various types of knot vectors are given in Appendix 10.6.

APPENDIX 11.4

```
subroutine rational B-spline_Surface()
#CPi,j -> is the (i,j)'th control point on the surface
#Hi,j -> weight assigned at the (i,j)'th control point
begin
      for i=0 to n do
            for j=0 to m do
                  Read control point CPi,j
                  Read Hi,j
            next j
      next i
      Read degree of surface
      for s=0.0 to 1.0 insteps of 0.05 do
            MOVE_FLAG=TRUE
            for t = 0.0 to 1.0 insteps of 0.05 do
                  P(s,t)=
```

$$\frac{\displaystyle\sum_{i=0}^{n}\sum_{j=0}^{m} N_{i,k}(s) * N_{j,k}(t) * CP_{i,j} * H_{i,j}}{\displaystyle\sum_{i=0}^{n}\sum_{j=0}^{m} N_{i,k}(s) * N_{j,k}(t) * H_{i,j}}$$

```
                  if P(s,t) is starting point
                        then
                              begin
                                    Move_To(P(s,t))
                                    MOVE_FLAG=FALSE
                              end
                        else
                              Draw_To(P(s,t))
                  end if
            next t
      next s
```

(continued on next page)

```
for t=0.0 to 1.0 insteps of 0.05 do
     MOVE_FLAG=TRUE
     for s = 0.0 to 1.0 insteps of 0.05 do
          P(s,t)=
```

$$P(s,t)=\dfrac{\sum\limits_{j=0}^{m}\sum\limits_{i=0}^{n} N_{i,k}(s)*N_{j,k}(t)*CP_{i,j}*H_{i,j}}{\sum\limits_{j=0}^{m}\sum\limits_{i=0}^{n} N_{i,k}(s)*N_{j,k}(t)*H_{i,j}}$$

```
          if P(s,t) is starting point
               then
                    begin
                         Move_To(P(s,t))
                         MOVE_FLAG=FALSE
                    end
               else
                    Draw_To(P(s,t))
          end if
     next s
next t

return
end
```

Note: Details on the computation of the blending functions N and various types of knot vectors are given in Appendix 10.8.

Chapter 12

Solid Modeling

Solid objects can be represented as shown in Chapters 7 and 11 by using wireframe and surface modeling techniques. A third type of modeling representation is *solid modeling,* which gives a complete and unambiguous definition of an object, describing not only the shape of the boundaries but also the object's interior and exterior regions. This type of representation avoids the problems found with wireframe models. As shown in Figure 12.1, wireframe models can be ambiguous in the way they represent an object and are not suitable for mass property calculations, hidden surface removal, generation of shaded images, and so forth. Because of their computational efficiency they are mostly used for the quick verification of a design idea. Surface models are not so complete as solid models, since they do not allow points in space to be classified as inside or outside an object; only points on the boundary are considered.

Solid modeling systems provide the user with the means to create, store, and manipulate complete representations of solid objects with the potential for integration and improved automation [48,49]. Color Figures 1.15*a,*

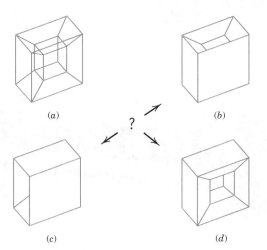

FIGURE 12.1 Ambiguity of wireframe models.

1.17*a*, 1.19, and 1.20 show examples of solid models used in engineering applications.

12.1 SOLID REPRESENTATION

The representation of solid models uses the fundamental idea that a physical object divides three-dimensional Euclidean space, E^3, into two regions—one interior and the other exterior to it—separated from each other by the boundary of the object. As shown in Figure 12.2, the boundary can be a closed surface (12.2*a*) or a group of open surfaces interconnected at specific locations (12.2*b*). All cases involve the idea of geometric closure, implying that the solid is formed by all points in its interior space and is geometrically enclosed by its boundaries. This concept of closure does not apply to wireframe and surface models, leading to ambiguity [50].

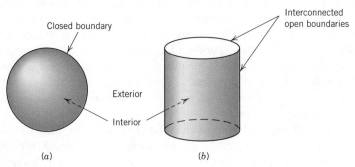

FIGURE 12.2 Examples of (*a*) closed boundary surface, and (*b*) open boundary surface.

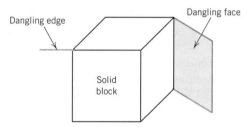

FIGURE 12.3 Homogeneous three-dimensionality avoids dangling edges or faces.

Solid models are mathematical models of objects in the real world that satisfy specific properties causing them to be

- *Bounded.* The boundary must limit and contain the interior of the solid.

- *Homogeneously three-dimensional.* No dangling edges or faces should be present (see Figure 12.3) so that the boundary is always in contact with the interior of the solid.

- *Finite.* The solid is not infinite in size and can be described by a limited amount of information.

These solids are, therefore, modeled by using subsets of E^3 that are

Bounded ⟶ no dangling edges
Regular
Semianalytic—do not oscillate infinitely fast within the E^3 space

Based on these properties, objects such as those in Figure 12.4 are considered invalid.

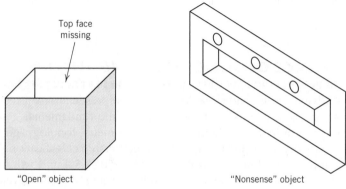

FIGURE 12.4 Examples of invalid objects.

The representation schemes, that is, the ways in which the solid model is actually described, are various and usually meet the requirements described above. A solid modeling representation scheme must produce an unambiguous model, representing no more than one object.

To be useful in geometric modeling, these representation schemes must satisfy some formal properties that can be stated as follows:

- *Domain or coverage.* Defines the class of object that can be represented.

- *Validity.* Each representation must produce a legal solid and avoid models such as those in Figure 12.4.

- *Completeness.* Each representation must produce a complete solid, with enough data to have any geometric calculation performed.

- *Uniqueness.* Given a solid, only one representation for it should be found within the representation scheme. This is a key factor in determining the equality of objects and is a property not found in all available representation schemes.

Some less formal properties must also be satisfied. Among these, efficacy of the model representation in the context of applications is of primary importance in engineering; that is, how effectively can the model be used by future application algorithms in the evaluation of various functions, such as mass and volume determinations?

Several representation schemes are available for the creation of solid models. Some of the most popular will be discussed in this chapter:

- Constructive Solid Geometry—CSG

- Boundary Representation—B-Rep

- Sweeping

- Spatial Enumeration

Each scheme, with its own properties and advantages/disadvantages, will be described in detail. A comparative study among them will also be done later in this chapter, with information on their use in existing solid modeling systems.

12.2   BASICS OF SOLID MODELING THEORY

Before studying the individual solid modeling representations listed in the previous section, it is important to understand the fundamental geometric principles present in these schemes, such as geometry, topology, geometric closure, set theory and operations, and set membership classification. Details on these topics are abundant in the literature [50,51,52] and will be only generally described here for an overall understanding of the solid representation schemes.

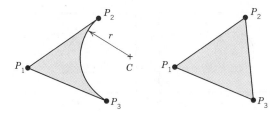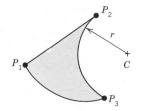

Geometry and Topology. In the context of model definition, geometry relates to the information containing shape defining parameters, such as the coordinates of the vertices in a polyhedral object. Adjacency topology, on the other hand, describes the connectivity among the various geometric components, that is, the relational information between the different parts of an object. The topology of the objects in Figure 12.5 is the same, although the geometry varies from case to case. The data structures used to create the three-dimensional models in Section 7.2.2 use both geometric and topological entities:

$$(x,y,x) \text{ coordinates of vertices} \rightarrow \text{geometry}$$
$$\text{connectivity matrix} \rightarrow \text{topology}$$

Geometric Closure. This concept is discussed in Section 12.1.

Set Theory. A set is defined as any collection of objects, called "elements" or "members." In the context of geometric representation, the basic element of a set is a point. Two sets are commonly represented: the universal set W, containing all the elements of all sets and the null set, $\varnothing$, containing no elements. In solid modeling, set W contains all points in E^3 space.

A set B is defined as a subset of set A if every element in B is also in A. This relationship is indicated by the symbol $\subset$, so that $B \subset A$ means that set B is a subset of A. Equality and inequality of sets pattern their algebraic counterparts. Two sets are equal if they contain exactly the same elements; inequality occurs otherwise.

Certain defined operations are performed on sets by combining their elements to create new sets. These operations are simple but powerful, and are commonly used in computer modeling applications. The set operations most often used in solid modeling are union, intersection, and difference. A convenient way to illustrate these operations is through the use of Venn diagrams, named for the British logician John Venn. These diagrams give a graphical interpretation of the operations that can be performed on sets. The E^3 points defining Euclidean space used in computer graphics and geometric modeling can be classified with Venn diagrams as being inside, outside, or on the boundary of a geometric object. Figure 12.6 shows these diagrams for the union ($\cup$), difference ($-$), and intersection ($\cap$) operations. The rectangle represents the universal set W, and each circular region represents a subset of the universal set. In the context of geometric modeling these subsets could

FIGURE 12.6 Venn
diagrams for various operations (a) Union (S ∪ T).
(b) Intersection (S ∩ T).
(c) Difference (S − T).

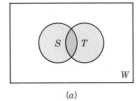

(a)

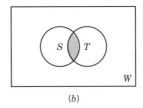

(b)

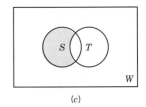

(c)

be points in space, surfaces, or solids. The shaded portion in the Venn diagram shows the result of each operation.

Regularized Set Operations. When using the set operations of union,
intersection, and difference in the theoretical context described above, problems dealing with the lack of geometric closure can occur, as shown in Figure
12.7. Regularization set operations, also known as *boolean operations*, ensure the validity of geometric models, thus avoiding the creation of nonsense
objects.

Geometric solids are normally represented by regular sets, or "r-sets,"
which can be viewed as solids without dangling faces or edges. As applied
to these r-sets, the differences between theoretical and regularized set operations are as follows (see Figure 12.8):

Union: Both the theoretic and the regularized union operations ensure
that the new solid will also be regular.

FIGURE 12.7 Differences
between theoretical and
regularized set operations.

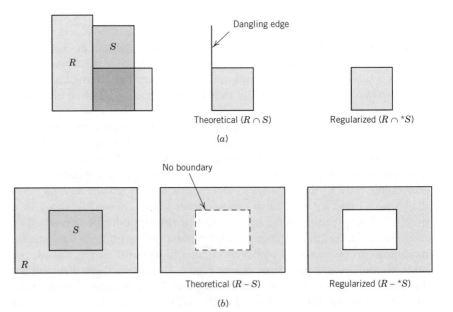

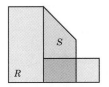

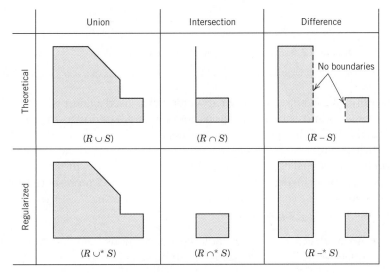

FIGURE 12.8 Conventional and theoretical set operations. (Two-dimensional objects used for simplicity).

Difference: The regularized operation ensures that the new solid will keep all needed boundaries, parts of which might be missing under the theoretic difference operation.

Intersection: Theoretic and regularized operations are equivalent unless solids have overlapping boundaries. In the latter case, the dangling parts obtained from the standard operation must be discarded.

Set Membership Classification. This type of classification can be studied as a simple generalization of the clipping operation described in Sections 5.2 and 8.5. The problem to be solved is

Given two sets X and S, check how various parts of X can be assigned to S as being on its interior, exterior, or on its boundaries.

This means that X is partitioned into subsets Xin$S$, Xon$S$, Xout$S$, respectively inside, on the boundary, or outside S. The function representing this partition is termed $M(X,S)$. Figure 12.9 shows the use of $M(X,S)$ in two-dimensional sets representing a line X and a polygon S. This is very similar to the operation

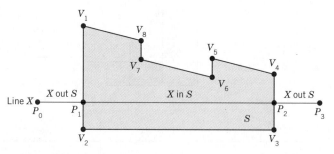

FIGURE 12.9 Example of set membership classification.

in Section 5.2.2, where a rectangular window was used against which to clip line segments and separate portions interior and exterior to the window boundaries by finding points of intersection.

In set membership classification, the checking can be done against two- or three-dimensional objects. As a simple example, consider the classification of line X shown in Figure 12.9 against the polygon S represented by its vertices and edges. To check which portions of X are "in," "on," or "out" of S, use the following algorithm:

- An intersection routine finds the intersections between X and the edges of S. These intersections can be calculated as, for example, in Section 5.2.2.

- A sorting procedure develops the boundary crossing list P_0, P_1, P_2, P_3.

- Line X is classified with respect to S. This can be done by first choosing a clockwise or counterclockwise direction in which to number the vertices of S. In Figure 12.9 a counterclockwise direction was chosen. It can be seen that the interior points of S lie to the left of the boundary as it is traversed from V_1 to V_8. Representing each edge of S by its bounding vertices V_i and V_{i+1}, the classification can be established as follows:
    If, at the boundary where an intersection occurs, vertex V_i is above and V_{i+1} is below line X, an "in" segment is flagged;
    If the opposite occurs, an "out" segment is flagged.

Based on this algorithm, the classification of line X with respect to polygon S is:

$$[P_0, P_1] \longrightarrow X \text{out} S$$

$$[P_1, P_2] \longrightarrow X \text{in} S$$

$$[P_2, P_3] \longrightarrow X \text{out} S$$

as shown in Figure 12.9.

12.3 CONSTRUCTIVE SOLID GEOMETRY—CSG

Constructive Solid Geometry (CSG) is one of the most popular representation schemes for solid modeling because it is well understood, and easy to interface with the user and to check for validity.

A CSG model assumes that physical objects can be created by combining basic elementary shapes through specific rules. These basic shapes form what are commonly known as primitives, which are themselves valid, bounded CSG models represented by r-sets. A wide variety of primitives are available in solid modeling systems, but the most commonly used are blocks, cylinders, cones, and spheres, as shown in Figure 12.10. The solid primitives in the CSG representation are defined mathematically as the combination of unbounded geometric entities separating the E^3 space into infinite portions. These entities are called *half-spaces*. The most commonly used half-spaces are planar, cylindrical, spherical, and conical, and relate to the natural quadric surfaces [53,54].

CSG primitives are represented by the intersection of a set of half-spaces (see Figure 12.11). The primitive block is formed by the regularized intersection of six planar half-spaces. Each half-space is expressed by one limit of the three inequalities forming the primitive. A solid modeler supporting these primitives must be able to calculate the intersections of the given half-spaces. More details on the creation of quadric primitives and calculation of quadric intersections are given in Section 12.12.

Quadric surfaces are commonly used in CSG because they represent the most commonly used surfaces in mechanical design produced by the standard operations of milling, turning, rolling, and so forth. For example, planar surfaces are obtained through rolling and milling, cylindrical surfaces through turning, and spherical surfaces through cutting done with a ball-end cutting tool.

From the user's point of view, and regardless of how the primitive is created internally by the system, only its location, geometric data, and orientation data are needed. The location data for each primitive encompasses the establishment of a local coordinate system and the position of the origin. The geometric and orientation data are usually input by the user. All primi-

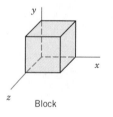
Block

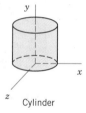
Cylinder

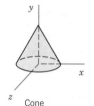
Cone

Sphere

(all unit size by default)

FIGURE 12.10 Examples of primitives used in CSG.

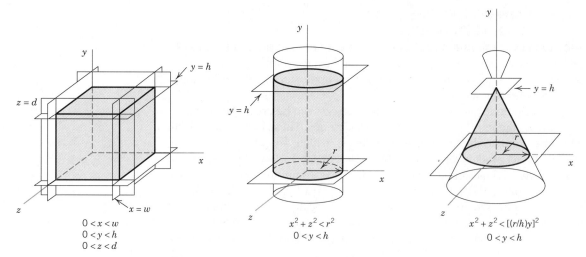

$$0 < x < w$$
$$0 < y < h$$
$$0 < z < d$$

$$x^2 + z^2 < r^2$$
$$0 < y < h$$

$$x^2 + z^2 < [(r/h)y]^2$$
$$0 < y < h$$

FIGURE 12.11 Primitives created by the intersection of half-spaces.

tives have a default size guaranteed by most modeling systems. Figure 12.10 shows a possible default size and location for the primitives.

The boolean operations—union, difference, intersection—described in Section 12.2 are used to combine the r-sets formed by the solid primitives. Figure 12.12 shows an example of this process.

Data structures for the CSG representation are based on the binary tree structure described in Section 7.2.7. The CSG tree is a binary tree with leaf

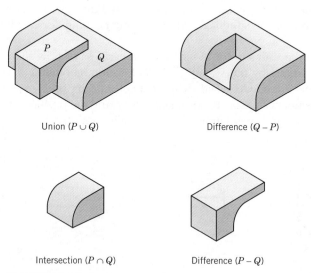

Union ($P \cup Q$) Difference ($Q - P$)

Intersection ($P \cap Q$) Difference ($P - Q$)

FIGURE 12.12 Boolean operations.

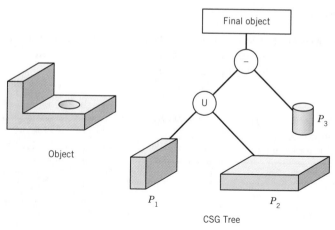

FIGURE 12.13 CSG tree.

nodes as primitives and interior nodes as boolean operations, as shown in Figure 12.13. The total number of nodes in the tree is a function of the number of primitives used.

The creation of a model in CSG can be simplified by the use of a table summarizing the operations to be performed. The following example illustrates the process of model creation used in the CSG representation.

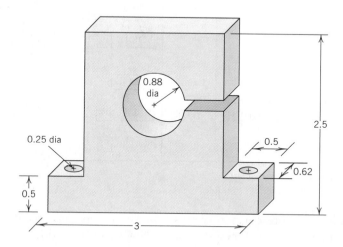

Example 12.1

Create a CSG table for the object shown in the accompanying figure and output the model using a solid modeling system available to you. See accompanying table.

Solution

The accompanying table gives one possible solution to the problem. Note that this solution is not unique and could have been found through the use of different primitives and boolean operations.

CSG Table

Primitive No.	Primitive Type	Transformations $S(x,y,z)$ $T(x,y,z)$ $R(x,y,z)$		Boolean (U, D, I)	CSG Tree	Sketch
1	Block	$S(3.0,2.5,.62)$				
2/3	Block	$S(0.5,2.0,.62)$ $T(2.5,0.5,0.0)$	$\|\|$ $S(0.5,2.0,.62)$ $T(0.0,0.5,0.0)$	D/D		
4	Cylinder	$S(r = 0.44, h = 0.62)$ $T(1.5,1.5,0.0)$		D		
5	Block	$S(0.56,0.12,0.62)$ $T(1.94,1.44,0.0)$		D		
6/7	Cylinder	$S(r = 0.125, h = 0.5)$ $T(0.25,0.0,0.31)$ $R(90.0,0.0,0.0)$	$\|\|$ $S(same)$ $T(2.75,0.0,0.31)$ $R(same)$	D/D		

*Default primitives have origin as shown in Figure 12.10, and unit size.

The CSG representation creates a procedural model, specifying how solid primitives are combined to create a new solid, but it does not specify quantitative values for the new solid. The model is said to be "unevaluated." More information is usually needed for display purposes or calculation of engineering properties. The new model must be checked through a *boundary evaluation* routine which will supply quantitative information about its vertices, edges, faces, and so forth. This requires the calculation of intersections in the form of curve/curve, curve/surface, or surface/surface intersections, and routines must be available in the solid modeler to perform these calculations. The boundary evaluator determines where faces or edges of the original primitives must be truncated to create the combined solid. It does this by various means, including set membership classification. It must also create or delete new vertices or edges and merge into a single element overlapping boundary elements. Details on procedures for boundary evaluation are beyond the scope of this text but are available in the literature [55,56].

12.4 BOUNDARY REPRESENTATION—B-REP

The boundary representation is built on the idea that a physical object is enclosed by a set of faces, which themselves belong to closed and orientable surfaces. Orientation as applied to surfaces indicates that it is possible to distinguish between the two sides of the surface, so that a solid model created with them will have an interior and an exterior region. The orientation is usually established by the direction of a normal vector, as stated in section 11.3.1. Figure 12.14 shows the B-rep model of an object. In this model, each face is bounded by edges and each edge is bounded by vertices. There is a separation between geometry and topology, as follows:

Geometric Entities	Topological Entities
Point	Vertex
Curve	Edge
Surface	Face

Figure 12.15 illustrates these entities.

Information on both geometric and topological elements is stored in the B-rep database. To ensure topological validity of the boundary model, special operators are used to create and manipulate the topological entities described above. These are called Euler operators and apply to polyhedral-like objects that satisfy Euler's law. The Euler–Poincaré law gives a quantitative relationship among faces, edges, vertices, faces' inner loops, bodies, or through holes ("genus") in solids:

$$F - E + V - L = 2(B - G) \tag{12.1}$$

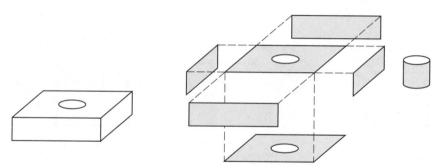

FIGURE 12.14 Boundary representation (B-rep).

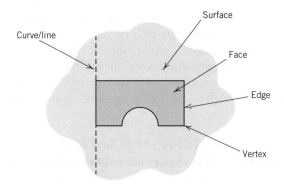

FIGURE 12.15 Difference between geometric and topological entities.

In its simplest form

$$F - E + V = 2 \qquad (12.2)$$

it applies to simple polyhedra as shown in Figures 12.16*a* and *b*. Figure 12.16(*c*) shows an application of the general Euler's formula. It is important to remember that Euler's law is not restricted to solids with planar faces. In the case of curved objects, that is, objects with closed curved faces or edges such as cylinders, for example, the same rules apply. The cylinder in Figure 12.17 has

- Two vertices
- Three edges—two circular edges at the top and bottom and one vertical edge (Any additional vertical edges, called *silhouette edges*, are used only for display purposes and are not real edges of the object.)
- Three faces—two planar ones at the top and bottom and one cylindrical one

The formula $[F - E + V = 2]$ applies to this cylinder $[3 - 3 + 2 = 2]$.

FIGURE 12.16 Euler's law applied to polyhedral objects.

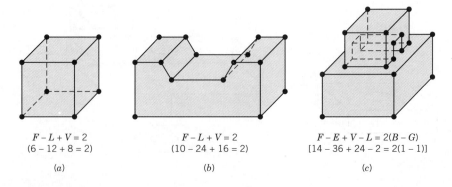

$F - L + V = 2$
$(6 - 12 + 8 = 2)$

(a)

$F - L + V = 2$
$(10 - 24 + 16 = 2)$

(b)

$F - E + V - L = 2(B - G)$
$[14 - 36 + 24 - 2 = 2(1 - 1)]$

(c)

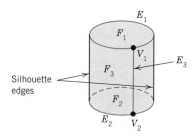

FIGURE 12.17 Euler's law for objects with curved faces or edges.

Solids formed by any closed surfaces represented by patches, curve segments, and vertices also obey Euler's law. These could be solids represented by the standard freeform surfaces such as Bezier, B-spline, and the like.

Information needed for a boundary representation is commonly obtained through user input or through a boundary evaluation of CSG data. In a B-rep model, the geometry is created and the topological validity of the model simultaneously ascertained. The topological information serves as the glue that keeps all the geometric information together. Various types of data structures have been developed to represent the topological information. Their description goes beyond the scope of this text, but is easily found in the literature [53,54].

12.5 FACETED REPRESENTATION

When curved objects are stored in a B-rep model by the equations that represent their edges and faces, a complete or exact B-rep scheme is obtained. However, an approximated scheme is often used, usually referred to as "faceted B-rep." In this case, curved surfaces are approximated by planar facets and curves become strings of line segments. Figure 12.18 shows a cylindrical

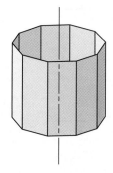

FIGURE 12.18 Faceted boundary representation.

surface in a faceted boundary representation. This approach has advantages and disadvantages. It is easy, for example, to add new surface types, and a small amount of very simple geometric data will satisfy all the needs. The problem of surface-to-surface intersection is reduced to calculating the intersection of two planar surfaces. On the other hand, a very large quantity of data may have to be generated to keep an acceptable level of accuracy in the model. An example showing the creation of solids using this type of representation is given in Section 12.12.2.

12.6 SWEEP REPRESENTATION

Solids that have a uniform thickness in a particular direction and axisymmetric solids can be created by what is called *translational* and *rotational sweeping*. Figure 12.19 shows examples of these types of solids.

Sweeping requires two ingredients—a surface to be moved and a trajectory, analytically defined, along which the movement should occur. General guidelines for this process were given in Section 11.2 for the creation of swept surfaces and need only be generalized to solids. Sweeping is usually available in B-rep or CSG-based systems as an additional tool for solid creation. There are no sweeping-based solid modeling systems because of the limited domain of the representation [57].

In engineering applications sweeping can be used to detect possible interference between moving parts, or simulate and analyze material removal operations in manufacturing. In the first case, a moving object collides with a fixed object if the swept volume resulting from the motion intersects the fixed object. In material removal operations, the volume swept by the tool moving along a predefined path intersects the raw stock of the part. Figure 12.20 shows an example.

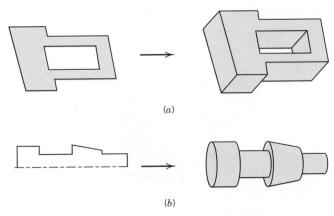

(a)

(b)

FIGURE 12.19 Sweeping (*a*) Translational. (*b*) Rotational.

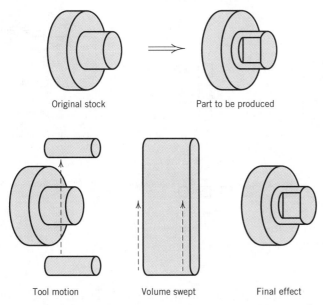

Original stock   Part to be produced

Tool motion   Volume swept   Final effect

FIGURE 12.20 Use of sweeping to simulate material removal operations in engineering manufacturing.

12.7   SPATIAL ENUMERATION SCHEMES

Any physical object can be modeled as the sum of a number of spatial cells in which the object is assumed to be decomposed. If these cells are cubes of equal size, the modeling scheme is called "spatial enumeration" (see Figure 12.21). The equal cells forming the model can be described by the location of their centroids within a fixed spatial grid. If the object has curved boundaries, the accuracy of the model will depend on the size of the cell. The smaller the cell the more accurate the model. This will also produce a large volume of data, however, so this type of representation can be computationally expensive. Spatial enumeration schemes have the advantage of easy access to any part of the model and the assurance of spatial uniqueness [58].

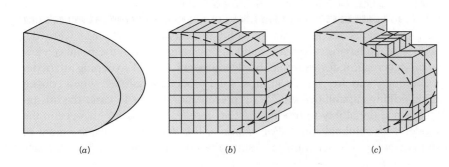

(a)   (b)   (c)

FIGURE 12.21 (a) Solid. (b) Spatial enumeration scheme. (c) Octree.

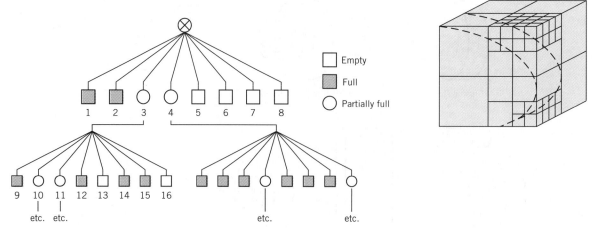

FIGURE 12.22 Tree structure for an octree.

The scheme can be made more efficient by the use of the *octree* system, or its two-dimensional counterpart, the *quadtree*, briefly described in Section 7.27. Here, the cells forming the model may have variable sizes. Octrees have a hierarchical structure, with a recursive subdivision of space into variably diminishing cubes.

Figure 12.21 compares the general spatial enumeration scheme—cells of equal size—with the octree scheme—cells of variable size. In the octree scheme the object is first enclosed into one cubical region and then recursively subdivided into eight octants. If any of these octants is full or empty, no further subdivision is needed; for octants partially full, the subdivision process continues until all regions are full or empty, or a predetermined level of resolution is reached. The data structure described in Section 7.2.7 for quadtrees can be generalized for octrees, using cubes instead of squares. The tree shown in Figure 12.22 has the same type of structure as the one given for quadtrees in Figure 7.19, except that each partially full node has eight children. The octree scheme is suitable for image representation and for fast computation of mass properties or interference detection.

12.8 SOLID MODELING SYSTEMS

In the previous sections various solid representation schemes were described, each having advantages and disadvantages. From the point of view of model creation, for example, boolean operations and sweeping are better techniques, and are present in most solid modeling systems. When considering editing capabilities the CSG representation seems to carry the advantage, since the ability to modify the CSG tree leads to major changes in the model with minimal input. For example, the deletion or displacement of primitives is easily accomplished since the history of creation is completely

TABLE 12.1 Characteristics of CSG and B-rep

	Storage of Model	Detail Level
CSG	Implicit	Low
B-rep	Explicit	High

maintained in the combinatorial binary tree. On the other hand, there are certain methods inherent to the boundary representation that cannot be implemented in a pure CSG context. For example, local changes on the model, such as chamfering and rounding of edges, is done very simply in a boundary representation. In addition, in an interactive environment it is generally the faces, edges, and vertices of the model that the user/designer wants to manipulate, and these are the very core of the B-rep data structure. Tables 12.1 and 12.2 summarize the general characteristics and the advantages and disadvantages of CSG and B-rep [59].

Since none of the solid representations is shown to be clearly superior to the others, conversion among them is of great practical importance. Figure 12.23 shows how some of the solid representations convert algorithmically to others. Note that in some cases the conversion is not possible. For example, CSG cannot be converted to sweeping because their domains are different. Some of the conversions shown in Figure 12.23 are simple. Spatial enumeration converts exactly to B-rep by selecting cell faces which belong to only one cell throughout the recursive decomposition. These faces form the boundary of the object. The conversion of simple sweep to B-rep is also very easy: Advantage is taken of the fact that there is a direct correspondence between the bounding edges of the two-dimensional set used in sweeping and the faces in the boundary representation of the final solid.

Not so simple is the exact conversion from CSG to B-rep. As mentioned in Section 12.3, this is done through a boundary evaluator, using the concept of set membership classification. The approximate conversion from various representations to the spatial enumeration scheme is also done by set membership classification. This conversion becomes exact for some polyhedral objects.

TABLE 12.2

	Complexity	Uniqueness	History of Construction	Use in Interactive Environment	Local Operations
CSG	*A*	*D*	*A*	*D*	*D*
B-rep	*D*	*A*	*D*	*A*	*A*

A = advantage; *B* = disadvantage.

FIGURE 12.23 Conversion among representations.

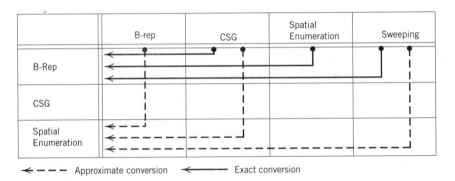

	B-rep	CSG	Spatial Enumeration	Sweeping
B-Rep				
CSG				
Spatial Enumeration				

◄ − − − Approximate conversion   ◄——— Exact conversion

The architecture of solid modeling systems depends on the types of conversion algorithms available to the solid modeler. In general, solid modeling systems are characterized as "mostly CSG" or "mostly B-rep." Figures 12.24 and 12.25 show the general architecture of these modelers. In the mostly CSG approach, model creation and editing is done only in the CSG form. Once the model is created, a boundary evaluator algorithm is used to obtain a boundary representation, which is then stored internally along with the CSG tree. The user can query any of the two major representations—CSG or B-rep. Algorithms used to compute properties of the model, for example, or to perform simulation can work from one or the other of these two representations. This type of architecture is also known as "dual representation" of a solid model, since both the CSG and B-rep are maintained by the system. In the mostly B-rep approach, the user can create the model in either CSG or B-rep, but the CSG representation is discarded by the system.

12.9 RECENT ADVANCEMENTS IN SOLID MODELING—NURBS

In recent years, solid modelers have been developed to handle not only polyhedral and quadric models, but also the wealth of freeform surface definitions described in Chapter 11. Some of these modelers keep two separate sets of algorithms internally, one to deal with the quadric surfaces and another with the freeform surfaces. A better and more recently developed ap-

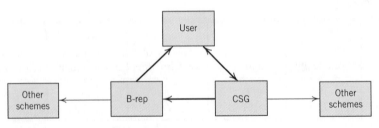

FIGURE 12.24 Mostly CSG architecture

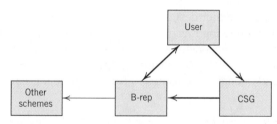

FIGURE 12.25 Mostly B-rep architecture

proach is to support the various curve and surface forms in a single representation, and thus minimize the amount of geometric software required in the modeler. The use of nonuniform rational B-splines (NURBS), as described in Section 11.3.6, has been adopted in some solid modelers for this purpose. NURBS can exactly represent quadric surfaces, so internal operations in the modeler, such as the calculation of surface–to–surface intersections, are accomplished with a single algorithm. The surfaces are first specified by the designer and then translated into the common internal form. Primitives can be created with NURBS and used for model development in a CSG representation. The B-rep can also be maintained in these systems, allowing a large variety of geometric forms to be handled with a manageable amount of computer code.

12.10   FEATURE MODELING

Feature modeling is an extension of the solid modeling schemes described in the previous sections. In an effort to link CAD and CAM in an efficient way, this method identifies, by means of features, the manufacturing requirements of a part. The modeler contains not only a geometric and topological structure, as in the conventional solid modeling systems, but can also support high level information such as the geometric characteristics of a part, that is, the shapes of holes, cutouts, slots, chamfers, ribs, and so forth, as shown in Figure 12.26. This approach provides the designer with a set of features that

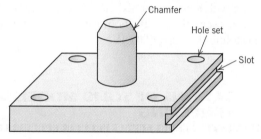

FIGURE 12.26 The shape of holes, slots, and so on is part of a feature modeler.

have significance for either design, analysis, or manufacturing, and contains a well defined engineering meaning. Instead of using a model consisting of graphic primitives such as cylinders or blocks, the designer has access to a set of features from which manufacturing operations can be derived [60].

Three fundamental approaches to feature modeling have been developed:

1. *Human-Assisted Feature Recognition.* In this method, a geometric model of a part is created and the results are displayed on a graphics screen. The user interactively selects the groups of items that belong to each form feature and adds any nongeometric information required, such as tolerances or surface finish. This information is then stored in the database and later used by process planning systems.

2. *Automatic Feature Recognition.* In this approach, a feature recognition program examines the model created by a solid modeling system and attempts to find and extract form features that correspond to some predefined geometric pattern. This is done by

- Using some form of geometric reasoning in a boundary representation of the model
- Decomposing the model into various volumes
- Manipulating the binary tree in a CSG representation of the model

This approach is very difficult as it essentially tries to synthesize a high level of abstraction from a mass of low level detail. It can be compared to trying to generate a FORTRAN program from the object code.

3. *Design by Feature.* In this case, designers create models directly from predefined features, an approach that best captures the intent of the designer in modeling a part. The features are usually placed into the model by referring to existing portions of the object's boundary to establish datum planes, reference lines, and so forth.

Feature modeling capabilities are built into the architecture of solid modeling systems. Feature design seems to be performed best in the language of boundary representation. However, editing a design by altering feature parameters gives rise to the need for a history of construction, as available in a CSG tree. Designing with features seems, therefore, to require the availability of both types of representations. Efforts in this area have been well documented in the modeling literature [60,61].

12.11 APPLICATIONS OF SOLID MODELING TO ENGINEERING

Solid modeling is commonly used in engineering to aid visual analysis of a design idea, mass property calculations, and static interference analysis. The following examples show the use of this technology in the solution of a few simple problems.

Example 12.2

A standard application of solid modeling is help in interference detection through the boolean interference operator. In many cases a simple static analysis is sufficient. An example is shown in Figure 12.27. Rod *AB* is attached to the pin of a clevis and rotates inside the opening cut on the base block. To check if any interference occurs, the object is modeled with a solid modeling system, and three extreme positions are checked for interference using boolean operators.

Example 12.3

There are many computer programs that perform construction estimates of structural elements in civil engineering projects. These programs can be interfaced with a solid modeling system to allow the user to visually verify that the quantities generated actually represent the structure [62]. The column footings shown in Figure 12.28 can be constructed through a CSG interface. *Quantity visual verification* can prevent costly estimating mistakes by allowing the engineer or estimator to perform checks by visual inspection.

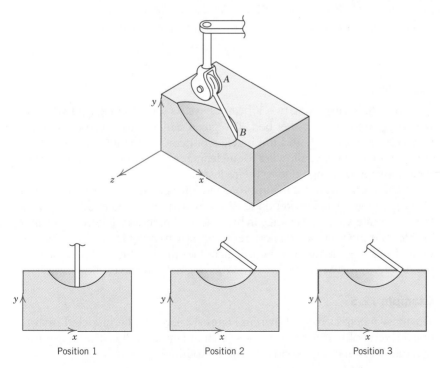

FIGURE 12.27 Static interference check at three likely positions.

Position 1   Position 2   Position 3

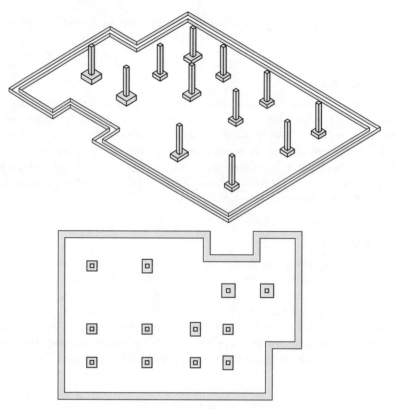

FIGURE 12.28 Quantity visual verification using solid modeling.

Example 12.4

A countershaft supporting two V-belt pulleys, as shown in Figure 12.29a and b, is supported by a bracket bed. The given dimensions cause interference between the pulley P_2 and the bracket B. Remove this interference by re-designing the bracket, allowing for a clearance of 10 mm, and find the volume of material change due to the redesign.

The problem shows the approach to interference detection using boolean operations. The bracket dimensions must be changed to accommodate the large pulley, P_2. The change in the bracket dimensions is shown in Figure 12.29c, and the volume of interference is shown in Figure 12.29d. The volume of material change can be calculated by the solid modeling system as the difference between the new and the original volume of the bracket.

Example 12.5

The axisymmetric object shown in Figure 12.30a is to be modeled by rotational sweep of the planar surface shown in Figure 12.30b. The transformation that will create this solid must be established.

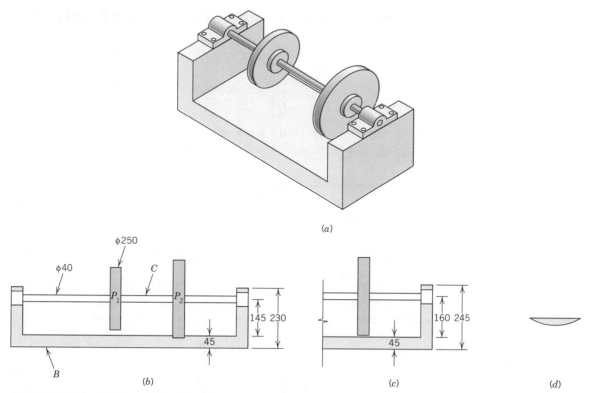

FIGURE 12.29 (*a*) Object. (*b*) Original dimensions (units-mm). (*c*) New dimensions. (*d*) Interference volume.

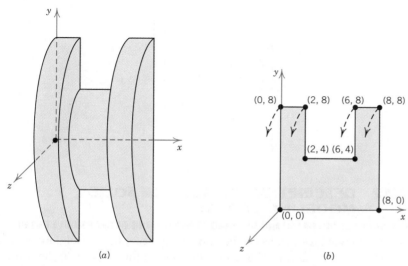

FIGURE 12.30 Rotational sweep of a planar surface.

Since the rotation is to occur about the x axis, the following transformation matrix is used:

$$T(S) = \begin{bmatrix} 1 & 0 & 0 & 0 \\ 0 & \cos(2\pi s) & \sin(2\pi s) & 0 \\ 0 & -\sin(2\pi s) & \cos(2\pi s) & 0 \\ 0 & 0 & 0 & 1 \end{bmatrix}$$

Multiplying this matrix by the point matrix

$$\begin{bmatrix} 0 & 0 & 0 & 1 \\ 0 & 8 & 0 & 1 \\ 2 & 8 & 0 & 1 \\ 2 & 4 & 0 & 1 \\ 6 & 4 & 0 & 1 \\ 6 & 8 & 0 & 1 \\ 8 & 8 & 0 & 1 \\ 8 & 0 & 0 & 1 \end{bmatrix}$$

and incrementing the value of s between 0 and 0.5 will describe the swept solid. For $s = 0.5$, for example, the transformed points become

$$Q(s=0.5) = \begin{bmatrix} 0 & 0 & 0 & 1 \\ 0 & 8 & 0 & 1 \\ 2 & 8 & 0 & 1 \\ 2 & 4 & 0 & 1 \\ 6 & 4 & 0 & 1 \\ 6 & 8 & 0 & 1 \\ 8 & 8 & 0 & 1 \\ 8 & 0 & 0 & 1 \end{bmatrix} \begin{bmatrix} 1 & 0 & 0 & 0 \\ 0 & -1 & 0 & 0 \\ 0 & 0 & -1 & 0 \\ 0 & 0 & 0 & 1 \end{bmatrix}$$

$$= \begin{bmatrix} 0 & 0 & 0 & 1 \\ 0 & -8 & 0 & 1 \\ 2 & -8 & 0 & 1 \\ 2 & -4 & 0 & 1 \\ 6 & -4 & 0 & 1 \\ 6 & -8 & 0 & 1 \\ 8 & -8 & 0 & 1 \\ 8 & 0 & 0 & 1 \end{bmatrix}$$

12.12 DESCRIPTION OF A SIMPLE SOLID MODELING SYSTEM

This section will give details on the construction of a simple solid modeling system, based on the use of quadric surfaces. In this approach, the representation available for user input is CSG which is then internally converted to a faceted boundary representation for purposes of rendering and possible manufacture. As mentioned in Section 12.5 describing the faceted representation, this approach simplifies the calculation of surface–to–surface intersections, which reduce to intersections between pairs of planes.

The implementation of the solid modeling system involves the development of several components:

- Creation of the quadric primitives based on user input
- Conversion to a faceted representation
- Intersection calculations—boolean operations
- Rendering techniques

All these components will be described in detail in the following subsections [63].

12.12.1   Quadric Primitives

Quadric primitives such as blocks, cylinders, and the like, are created in this solid modeler as CSG half-spaces (see Section 12.3). A general half-space is described as the region defined by the quadric inequality

$$Ax^2 + By^2 + Cz^2 + 2Dxy + 2Eyz + 2Fxz + 2Gx + 2Hy + 2Jz + K \le 0$$

This expression can also be written in matrix form as

$$[x \; y \; z \; 1] \begin{bmatrix} A & D & F & G \\ D & B & E & H \\ F & E & C & J \\ G & H & J & K \end{bmatrix} [x \; y \; z \; 1]^T \le 0 \qquad (12.3)$$

Primitive solids are obtained by intersection of the appropriate half-spaces. For example, a cube is obtained by intersecting six planar half-spaces and a cylinder is the intersection of two planar and one cylindrical half-spaces (see Figure 12.11). A quadric surface would be defined as the equality of Eq. 12.3. By assigning values to the coefficients $A, B, C, \ldots K$, different types of quadrics, with varying positions and orientations, can be obtained. A planar surface, for example, is formed by setting all coefficients to zero except $G, H, J,$ and K.

All primitive solids are created in a default position, in their standard form, as shown in Figure 12.31, and have unit size. The primitive's information is thus expressed in terms of its own local coordinate system. The matrix of coefficients for the quadric equation relating to various primitives, and the expressions for their creation in the default position, are also shown in Figure 12.31. Starting with these default solids, the primitives are transformed based on user input defining the dimensions and positions required for the design. These user-defined values are multiplied by the default values

UNIT PRIMITIVES

Primitive	Bounded Half-Space	Quadric Equation Coeffs. Matrix	
CUBE	$0 \leq x \leq 1$ $0 \leq y \leq 1$ $0 \leq z \leq 1$	$\begin{bmatrix} 0 & 0 & 0 & \$ \\ 0 & 0 & 0 & 0 \\ 0 & 0 & 0 & 0 \\ \$ & 0 & 0 & 0 \end{bmatrix}$ (For $x = 0$)	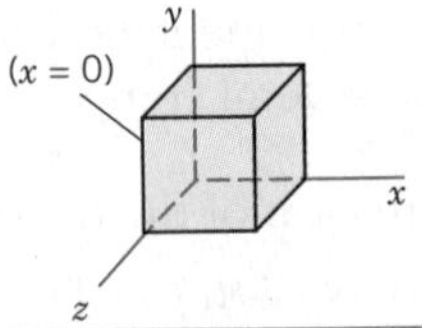
CYLINDER	$x^2 + y^2 \leq r^2$ $0 \leq z \leq 1$	$\begin{bmatrix} 1 & 0 & 0 & 0 \\ 0 & 1 & 0 & 0 \\ 0 & 0 & 0 & 0 \\ 0 & 0 & 0 & -r^2 \end{bmatrix}$ (For cylindrical shell)	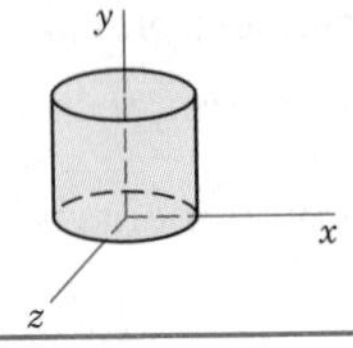
CONE	$x^2 + y^2 \leq (r^2z^2)$ $0 \leq z \leq 1$	$\begin{bmatrix} 1 & 0 & 0 & 0 \\ 0 & 1 & 0 & 0 \\ 0 & 0 & -r^2 & 0 \\ 0 & 0 & 0 & 0 \end{bmatrix}$ (For conical shell)	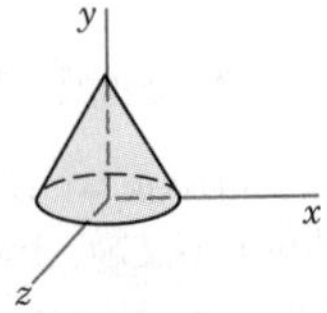
SPHERE	$x^2 + y^2 + z^2 \leq r^2$	$\begin{bmatrix} 1 & 0 & 0 & 0 \\ 0 & 1 & 0 & 0 \\ 0 & 0 & 1 & 0 \\ 0 & 0 & 0 & -r^2 \end{bmatrix}$	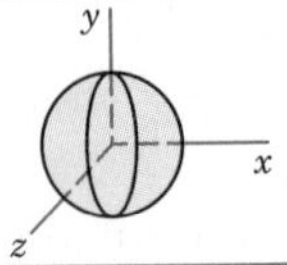

FIGURE 12.31 Primitives created in default positions.

to obtain a new matrix of coefficients for the quadric equation:

$$\begin{bmatrix} \text{Default} \\ \text{quadric} \\ \text{coefficient} \end{bmatrix} \begin{bmatrix} \text{Transformation} \\ \text{matrix} \end{bmatrix} = \begin{bmatrix} \text{New} \\ \text{quadric} \\ \text{coefficient} \end{bmatrix} \qquad (12.4)$$

The transformation family of operations may involve scalings, translations, and/or rotations, and is represented by a [4 × 4] homogeneous matrix (see Chapter 6). The newly found coefficients are stored in an array for further use and recall.

12.12.2 Faceted Boundary Representation

A faceted B-rep approximates each primitive by a number of planar facets. The level of the approximation is user controlled, thereby allowing the best balance between the number of facets generated and the level of model approximation required by future applications. The procedure is implemented by using incremental values in a parametric direction, and calculating the coordinates of the points found as vertices of each individual plane. In

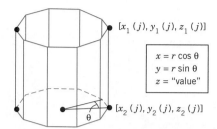

$$x = r \cos \theta$$
$$y = r \sin \theta$$
$$z = \text{"value"}$$

FIGURE 12.32 Parametric equations used in the faceted representation of a cylinder.

the case of a cylinder, for example, the parametric representation given in Figure 12.32 can be used. The value of the rotation angle θ is increased from $0°$ to $360°$ by increments, as shown in Figure 12.32, and lines are drawn

from $x_1(j)$, $y_1(j)$, $z_1(j)$ to $x_2(j)$, $y_2(j)$, $z_2(j)$; from $x_1(j)$, $y_1(j)$, $z_1(j)$ to $x_1(j + 1)$, $y_1(j + 1)$, $z_1(j + 1)$, and from $x_2(j)$, $y_2(j)$, $z_2(j)$ to $x_2(j + 1)$, $y_2(j + 1)$, $z_2(j + 1)$.

The same approach can be used to facet the other primitives. The rectangular facets resulting from this operation are then triangulated to improve the accuracy of the model. The planar triangular facets are directly used to perform intersection computations.

12.12.3   Intersection Calculations

Once the triangulation of all user-defined primitives is performed, a simple check detects possible intersections among them. Figure 12.33 depicts a flowchart giving the logic of this approach. To avoid unnecessary calculations, the first step in the solution is the elimination of planes that cannot possibly intersect. This is done by using the bounding box (minimax) test, as described in section 9.1.2. The bounding box of a triangular facet is defined by two points (Q_0, Q_1), where $Q_0 = (x_{min}, y_{min}, z_{min})$ and $Q_1 = (x_{max}, y_{max}, z_{max})$. Therefore, any point (x, y, z) on the facet satisfies the following:

$$x_{min} \le x \le x_{max}$$

$$y_{min} \le y \le y_{max}$$

$$z_{min} \le z \le z_{max}$$

Figure 12.34 shows this bounding box. In the event of intersection between the facets, an overlap of the bounding boxes will occur. This simple test eliminates trivial conditions of nonintersecting facets. For the facets that pass the bounding box test, actual intersection calculations are performed. This involves plane-to-plane intersection calculations for every two triangular facets of different primitives.

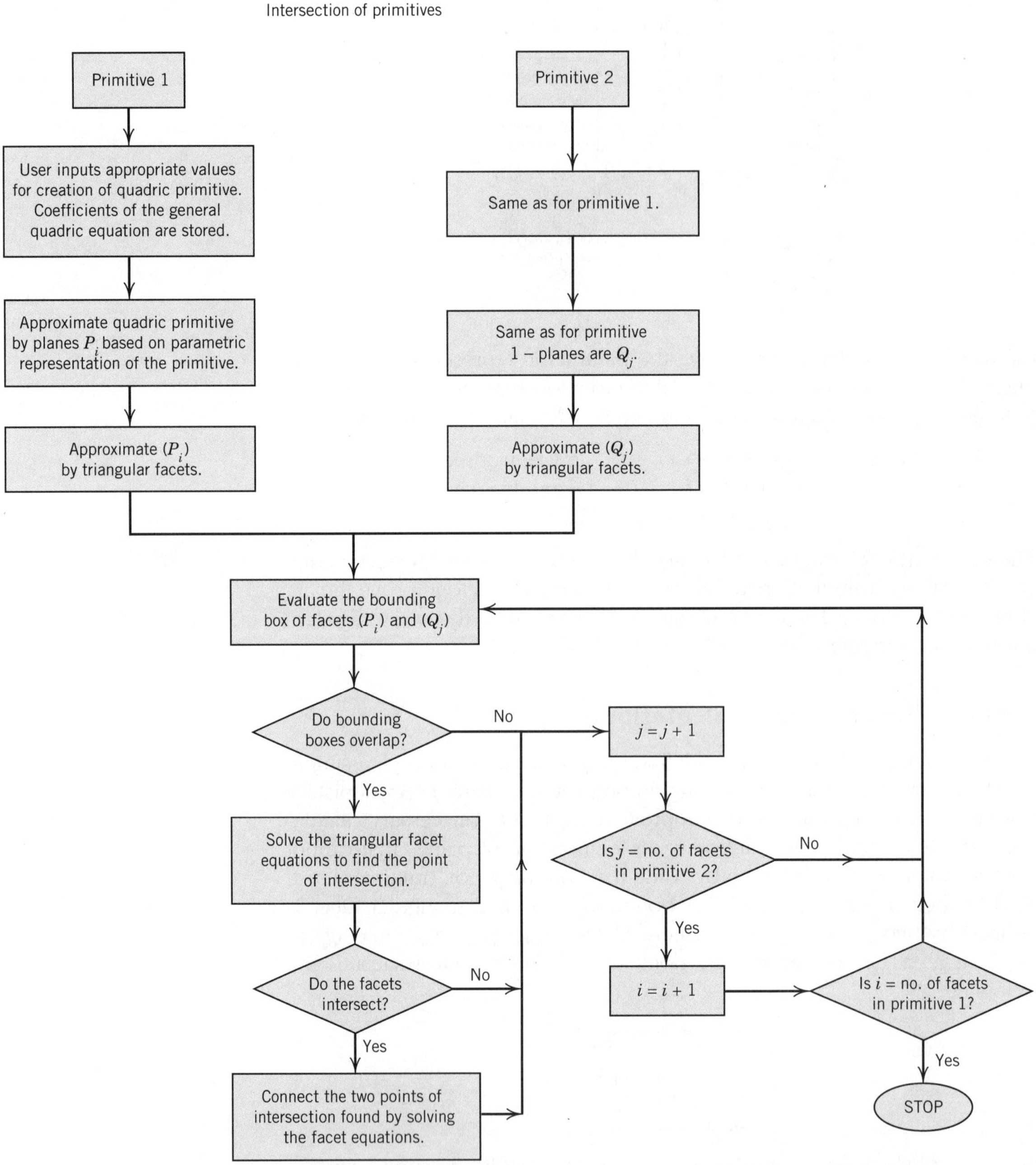

Intersection of primitives

FIGURE 12.33 Flowchart for intersection calculations between primitives.

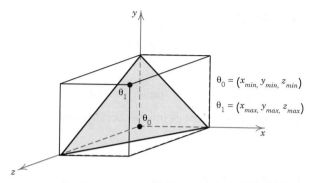

FIGURE 12.34 Bounding box test for a triangular facet.

The mathematical formulation of triangular facet intersection uses vector equations expressed in parametric form for the planes forming the two facets in question [64]. If these are represented by their three vertices A_0, A_1, A_2, and B_0, B_1, B_2 the vector equations become

$$\mathbf{A}(u,v) = \mathbf{A}_0 + u\,(\mathbf{A}_1 - \mathbf{A}_0) + v\,(\mathbf{A}_2 - \mathbf{A}_1) \qquad 0 \le u,\, v \le 1 \quad (12.5)$$

$$\mathbf{B}(s,t) = \mathbf{B}_0 + s\,(\mathbf{B}_1 - \mathbf{B}_0) + t\,(\mathbf{B}_2 - \mathbf{B}_1) \qquad 0 \le s,\, t \le 1 \quad (12.6)$$

The facet-to-facet intersection is defined by the equation:

$$\mathbf{A}(u,v) - \mathbf{B}(s,t) = 0 \qquad\qquad (12.7)$$

This vector equation corresponds to three scalar equations (one for each x,y,z component of the vectors) in four variables, u, v, s, and t, which is an overspecified problem. To solve it, the parameter values are constrained within the limits of zero and one, and two more constraints are imposed:

$$u + v \le 1 \qquad\qquad (12.8)$$

and

$$s + t \le 1 \qquad\qquad (12.9)$$

The three scalar equations are solved eight times for the parameters u, v, s, and t, each being equal to zero and one. For example, setting the parameter $u = 0$ and eliminating parameter v, the scalar equations reduce to:

$$m_1 s + m_2 t + m_3 = 0 \qquad\qquad (12.10)$$

$$n_1 s + n_2 t + n_3 = 0 \qquad\qquad (12.11)$$

From Eq. 12.10,

$$s = -\,(m_3 - m_2 t)/m_1 \qquad\qquad (12.12)$$

which can be substituted into Eq. 12.11 to give the value of t.

$$t = (n_1 m_3 - m_1 n_3)/(n_2 m_1 - n_1 m_2) \qquad\qquad (12.13)$$

The solution is valid only if

$$0 \le u, v, s, t \le 1$$

and

$$u + v \le 1 \quad \text{and} \quad s + t \le 1$$

which results in a single segment of intersection between the two triangular facets.

12.12.4 Boolean Operations

Once the line of intersection between two primitives has been obtained, boolean operations (union, difference, intersection) can be performed. The procedure followed in these operations makes use of the faceting approach to model creation. The flowchart in Figure 12.35 gives the logic of this procedure for a union operation. Similar logic is followed when performing intersection or difference operations.

12.12.5 Rendering

A procedure for hidden surface removal is applied to the new primitive obtained from the boolean operations. The ray tracing technique can be used on the facets, and the problem is then reduced to one of finding a line-plane intersection. If the ray to a facet intersects any other of the surfaces forming the object, the facet under consideration is hidden. This process is implemented for all the facets forming each quadric primitive. The rays from the viewpoint (eye of the observer) are varied along a parametric direction and checked for intersection with all the facets, as shown in Figure 12.36.

The mathematical formulation for this procedure is simple. If the position of the viewpoint and the point at which visibility has to be determined in world coordinates are given as (x_1, y_1, z_1) and (x_2, y_2, z_2), then the ray joining the vertices of each facet and the viewpoint will have the equations:

$$(x - x_1)/(x_2 - x_1) = (y - y_1)/(y_2 - y_1) = (z - z_1)/(z_2 - z_1)$$
(12.14)

or

$$x = x_1 + t(x_2 - x_1)$$
$$y = y_1 + t(y_2 - y_1) \qquad (12.15)$$
$$z = z_1 + t(z_2 - z_1)$$

where $0 \le t \le 1$ for a line defined between the coordinates (x_1, y_1, z_1) and (x_2, y_2, z_2). The problem of finding the intersection between this ray and the facet has been mentioned extensively in the literature [53,54]. The approach used here makes use of the formulation where both the patch and the ray are in parametric form.

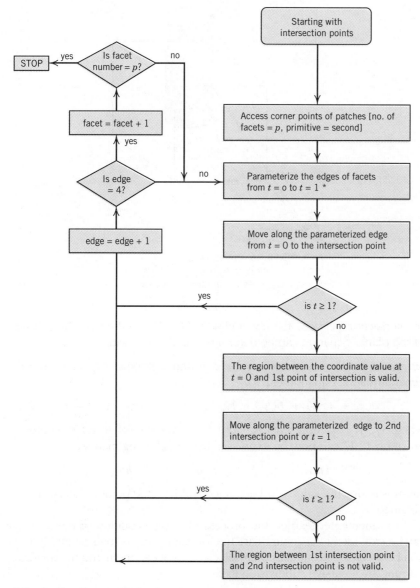

* The direction of parameterization for each edge is fixed by the bounding box test, so that $t = 0$ remains outside the first primitive.

FIGURE 12.35 Flowchart for a union operation.

The general equation of a patch is defined as

$$f(x, y, z) = ax + by + cz + d = 0 \qquad (12.16)$$

where a, b, c, and d are arbitrary real constants.

Different values of the algebraic coefficients a, b, c, and d will produce different types of planes with different positions and orientations. The points

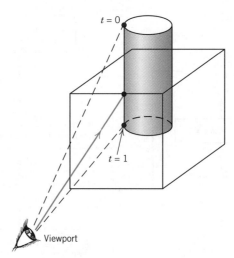

FIGURE 12.36 Ray tracing implementation, with the rays varying along a parametric direction on the facets.

of intersection between the ray equations (12.15) and the bounding surface of the planar equation can be determined in the following manner.

Substitute the three expressions for x, y, and z given in Eq. 12.15 into the general quadric equation (12.16),

$$a(x_1 + tx_{12}) + b(y_1 + ty_{12}) + c(z_1 + tz_{12}) + d = 0 \quad (12.17)$$

where x_{12}, y_{12}, z_{12} represent $(x_2 - x_1)$, $(y_2 - y_1)$, and $(z_2 - z_1)$, respectively. Equation 12.17 can now be expressed in the following manner:

$$t = -(ax_1 + by_1 + cz_1 + d)/(ax_{12} + by_{12} + cz_{12})$$

By substituting the value of t back into Eq. 12.15, the point of intersection is obtained.

As mentioned earlier, the process of implementation of the modeler can be extended to accommodate freeform surfaces, as long as the intersection between these surfaces themselves, or between them and the quadrics, is found by recursive subdivision [65].

SUMMARY

This chapter described the basics of solid modeling theory and details on the most common representation forms: CSG, B-rep, sweeping and spatial enumeration. Issues of architecture and conversion between representations were also addressed, with emphasis on the use of NURBS in contemporary solid modeling systems. Basic approaches to feature modeling, as an extension of solid modeling, were mentioned.

EXERCISES

1. Establish a CSG table that will create the models in Figure 7.21, and output them using a CAD system.

2. A cylinder of radius 4 units and height 10 units is to be approximated on a solid modeler, using faceted boundary representation. Find the percentage of error in its volume calculation due to the approximation:

   (a) When the number of facets, $n = 10$.
   (b) When $n = 30$.

3. Create an octree for the object shown in the accompanying figure.

4. Use a CAD system to verify the problem given in Example 12.4.

5. Use a CAD system to create the swept solid given in Example 12.5.

Chapter 13

General Engineering Applications

The information presented in the previous chapters can be used to solve a variety of engineering problems. This chapter illustrates some of those engineering applications and provides flowcharts to facilitate their implementation. The use of a graphics library is recommended during this implementation stage.

Three problems will be studied in detail, relating to contouring, robotics, and finite element mesh generation. In addition, suggestions will be made for other possible applications.

13.1 CONTOURING

Contouring is a standard and well-used technique to represent a three-dimensional surface in two dimensions. Such plots have for a long time been drawn by manual methods and used in the form of simple topographic maps. Contour plots are created by connecting points of equal z value in an xy

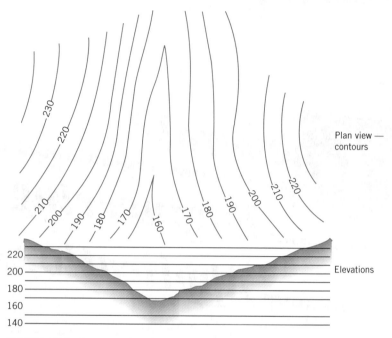

FIGURE 13.1 Contour plot with appropriate elevations.

plane. Curves representing contours are obtained by the intersection of a series of parallel planes with the three-dimensional surface in consideration, as shown in Figure 13.1. Contour plots have the advantage that one can obtain numerical z values by interpolation between contour lines. The contouring technique can be applied in various areas of engineering to show, for example, stress or temperature distributions in a domain, or elevations in a survey map. Figure 13.2a shows the plot of a terrain in which the elevations of the contours have been marked, whereas stress contours on a plate are shown in Figure 13.2b.

Although contours can be drawn for a continuous mathematical function $z = f(x, y)$, a more common case in engineering involves the creation of contour plots from a discrete set of data points. In the latter case, it is often convenient to interpolate the given data onto a regular rectangular grid with equally spaced x and y points, and then draw the contour lines from the gridded data. It can be seen that the first step requires fitting the available data onto a regular grid. There are several methods for the solution of this problem; one of the simplest involves the use of a distance-weighted linear interpolation described as follows.

13.1.1 Grid Interpolation

For simplicity, let us consider the application of contouring in survey maps. Typically, the surveyor determines the height of the terrain at arbitrary points,

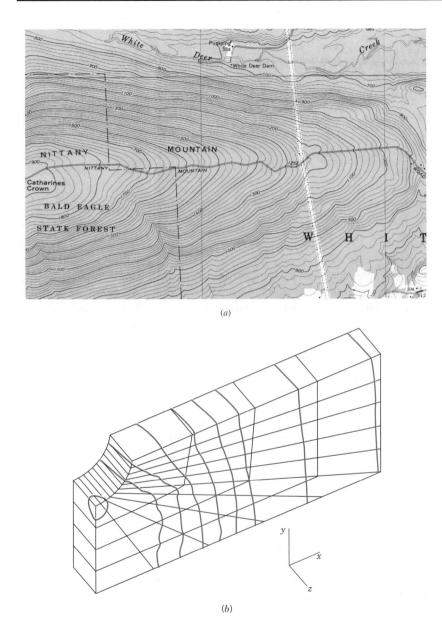

(a)

(b)

FIGURE 13.2 (a) Terrain contour plot. (b) Stress contours on a plate.

and takes more numbers of readings at locations with large variations of slope. It is important to note that the points at which readings are taken are arbitrarily chosen. When using computational methods, these arbitrary points can be related to a large number of reference points forming a regular rectangular grid.

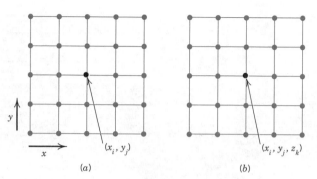

FIGURE 13.3 Grid mesh (*a*) Before interpolation. (*b*) After interpolation.

A simple algorithm to interpolate the scattered data to the regular grid makes use of a distance-weighted linear interpolation technique [66]. Let (x_p, y_p, z_p) for $p = 1$ to m represent the coordinates of m arbitrarily selected points. If each point on the regular grid is represented by $[x(i), y(j)]$, then the z value for the grid points is given by

$$
z_{i,j} = \frac{\displaystyle\sum_{p=1}^{m} \frac{z_p}{[(x_i - x_p)^2 + (y_j - y_p)^2]}}{\displaystyle\sum_{p=1}^{m} \frac{1}{[(x_i - x_p)^2 + (y_j - y_p)^2]}}
\tag{13.1}
$$

Note that the denominator of each fraction in Eq. 13.1 is the square of the distance between the grid point and any arbitrary input data point. Figure 13.3 shows the format of the grid mesh before and after the interpolation.

The procedure just described can be made more accurate by using only a limited number of input points close to the grid location under consideration. The choice of arbitrarily placed input points depends on the curvature of the surface. Such restriction totally eliminates the effect of faraway points during the grid interpolation. Figure 13.4 gives a pseudocode for the implementation of this technique.

13.1.2 Contouring over Regular Rectangular Grids

After all the height data have been mapped to the regular grid, one is ready to produce a contour map. Contours of a given height can be created in one of two ways:

Method 1. Examine each square of the grid and draw the part of the contour located inside the square with a straight line.

ALGORITHM 13.1

FIGURE 13.4 Flowchart for grid interpolation.

```
subroutine Grid_Interpolation( )

begin
     Open input data file and read number of data
          points (n, m)
     Read arbitrary data x(i), y(i) and z(i)
     for i = 1 and i < m do
          for j = 1 and j < n do
               Compute x,y for grid as
               Xg = Xo + (i - 1) * Xincrement
               Yg = Yo + (j - 1) * Yincrement
               Compute Z [i,j] based on equation 13.1
          next j
     next i

     Print data to output file
     end

end
```

Method 2. Locate the intersection of the contour with the side of one grid cell and then trace the rest of the contour throughout the entire grid. Various contour heights are sought in turn and are traced throughout the grid. The contours may be plotted directly by joining the points with straight lines, or are stored for later output with a curve fitting routine.

Method 1. It is convenient in this case to triangulate the grid and define an array of cells that are triangular instead of rectangular, as shown in Figure 13.5. A contour line is created by checking whether height h crosses the line segment between two grid points forming a cell. If one of the grid points has a height less than h and the other has a height greater than h, the contour will intersect the grid line and its location on the line is calculated. Assuming

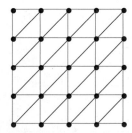

FIGURE 13.5 Triangulation of grid.

that the grid points are located sufficiently close to one another and no contour line crosses each grid line more than once, a good approximation to the point of intersection can be found by simple linear interpolation, as follows (see accompanying figure):

$$x = x_1 + (x_2 - x_1)\left(\frac{b - z_1}{z_2 - z_1}\right)$$

$$y = y_1 + (y_2 - y_1)\left(\frac{b - z_1}{z_2 - z_1}\right)$$

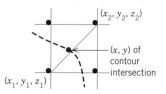

It is expected that whenever a contour point is located along one of the boundary lines of a triangular cell, it also crosses another boundary. Each contour segment inside a triangular grid cell is obtained by straight line connection between two points. The contour line is completed by connecting a series of isolated straight line segments, as shown in Figure 13.6. A flowchart for this problem is given in Figure 13.7.

Method 2. The assumption is again made that no contour crosses a grid line more than once, and linear interpolation is used to locate the position of the contour intersection with the grid line. After a desired starting point for the contour has been found, an appropriate scheme is employed to trace the complete contour line.

Several approaches have been used in the solution of this problem [67], one of which will be described in detail in this section. This solution uses rectangular cells and is based on the understanding that all contour lines must cross either the boundary or a horizontal grid line. A search along the boundary lines for a contour intersection is performed first through the inequality:

$$z(G_1) < b \leq z(G_2) \tag{13.2}$$

FIGURE 13.6 Straight line connection of contour points.

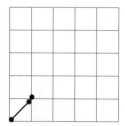 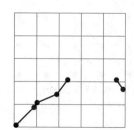 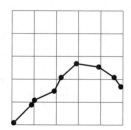

ALGORITHM 13.2

FIGURE 13.7 Flowchart for contouring problem—Method 1.

```
subroutine Generate_Contours_1 ( )
#Xo,Yo        —grid origin
#m,n          —number of grid points along the x,y-
                directions
#dX,dY        —grid increments
#Z[i,j]       —grid heights
#h            —contour height
#N            —number of different contour heights
begin
      Initialize graphics
      for k=0 and k<N
            for j=0 and j<n do
                  for i=0 and i<m do
                        L=i+1
                        P=j+1
                        call Test ( )
                  next i
            next j
            Label contour line
      next k
      Generate hard copy
      return
end

subroutine Test ( )
begin
      CHECK=0
      for each side of the current grid
            if(Z[i,j]<h<Z[L,j]) OR (Z[i,j]>h>Z[L,j])
                  then
                        begin
                              Interpolate to find contour point, using dX
                              and dY  Move to point
                              CHECK=1

                        end
                  else
                        begin
                              if(Z[L,j]<h<Z[L,P]) OR (Z[L,j]>h>Z[L,P])
                                    then
                                          Interpolate_
                                          if(CHECK=1)
                                                then
                                                      begin
                                                      Draw to point
                                                      CHECK=0
```

FIGURE 13.7 (Continued)

```
                                                           end
                                           else
                                               begin
                                                    Move to point
                                                    CHECK=1
                                               end
                                           end if
                               end if
                   end if
             end if
       next side
       return
end
. . . . .
. . . . .
(continue until all sides of two triangular cells are checked.)
```

where G_1 is taken as the grid immediately preceding G_2 in the scanning path shown in Figure 13.8. Each time a contour intersection is found, the complete contour is traced from this original point. Since the inequality in Eq. 13.2 is used only when G_1 precedes G_2, that is, G_1 is lower than G_2, only one end of the open contour is picked up at each time, as shown in Figure 13.9. As the open contours are traced, all horizontal grid lines which have been crossed are stored in a separate array for a check at a later time.

When all open contours are found, a search for possible closed contours is started by scanning horizontal grid lines from left to right to look for those that satisfy Eq. 13.2. When such a horizontal line is found, it is checked against the stored array to see if this line has previously been used. If so, the line is discarded and the search is continued until a new one is found. This is then used as a starting point (or entry point) for the closed contour. Again, all intersections of the contour with horizontal lines are stored. The process is repeated until the whole grid has been scanned and no new intersections are found.

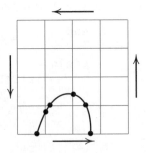

FIGURE 13.8 Scanning path for boundary lines search.

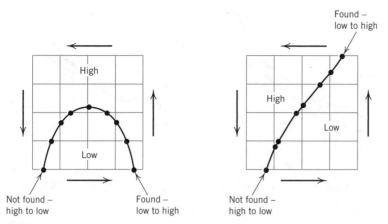

FIGURE 13.9 Only one end of each open contour is selected at each time.

Once an entry point into the contour line is found, the tracing is per-formed by searching the sides of the rectangular cell where the contour starts. For example, assume that the first contour point is C_1, in Figure 13.10a. This is the entry point of the contour into the cell shaded in the figure. To find the exit point, the sides of the cell are searched in the order right, top, left—all relative to the entry side—and the first contour point encountered is used as the exit point. This procedure is based on the principle of "high ground on the right," which is implied by the inequality given in Eq. 13.2. If the exit point is found as C_2, as shown in Figure 13.10b, the process is con-tinued by assuming that this is the entry point into a new cell (shaded in Figure 13.10b). The cell is scanned starting on side I—high side of entry line—and continuing to sides II and III. If point C_2 had been found in the location shown in Figure 13.10c, the scanning of the shaded cell would start on the high side and follow the pattern I → II → III shown. It is important to remember that the first cell line checked during each tracing step is on the high side of the entry cell line.

Once the contour points have been found and stored in sequence, a curve-fitting algorithm can smooth the contour line. The cubic spline routine

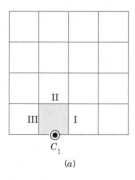

(a)

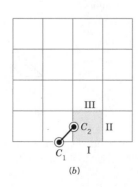

(b)

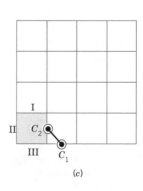

(c)

FIGURE 13.10 Various possible entry points into a cell and tracing orders.

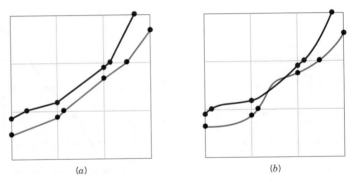

FIGURE 13.11 (*a*) Straight line connection. (*b*) Curve fitting routine.

described in Section 10.4.4, for example, would give good results. It is important to note, however, that this curve fitting solution may occasionally create problems, as shown in Figure 13.11, where contours of different heights are shown to cross each other, an obvious impossibility. This problem could be solved by the use of splines under tension, as described at the end of Section 10.9.4, with the tension factors specified by the user to increase or decrease the curvature of the contours until they no longer cross each other [67].

A flowchart for the implementation of this algorithm is given at the end of this chapter, as Appendix 13.1.

13.2 SIMPLE SURFACE DEVELOPMENT

The gridded x_g, y_g, z_g data obtained from the interpolation described in Section 13.1.1 can be used to develop a three-dimensional wire mesh type of surface through a very simple routine.

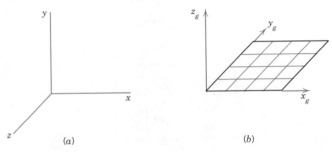

FIGURE 13.12 (*a*) Right-handed system in standard orientation. (*b*) Right-handed system in orientation needed for surface development.

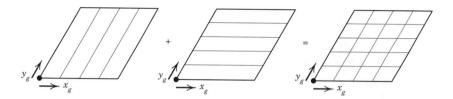

FIGURE 13.13 Process of surface creation.

As seen in Section 8.1.3, a point in an oblique projection to the xy plane, in a right-handed coordinate system (Figure 13.12a), is given by

$$[(x + z \cos \theta) \quad (y + z \sin \theta) \quad 0 \quad 1] \tag{13.3}$$

In the case of our data, the right-handed system is as shown in Figure 13.12b, with the grid on the horizontal xy plane and the z values shown along the vertical axis.

Using Eq. 13.3 for this case yields

$$[(x_g - y_g \cos \theta) \quad (z_g - y_g \sin \theta) \quad 0 \quad 1] \tag{13.4}$$

Application of this transformation to the gridded data will produce the surface. The flowchart in Appendix 13.2 describes the surface generation. Lines for each fixed x value are created first by varying y values, followed by the reverse procedure, as shown in Figure 13.13. An implementation of this routine for a set of data values is shown in Figure 13.14.

13.3   GRAPHICAL SIMULATION OF AN ARTICULATED ROBOT

Articulated robots, also known as elbow manipulators, have an arrangement as shown in Figure 13.15. The movement of the robot's parts is accomplished by rotation about three axes, with two axes, z_1 and z_2 in Figure 13.15, parallel

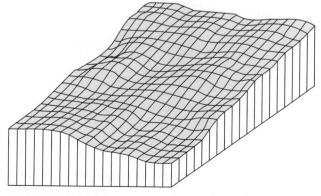

FIGURE 13.14 Surface description from gridded data.

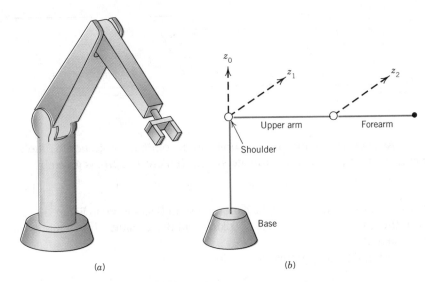

(a)   (b)

FIGURE 13.15 (*a*) Elbow manipulator. (*b*) Schematic diagram.

to each other and the third axis perpendicular to the other two. The total volume swept by the end of a robot as all possible motions are performed is called the *workspace*. The workspace for the resolute configuration described above is shown in Figure 13.16. With the base kept stationary, this workspace encompasses all the points that can be reached by the robot.

Figure 13.17 shows the "home" configuration of the articulated robot, that is, the configuration before any rotation takes place. The three angles

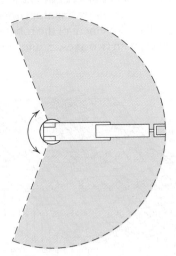

FIGURE 13.16 Total volume swept by end of robot, viewed from the top.

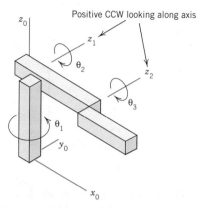

Positive CCW looking along axis

FIGURE 13.17 "Home" configuration
of the articulated robot.

of rotation (θ_1, θ_2, θ_3) that move the robot to the desired position are also
indicated in the figure.

A standard problem in robotics is to find the configuration an articulated robot must take in order to reach a specific point within its workspace.
Given the coordinates of this point, the three angles of rotation that will place
the robot in the required orientation must be calculated. For this calculation,
it is helpful to view the robot from different directions, as shown in Figure
13.18. From Figure 13.18b, the value of θ_1 is

$$\theta_1 = \tan^{-1}\left(\frac{P_y}{P_x}\right) \tag{13.5}$$

All points in the robot's workspace can be reached by this rotation, except
for points where $P_x = P_z = 0$, since Eq. 13.5 is undefined for these values.
This exception can be removed by the inclusion of an offset as described in

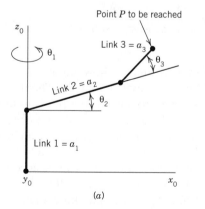

(a)

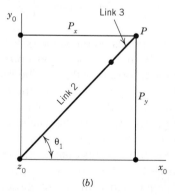

(b)

FIGURE 13.18 Viewing directions (a) Along the y_0 axis. (b) Along the z_0 axis.

FIGURE 13.19 Two possible orientations in which a robot can reach a designated point.

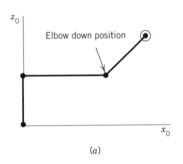

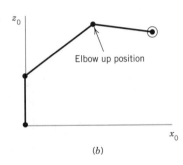

[68]. Once θ_1 is obtained, the angles θ_2 and θ_3 are found by considering the plane formed by the second and third links of the manipulator, as shown in Figure 13.18a. Using the law of cosines the angle is given by

$$\cos \theta_3 = \frac{P_x^2 + P_y^2 - a_2^2 - a_3^2}{2a_2a_3} = M \qquad (13.6)$$

or

$$\theta_3 = \cos^{-1}(M) \qquad (13.7)$$

Since it is necessary to obtain a unique value for each angle, the use of the arctangent function is more appropriate for this problem. Knowing that

$$\sin(\theta_3) = \pm\sqrt{1 - M^2} \qquad (13.8)$$

the angle θ_3 becomes

$$\theta_3 = \tan^{-1}\left[\frac{\pm\sqrt{1 - M^2}}{M}\right] \qquad (13.9)$$

The plus and minus signs indicate whether the point is reached by the robot with the elbow up or the elbow down, as shown in Figure 13.19.

The value of θ_2 is given by [68]

$$\theta_2 = \tan^{-1}\left[\frac{P_y}{P_x}\right] - \tan^{-1}\left[\frac{a_2 \sin \theta_3}{a_1 + a_2 \cos \theta_3}\right] \qquad (13.10)$$

and depends on the value of θ_3.

With this information a program can be written to show graphically the different positions that can be reached by an elbow manipulator. The flowchart in Figure 13.20 gives the logic of such a program. The input is in the form of coordinates of point $P(P_x, P_y, P_z)$ to be reached, and the geometry of the robot, that is, the data for each link. When calculating the three angles of rotation given by Eqs. 13.5, 13.9, and 13.10, care should be taken to flag the user for points outside the reach of the robot's arms. This can be accomplished by checking the value of $(\cos \theta_3)$ as given by Eq. 13.6. If this value is larger than 1, the point chosen is out of reach. Once the three angles of

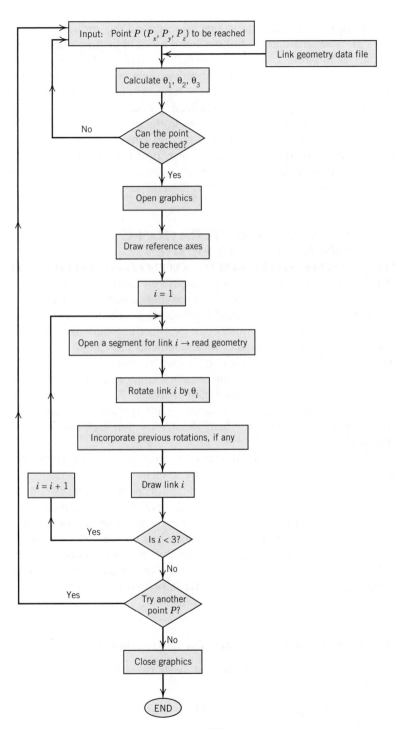

FIGURE 13.20 Flowchart for robot problem.

rotation are known, the data values representing the surfaces forming the robot's arms are manipulated to place the robot in its final orientation. The geometry of the arms can be represented in the form of polygons, through a list of vertex coordinates and connectivity as mentioned in Section 7.2.2. This information should be stored in a separate file and linked to the program. The final image of the manipulator is obtained in three stages, with each represented by a separate segment in the program. The vertical arm is first rotated by θ_1 and displayed. The second arm is rotated by θ_2 about its local axis and has the rotation of the first arm superimposed on it before display. The third arm is rotated by θ_3 about its own axis, has the rotation of the first two arms incorporated, and is then displayed.

13.4 AUTOMATIC GENERATION OF FINITE ELEMENT MESHES

The Finite Element Method has been extensively used in engineering to solve structural, fluid mechanics, and electromagnetics problems. The basic idea behind the finite element method is to divide a structure, body, or region being analyzed into a large number of two- or three-dimensional finite elements. The connecting points of these elements are called *nodes*. A set of simultaneous algebraic equations are formed in terms of the unknown nodal field variables, which can be displacements, temperatures, or velocities, depending on the type of problem being analyzed. Finally, the simultaneous equations are solved for the nodal variables. Interpolation functions are used to describe the variation of the field variables within each element in terms of the nodal variables.

The process of dividing the structure or object into a number of finite elements, finding the connectivity of these elements in terms of nodes, and generating the coordinates of the nodes in a global system is collectively called "mesh generation." Manual procedures for mesh generation are time consuming, error prone, and tedious. The overall efficiency of the finite element method can be improved substantially if the process of mesh generation is automated and a graphical output of the mesh is obtained. In recognition of this need, a number of methods have been devised to automate the mesh generation process [69,70]. Basic procedures for creation of finite element meshes are described in this section.

13.4.1 Simple Procedures for Mesh Generation

In the generation of any finite element mesh, two basic procedures must be defined:

1. Numbering and location of the nodes.
2. Connectivity of the nodes to create each element.

Consider, for example, the quadrilateral region shown in Figure 13.21. A finite element mesh will be created for this region with the following user-defined information:

- Coordinates (x, y) of corner points.
- Number of nodes desired at each boundary, noting that the number of nodes on the opposite boundaries must be the same. In addition, the distances between nodes along any line are equal.

A simple algorithm for node generation follows:

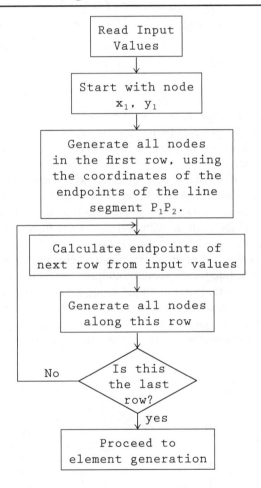

Once all nodes are located and numbered sequentially, finite elements are generated using the appropriate nodal connectivity. Assume that N nodes are present along each row, as defined by the user. The first row, for example, goes from node 1 to node N, the second from $(N+1)$ to $2N$, and so on, as shown in Figure 13.22a. If a CCW direction for connectivity is fol-

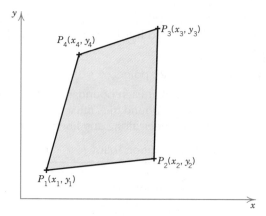

FIGURE 13.21 Quadrilateral region.

lowed, each element has nodes as shown in Figure 13.22*b*, and a connectivity procedure and element numbering can be established. Using the values of the nodal coordinates and element connectivity, a graphical output of the mesh is obtained.

This simple procedure can be modified to fit many special applications. Consider, for example, Figure 13.23*a*, which shows the cross-section of a rectangular furnace. A finite element analysis is to be performed in order to determine the temperature distribution across the furnace cross-section for a given temperature and at specific locations.

The procedure for node numbering and element connectivity just described can be applied with some modifications to create a finite element mesh for this problem. For node numbering, for example, the cross-section is divided into four regions, as shown in Figure 13.23*b*. The node generation is performed in each region by rows, as previously explained and, to account for the center opening, the following algorithm is used:

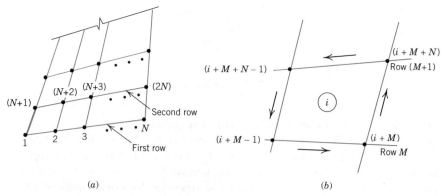

(a)   (b)

FIGURE 13.22 Mesh generation (*a*) Node numbering. (*b*) Element connectivity.

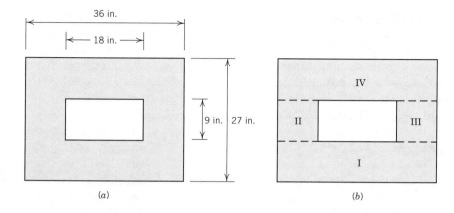

GENERATION OF NODES FOR EACH REGION

```
For each region DO
  For each row DO
    Determine coordinates of each new node.
    If not first row of region
    THEN
      Begin
        Compare last node in this row with extreme
        nodes (y_min and y_max) of all other regions.
        IF ( y_min ≤ y_current) AND ( y_max ≥ y_current)
        THEN
        Add to the next row the number of nodes
        present in the current row of the compared
        region
      END
    END FOR
  END FOR
Plot all nodes.
```

Figure 13.24 shows the corresponding finite element mesh generated for this problem.

The finite element mesh generation examples just described are simplistic in nature. Much more complex problems in engineering are solved using this technique and utilizing the various model representations studied in the previous chapters, including surface and solid models. Contemporary CAD systems have automatic meshing utilities that can be used to solve two- or three-dimensional problems. In their first stages of development, these automatic mesh generation algorithms operated on wireframe models, requiring considerable user input. More fully automated algorithms were later developed, using solid modeling as the representation scheme, and can be divided into two general types: triangulation and recursive spatial subdivi-

FIGURE 13.24 Graphical display of a quadrilateral mesh.

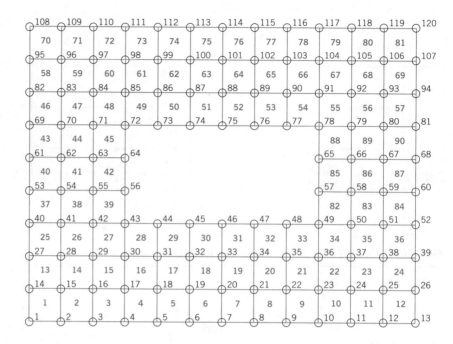

sion algorithms [69]. One of the triangulation schemes for solids operates by first performing surface triangulation of the boundary, and then solid triangulation of the interior. Tetrahedral meshes result from this implementation [70]. In recursive spatial subdivision algorithms, the quadtrees and octrees described in Chapter 12 are used, with inside cells converted directly into mesh elements and boundary cells further processed to adapt them into acceptable mesh elements [69]. The reader is encouraged to explore the mesh generation procedures of available CAD systems.

SUMMARY

This chapter described in detail three problems related to the engineering disciplines. Although narrow in scope, these problems should serve as an indication to the reader of the many possible engineering applications of computer graphics and geometric modeling.

EXERCISES

1. Develop a computer program that outputs moment and shear diagrams for various loading conditions on simply supported and cantilever beams.

2. Create graphical user interfaces for manipulating the following:

   (a) Control parameters for bicubic curves—Bezier and B-spline.

(b) Control parameters for bicubic surfaces—Bezier and B-spline.

(c) Modeling and viewing operations for polyhedral objects.

3. Develop a procedure to create a finite element mesh on a free form surface, given the geometry of the surface.

4. Implement the contouring algorithms given in Figure 13.7 for any set of data points.

5. Use the same data points of Exercise 4, and implement the surface algorithm given in Appendix 13.2

6. Implement the robotic algorithm given in Figure 13.20, defining the robot's arms as simple polyhedrals.

7. Adapt the algorithms of Section 13.4 to create a triangular finite element mesh for the rectangular surface of Figure 13.23*a*.

8. Create a mesh generation algorithm for a region with curved (circular arcs) boundaries.

APPENDIX 13.1

▌▊▌

```
subroutine Generate_Contours ()
#assume no contour enters and exits the same side of a grid cell
#Grid[i,j]—is a two-dimensional array of size Nx * Ny containing the
interpolated heights
#Point    —is a 3D-point <x,y,h> containing x,y coordinates and the
height h at location x,y
#hc       —is the current contour height
begin
      #begin along boundary y=0
      j=1
      for i=0 to (Nx-1) do
            if (Grid [i,j].h < hc <= Grid [i+1,j].h)
                  then
                        contour intersection found
                        entry_side=4
                        call Trace(i,j,entry_side)
            end if
      next i


      #begin along boundary x=dx*Nx
      i=Nx
      for j=0 to (Ny-1) do
            if (Grid [i,j].h <hc <= Grid [i,j-1].h)
                  then
                        contour intersection found
                        entry_side=1
                        call Trace(i,j,entry_side)
            end if
      next i

      # begin along boundary y=dy*Ny
      j=dy*Ny
      for i=Ny to 2 insteps of -1 do
            if (Grid [i,j].h < hc <= Grid [i-1,j].h)
                  then
                        contour intersection found
                        entry_side=2
                        call Trace(i,j,entry_side)
            end if
      next i
```

```
#begin along boundary x=0
i=1
for j=Ny to 2 insteps of -1 do
      if (Grid [i,j].h < hc <= Grid [i,j-1].h)
            then
                        contour intersection found
                        entry_side=3
                        call Trace(i,j,entry_side)
            end if
      next j
```

```
#Now check for closed contours

      for i=1 to (Nx-1) do
            for j=1 to (Ny-1) do
                  if (Grid [i,j].h < hc <= Grid [i,j+1].h
                        then
                                    check if it was already processed
                                    if not processed
                                          then
                                                      entry_side=4
                                                      call Trace(i,j,entry_side)
                                          end if
                        end if
                  next j
            next i

      return

end
subroutine Trace (i,j,entry_side)-Assumes that a subroutine can call
itself.
#Grid[i,j] is the lower point in the grid
#entry_side is the side of the grid in which the contour enters
begin

      if (entry_side=4)
            then
                  begin
                        Check intersection with side 1
                        if intersection found
                              then
                                    begin
                                          store intersection point
                                          entry_side=3
```

```
                                                i=i+1 # j remains same
                                                call Trace (i,j,entry_side)
                                    end
                    end if

                    Check intersection with side 2
                    if intersection found
                            then
                                    begin
                                            store intersection point
                                            entry_side=4
                                            j=j+1 # i remains same
                                            call Trace (i,j,entry_side)
                                    end
                    end if

                    Check intersection with side 3
                    if intersection found
                            then
                                    begin
                                            store intersection point
                                            entry_side=1
                                            i=i-1 # j remains same
                                            call Trace (i,j,entry_side)
                                    end
                    end if
            end
    end if

    else if (entry_side=1)
            then
                    begin
                            Check intersection with side 2
                            if intersection found
                                    then
                                            begin
                                                    store intersection point
                                                    entry_side=4
                                                    i=i-1
                                                    j=j+1
                                                    call Trace (i,j,entry_side)
                                            end
                            end if

                            Check intersection with side 3
                            if intersection found
```

```
                       then
                              begin
                                     store intersection point
                                     entry_side=1
                                     i=i-2 # j remains same
                                     call Trace (i,j,entry_side)
                              end
                   end if

                   Check intersection with side 4
                   if intersection found
                          then
                                 begin
                                        store intersection point
                                        entry_side=2
                                        i=i-1
                                        j=j-1
                                        call Trace (i,j,entry_side)
                                 end
                   end if
              end
    end if

    else if (entry_side=2)
          then
              begin
                   Check intersection with side 3
                   if intersection found
                          then
                                 begin
                                        store intersection point
                                        entry_side=1
                                        i=i-2
                                        j=j-1
                                        call Trace (i,j,entry_side)
                                 end
                   end if

                   Check intersection with side 4
                   if intersection found
                          then
                                 begin
                                        store intersection point
                                        entry_side=2
                                        j=j-2
                                        i=i-1
                                        call Trace (i,j,entry_side)
```

```
                                end if

                                Check intersection with side 1
                                if intersection found
                                        then
                                                begin
                                                        store intersection point
                                                        entry_side=3
                                                        j=j-1 # i remains same
                                                        call Trace (i,j,entry_side)
                                                end
                                end if
                        end
            end if

            else if (entry_side=3)
                  then
                        begin
                                Check intersection with side 4
                                if intersection found
                                        then
                                                begin
                                                        store intersection point
                                                        entry_side=2
                                                        j=j-2 # i remains same
                                                        call Trace (i,j,entry_side)
                                                end
                                end if

                                Check intersection with side 1
                                if intersection found
                                        then
                                                begin
                                                        store intersection point
                                                        entry_side=3
                                                        j=j-1
                                                        i=i+1
                                                        call Trace (i,j,entry_side)
                                                end
                                end if

                                Check intersection with side 2
                                if intersection found
                                        then
```

```
                                begin
                                    store intersection point
                                    entry_side=4
                                    i=i+1
                                    j=j+1
                                    call Trace (i,j,entry_side)
                                end
                        end if
                    end
            end if

            return

end # end of subroutine Trace( )
```

APPENDIX 13.2

▐▌▌▐▌▐▌▌▐▌▌▌▐▌▌▐▌▌▐▌▌▐▌▌▐▌▐▌▌▐▌▌▐▌▌▐▌▐▌▌▐▌▌▐▌▌▐▌▐▌▌▐▌▌▐▌▌▐▌▌▐▌▐▌▌▐▌▌▐▌▌▐▌▐▌▌▐▌▌

```
subroutine Generate_Surface_Mesh()
#Zg[i,j] -Z coordinate at each grid point
#m,n     -grid dimension
#dX,dY   -grid increment
#THETA   -angle of oblique projection
#Xo,Yo   -initial point on grid

begin
      for i=0 and i<m do
            Xg=Xo+i*dX
            Yg=Yo
            Move to point ((Xg-Yg*COS(THETA)),(Zg[i,j]-Yg*SIN(THETA) ))
            for j=0 and j<n do
                  Yg=Yo+j*dY
                  Draw line to ((Xg-Yg*COS(THETA)),(Zg[i,j]-
                  Yg*SIN(THETA) ))
            next j
      next i
      for j=0 and j<n do
            Yg=Yo+j*dY
            Xg=Xo
            Move to point ((Xg-Yg*COS(THETA)),(Zg[i,j]-Yg*SIN(THETA) ))
            for i=0 and i<m do
                  Xg=Xo+i*dX
                  Draw line to ((Xg-Yg*COS(THETA)),(Zg[i,j]-
                  Yg*SIN(THETA) ))
            next i
      next j

      return

end
```

Appendix A

Object Oriented Graphics

The concept *object-oriented* has gained popularity in all computing areas in the last few years [71] and has been used to solve a number of graphics problems. The object-oriented abstraction comprises some basic concepts, described as follows:

Objects are entities in an object-oriented system formed by a collection of internal data that represent their active state, and transparent to the outside. All objects are given names with which they are addressed.

Messages are means by which the objects are addressed. In response to a message, the object may change or return another object or value, and so on.

Methods are means by which the objects react to the messages received.

Classes are entities to which objects belong. Objects are instances of a class, and their behaviour depends on the methods defined for the class.

Inheritance is an important characteristic of object-oriented systems, permitting the specification of inheritance of both methods and variables among classes. Inheritance can be specified through various mechanisms. For example, through a tree structure, hierarchical inheritance specifies a one-to-one relationship. Through a directed graph, on the other hand, multiple inheritance from several classes is allowed to occur.

Data abstraction means that information relating to the implementation of an object is hidden from other objects. To access an object, only its class or type need be known. Data structures and algorithms are kept behind an interface that specifies the function of an object, but not how it functions.

Polymorphism is the ability to send the same messages to various types or classes of objects.

Many object-oriented programming languages have been developed, such as Smalltalk and LIST-derived languages, C++ and Object Pascal, using most or all of the basic concepts previously listed. In all these languages objects are addressed by means of messages, without regard to each object's internal representation. In this sense, an object-oriented program can be seen as a network of objects linked via a stream of messages. An object's interface is specified so that the object itself can be replaced or improved without affecting the overall program structure.

Another way of manipulating objects is through class inheritance, where classes contain *templates* for the creation of object instances. For example, a "quadric" class could define data fields such as the coefficients of the general quadratic equation and allow instances of various quadric primitives, such as spheres, cones, and so forth. These data are taken as *instance variables*, and the various algorithms that operate on them are the *methods*. Actual instances of the various quadric primitives would be created by the application program through the use of these templates.

Various graphics libraries and frameworks have been developed and are described in the literature [72] that support an object-oriented approach to computer graphics programming. GO‖, for example, provides a hardware and software independent object-oriented graphics system. The GO‖ specification allows graphical algorithm development through an object-oriented language with multiple inheritance, graphical class hierarchies, polymorphism, and so on. The two- and three-dimensional class hierarchy of GO‖ is shown in Figure A-1. Notice that, in this particular implementation, no free-form class exists. Its incorporation, however, should be relatively simple due to the inherent benefits of object-oriented design, that is, modularization and resource sharing.

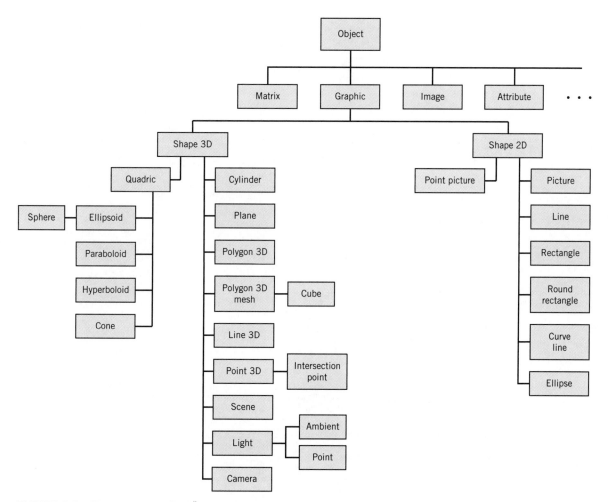

FIGURE A.1. Class hierarchy of GO‖.

A new effort in the development of second generation graphics standards, comprising the capabilities of existing standards (GKS and PHIGS) and addressing the needs of a variety of applications, is under development at this time [73]. Recommendations for the use of the object-oriented philosophy have been made and are presently under study.

Review of Vector and Matrix Algebra

Various mathematical techniques are consistently used in the fields of computer graphics and geometric modeling because of their adaptability to computational solutions. Among these are vector and matrix algebra, which are used extensively throughout this textbook. A short review of these techniques will be given in this appendix.

VECTOR ALGEBRA

The concept of vectors has a number of applications in computer graphics, such as geometric transformations, planar projections, or the determination of surface orientation. Vectors are defined by a magnitude and a direction, and are independent of any coordinate system.

A vector can be shown graphically as a directed line segment whose length is proportional to the vector's magnitude. The sense of the vector is indicated by an arrow, as shown in Figure B.1.

FIGURE B.1.

FIGURE B.2.

FIGURE B.3.

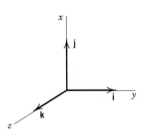

FIGURE B.4.

The following laws of vector algebra apply to all vector operations:

Equality occurs when two vectors have the same magnitude, direction, and sense.

Addition can be defined in graphical form as shown in Figure B.2, by placing the vectors in a tip-to-tail order.

Subtraction is defined by

$$\mathbf{p} - \mathbf{q} = \mathbf{p} + (-\mathbf{q})$$

where $(-\mathbf{q})$ represents a vector with the same magnitude and direction as $\mathbf{q}$, but opposite sense.

Scalar multiplication results in a vector with the same direction and sense as the original vector, but different magnitude. For example, given vector $\mathbf{p}$ in Figure B.3, multiplication by a scalar a would result in $a\mathbf{p}$.

A *unit vector* in the direction of any given vector $\mathbf{p}$ can be found as

$$\mathbf{u} = \frac{\mathbf{p}}{|\mathbf{p}|}$$

In this case, vector $\mathbf{p}$ is said to have been normalized. It is now possible to define unit vectors along the axes of a cartesian system, labeled $\mathbf{i}$, $\mathbf{j}$, $\mathbf{k}$, as shown in Figure B.4.

Any vector $\mathbf{p}$ can be represented as

$$\mathbf{p} = p_x\mathbf{i} + p_y\mathbf{j} + p_z\mathbf{k}$$

where p_x, p_y, p_z are the cartesian components of vector $\mathbf{p}$ (see Figure B.5).

The unit vector, $\mathbf{u}$, in the direction of $\mathbf{p}$ has three cartesian components representing the cosines of the angles formed by the vector $\mathbf{p}$ and the x, y, z coordinate axes, so that

$$\mathbf{u} = \cos\theta_x\mathbf{i} + \cos\theta_y\mathbf{j} + \cos\theta_z\mathbf{k}$$

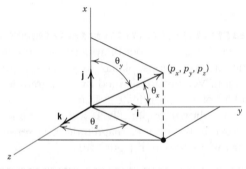

FIGURE B.5.

These components are usually called *direction cosines.*

The *dot-product* of two vectors

$$\mathbf{p}(p_x, p_y, p_z)$$

$$\mathbf{q}(q_x, q_y, q_z)$$

is a scalar given by

$$\mathbf{p} \cdot \mathbf{q} = p_x q_x + p_y q_y + p_z q_z = |p| |q| \cos \theta$$

where θ is the angle between the two vectors. The dot-product can be positive or negative, depending on whether or not $0 \leq \theta \leq \pi/2$.

The *cross-product* of vectors $\mathbf{p}$ and $\mathbf{q}$ is defined as

$$\mathbf{p} \times \mathbf{q} = (p_y q_z - p_z q_y)\mathbf{i} + (p_x q_z - p_z q_x)\mathbf{j} + (p_x q_y - p_y q_x)\mathbf{k}$$

$$= |\mathbf{p}| |\mathbf{q}| \sin \theta$$

and represents a vector in a direction perpendicular to the plane containing the two original vectors. The sense of the cross-product is obtained by applying the right-hand rule.

MATRIX ALGEBRA

Matrices are rectangular arrays of elements that share certain properties. In computer graphics/geometric modeling applications, these elements can represent coordinates of points, transformation components, and so on.

In general, a matrix M is represented as

$$[M] = \begin{bmatrix} a_{11} & a_{12} & a_{13} & \cdots & a_{1n} \\ a_{21} & a_{22} & a_{23} & \cdots & a_{2n} \\ \vdots & \vdots & \vdots & & \vdots \\ a_{m1} & a_{m2} & a_{m3} & \cdots & a_{mn} \end{bmatrix}$$

with m rows and n columns, or $M(m,n)$. If $m = n$, the matrix is square. Any element in the matrix can be represented as a_{ij}, where i is the row number and j the column number. Elements $a_{11}, a_{22}, \ldots, a_{ii}$ form the principal diagonal.

Matrices can be added if they have the same number of rows and columns, so that

$$[c_{ij}] = [a_{ij}] + [b_{ij}]$$

This implies that each element of one matrix is added to the corresponding element of the other matrix. Subtraction between matrices follows the same principle.

The transpose of a matrix $[A]$ is $[A]^T$, so that for each (a_{ij}) element of $[A]$ the corresponding element of $[A]^T$ is (a_{ji}). The transpose of a row matrix is, therefore, a column matrix.

The multiplication of two matrices is possible if the number of columns in one of them equals the number of rows in the other. For example:

$$[A(m,n)][B(n,p)] = C(m,p)$$

and the elements of $[C]$ are given by:

$$c_{jk} = \sum_{i=1}^{n} a_{ji}b_{ik}, \text{ where: } \begin{matrix} j = 1, \ldots, m \\ k = 1, \ldots, p \end{matrix}$$

It should be noted that matrix multiplication is not commutative, that is:

$$[A][B] \neq [B][A]$$

The inverse of a square matrix $[A]$ is $[A]^{-1}$, such that

$$[A][A]^{-1} = [I]$$

where $[I]$ is referred to as the identity matrix and is a square matrix where the elements along the principal diagonal are equal to one and all other elements are zero. The inverse of a matrix $[A]$ can be computed as follows:

$$[A]^{-1} = \frac{1}{\det[A]} \|A\|^T$$

as long as the determinant of $[A]$ is not zero; otherwise, matrix $[A]$ is said to be singular. The term $\|A\|$ is obtained from $[A]$ by replacing each element by its cofactors, and is called the matrix of cofactors. The cofactor of any element (a_{ij}) is

$$(-1)^{i+j}[M_{ij}]$$

where $[M_{ij}]$ is the minor of the element (a_{ij}), obtained by deleting the ith row and jth column from $[A]$. A numerical example will help understand this principle. Given matrix

$$[A] = \begin{bmatrix} 1 & 2 & 3 \\ 1 & 3 & 5 \\ 1 & 5 & 12 \end{bmatrix}$$

find its inverse, if it exists.

The determinant of $[A]$ is found first, to check for singularity:

$$\det[A] = 1\begin{vmatrix} 3 & 5 \\ 5 & 12 \end{vmatrix} - 2\begin{vmatrix} 1 & 5 \\ 1 & 12 \end{vmatrix} + 3\begin{vmatrix} 1 & 3 \\ 1 & 5 \end{vmatrix} = 3 \neq 0$$

The inverse, therefore, exists.

The various cofactors are found next:

$$A_{11} = \begin{bmatrix} 3 & 5 \\ 5 & 12 \end{bmatrix} = 11$$

$$A_{12} = -\begin{bmatrix} 1 & 5 \\ 1 & 12 \end{bmatrix} = -7$$

$$A_{13} = \begin{bmatrix} 1 & 3 \\ 1 & 5 \end{bmatrix} = 2$$

and so on, to yield:

$$A_{21} = -9, A_{22} = 9, A_{23} = -3, A_{31} = 1$$

$$A_{32} = -2, A_{33} = 1$$

The matrix of cofactors becomes:

$$\|A\| = \begin{bmatrix} 11 & -7 & 2 \\ -9 & 9 & -3 \\ 1 & -2 & 1 \end{bmatrix}$$

And the inverse is:

$$[A]^{-1} = \frac{\|A\|^T}{\det[A]} = \frac{1}{3}\begin{bmatrix} 11 & -9 & 1 \\ -7 & 9 & -2 \\ 2 & -3 & 1 \end{bmatrix}$$

References

[1] Herzog, Bertram (organizer). Introduction to computer graphics. *ACM SIGGRAPH 86.* Course notes. Dallas, TX, 1986.

[2] Hobbs, D. An introduction to computer color graphics—Concepts and guidelines for users and programmers. *TEK Users Handbook.* Beaverton, OR: Tektronix, Inc., 1985.

[3] Foley, James D., A. Van Dam, S. Feines, and J. Hughes. *Computer Graphics—Principles and Practice.* Reading, MA: Addison-Wesley, 1990.

[4] Crane, T. Frame buffer architecture. *ACM SIGGRAPH 86.* Course notes on introduction to color raster graphics. Dallas, TX, 1986.

[5] Rogers, David F., and J. A. Adams. *Mathematical Elements for Computer Graphics,* 2nd ed. New York: McGraw-Hill, 1990.

[6] Hogan, M. Laptops in living color. *PC World* **9**(2) (February 1991):77–78.

[7] Krouse, John K. Selecting a graphic input device for CAD/CAM. *Machine Design* **55**(23):74–80 (October 1983).

[8] McGrath, Michael B., and M. L. Merickel. Evaluation of virtual reality technology as a scientific visualization medium. Presented at Compugraphics '91, Sesimbra, Portugal, September 1991.

[9] Chin, Janet, T. Reed, and K. Chauveau. The computer graphics interface—The next international graphics standard. *ACM SIGGRAPH 89*. Course notes. Boston, 1989.

[10] Carson, George S., and E. McGinnis. The reference model for computer graphics. *IEEE Computer Graphics and Applications* **6**(8):17–23 (August 1986).

[11] Bono, Peter. Understanding the CGI. *ACM SIGGRAPH 86*, Course notes. Dallas, TX, 1986.

[12] Brown, Maxine. Understanding PHIGS. *Megatek Corporation*. San Diego, CA, 1985.

[13] American National Standards Institute (ANSI). American national standard for the functional specification of PHIGS. *ANSI Document X3H3/85-21*. February 18, 1985.

[14] Enderle, Gunther, K. Kansy, and G. Plaff. *Computer Graphics Programming— GKS, the Graphics Standard*. New York: Springer-Verlag, 1984.

[15] Shuey, David, D. Bailey, and T. Morrissey. PHIGS: A standard, dynamic, interactive graphics interface. *IEEE Computer Graphics and Applications* **6**(8) (August 1986):50–57 .

[16] Steinhart, Jonathan. Introduction to window management. *ACM SIGGRAPH 89*. Course notes. Boston, 1989.

[17] Scheiffer, R.W., and J. Gettys. The X Window system. *ACM Transactions on Graphics* **5**(2): (1986):79–109.

[18] Pao, Y. C. *Elements of Computer-Aided Design and Manufacturing*. New York: Wiley, 1984.

[19] Zeid, Ibrahim. *CAD/CAM Theory and Practice*. New York: McGraw-Hill, 1991.

[20] Gere, James M., and S. Timoshenko. *Mechanics of Materials*. Boston: PWS-Kent, 1990.

[21] Plastock, Roy, and G. Kelley. *Computer Graphics*. Schaum's Outline Series. New York: McGraw-Hill, 1986.

[22] Rogers, David F. *Procedural Elements for Computer Graphics*. New York: McGraw-Hill, 1985.

[23] Hoffman, Joe D. *Numerical Methods for Engineers and Scientists*. New York: McGraw-Hill, 1992.

[24] Pokorny, Cornel K., and C. F. Gerald. *Computer Graphics: The Principles Behind the Art and Science*. Irvine: Franklin, Beedle and Associates, 1989.

[25] Lipschutz, Seymour. *Data Structures*. Schaum's Outline Series. New York: McGraw-Hill, 1986.

[26] Carlbom, Ingrid, and J. Paciorek. Planar geometric projections and viewing transformations. *ACM Computing Surveys* **10**(4) (1978):465–502.

[27] Clark, J. The geometry engine—A VLSI geometry system for graphics. *SIGGRAPH 82* (1982):127–133.

[28] Schwarz, M. W., W. B. Cowan, and J. C. Beatty. An experimental comparison of RGB, YIQ, LAB, HSV and opponent color models. *ACM Transactions on Graphics* **6**(2) (1987):123–158.

[29] Yang, C. G. Illumination models for generating images of curved surfaces. *CAD* **19**(10) (1987):544–554.

[30] Sederberg, T. W., D. C. Anderson, and R. N. Goldman, Implicit representation of parametric curves and surfaces. *Computer Vision, Graphics and Image Processing* **28**(1) (1984):72–84.

[31] Goldman, R. N., T. W. Sederberg, and D. C. Anderson. Vector elimination: A technique for the implicitization, inversion, and intersection of planar parametric rational polynomial curves. *Computer-Aided Geometric Design* **1**(4) (1984):327–356.

[32] Dresden, A. *Solid Analytical Geometry and Determinants.* Mineola, NY: Dover, 1964.

[33] Farin, Gerald. *Curves and Surfaces for Computer-Aided Geometric Design.* Orlando, FL: Academic Press, 1988.

[34] Forrest, A. R. Curves and surfaces for computer-aided design. Ph.D. thesis, University of Cambridge, Cambridge, UK, 1968.

[35] De Boor, Carl, On calculating with B-splines. *Journal of Approximation Theory* **6**(1) (1972):50–62.

[36] Bohm, Wolfgang, G. Farin, and J. Kahmann. A survey of curve and surface methods in CAGD. *Computer-Aided Geometric Design* **1**(1):1–60 (1984).

[37] Piegl, L. Key developments in computer aided geometric design. *CAD,* **21** (5) (1989):262–273.

[38] Cook, R. *Patch Work.* Computer Division, Lucasfilm, Ltd., CA, Technical Memo No. 118. June 30, 1985.

[39] Barsky, B. A. The Beta-spline: A local representation based on shape parameters and fundamental geometric measures. Ph.D. thesis, University of Utah, Salt Lake City, December 1981.

[40] Barsky, B. A., and J. C. Beatty. Local control of bias and tension in beta-splines. *ACM Transactions on Graphics* **2**(2) (1983):109–134.

[41] Tiller, W. Geometric modeling using nonuniform rational B-splines: Mathematical techniques. *ACM SIGGRAPH 86.* Course notes. Dallas, TX, 1986.

[42] Farin, G. Algorithms for rational bezier curves. *CAD* **15**(2):73–77 (1983).

[43] Piegl, L., and W. Tiller. Curve and surface constructions using rational B-splines. *CAD* **19**(9) (1987):485–498.

[44] Barnhill, R. E. Surfaces in Computer Aided Geometric Design: A Survey with New Results. *Computer-Aided Geometric Design* **2** (1):1–17 (1985).

[45] Yamaguchi, Fujio. *Curves and Surfaces in CAGD.* New York: Springer-Verlag, 1988.

[46] Faux, I. D., and M. J. Pratt. *Computational Geometry for Design and Manufacture.* New York: Wiley, 1985.

[47] Bartels, R., J. Beatty, and B. Barsky, *An Introduction to Splines for Use in Computer Graphics and Geometric Modeling.* Los Altos, CA: Morgan Kaufman, 1987.

[48] Requicha, A.A.G., and H. B. Voelcker. Solid modeling: A historical summary and contemporary assessment. *IEEE Computer Graphics and Applications* **2**(2):9–24 (March 1982).

[49] Allen, George. Introduction to solid modeling. *ACM SIGGRAPH 86.* Course notes. Dallas, TX, 1986.

[50] Requicha, A.A.G. Representations for rigid solids: Theory, methods and systems. *Computing Surveys* **12** (4) (1980):437–464.

[51] Tilove, Bruce R. Set Membership Classification: A Unified Approach to Geometric Intersection Problems. *IEEE Transactions on Computers* **29**(10) (1980):874–883.

[52] Wilson, P. R. Euler Formulas and Geometric Modeling. *IEEE Computer Graphics and Applications* **5**(8):24–36 (August 1985).

[53] Mantyla, M. *Introduction to Solid Modeling*. Rockville, MD: Computer Science Press, 1988.

[54] Mortenson, M. E. *Geometric Modeling*. New York: Wiley, 1985.

[55] Miller, James. A boundary evaluation algorithm. *ACM SIGGRAPH 89*. Course notes on solid modeling. Boston, 1989.

[56] Requicha, A. A. G., and H. B. Voelcker. Boolean operations in solid modeling: Boundary evaluation and merging algorithms. *Proceedings of IEEE* **73**(1) (1985):30–44.

[57] Tan, S. T., M. F. Yuen, and K. C. Hui. Modeling solids with sweep primitives. *Computers in Mechanical Engineering* **6**(2):60–73 (Sept./Oct. 1987).

[58] Fujimura, K., H. Toriya, and K. Yamaguchi. Octree Algorithms for Solid Modeling. In *Computer Graphics—Theory and Applications*, T. Kunii, ed. New York: Springer-Verlag, 1983.

[59] Miller, James. Solid modeling: Architectures, mathematics and algorithms. *ACM SIGGRAPH 89*. Course notes. Boston, 1989.

[60] Wilson, Peter. Feature modeling overview. *ACM SIGGRAPH 89*. Course notes on solid modeling. Boston, 1989.

[61] Pratt, M. J. Solid modeling and the interface between design and manufacture. *IEEE Computer Graphics and Applications* **4**(7) (1984):52–59.

[62] Rodriguez, Walter, L. Riggs, and T. Wade. *Quantity visual verification of structural components with GPL/CSG system interface*. Georgia Institute of Technology, Civil Engineering Department Technical Report. Atlanta: 1990.

[63] Babu, Aravinth. An automated interface between CAD and CAM, based on feature technology, solid modeling and freeform surface modeling. M.S. thesis, Clemson University, June 1990.

[64] Aziz, N. M., R. Bata, and S. Bhat. Bezier surface/surface intersection. *IEEE Computer Graphics and Applications* **10**(1) (January, 1990):50–58.

[65] Lasser, D. Intersection of parametric surfaces in the Bernstein-Bezier representation. *CAD* **18**(4) (1988):162–192.

[66] Dewey, Bruce R. *Computer Graphics for Engineers*. New York: Harper & Row, 1988.

[67] Sutcliffe, D. C. Contouring over rectangular and skewed rectangular grids—An introduction. In *Mathematical Methods in Computer Graphics and Design*, K. W. Brodie, ed. Orlando, FL: Academic Press, 1980.

[68] Spong, Mark W., and M. Vidyasagar. *Robot Dynamics and Control*. New York: Wiley, 1989.

[69] Kela, Ajay, R. Perucchio, and H. Voelcker. Toward automatic finite element analysis. *Computers in Mechanical Engineering* (July 1986).

[70] Wordenweber, B. Finite element mesh generation. *CAD* **16**(5) (1984):285–291.

[71] Purgathofer, W., and J. Schonhut, eds. *Advances in Computer Graphics V*. New York: Springer-Verlag, 1989.

[72] Cunningham, Steve, N. K. Craighill, M. W. Fong, and J. R. Brown, eds. *Computer Graphics Using Object-Oriented Programming*. New York: Wiley, 1992.

[73] Kansey, K., and P. Wisskirchen. *An object-oriented approach towards a new API for computer graphics*. Document ISO/IEC JTC1 SC24 WG1 N94, 1989.

Index